Aristocratic Women in Medieval France

THE MIDDLE AGES SERIES

Ruth Mazo Karras, General Editor

Edward Peters, Founding Editor

A complete list of books in the series
is available from the publisher.

Aristocratic Women in Medieval France

Edited by Theodore Evergates

PENN

University of Pennsylvania Press

Philadelphia

10 9 8 7 6 5 4 3 2 1

Published by
University of Pennsylvania Press
Philadelphia, Pennsylvania 19104-4011

Library of Congress Cataloging-in-Publication Data
Aristocratic women in medieval France / edited by Theodore Evergates.
p.   cm. — (Middle Ages series)
Includes bibliographical references and index.
ISBN 0-8122-3503-7 (cloth : alk. paper). — ISBN 0-8122-1700-4
(pbk. : alk. paper)
1. Upper class women — France — History.   2. Upper class women —
France — Social conditions.   3. Women — History — Middle Ages,
500–1500.   4. France — History — Medieval period, 987–1515.
I. Evergates, Theodore.   II. Series.
HQ1147.F7A75   1999
305.48'9621 — dc21   99-24086
                                                                      CIP

Maps and genealogical tables prepared by Gordon Thompson.

Contents

Maps and Genealogical Tables

Preface

This volume originated in a remark and an invitation by Fredric L. Cheyette in 1993. Despite the current interest in medieval women, he observed, there still lacked close studies of women's lives and their exercise of lordship in the central Middle Ages. Was it not time for historians working "on the ground," as it were, to explore the lives and actions of women within their regional settings, especially in France where women were conspicuously absent from recent works of medieval social history? To that end, the authors of this volume were invited to prepare chapters on aristocratic women in the regions of France they already knew well.

Our undertaking took us far beyond what seemed initially a straightforward task. As we reread familiar source materials with our new questionnaire, we were forced to discard powerful older, but clearly outmoded, interpretive models of medieval social and familial organization in order to form a coherent view of aristocratic women consonant with the documentary evidence. Our chapters also reflect the shared insights and approaches that emerged in a most collegial interchange of reading and commenting on one another's contributions. In appreciation for this opportunity to explore beyond the seemingly known and certain, we dedicate this volume to Fred.

Introduction

Kimberly A. LoPrete and Theodore Evergates

IN A MILESTONE ARTICLE a quarter century ago, Jo Ann McNamara and Suzanne Wemple concluded that in Western Europe before the twelfth century there existed "no really effective barriers to the capacity of women to exercise power; they appear as military leaders, judges, castellans, controllers of property."[1] But in the twelfth and thirteenth centuries, McNamara and Wemple speculated, women lost those capacities because aristocratic families, responding to the encroaching powers of territorial principalities and monarchical states, restricted women's property rights in favor of a single male heir, and excluded women from the exercise of "public" powers associated with lordship and governance within those nascent states.

Such a scenario of women's declining roles and rights in the central Middle Ages accorded well with the influential views of the French historian Georges Duby, who in a series of essays beginning in the 1960s posited a fundamental transformation of the aristocratic family in the eleventh century. The family became organized as a patrilineage, he argued, in which eldest sons inherited virtually the entire patrimony; younger sons, who were effectively dispossessed, joined gangs of wandering knights while daughters, if not relegated to convents, became objects of exchange between male lineages. As virtual appendages to their husbands' lineages and necessary only to produce male heirs with unsullied lines of paternal descent, wives were confined to the inner chambers of castles, except for the ceremonial occasions when they were displayed to enhance the status of their husbands.[2]

In the absence of detailed studies of the lives of women in the eleventh through thirteenth centuries, such a depiction of nobleborn women, reinforced by studies of misogynist literature, has achieved wide currency. Even historians in the vaunted *Annales* tradition of social history, who might have been expected to pioneer the new field of women's history, adopted instead the social models of structural anthropologists, preferring to investigate "mental attitudes" rather than the actual lives and actions of women in medieval society.[3] The process of building a secure base of knowledge about nonroyal aristocratic women in France began slowly, but already it is yielding a picture of women's roles and lives in noble households substantially different from the one depicted so vividly by Duby.[4]

The essays in this volume continue that enterprise. They depict women of diverse ranks within the landholding elite from the mid-eleventh through the thirteenth century in several regions of medieval France: Blois-Chartres in the northwest, Champagne in the northeast, Flanders in the far north, and Occitania in the south. Together they demonstrate that it is not the lack of sources that accounts for the "oddly ahistorical" women who appear in recent works of medieval social history,[5] but rather the failure of historians to exploit the vast and varied source materials that do exist. Fundamental in this regard are the voluminous collections of ecclesiastical charters, the title-deeds of ecclesicatical institutions that furnish the main source of information about the lives of men and women below princely rank in this period. These are supplemented by chronicles, episcopal letters, and poetry, as well as secular records from the late twelfth century such as administrative registers, notarial acts, and baronial letters. There exists, in short, a large and varied base of information about aristocratic women in their roles as daughters, wives, widows, and nuns.

The volume opens with Kimberly LoPrete's account of the life and career of Adela of Blois, the youngest daughter of William the Conqueror, who by marriage became countess of Blois, Chartres, and Meaux (ca. 1083–1120). From an analysis primarily of ecclesiastical charters and episcopal letters, LoPrete shows how Adela used her status and lordly powers, extended family ties, and personal abilities (Latin literacy, diplomatic acumen, and administrative skills) to play a decisive role in the princely politics of her day. She first acted as virtual co-count with her husband; after his death she ruled as countess and head of her affinal family for almost two decades until she retired to a monastery, leaving the countship to her thirty-year-old second son, whom she had designated to succeed. Although a female lord, Adela was acknowledged by contemporaries to have played a critical role in preserving and extending the powers of both her natal and affinal families.

Amy Livingstone discusses the activities of aristocratic women below the rank of countess in the counties of Blois and Chartres. Using the rich collection of ecclesiastical charters available from this region, Livingstone demonstrates that women of the landholding elite were treated as members of both their natal and affinal families, even after marriage, and inherited both titles and properties (feudal as well as allodial) that they transmitted to their children. Their titles and property rights involved women as litigants and adjudicators in property disputes and served as the basis of networks of patronage and alliance that women forged with neighboring lordly families and religious houses. Tracing women's actions through their successive life stages, Livingstone shows how aristocratic women of the Chartrain participated in a wide range of familial and lordly activities in the eleventh and twelfth centuries.

Theodore Evergates analyzes conditions in the county of Champagne, a region best known for its court and the romances of Chrétien de Troyes. Evergates first discusses the lives and contributions of the seven countesses during the county's existence as an independent principality (1152–1285). He then turns to the regional customary practices that accorded aristocratic women basic rights flowing from noble birth (inheritance/dowry) and marriage (joint property, dower, and wardship), rights that made women property holders of both fiefs and allods, and gave them sole authority within their families during the absences and after the deaths of their husbands. Despite those common practices, the life experiences of aristocratic women were quite diverse, as brief biographies of seven women illustrate. Evergates concludes his survey with female monastic life in Champagne, a region profoundly marked by a wave of spirituality that fueled an extraordinary expansion of both male and female monasticism.

Karen Nicholas surveys the varied life experiences and political activities of twelve countesses of Flanders between 1067 and 1280. On the basis of regional chronicles as well as ecclesiastical and comital charters, she shows how the countesses controlled diverse types of property, actively assisted their husbands and other relatives, ruled as regents or heiresses, and effectively defended their rights, lands, and people. Although the activities of individual countesses varied widely as a result of personal and familial circumstance as well as political opportunities, the powers of the countesses, claims Nicholas, increased as governance became more centralized, towns and trade influenced comital politics, and dynastic demographics produced heiresses to Flanders in 1191, 1205, and 1244. In fact, two sister countesses ruled Flanders for most of the thirteenth century.

The final chapter turns to Occitania, what is now southern France, where courtly lyric flourished. Fredric Cheyette confronts the interpretive problems raised by such poetic songs and argues that they are best understood within their particular socio-political context. Thus, on the basis of charters, wills, oaths, and other notarial documents, Cheyette depicts the world of the powerful and competitive lordly families who formed the primary audience of the troubadours. He describes how members of those families routinely partitioned properties, expanded fortunes through commercial investment, expected women to control and defend patrimonies even after marriage, and frequently found themselves swearing oaths of fealty to, or receiving such oaths from, women. With special reference to the court and career of Ermengard, viscountess of Narbonne from 1134 to 1192/93 and herself immortalized in lyric song, Cheyette argues that the poetic language of loving service to aristocratic "ladies" belongs to a continuum of verbal usage that is commonplace in documents of practice that record the activities of powerful female lords. He thus suggests that lyric's eroticization of aristocratic values such as faith and loyalty might actually have served to bolster the legitimacy of these lordly women.

These essays underscore not only the diversity of life experiences of French aristocratic women in the eleventh, twelfth, and thirteenth centuries but also the range of social and political roles open to them. It is no longer possible to depict well-born women as powerless in medieval society, marginalized by purported changes in family structure and growing public powers exercised by territorial princes. As the authors clearly demonstrate, aristocratic families continued to be viewed in cognatic or bilateral terms, with women regarded as full members of both their natal and affinal families. Women were never entirely excluded from inheriting and controlling property, not even fiefs, although the extent of their rights varied according to regional customs and familial circumstances. Moreover, dowries did not prevent women from inheriting other natal family possessions, and dowers, which became increasingly important resources for women, could remain in their hands even after remarriage or entry into convents.

In the aristocratic household based on the conjugal unit, women engaged in a variety of activities: supervising the rearing and marriage of children, dispensing patronage and gifts, receiving visiting dignitaries, assisting husbands with lordly responsibilities (as at court), performing lordly functions in their husbands' absence, and serving as guardians and regents. It was their right to fiefs, titles, and wardship over minor heirs that particularly drew women into the extra-familial networks of relations between lords and followers and into the realms of politics and lordly rule. Although their husbands or other men usually performed the personal military services owed for fiefs, women across France exchanged the customary oaths for fiefs and assumed responsibilities for enfeoffed knights. As feudal lords, women settled disputes involving vassals, garrisoned and fortified castles, raised and commanded troops, and sometimes even rode into battle at the head of the host.

Aristocratic women were also actively involved with religious institutions. They made donations to monasteries for the spiritual well-being of family members, founded new houses, and promoted church reform; they could also, like men, contest donations, oppress monasteries, and use ecclesiastical patronage for strategic political ends. Their roles as patrons and advocates drew them into the sacred precincts of male monasteries and into contact with bishops, abbots, and other male religious. While some women favored women's houses, others patronized male and female establishments alike. A religious calling could motivate daughters and wives, as well as widows, to enter convents, often the very ones they had endowed or where other family members already lived. Just as they played leading roles in lay society, aristocratic women frequently took the lead in monastic administration upon conversion to a fully religious life.

The pivotal position French aristocratic women occupied in lordly families assured their continuing participation in the "male" domains of controlling property, dispensing justice, enforcing peace, and waging war. Neither the formation of territorial principalities nor the growing powers of the French kings prevented aristocratic women from exercising the same lordly powers as their male peers, even though they did so less frequently than men. In drawing attention to the roles and lives of these aristocratic — and therefore lordly — women in several regions of France, the authors of these essays hope to encourage further exploration of the rich veins of documentary evidence from which the lives and actions of aristocratic women can be restored to their proper place in the history of medieval France.

I

Adela of Blois:
Familial Alliances and Female Lordship

Kimberly A. LoPrete

POWERFUL ARISTOCRATIC FAMILIES long used the marriage of daughters to forge and strengthen alliances. But how did such alliances work in practice? Did the creation of new family ties actually result in mutual political, military, or economic support? To answer these questions, historians must look beyond abstract models of socio-political organization to particular marriage alliances in their specific historical contexts. They must attempt to reconstruct the events leading to an alliance, the aims of the parties involved, and the actions of all the participants in maintaining or breaking the alliance. At this level of analysis, the sources often reveal that women who embodied the joining of two families through marriage and childbearing were not merely passive pawns in power relations among groups of men; rather, they were active participants whose actions could profoundly effect the shape of those relations and the course of politically significant events.[1]

This chapter presents a contextual analysis of one such familial alliance, the one reinforced by the marriage of Adela, the youngest daughter of William the Conqueror, to Stephen-Henry, the eldest son of Thibaut III, count of Blois, Chartres, Meaux, and Troyes. Adela linked two of the most powerful families in northern France. Born to the first Norman duke to become king of England, she married into the Thibaudian family that controlled multiple counties lying west, south, and east of the lands ruled directly by the kings of France. Stephen-Henry's death while defending the Latin kingdom of Jerusalem left Adela a widow with young children. Both while her husband lived and after his death Adela legitimately exercised the powers of comital lordship and played an active role in sustaining the alliance confirmed in her marriage. That alliance brought benefits to both her

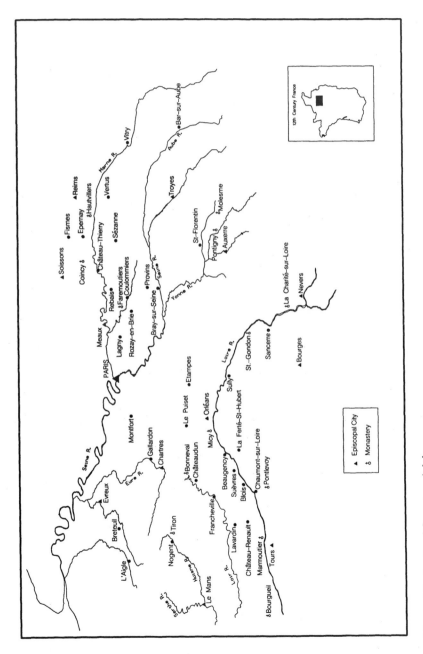

Map 1. The lands of Countess Adela.

families and placed Adela in a position to intervene decisively in the tumultuous power politics of her day.

The sources for a reconstruction of Adela's life, like that for her male peers, are fragmentary, but fall into the main categories of written texts available to historians of this period. They include ecclesiastical charters and necrologies (listings of the dead for whom prayers were offered, sometimes describing gifts made to endow the anniversaries); letters to and about the countess by high-ranking churchmen, her husband, and a castellan (and even two letters sent by Adela herself after her retirement); historical and hagiographical narratives composed by male clerics; and Latin poems either about Adela or addressed to her.[2] Each type of source presents interpretive problems. Discerning Adela's personal opinions and perceptions in them is a particularly delicate task since most were composed by churchmen, addressed to a broad audience, and treat public affairs. Yet by examining all the sources the historian can discover many of Adela's actions and trace their political consequences, in addition to learning how she was perceived by contemporaries. The sources also reveal that Adela acted in a familial context based on bilateral kin reckoning. She could tap into shared interests and a network of obligations among members of her natal and affinal families, as well as the two branches of her affinal family, in a wide variety of situations.

Because Adela and her fellow family members were among the highest-ranking, wealthiest, and most powerful people of her time, historians have far more information about their activities than is available for individuals of lower-ranking lordly families, such as counts (or countesses) of single or small counties, holders of honors and titles like viscount (or viscountess), lords of castles (castellans), and knightly lords of small estates. The range of lordly powers and the opportunities to influence important events were greater at the top of this lordly ladder than at the bottom. Nevertheless, lords of all rank exercised powers of command over lands and persons and used similar strategies to further their interests. Thus, while the extent of Adela's powers and the political impact of her actions were exceptional for a woman of her day (and indeed for most men), the sources of her powers and the activities she engaged in were not fundamentally different from those of other women of lordly rank, whose lives are less well-documented. This chapter therefore highlights features of Adela's experience that she shared with other lordly women. Many female lords exercised less power than Adela; nonetheless, often acting in analogous situations and doing similar things, they too affected the lives of men and the course of historically-significant events.[3]

Family Politics

Turbulence and armed conflict marked eleventh-century politics in France, as powerful lords strove to increase the lands they controlled directly and to enforce peace among other landholders in the territories they claimed to rule. Fundamental to any lord's effective power were inherited lands and the loyalty of fighting men, many of whom were themselves lords of land and men. Inheritances were frequently contested, in which case claimants often took up arms to assert their rights. Fighting men who controlled sizable estates could entrench their power by building a castle from which they could act almost independently, especially if their lands lay at the peripheries of territories dominated by more powerful lords. Still, such lesser lords were vulnerable to attacks from their neighbors, and they would pledge their loyalty and agree to serve more powerful lords, who could defend them and provide opportunities for further gains. More powerful lords, in turn, sustained the loyalty and service of lesser lords by acting as effective protectors and generous patrons, or else risked seeing such men switch allegiance to their rivals.

Beneath this stormy political surface, however, lay a society ordered by a hierarchical array of ranks and personal status.[4] While neither immutable nor fixed in law, rank and status were grounded in birth as well as landed wealth, promoted by titles, and sustained by deeds.[5] It was expected that those of higher rank or status would be treated with deference and respect by those of lower rank or status, even if their actual power was not necessarily greater. At the same time, however, if individuals demeaned or dishonored themselves by behaving in ways that others thought were inappropriate, their ability to command respect and service — and hence their political power — would suffer.

Adela was born into this volatile world sometime in late 1067–68 after her father, duke William "the Bastard" of Normandy, had successfully asserted his claim to the throne of England. The key source for Adela's birthdate, a letter in verse written by Godfrey of Reims, a high-ranking churchman with personal ties to the courts of both the Anglo-Normans and the Thibaudians, went so far as to claim that the Fates had arranged for William to conquer England so that Adela would be born to a crowned king instead of to a mere count.[6] Though Godfrey's conceit is flattering hyperbole, his information about Adela's birth is confirmed by Ivo of Chartres, who asserted that Adela's royal blood from *both* lines marked her as noble in the eyes of the world.[7] Her royal status was proclaimed by the very name she bore: that of her maternal grandmother, the daughter of the Capetian king Robert II. Adela was thus distinguished from her older siblings by the fully royal blood flowing in her veins. Above and beyond her rank as a king's daughter, it was this indelible mark she would transmit to any children.

With three older brothers and one younger, Adela was not likely to be an heiress to her father's honors, but her royal blood would be an asset prized by any suitor of lower rank hoping to increase both his own status and prestige and that of his children. Not surprisingly, the earliest surviving reference to Adela is Godfrey's poem, written about the time of her betrothal to Stephen-Henry, arranged around 1080. Although the two sources for Adela's betrothal and marriage describe different aspects of these events, both present the match as a political act of alliance between the Anglo-Normans and the Thibaudians.[8]

Two geo-political factors shaped this alliance and many of Adela's later actions. The first was the configuration of the counties and other properties controlled by the Thibaudians. The second was the strategic importance for both the Anglo-Normans and the Thibaudians of the county of Maine, which lay just to the west of Blois-Chartres and between Normandy and the counties controlled by the powerful counts of Anjou.

At the time of Adela's marriage, her father-in-law, Thibaut III, controlled the totality of the Thibaudian domains. These included most of the family's oldest lands, the counties of Blois, Châteaudun, and Chartres (lying largely to the west of the royal domain), counties Thibaut had inherited from his father in 1037 (see Map 1). Thibaut also inherited his father's counties centered on Provins, Château-Thierry, and Reims, in addition to castles and rights in northeastern Berry, northern Burgundy, and Lorraine. All those lands and rights lay largely to the south or east of the royal domain and included an important core of the future county of Champagne.[9] After the premature death of his younger brother Stephen in 1045–48, Thibaut also assumed responsibility for his brother's share of their father's lands: Champenois castles and counties around Meaux, Epernay, Châlons-sur-Marne, and Troyes (Genealogical Table 1).[10] Uniquely among the most powerful counts in France, the Thibaudians faced the king as their immediate neighbor on several fronts.

In 1044, despite support from his brother Stephen, Thibaut lost the

Odo II (d. 1037) = (2) Ermengard of Auvergne (d. c. 1048)

(1) Gersent of Le Mans = Thibaut III (d. 1089) = (2) ?Agnes of Burgundy (no issue)

(3) Adelaide of Valois (d. by 1100)

(1) Alan of Brittany (d. 1040) = Bertha (d. 1085) = (2) Hugh IV Ct. of Le Mans (d. 1051)

Stephen (d. 1045–48)

Adela (d. 1137) = Stephen-Henry (d. 1102)

Philip Bp. of Châlons-sur-Marne (d. 1100)

Odo Ct. of Troyes (d. 1093)

(1) Constance of France = Hugh Ct. of Troyes (d. 1130) = (2) Elizabeth of Burgundy

Odo "of Champagne" (d. c. 1096)

Agnes of Sully = William (d. 1126–36)

Thibaut IV (d. 1152)

Stephen K. of England (d. 1154)

Odo (d. after 1107)

Henry Bp. of Winchester (d. 1171)

Matilda (d. 1120)

Agnes

daughter

Genealogical Table 1. The Thibaudians.

family's original patrimonial honor, the county of Tours, to the count of Anjou.[11] Regaining Tours remained an important objective of the Thibaudians for well over a century,[12] though one they had to pursue in the context of changing geo-political circumstances. New responsibilities and new threats motivated Thibaut's own matrimonial politics and led to Thibaudian cooperation with the rising power in the northwest, William of Normandy. This cooperation emerged in the interaction of the two families and their respective allies in Maine, a region that could shield the core patrimonial domains of both families against the expansionist ambitions of the counts of Anjou.

Immediately after the loss of Tours, Thibaut III moved to increase the odds that the counts of Maine would be loyal relatives: his widowed sister Bertha married the young count while Thibaut married the count's eldest sister.[13] Adela's future husband, Stephen-Henry, was born by 1049, around the time Thibaut's brother Stephen died, leaving Thibaut alone responsible for preserving the full extent of the Thibaudian domains. Because powerful neighbors contested his position in the east, Thibaut repudiated his first wife in order to contract a marriage that would strengthen his position in that region.[14] In the early 1050s, while Thibaut was campaigning against his eastern rivals, the premature death of the count of Maine left his sister a widow with young children once again. The count of Anjou, actively battling against William in Normandy, allied himself to the king of France and moved to seize Le Mans. With Thibaut still engaged primarily in the east, the Thibaudians looked to William for support in the west.[15] Thibaut's sister, Bertha, took refuge at the Norman court and arranged the engagements of her children to two of William's. The deaths of Bertha's children prevented the celebration of the marriages, but the betrothal terms gave William a claim to Maine. In 1063 he successfully asserted it against a claimant backed by the count of Anjou; the Thibaudians, in turn, made no move to assert the claim of the now adolescent Stephen-Henry to the county.

Thibaut associated Stephen-Henry in comital rule so that he could continue campaigning in the east while assuring closer oversight of affairs in the west. In 1068–69, Stephen-Henry, supported by men from Maine and the king of France, wrested recognition of the Thibaudians' right to Tours from the new count of Anjou. William, meanwhile, conquered England. His host included Thibaut's nephew as well as several castellans with ties to the Thibaudians.

Despite the new rank, enhanced status, and increased wealth acquired by William in 1066, events of the 1070s strained the limits of his power.

In 1073 he had to reassert control over Maine against claims brought by Stephen-Henry's mother, who had journeyed from Italy with her second husband and their adolescent son to assert them.[16] In 1076 the combined forces of the count of Anjou and the king of France defeated William in Brittany and the count pursued his advantage with a campaign against Norman allies in Maine. The next year, William's own son, supported by the count of Anjou and the king, tried to assert independent rule in Maine and Normandy. After another major defeat, William began, in January 1079, to seek a negotiated settlement to these hostilities.

Those negotiations continued into the years Adela's marriage was arranged. Two of the negotiators, Geoffrey of Chaumont-sur-Loire and Thibaut III's brother-in-law, the knight-turned-monk Simon of Crépy, had close contacts with both families at this time.[17] William's willingness to marry Adela to Stephen-Henry thus appears linked to his concerns to stabilize his position after the hostilities of the 1070s. The count of Anjou, a major threat to William's power in Normandy and Maine, was also the target of Thibaudian attempts to regain Tours; for both families Maine was a critical buffer against the Angevins. The marriage of William's youngest daughter to Thibaut's eldest son reinforced decades of cooperation against the count of Anjou. While Thibaut was not expected to renounce all ties to the king of France, he could provide William support for his claims in Maine. And, in light of William's recent defeats, the Thibaudians may well have bargained successfully for William's one daughter, whose fully royal blood would enhance their prestige in relation to other powerful lords with whom they competed for the loyalty of leading castellans, especially in their far-flung border zones.[18] Those border lords who looked to both the Anglo-Normans and Thibaudians for protection and patronage, would, with their lords in alliance, have less cause to be drawn to the count of Anjou or the king of France.

As the higher-ranking and more powerful of the two families, the Anglo-Normans do not appear to have given Adela a landed dowry; she was, however, undoubtedly endowed with a healthy wedding gift of cash and other movable goods from the prodigious store of Anglo-Norman wealth.[19] From the Thibaudians, Adela received a landed dower that included an immense tract of forest in the critical frontier zone with Maine.[20] The precise dates of Adela's engagement and wedding are not known, but her formal betrothal, probably in 1081–82, at Breteuil on the Norman border, signaled the reconciliation of William the Conqueror and the lord of Breteuil, who had supported William's rebellious son.[21] Adela's marriage was celebrated in Chartres cathedral, most likely sometime between January 1083 and her mother's death in November of that year, shortly after her fifteenth birthday.[22]

Husband and Wife

The two sources for Adela's marriage, lengthy narratives chronicling regional ecclesiastical affairs and the political fortunes of lordly families, stress the political aspect of the match.[23] Neither records what the adolescent Adela or her husband, then in his mid-thirties, felt about it (or each other), though both would have been raised in ways that emphasized respect for parental authority and demonstrated the importance of family ties for individual well-being in the world. Little is known about the childhood years of either spouse, but it appears that Adela, at least, received formal instruction in Latin letters. Her education would have included elementary training in the liberal arts based on standard textbooks and both poetical and historical works commonly used when teaching these disciplines in her day. Adela's mother came from a family with a generations-old tradition of Latin literacy and several of Adela's siblings are known to have received at least the rudiments of a literary education, either from household tutors or at religious establishments.[24]

Since Adela's mother was a ruling countess who perambulated across Normandy while assisting her husband, it is likely that Adela spent much of her childhood and was educated at a monastery, most probably La Trinité in Caen. La Trinité was a family foundation where her oldest sister, Cecilia, had been dedicated to God and another literate sister may have lived for a time; Cecilia's tutor there was a noted orator, well versed in the liberal arts.[25] Fostering children in monasteries, far from a form of child abandonment, was one way that itinerant parents assured that their children would experience stability and a uniformly-structured daily life, in addition to receiving a religious and literary education. At La Trinité, Adela could have enjoyed special attention from her sister(s) as well as visits from her parents, for at this time monastic precincts, especially those of family foundations, remained permeable and were frequently the sites of family gatherings. Thus even at La Trinité the young Adela would not have been isolated from the outside world and she occasionally might have joined her mother's household, with its staff of tutors and other clerics employed in part to oversee the education of ducal children.

Little is known of Adela's activities as the teenaged bride of a mature man whose father was still alive. She once appeared alongside her husband when he saw to the implementation of a pious bequest and was formally received, as countess, into the monks' prayer society.[26] She also began to bear children. Adela certainly gave birth to one son (named for her royal father) before her father-in-law died; she bore at least six, and perhaps eight children who lived beyond infancy during the approximately fifteen years she lived with her spouse.[27]

Yet Adela's other activities indicate she was treated by her in-laws as more than a child-bearing vessel, however much her son assured her place in her new family. Both Adela's status, which was higher than her husband's, and her literate skills, which she saw were transmitted to at least some of her children, were tapped to good effect after her husband became head of the Thibaudian family.[28] Adela became an active participant in comital rule and, despite an age difference of at least eighteen years, the couple appear to have developed a relationship based at least on trust and mutual respect if not affection.[29]

Stephen-Henry, an eldest son who had been ruling with his father for over twenty years, was Thibaut's principal heir on his father's death in 1089. He inherited both the western and eastern domains Thibaut had inherited, as well as his father's lands, castles, and rights in northeastern Berry and northern Burgundy. In addition, Stephen-Henry received the lands and rights centered on Meaux, which had been inherited by Thibaut's brother in 1037.[30] Stephen-Henry and Adela were thus known to contemporaries as the count and countess of Blois, Chartres, and Meaux.

Yet, like his father before him, Thibaut granted a share of his family's extensive possessions to a younger son. Stephen-Henry's younger half-brother, Odo, received what remained of the domains inherited by Thibaut's younger brother, centered on Troyes and Epernay. To compensate for Meaux, Odo also received all his father's castles in Lorraine, while he stood to inherit Bar-sur-Aube and Vitry from his own mother. When Odo died, unmarried, four years after his father, Stephen-Henry saw that his inheritance passed to Odo's younger brother Hugh, known as the count of Troyes (Genealogical Table 1). Hugh soon married Constance, the daughter of the king of France, but could be relied upon to support the senior branch of his natal family.[31]

When Stephen-Henry became count in his own right in September 1089 he was over forty while Adela was in her early twenties. She immediately joined Stephen-Henry on a tour through their widespread domains to display Stephen's new status to all his followers and dependents. Appearing publicly alongside her husband at Blois in November and at Coincy (in the county of Meaux) on Christmas, Adela consented to his donations to two monasteries.[32] One grant was made for their fathers' and mothers' salvation, the other for their own souls. Stephen clearly saw as one of his lordly responsibilities care for the spiritual well-being of male and female kin, whether related by blood or by marriage, and considered both his mother and his wife as members of his family. That Stephen appeared publicly with Adela, whose rank as a royal daughter was underscored in one of the documents, shows how Adela's prestige enhanced his own. The couple's son, still probably a toddler, did not appear on these ceremonial occasions, but Stephen's stepmother, the widowed countess Adelaide, joined them at Blois before taking up residence with her sons in Troyes. Adela could henceforth manage her husband's household without interference from a female in-law.[33]

Adela continued to play an active role in comital affairs while maintaining relations with her natal family. In about 1091, the new bishop of Chartres agreed to Adela's request to intervene in the case of her distant cousin's adulterous liaison with the childless lord of Breteuil. Though the bishop politely rebuked the countess for condoning the couple's adultery, he acceded to her request — probably to legitimize the couple's sons, who later became key supporters of Adela's brother in Normandy.[34]

In 1092 Adela and Stephen-Henry presided over the court that adjudicated a dispute between the comital provost for Blois and the monks of Marmoutier.[35] Shortly thereafter Adela, alone and on her own initiative, swore an oath binding both herself and her husband to protect the bishop of Chartres, who was then embroiled in a dispute with the king of France.[36] In 1094 and in 1096 she acted alongside her husband when the couple consented to the sale of houses in Blois and persuaded the bishop of Soissons to grant an altar to a Parisian monastery.[37] The documents show the young countess participating in judicial affairs and property transfers of comital followers, as well as sharing in decisions regarding reform-motivated bequests. The bishop of Chartres, for one, assumed that her oath could bind her husband in the lordly prerogative of protecting churchmen.

In October 1095 Adela appeared prominently at the monastery of Hautvillers, outside Epernay, when the monks celebrated the translation of the relics of the empress Helen (the mother of the first Christian emperor, Constantine). Adela, alone of the lay people present, joined the officiating bishops on the platform specially constructed for this event. When the relics were transferred from the old to a new reliquary (probably one provided by the comital family), Adela read out loud to the assembled multitude the identifying label. Stephen-Henry, together with his half-brother, the bishop of Châlons-sur-Marne, and his sister-in-law Constance, then established a weekly market for the monks; Adela was undoubtedly among the unnamed persons who confirmed the arrangements by swearing an oath on the newly-translated relics.[38] In the eyes of the monk who reported these events, the rank and Latin literacy of the countess allowed her to represent the extended comital family alongside bishops in the religious ceremony designed to honor the sainted female patron and protector of his monastery. By honoring the saint and her monastic guardians through both the translation ceremony and the market grant, the comital couple, as the earthly protectors of the monks, demonstrated that they knew how to act as honorable lords and patrons to their assembled lay followers as well.

Adela appeared with her husband on other occasions. According to the necrology of the cathedral of Reims, the countess, assisted by her husband, renewed the arrangement whereby the Thibaudians held the castle of Vertus and permanently granted other land to the canons. Since a similar arrangement, which expired on the death of Thibaut III, had been made for Vertus by count Odo II's widow (after 1037), it is likely that the castle was part of Adela's dower and these transactions occurred shortly after Thibaut's death. In any event, the canons remembered the countess as the principal actor in exchanges concerning an important comital castle and the alienation of property.[39]

Adela also acted jointly with her husband in authorizing a knight's donation of land to Chartres cathedral and in granting a female serf and her offspring to the monks of Saint-Père of Chartres.[40] On another occasion count and countess, again presented as co-actors, remitted to the inhabitants of Blois the tax on wine sold there, on condition that they take responsibility for closing the town gate. No document recording this privilege has survived, but its terms were engraved on the gate for all to see.[41]

When the comital couple attended the translation of the relics of Saint-Ayoul in Provins, Stephen acted on Adela's advice and with her consent in granting the monks half of the comital revenues from the annual Provins fair. The hagiographical narrative written to record these events presented the couple as acting publicly together to honor an important saint and to endow his earthly guardians.[42] When Stephen dispossessed an advocate for abusing his charge, Adela appeared with two of their sons, swore to uphold her husband's dispositions, and subscribed the document recording them.[43]

The count clearly thought his wife should be as responsible as his young sons for upholding decisions concerning important comital prerogatives.

The sources reviewed here are the only direct traces of Adela's activities prior to her husband's decision to depart on the First Crusade. Only one charter has survived in which Stephen, without Adela, was the principal actor. It records how Stephen, when temporarily encamped at Suèvres, resolved a question relating to the 1092 dispute mentioned above; the charter underscored the subsidiary nature of this intervention, which did not change an earlier judgment in which Adela had been involved.[44]

The surviving evidence makes it impossible fully to reconstruct Adela's early activities as countess of Blois, Chartres, and Meaux; still, it does provide significant indications of the important roles she played. While continuing to bear children, Adela traveled regularly with her husband across the full extent of the Thibaudian domains, even though she did not always accompany him on short trips from the couple's major castle-residences to oversee local affairs. Although charters recording land grants tend to present Adela in the seemingly subordinate role of consenting to her husband's decisions, she was always present with him when the grants were publicly implemented, and she always subscribed or otherwise validated the relevant documents. Whenever there exist detailed descriptions of the context of such donations, churchmen presented Adela as an active and valued participant in public events of which the grants themselves were just one part. And she was remembered as the principal actor in exchanges involving what were probably dower properties — which included a castle.

Yet in other activities of the comital court — adjudicating disputes, granting privileges, and authorizing donations or sales made by others — Adela, bearing the title of countess, was represented as acting in the same capacity as her husband, the count. She also acted independently in swearing an oath to defend the bishop of Chartres. Taken as a group, these sources reveal Adela as an active and acknowledged participant in comital lordship who routinely advised her husband, implemented their joint decisions, and collaborated with him in the public business of the comital court. Stephen showed concern for the spiritual well-being of his wife's natal family, as well as his own conjugal family, while Adela intervened in affairs of her natal family in addition to her activities as countess of Thibaudian domains. Moreover, the authority-enhancing prestige and literate skills of the high-born and educated countess impressed contemporaries. Adela's royal rank was noted in charters and the poet-prelate Baudry of Bourgeuil, who may have been present at the Hautvillers translation ceremony, claimed that

Adela actually surpassed the *virtus* (meaning both power and moral virtue) of her conquering father because of her Latin literacy.[45]

In addition to her manifest abilities, high status, and literate skills, another factor undoubtedly contributed to Adela's prominent role in the exercise of comital lordship. Since Stephen-Henry did not begin to act as count in his own right until he was in his early forties, there was a strong possibility that he might predecease his wife and leave very young heirs. What better way to give his wife experience and bolster her ability to command the respect of comital followers than to associate her in acts of comital rule? Aging counts routinely associated designated heirs in lordship, both to gain assistance for themselves and to allow their successors to acquire important experience.[46] The sources indicate that Stephen-Henry, whose sons were too young to take significant decisions independently, willingly associated his younger, literate, and high-born wife in all aspects of comital lordship from the start of his tenure as count.

In late 1095–96 crusading fervor swept over France after the pope launched his appeal for an armed pilgrimage to assist the embattled Christians in the Holy Land. Stephen-Henry, then in his late forties, heeded the call.[47] That he could depart without fear of diminishing his power, fortune, or patrimony was due, in large part, to the wealth and abilities of his wife, Adela, then in her late twenties. On Stephen's own admission, Adela provided much of the cash to underwrite this expensive undertaking, and he departed without mortgaging lands to raise funds.[48] Stephen expected his wife to rule during his absence, as he revealed in a letter written during the siege of Antioch, in which he enjoined Adela to "act well, order your land illustriously, and treat both your children and your men honorably, as befits you."[49] Orderic Vitalis claimed that Adela "honorably governed (*honorifice gubernauit*) her husband's county (*consulatum*) after his pilgrimage" while the author of the "Deeds of the lords of Amboise" asserted that Adela "ruled (*regebat*) the county of Blois," indicating that clerical chroniclers acknowledged the countess's ruling powers.[50]

Stephen's situation can be contrasted with other crusading magnates, most notably Adela's own brother, Robert Curthose, the unmarried duke of Normandy, and Helias, Stephen's maternal cousin and count of Maine. Robert, who had been struggling to maintain his hold on Normandy against his brother, William Rufus, the king of England, mortgaged Normandy to Rufus for 10,000 marks to subsidize his crusading venture.[51] Helias, who took advantage of Curthose's weak rule in Normandy and became count of Maine in 1092, asked Rufus to respect his position after he took the cross. When Rufus instead threatened to retake Maine, Helias decided not to depart. Although the count of Anjou did not join the crusaders and supported Helias, Stephen, who had studiously avoided entanglement in these complex disputes, could rely on Anglo-Norman power to keep the Angevins contained, and, indeed, William Rufus was master of Le Mans when he died in 1100.[52]

Before Stephen's departure the comital couple founded a new Marmoutier priory on Adela's dower lands in the Long Forest, the first gift of land from the Thibaudians' western domains to these monks in over thirty years. The lengthy document recording the foundation, composed by monks from Marmoutier and ratified after Stephen's departure, illuminates the complex motives for this major undertaking at an important juncture in the couple's relationship. The various voices used to recount events also reveal how these monks viewed Adela's place and powers in the comital household.[53]

The text opens in the names of count Stephen and his wife Adela speaking together. Stephen is introduced as the "son and heir of the celebrated (*inclitus*) palatine count Thibaut [III]," Adela as the "daughter of the illustrious king of the English and most noble duke of the Normans, William." A lengthy narrative follows, spoken by Stephen alone in the past tense. He summarized prior Thibaudian relations with Marmoutier, where three of his ancestors had been buried before his father lost Tours.[54] Stephen then explained how, after Thibaut III's death, he discussed with his wife (*coniugis*), "friends" (*amici*), and retainers (*familiares*) what he, as heir to Thibaut's lordship (*dominium*) over Marmoutier, might do to avoid offending his father. After describing the monks' repeated requests for a donation and his crusade preparations, Stephen announced: "I gave (*dedi*) [to the monks] our [land in the Long Forest], not only with my wife's consent and at her suggestion, but indeed at her behest (*non solum assensu ejus et ammonitione, sed etiam prece*)."[55] Although he made the grant especially for the souls of his father, himself, and his wife, Stephen also expressed his hope that the monks' prayers would assure him divine protection during his pilgrimage and keep his wife and children safe during his absence, in addition to aiding the souls of past, present, and future relatives (*parentes*) of both Adela and himself.

In the ensuing exposition of the terms of the donation, the drafters reverted to plural subjects and verbs as count and countess explain how the land is to be settled by men under the monks' supervision; they refer repeatedly to "our" officials, court, land, and alms. Not only did these terms confirm the superior jurisdiction of the comital court by referring disputed cases in the new settlement to it, but they also assured cash profits for the couple through taxes on forest products marketed by the settlers. This section concludes with a passage beginning "all these things, I count Stephen, and my wife, countess Adela, give (*damus*) to them," and expressing the couple's hope that their heavenly treasures will be all the greater to the extent that the land donated, earlier described as infertile and unproductive, "would be built up into something better."

The comital couple clearly hoped to reap both heavenly and earthly rewards from this pious bequest. In addition, the terms of the grant reflect Stephen's and Adela's view of their family, in which patrilineal affiliation was only one identifying feature within a wider cognatic kindred centered on the conjugal unit. Moreover, the alternation of person and tense by the drafters of the document underscores Adela's instigating role in the decision and the couple's joint exercise of comital prerogatives, even as it reflects these monks' view that husbands' formally alienated their wives' property after due consent was obtained. But the document was still not complete and the donation not yet fully implemented.

The final section presents Adela herself as speaking subject, as the drafters recorded the formal implementation of the grant and the ratification of the document. Adela here recounts how, after her husband's departure, she had the land measured off, as Stephen had instructed, and ceremonially transferred it to the monks. She then, "on the authority of my husband and myself," has the document sealed with her sign and ratified by her children, who make "the Lord's sign of the cross" on it in the presence of thirty-two witnesses; finally, she gives the document to the monks.[56] Four distinct hand-drawn crosses are visible on it, along with Adela's name written by her own hand next to where Stephen's seal was applied; slits in the parchment suggest that another seal was once attached to the document.[57]

Comital seals were new at this time and Stephen did not routinely seal documents; no personal seal of Adela has survived, but there is evidence that she used one, at least after her retirement.[58] Still, Adela had access to Stephen's seal and used both it and other symbolic forms of ratification fully to authorize this important grant from her dower. The monks who benefited from Adela's desire to see her lands used more profitably, agreed to regulate certain affairs in their new settlement at the comital court now under her headship; they prayed to protect her conjugal family in this life and to save her extended cognatic kindred in the next; they had no doubt that Adela could impose her will on her husband and that she exercised full

comital authority during his absence on crusade. By 1099 the new settlement, named Francheville ("Freetown") by Adela, was flourishing to such
an extent that the countess persuaded the bishop of Chartres to let the
monks build a new parish church there, free from episcopal dues.[59]

Three other charters and letters of Ivo of Chartres reveal more of
Adela's activities during Stephen's absence (between October 1096 and
sometime in 1099). None mention any of the couple's sons (the oldest was
about ten), thus confirming that Adela exercised full comital authority.
They also show that she, like any effective medieval lord, personally toured
her domains, dispensing justice and defending the church. Indeed, her
earlier defense of bishop Ivo brought Adela his support when he arranged
for a diocese-wide peace to be sworn at a special synod in the very month of
Stephen's departure. With this solemn renewal of the peace, Ivo brought
the weight of the church to bear on any who might have considered the
count's absence an opportunity to disrupt good order in the Thibaudians'
western domains.[60]

In Chartres, Adela renounced minor comital customs and persuaded a
Chartrain castellan to renounce similar customs, in response to complaints
from monks at the Marmoutier priory there.[61] In Blois and Châteaudun,
the countess presided over the comital court and imposed settlements in
two disputes between priories of Marmoutier and powerful comital followers. On both occasions she decided against the lay disputants, who were
obliged to renounce their claims outright.[62] Clearly, Stephen's absence did
not impede the discharge of comital justice, even when it ran counter to the
interests of powerful castellans. When in her eastern domains, Adela became aware of scandalous behavior by the nuns at Faremoutiers; she com-
municated her concerns to bishop Ivo, who asked his episcopal colleague in
Meaux to have the nuns reform themselves, which they eventually did.[63]

Meanwhile, Stephen-Henry, probably after a serious illness, left the
protracted and demoralizing seige of Antioch in June 1098, eventually making his way back to France. After the crusaders' near miraculous capture of
Jersualem (July–August 1099), Stephen and others who had left Palestine
earlier were seen as deserters and faced ecclesiastical sanctions for failing to
complete their pilgrims' vows.[64] Though he was over fifty and his experiences had disabused him of any notion that crusading was a glorious adven-
ture, Stephen had little choice but to return to the Holy Land. Adela,
dubbed "a wise and spirited woman," is reported to have appealed to the
valor of her husband's lost youth in a successful attempt to persuade him to
take up arms once again for the Christian cause; Stephen recruited a large

host of bishops and barons to join him.[65] Prior to his departure, Stephen and Adela (then in her early thirties) took several measures to consolidate comital authority should the aging count not return fit to rule.

The comital couple publicly renounced their right to control episcopal properties at the death of the bishop of Chartres in response to the urgings of bishop Ivo. They received in exchange annual anniversary prayers and a written guarantee that Ivo's new stone residence not be fortified. The bishop also provided a valuable countergift, but he was wisely ambiguous about its precise nature when later writing to the pope to request confirmation of the privilege.[66] By championing church reform when Stephen was under threat of excommunication and as Adela again would be ruling without her husband, the couple enhanced their authority as the true respecters of divine law in a diocese where they competed for power with a then excommunicate king.[67] Similarly, in their holdings in northern Burgundy, the couple saw to the institution of Cluniac customs at Saint-Germain, Auxerre, on terms that settled an intermonastic dispute which had erupted in the mid-1090s. The public implementation of this internal reform explicitly confirmed the couple's economic rights as the monks' advocates in the presence of several powerful lay and ecclesiastical lords who could contest them, and thus served to bolster the Thibaudian position in this strategic region.[68]

The couple's eldest son, William, was also approaching adulthood at this time. Following traditional aristocratic practice, Stephen and Adela designated him as principal heir and publicly displayed his new status in a tour of their domains.[69] During this tour Stephen's chaplain Alexander, who had accompanied Stephen on the first crusade and would return to the Holy Land with him, drafted a charter to record a pious gift of customs from estates on the northern border of the family's eastern domains. As a document written by a member of the comital household instead of by the churchmen who benefited from comital largess, it is especially valuable. Short as well as formulaic, it pays particular attention to the military services that would still be owed after the grant. Alexander represents Stephen, Adela, and William as speaking in unison; all three subscribe the charter in front of witnessess, but only Stephen and Adela use the comital title.[70] The very form of this document thus underscores the real powers wives could exercise in their conjugal households: husband, wife, and eldest son jointly granted customs and received military services from tenants on family land, though ultimate authority remained in the hands of both parents during their son's minority.

As in the years prior to Stephen-Henry's departure on the First Crusade, in the years between his trips to the Holy Land Adela actively participated with her husband in all aspects of comital lordship throughout the Thibaudian domains, regardless of any formal subordination to him in the eyes of monks when disposing of family lands. Although Stephen appears to have traveled somewhat more frequently than Adela to oversee comital affairs, she was nonetheless publicly involved in all the affairs he is known to have treated, and she joined him on grand tours of their widespread domains undertaken to display and reinforce comital authority at critical junctures. During Stephen's almost three-year absence, Adela proficiently and energetically exercised full comital authority. Her own wealth and abilities, her own authority-enhancing status, and her age relative to that of her spouse and children, led to Adela ruling as an acknowledged co-count with her husband, even during his lifetime.

Family Head and Female Lord

When Stephen-Henry left again for the Holy Land late in 1100, his sons were still boys. Adela thus continued to rule as countess. Though she was not accorded the title of regent in any surviving source, Adela's ruling powers were acknowledged in the dating clause of two charters issued by others, one in 1102, "when count Stephen [then in the Holy Land] and his wife Adela were ruling (*regnantes*)," the other in 1107, "when countess Adela was ruling (*principans*) and present."[71]

In 1101 and 1102, Adela and three of her sons met with her brother-in-law, Hugh of Troyes, and his wife Constance, at Epernay and Coulommiers, where they consented to Hugh's and Constance's donations to the monks at Molesme.[72] In seeking consent from the wife of his absent older brother, Hugh acknowledged Adela's place in the Thibaudian family as a whole. By 1103 Adela had entrusted her second son, Thibaut (then about ten), to Hugh and Constance (still childless after almost a decade of married life) to be groomed as his paternal uncle's potential successor. Hugh's lands and titles would thus be kept in Thibaudian hands while Adela was relieved of the responsibility for her son's military training.[73] Such family solidarity continued after Hugh's and Constance's marriage was annulled and both partners remarried.

The heir-designate William also came of age in about 1103, the year news was received of Stephen-Henry's death (in May 1102) on crusade. William, married in 1104, continued to act as heir-designate until 1107, when Thibaut was knighted and chosen by Adela to be their father's principal heir.[74] Even so, Adela continued to exercise comital authority after her oldest sons came of age. Though young Thibaut played an increasingly active role in affairs, especially during the war-torn second decade of the twelfth century, charters reveal that Adela still acted with full authority without her son until she retired to a monastery in the spring of 1120. The chronicler Robert of Torigni depicted Adela as nobly ruling while her sons were less able to govern; by linking their full adulthood to Adela's taking the veil, he indicated that she ruled until that moment.[75] Indeed, in 1128 Thibaut himself stated that the lordship of the county of Chartres did not come into his hands until his mother took monastic vows.[76] Though Thibaut, when in his early twenties, occasionally acted alone there, it was simply because Adela was active elsewhere in the family's domains.[77] Thus it appears that the countess, like her male peers, simply associated her sons in comital rule until she chose to devote herself to God.

William and Thibaut had three younger brothers. Stephen probably came of age around 1109, about two years after the last dated appearance of his brother Odo, who was apparently always of fragile health and died in his teens. Adela employed a doctor to care for Odo and endowed anniversary prayers for his salvation.[78] She dedicated to God her youngest son, Henry, who was most likely conceived between Stephen-Henry's Holy Land campaigns, at the Cluniac priory of La Charité-sur-Loire, near the family's lands in northeastern Berry, shortly after his father's death.[79] Adela also had at least one daughter, named Matilda like Adela's own queenly mother.[80] She may well have been the mother of two other girls, Agnes and one whose name is not known, though it is possible that she acted simply as their stepmother. None of these girls appear by name in any extant document during their childhood years; eventually they all came to play important roles in Adela's political alliance building.

After news of her husband's death reached France, Adela and her brother-in-law Hugh made several pious bequests to endow anniversaries for Stephen. Adela's grants were mostly minor and frequently made when she was treating other comital affairs.[81] While Adela thus arranged for monks long patronized by the Thibaudians to pray for her husband, she did not allow her religious concern for his salvation to overwhelm her sense of practical administrative realities. At the same time, she endowed prayers for herself and her children. Nor did she forget her own parents in other bequests.[82] Like Stephen-Henry, Adela felt primarily responsible for the spiritual well-being of members of her conjugal family, but also showed concern for the salvation of both natal and affinal kin.

Adela appears to have been most active in the years 1101–9, when in her thirties (though this may simply be an impression arising from the vagaries of document survival). Twenty-five charters dated to 1101–9 and another fourteen documents most likely datable to this time testify to her activities during these years, compared to eighteen documents datable to the next decade. Adela's actions are also described in letters, chronicles, and other narrative texts. In addition, Adela suffered at least two serious illnesses, first sometime 1100–1102, then in the spring of 1105. It was perhaps in 1100–1102 that she was miraculously healed at Rebais through the relics of Saint Aile, after the best French, Norman, and "overseas" doctors failed to cure her life-threatening fevers.[83]

The countess perambulated through her widespread domains until her retirement. She held court to settle disputes, consented to donations by comital followers, founded and regulated fairs, and sponsored limited ecclesiastical reform. She acted as lord to lay followers as well as cultivating relations with traveling churchmen, her multiple diocesan bishops, and religious houses of various orders, several of which formally acknowledged her lordly role as protector.[84] She gave special attention to expanding the new settlement of Francheville and organized similar clearance and settlement programs elsewhere in the Thibaudian domains.[85] These ventures, together with her fostering of trade, show how Adela worked to increase comital revenues by promoting economic growth. Household officials, some of whom she herself appointed, and men of knightly rank with landed estates in one region of the Thibaudian domains often accompanied her to other parts of her domains, showing that she, like her father-in-law and husband before her, could rely on the service of powerful men from across the family's multiple counties. And, like earlier counts, the countess continued to rely on local agents resident in specific locations.[86]

Contemporary observers acknowledged that Adela exercised the same authoritative powers as her male peers.[87] Orderic Vitalis reveals that she had the authority to command fighting men when he described how the countess ordered one hundred knights to take the field with the co-king Louis.[88] In his letters, Ivo of Chartres referred to Adela's princely rule (*principatus*), the peace oaths she swore, and precepts and privileges she issued. He also discussed her jurisdiction over monasteries and her judgment at the comital court in a land dispute between castellans.[89] The poet-prelate Hildebert, bishop of Le Mans, praised Adela as an able administrator who embodied all that was required for governing in a letter urging her to cultivate clemency when exercising her princely power to punish others.[90] In another letter he asked her to deploy her protective power (*patrocinium*) by granting him an armed escort.[91]

Laymen also looked to Adela as their lord (*dominus/domina*), understood as one who had the right to grant and oversee the transmission of fiefs and honors, as well as the authority to settle disputes in which people holding such properties became involved. In 1102–4 the castellan of Château-Renault took his dispute with the monks of Marmoutier "to the court of his *domina*, the countess of Blois" for judgment; she persuaded the monks to restore the disputed goods to him.[92] In January 1105 Sanche of La Ferté-Hubert, who donated properties held in honor from the Thibaudians, had his brother-in-law go to Blois to obtain consent from his "*domina*, the countess"; Adela consented and then formally invested the recipients (the monks of Micy) with the properties granted.[93] Sometime after August 1108 a certain Gerard "of the tower" acted at the behest of his "*domina*, countess Adela" in giving his garden to the monks of the Conques priory in Coulommiers.[94] Adela also persuaded Gerard to give the monks other land he held in fief from her.[95] Gerard had been one of her sergeants (*servientes dominæ*) when he witnessed alongside the countess's chaplains, barons, and knights (*milites*) the judicial proceedings she presided over that confirmed Conques' possession of the priory.[96] The documents recording these events confirm that Adela acted as the feudal lord of powerful men even after her sons had come of age.[97]

Bishop Hildebert's letter portraying Adela as a *domina* with the power to grant an armed escort is especially revealing for contemporary perceptions of female lords.[98] According to Hildebert, successful ruling depended more on intellectual than bodily endowments. He appealed both to Adela's powers of discernment (she would know he was worthy of such a benefit) and her intellectual training (by citing a classical author). But when he assumed that Adela certainly would grant his request because she embodied "service to honorable conduct" and was "both an example and an instrument of virtue (*virtus*)," he artfully moved from the level of comital authority to the plane of political morality: it was the duty of Christian lords to use their power (*virtus*) to protect bishops. He thus elevated the virtuous countess to the status of an exemplary lord, who glorified her sex and acted with the dignity of her ruling ancestors. Hildebert may not have been able to overlook the fact that Adela was both a woman and a lord, but her female body did not prevent her from applying her mind to the task of exercising authoritative comital powers in a morally responsible way.

Hugh the Chanter, writing his history of the church of York some eight years after meeting Adela, also described the countess in the language of lordship. Recounting how he and his exiled archbishop Thurstan had been "joyfully received with due honor" by the countess and her son Thibaut, Hugh introduced Adela to his English audience as the sister of Thurstan's lord (*dominus*), king Henry I, who loved (*diligebat*) Thurstan as if *she* were his lord (*domina*).[99] For him, it should be noted, the force binding lay lord to the clerical beneficiary of lordly patronage was a kind of love.

Bishop Ivo likewise invoked the love that bound lay and ecclesiastical lord together. Ivo would faithfully serve the countess he loved and churchmen would pray for her salvation, he wrote, if Adela used her power in ways that demonstrated her love and respect for ecclesiastical institutions. It was the bishop's love (*amor*) for Adela that caused him to refrain from excommunicating young William, who had threatened bishop and chapter with violence in 1103, and from laying an interdict on the diocese in 1107 during Adela's violent dispute with the cathedral canons.[100] So too the monks of Marmoutier spoke the language of love when recounting how the countess settled major disputes in their favor. They called Adela "our most dear (*karissima*) *domina*, countess of Blois," "our most beloved (*amatissima*) and assiduous benefactor," and even "our most fervent lover (*amatrix ferventissima*)."[101] In another charter they depicted themselves as the "beloved" (*amati*) of Adela's father, himself a Marmoutier patron, and claimed Adela wanted to emulate his love (*amor*) for the monks with her benefactions.[102]

However sensual the overtones of this language of lordly love, the historian should not assume that the love expressed was perceived as predominantly erotic. That would be to ignore the ways Adela's contemporaries used the language of love to depict a wide array of socio-political relationships and to highlight the importance of personal bonds at lordly courts.[103] Adela was indeed a woman, but she was far from being a mere object of sexual fascination to these churchmen; rather, she was a ruling countess whose lordly powers, they hoped, she would continue to exercise on their behalf. Though *litterati* like Hildebert and Baudry of Bourgueil artfully linked Adela's lordly powers to her desirable female body in their letters and poems to this *domina* and countess, they longed for Adela to love chastely, through her generous gifts, wise judgments, and honorable lordly behavior to all who depended on her power.[104]

Princely Politics

Adela continued to stay in touch with members of her natal family and important men in their domains. Indeed, it was through these contacts that she reactivated the alliance with the Anglo-Normans after her brother

Henry acceded to the English throne on August 5, 1100 and eventually proved capable of supporting her efforts to preserve the integrity of her widespread domains, particularly in the west where she faced the counts of Anjou. Yet, important as this alliance became in the second decade of the twelfth century, Adela, like her husband and father-in-law before her, also had to be mindful of the co-kings of France, her superiors in rank as well as her immediate neighbors on several fronts. She adroitly orchestrated comital relations with kings Philip and Louis, though she willingly resorted to arms when Louis threatened comital autonomy. By acting as a generous patron and able protector of churchmen and castellans across the Thibaudian domains, she also worked to strengthen comital authority. Ever alert to changing circumstances within her own two families as well as in the wider world around her, Adela used her comital powers and position in the comital family to assure that Thibaudian power would not be eclipsed after she retired from the active life.

Henry's claim to the English throne was disputed by his older brother, Robert Curthose, duke of Normandy, who invaded England in the summer of 1101, though the brothers soon came to terms by which Robert abandoned the contest. Adela's contacts with a cleric from Henry's court and the two papal legates sent, in part, to help mediate between her feuding brothers assured that she was informed of these important events in England and Normandy.[105] In that same year, the countess provided military support for young Louis's campaigns in the French royal domain.[106]

As Henry consolidated his power in England and Robert continued to rule ineffectually in Normandy, feuding broke out among castellans on the borders of Normandy, Maine, and the Chartrain. Among those caught up in the hostilities was Agnes of Ponthieu, the wife of Robert of Bellême. Robert had revolted against Henry and imprisoned Agnes, who, after escaping, sought refuge at Adela's court.[107] Agnes undoubtedly brought Adela up-to-date on these struggles that could disrupt the stability of her western domains. In the county of Maine, count Helias reasserted his independence on the death of William Rufus and then allied himself with Henry I against Robert Curthose in Normandy. This alliance augured well for the future, as Henry prepared to seize power from his brother and reunite England with Normandy.[108]

By the spring of 1103, however, Henry and Anselm, the archbishop of Canterbury, were embroiled in a dispute over the investiture of bishops that slowed the king's preparations. When Henry allowed Anselm to seek a settlement at the papal court, the archbishop set out for Rome. Traveling via Chartres, Anselm was honorably received by Adela and negotiated a cessation of hostilities between the countess and bishop Ivo, themselves embroiled in a violent dispute with the canons of Chartres cathedral.[109] Once in Rome, Anselm failed to resolve his dispute with king Henry, but he interceded with the pope on Adela's behalf, blaming the scandalous behavior of the cathedral canons for the conflict in Chartres and praising Adela as a prince who staunchly supported papal policies.[110] Adela's good standing with high-ranking churchmen served her well: the papally-mediated settlement to her multi-party dispute vindicated the claims of both countess and bishop against the canons and Ivo was authorized to promote members of Adela's household in the cathedral chapter.[111]

In late March 1104, Adela probably joined count Hugh of Troyes and young Thibaut at a legatine council in Troyes that treated several ecclesiastical affairs of concern to her.[112] By November she had journeyed to Sancerre, where she was joined by Hildebert, bishop of Le Mans, who undoubtedly briefed her on Henry's trip to his diocese to recruit allies against Robert Curthose.[113] Adela was in northern Berry to organize the marriage of her eldest son, William, to Agnes of Sully.

Adela's decision to marry William to Agnes was triggered by king Philip's reassertion of direct royal rule over Bourges and Dun in southern Berry, though it capped events initiated eight years previously. In 1096 Agnes's father, Giles, who held the honor of Sully from the Thibaudians and had no male heir, arranged for Stephen-Henry to inherit Sully and its dependent castles.[114] Giles then frequented Adela's court until his death soon after April 1100, when his younger daughter Agnes probably became a ward of the countess.[115] Around this same time, Giles's son-in-law, the viscount of Bourges, pledged his viscounty to king Philip in order to raise funds for a Holy Land campaign. Early in 1100 and again in 1102, when the viscount was presumed killed at the battle of Ramla, king Philip marched to Bourges to exercise his new authority personally.[116] Between the king's trips, Adela traveled to the Thibaudian domains in northern Berry, where she, followed by Agnes and young count William, confirmed arrangements made by Giles and Stephen-Henry for a Benedictine priory.[117]

However, in 1104, the viscount of Bourges, released from captivity at the hands of the Muslims, returned to France.[118] King Philip journeyed again to Bourges to receive the viscomital rights from the viscount, who retired to a nearby monastery.[119] By November Adela had arranged for William, her only son of marriageable age at the time, to marry Agnes so that he could exercise direct comital rule in Sully and its dependent castles.[120] Thus, as king Philip steadily moved to reassert royal rule in southern Berry, Adela matched his trips with her own personal displays of authority and orchestrated events to consolidate comital power in northeastern Berry, a region critical to securing passage between the western and eastern portions of the Thibaudians' domains.

While Adela was jockeying with the king of France, king Henry proceeded with his preparations to unseat Robert Curthose, even though his dispute with archbishop Anselm over investitures remained unresolved after Anselm's audience with the pope in 1103. Henry took the offensive against Robert in the spring of 1105 while Anselm, who had stayed in central France, received a papal letter excommunicating Henry's chief lay advisor and promising to pronounce on the king himself shortly. Rumors spread that Henry was to be excommunicated, leading to defections in his ranks.[121] At this point, Anselm, learning that Adela was ill at Blois, decided to visit her. According to the monk who accompanied him and later wrote an account of their travels, Anselm found Adela well on the way to recovery and spent several days discussing various spiritual and worldly affairs with her. In response to the countess's inquiries about what brought him north, Anselm revealed that he planned to excommunicate Henry. Adela was greatly disturbed and decided to do what she could to effect a reconciliation between her brother and his archbishop.[122]

No wonder Adela was disturbed by this news she had elicited. The countess, with no personal military experience, could not herself intervene directly in the armed conflicts on the borders of her western domains; events of her lifetime showed that only a strong ruler in both England and Normandy, allied with the Thibaudians, could limit Angevin influence there so as to assure the integrity of her western frontier. Her brother Robert was inept but her brother Henry had shown his mettle; thus she had to support Henry's efforts to control Normandy. Since even talk of excommunication weakened Henry's position, Adela had to ensure that sanctions were never pronounced.

Adela persuaded Anselm to accompany her to Chartres, where she sent messengers to Henry explaining the archbishop's position. After taking counsel, Henry asked Adela to bring Anselm to Normandy for negotiations, since he was prepared to accede to some of the archbishop's demands.[123] In July 1105 Adela accompanied Anselm to Laigle for the talks, which effected a personal reconciliation between king and archbishop.[124] Anselm later asserted that it was Adela's intervention that enabled him to meet Henry personally and gave him hope for a positive outcome to their discussions.[125] Although Henry and Anselm were not publicly reconciled until August 1106, Adela continued to keep in touch with Henry's main negotiator.[126] Within two months of their public reconciliation, Henry, with the crucial support of the count of Maine, defeated and imprisoned his brother and became duke of Normandy.[127] Both the monk Eadmer and Anselm himself claimed that Adela's actions were decisive in forcing a resolution to this dispute that cleared the way for Henry's takeover of Normandy. By employing her diplomatic skills to support Henry's cause, Adela reactivated the Anglo-Norman–Thibaudian alliance for the very purposes embodied in her marriage, namely, keeping Maine in the Anglo-Norman orbit and the Thibaudians' western frontiers stable so as to contain the Angevins.

King Philip did not remain idle as Henry worked to reunite Normandy and England. By December 1104 he negotiated the lifting of his decade-long excommunication for his marriage to Bertrada of Montfort, an ex-wife of the count of Anjou.[128] Within two weeks of Henry's victory in Normandy, Bertrada and Philip traveled to Angers, where they personally renewed their ties with the count. They also arranged for the count's son by Bertrada to be named his father's successor; the adolescent heir-designate to Anjou then joined his mother in the royal domain.[129]

Even though she supported Henry in Normandy, Adela could not risk provoking either the count of Anjou or her king. After consolidating the Thibaudian position in northern Berry, she placated the Angevins with a small grant to their family necropolis in Angers.[130] In the spring of 1106, just over a year after the childless marriage between Philip's daughter, Constance, and Hugh of Troyes had been annulled for consanguinity,[131] she hosted the royal family and Philip's large entourage of barons and bishops in Chartres for Constance's wedding to the crusading hero, Bohemond of Antioch. According to several sources, Adela spared no expense and thus acted publicly as a faithful vassal to her king at this time of shifting power relations in northwestern France.[132]

Adela also worked to secure the continued support of strong-armed castellans and influential churchmen. She had bishop Ivo confirm her restoration of the *libertas* of the canons of Bourgmoyen, in Blois.[133] When in Chartres, she enlisted Ivo's support for her proposed reform of a house of secular canons and granted special privileges to the agents of the new leper hospital, while Ivo prepared a new rule for the inmates.[134] Ivo, in turn, used his legal acumen to see that two vexed cases involving former crusading companions of Stephen-Henry, Rotrou III of Nogent and Raoul of Beaugency, were resolved in ways that respected Adela's earlier judgments and allowed these castellans to renew their ties to the Thibaudians.[135] Both Rotrou and Raoul were among the castellans with several lords who fought with the Thibaudians in the warfare of the next decade.

The year 1107 was an especially active one for Adela because it brought the pope on a tour of northern France to secure support from French princes in his dispute with the Emperor. Pope Paschal II and his entourage traveled from La Charité-sur-Loire through southern Berry, Tours, and the county of Blois, to arrive for Easter (April 14) at Chartres, where both Ivo and Adela honorably received them. Adela made generous donations to the papal mission and renewed her peace oath directly to the pope, while Paschal blessed the comital family and probably approved the countess's plans to reform the secular canons in Chartres.[136]

Between a brief meeting with the French kings at Saint-Denis, inconclusive negotiations with imperial emissaries at Châlons-sur-Marne, and the scheduled opening of a council in Troyes on 23 May, Paschal traveled through the comital towns of Lagny, Provins, and Meaux.[137] Although Suger, the abbot of Saint-Denis, has left historians vivid descriptions of his own interview with the pope at La Charité and the discussions between Paschal and the co-kings Philip and Louis, historians have not noticed that Paschal had similar discussions with Adela and actually spent more time and transacted more ecclesiastical business in her domains.[138] Adela was in Meaux sometime in 1107 and at Coulommiers in early July; at Provins in May, Paschal confirmed an earlier decision of her court.[139] Adela may even have hosted the council at Troyes, in the absence of her brother-in-law in the Holy Land.[140] Since the council excommunicated king Philip's candidate to the see of Reims and quashed Louis's engagement, it is not surprising that the royal historian Suger provides no details of these events.[141] Still, they confirm Anselm's earlier remarks about Adela's support for papal policies.[142] Like her father-in-law before her, Adela was adept at taking the moral high ground by implementing papally-sponsored church reform, thereby enhancing Thibaudian authority as truly Christian lords who deserved loyal service from their men.

In the aftermath of the council, which had on its agenda filling the vacant see of Dol (in eastern Brittany, bordering on Normandy), Adela used her influence with several high-ranking churchmen to secure the election of her correspondent Baudry, abbot of Bourgueil, in place of the cleric chosen at the council, who had refused the post. Contravening a decision of his predecessor, Paschal raised Dol from a bishopric to an archbishopric with jurisdiction over the other Breton sees, which were withdrawn from the authority of the archbishop of Tours (who was then allied with the king of France and count of Anjou).[143] With Baudry's appointment as archbishop, Adela effectively limited the powers of her political rivals and aided important allies of her brother.

In that same year (1107), Adela's second son, Thibaut, was knighted, participated in his first armed combat, and began to appear in documents as successor to his father in place of his older brother William.[144] William, about twenty and already married, was remembered by Orderic Vitalis as a "good and peaceful man, blessed with children and wealth."[145] This assessment suggests why Adela replaced him with Thibaut as designated heir: the adolescent Thibaut was already proving to be more adept at the martial skills required of a leading prince. With the young Thibaut able to lead troops in battle, the Thibaudians could begin to play a more active role in the armed hostilities on their borders and intervene militarily to protect their followers.[146] As this episode shows, the bias favoring first-born sons as principal heirs was not a hard and fast rule. Concerned to maintain comital power, Adela chose her second over her first-born son to succeed when events suggested that Thibaut would make the more effective ruler. William appears to have accepted his mother's decision without protest, as he had consented to her choice of his spouse.

Louis VI, who became sole king of France on August 3, 1108, immediately sought to reassert royal claims in Normandy and thus risked upsetting the delicate balance Adela had been able to maintain between Thibaudian support for her brother's strong rule there and comital relations with her kingly neighbor. Adela first steered the Thibaudians on a course of cooperation with the new king. In the spring of 1109 Thibaut accompanied Louis to the Norman-French border for an inconclusive showdown with his maternal uncle Henry.[147] Later in that year Adela attended king Louis's court in Paris and witnessed his donation to a monastery in Chartres.[148] The following year she had Louis ratify her settlement of a violent dispute with another Chartrain monastery and install Thibaut as the monks' defender to succeed Stephen-Henry.[149] Shortly thereafter, Thibaut attended Louis's court at Etampes and subscribed a royal diploma, dated with special reference to Adela, recording donations to canons in Chartres.[150]

While Adela and Thibaut frequented the royal court, however, the count of Anjou attacked Adela's border castellan, Hugh of Chaumont-sur-Loire, opening an armed conflict that continued after the count of Anjou's death in April 1109. Adela intervened incisively by repudiating charges of disloyalty brought against Hugh and then rallying the count of Maine, his cousin Raoul of Beaugency, and the men of Blois to take the field with her castellan.[151] The death of the count of Maine in 1110 intensified the conflict because it brought Maine into the hands of the new count of Anjou, the son of the dowager queen Bertrada, who had married the count of Maine's daughter and heir. Appealing to king Louis for support, the new count of Anjou battled against Norman supporters in Maine and, goaded by his maternal uncle, Amaury of Montfort, made raids into Normandy. In August 1111 Henry returned to the continent in order to defend Normandy and Anglo-Norman dominance in Maine.[152]

Yet in a sign of continued good relations between the king and the Thibaudians, Louis responded in early 1111 to Adela's and Thibaut's appeal to restrain the intransigent Hugh III of Le Puiset (a castellan who counted both the Thibaudians and Louis as his lords). After Hugh was condemned in absentia for seizing ecclesiastical properties, Louis and Thibaut successfully assaulted Le Puiset and captured him.[153] But in the aftermath of this victory, Louis attempted to limit comital castle-building in the Chartrain, claimed an inheritance claimed also by the defeated Hugh, and secured the excommunication of a Thibaudian follower.[154] Because these royal moves to limit comital autonomy came when Louis had reactivated the Capetian-Angevin alliance against her brother, Adela decided to break with Louis and join the Anglo-Normans on the field so that Thibaudian autonomy could be maintained.

Adela won Hugh of Le Puiset to the Thibaudian side with promises of help in his inheritance claim and marriage to her (step)daughter Agnes.[155] Dispatching a Chartrain castellan to Amaury of Montfort, Adela had him negotiate terms by which Amaury withdrew from the fighting in Normandy and persuaded two powerful castellans to take up arms with the Thibaudians.[156] These men, Amaury's son-in-law, Hugh of Crécy, and Hugh's cousin, Milo of Bray, held castles from the king and had recently been fighting in a family quarrel. Milo also held Bray-sur-Seine from the Thibaudians and was heir-designate to the viscounty of Troyes; he was given another (step)daughter of Adela in marriage to confirm his support.[157] Adela also visited her brother-in-law, Hugh of Troyes, who joined the combined Thibaudian–Anglo-Norman forces against the assertive Louis.[158] Raoul of Beaugency and still other men with ties to both the Capetian kings and Thibaudians also rallied to the Thibaudian cause.[159] Rotrou III of Nogent was captured early in the fighting, but the hermit Bernard of Tiron successfully negotiated his release in time for him to join king Henry and

Thibaut in the destruction of Bellême that brought three years of open warfare to a close.[160]

For all his energetic assertiveness, king Louis, the one clear loser of the 1111–13 conflict, had seriously underestimated the desires of his most powerful princes for freedom of action within their domains. The co-count Thibaut may have been young and hence thought amenable to royal persuasion, but Louis sorely miscalculated the authority, strength of extended familial ties, and diplomatic skills of the indomitable countess Adela. While Thibaut led troops in battle, Adela's well-timed visits and behind-the-lines diplomacy clearly influenced the course of the fighting. Neutralizing Amaury of Montfort was a strategic coup of first importance and Amaury was formally pardoned by Henry in 1113.[161] How much of Adela's prodigious wealth was added to her political currency of marriageable daughters has escaped the extant record, but the number of powerful castellans who rallied to their Thibaudian lord against their king should be noted.

The Anglo-Norman–Thibaudian victories had also brought the count of Anjou, Fulk V, to a separate peace. Fulk engaged his infant daughter to Henry's designated but still minor heir, thereby assuring Norman dominance in Maine and limiting the threat of direct Angevin attacks against Normandy and the Thibaudians.[162] Adela and Henry reinforced their family ties: Adela's son Stephen, who had been knighted by his maternal uncle and joined him in the fighting, was guaranteed an inheritance in Henry's realm, while Adela's daughter Matilda married Henry's powerful ward, Richard of Chester.[163] Adela's and Henry's mutual support of the leper hospital in Chartres and the hermit Bernard's new foundation at Tiron also helped assure the continued support of both Bernard and bishop Ivo for the family's political agenda.[164]

During the relative calm which followed the settlement of 1113, Adela and Thibaut journeyed to Reims to join their king at an ecclesiastically-sponsored peace synod in March 1114. Hugh of Troyes, recently remarried, also attended and asked Adela, Thibaut, and Louis to confirm at least one pious bequest before leaving on another trip to the Holy Land.[165] Adela then toured her eastern domains while Thibaut probably traveled to England with his brother Stephen.[166]

Would the peace last? Back in France in the autumn of 1115, Thibaut joined with Adela's seneschal to capture William II of Nevers as he returned home from a royal campaign.[167] William was not only in the midst of a dispute with Adela's seneschal in northern Burgundy but had also dissuaded Louis from accepting the homage of Henry's son for Normandy.[168] By refusing to accept this homage, Louis signaled that he, at the first opportune moment, would move to support the claims of Robert Curthose's son, William Clito, to Normandy and thus upset the Thibaudian–Anglo-Norman position. Despite the ecclesiastically-sanctioned peace, Ivo of Chartres refused to excommunicate Adela's son for his act of aggression against William, which Louis interpreted as a direct provocation by the Thibaudians.[169]

In early 1116 skirmishing broke out between Thibaut and king Louis; the following April Henry sailed to the continent to support his nephew. The fighting intensified in 1118 as Louis rallied a powerful coalition to win Normandy for William Clito.[170] Louis ravaged the Chartrain, but Adela, Henry, Thibaut, and Stephen met together at least once and swore to uphold the terms by which a local knight sold his inheritance to Thibaut, who then conferred it on a Norman follower of Henry.[171] Whatever else transpired at this family council, it indicates Adela's continued role in the behind-the-lines recruitment of allies in a time of armed conflict. Though Thibaut was proving to be an able prince, the renewal of hostilities raised the possibility that he might die in battle; the aging countess wisely chose not to relinquish her position as family head.[172]

In 1119, while the pope was making his way through the Thibaudian domains to the Council of Reims, Henry, Thibaut, and Stephen turned the tables on Louis and his powerful coalition.[173] Adela toured her eastern domains, at a safe distance from the heaviest fighting and where she could keep abreast of the council's proceedings. While her sons fought, Adela settled disputes, made donations to religious houses, and bought land to endow a new Cistercian monastery in a strategic frontier zone. Though Thibaut joined his mother on some of these occasions, when he could bring her up-to-date on the progress of the fighting, Adela also acted independently.[174]

King Louis hosted the council of Reims, which he hoped would condemn his rivals.[175] Because clerics from the Anglo-Norman realm ably defended their king, the pope postponed judgment on the belligerents until he heard Henry's version of events.[176] Lengthy and delicate negotiations ensued, eventually resulting in another settlement wholly favorable to king Henry and the Thibaudians. One of Henry's principal negotiators was the exiled archbishop of York, Thurstan, who supported Henry's Norman politics despite his ecclesiastical dispute with his king. As he shuttled through northeastern France, bargaining with the parties involved to resolve both conflicts, he visited Adela at least twice. Like Anselm more than a decade earlier, Thurstan discussed his plans and concerns openly with the countess and was reconciled to her brother shortly thereafter.[177] Adela clearly had lost none of her diplomatic acumen.

Soon after Easter 1120, Thurstan accompanied Adela, then in her early fifties, to the monastery of Marcigny, where she could keep one eye on the world while preparing for death in a style befitting her princely status.[178] Though the final settlement between Henry and Louis concerning Normandy was probably not formalized until after Adela's departure, negotiations on terms favorable to Henry were well advanced by Easter.[179] However, as in 1111–13, the Anglo-Norman–Thibaudian victories had already brought the count of Anjou to a separate peace. The wedding between Fulk V's daughter and Henry's designated heir, contracted in 1113, was celebrated in June 1119, with Maine granted as dowry by Fulk.[180] Thus, prior to her retirement, Adela could assume that Angevin agressiveness, whether against the Normans in Maine or the Thibaudians' western domains, would be contained. Her resolute pursuit of the Thibaudian–Anglo-Norman alliance, forged to limit Angevin expansion, allow the Thibaudians to consolidate their power, and enhance comital autonomy in face of their royal neighbors, could be deemed a success.

By this time Adela had also positioned her surviving children to advance in the world according to their abilities. Her eldest son William, who had proved less able than his younger brother to act as an authoritative and powerful count, was married and settled at Sully; several of his children would make their careers in their great-uncle Henry's domains.[181] Thibaut, then approaching thirty, was well-tried in battle and had been well-groomed in governance, by both his mother and paternal uncle, Hugh, who soon would name Thibaut his heir as well. Stephen, who stayed with Adela through 1110, served his military apprenticeship with his mother's brother and won a princely inheritance in Henry's realms, thereby virtually eliminating the possibility of power struggles with his brother Thibaut.[182] Adela's youngest son Henry was then a monk at Cluny, the brother house of Marcigny; his maternal uncle would see to his promotion in the English church.[183] Adela found for her daughter Matilda a husband befitting her status in king Henry's entourage; unfortunately, the childless couple drowned in the White Ship disaster about seven months after Adela retired. Adela's two other (step)daughters had been married to assure the support of men of viscomital rank in the Thibaudian domains. One saw a son advanced in the English church, the other soon saw her marriage annulled; her fate is unknown.[184] For the well-being and status of individual family members, Adela thus also used the Thibaudian–Anglo-Norman alliance to Thibaudian advantage. As a contemporary poet had proclaimed, "with [Adela] ruling as duke, the glory of the realm stands affirmed and flourishes."[185] Nothing in the historical record contradicts his claim.

Retirement and Death

Marcigny, founded in the mid-eleventh century as the sister house of Cluny, was praised by contemporaries as a haven for aristocratic widows seeking to devote themselves to God with a balanced regimen of hand work, psalmody, and prayer while avoiding the extremes of corporate poverty and ascetic severity.[186] It also served as a retreat for high-ranking churchmen, and was only about thirty miles from Cluny where Adela's youngest son was a monk. Its founder had been the godfather of Adela's brother-in-law, Odo, and Anselm of Canterbury had been well-received by the nuns in 1100.[187] This combination of international prestige, appeal to aristocratic tastes, and family ties most probably drew Adela to Marcigny.

During her seventeen years as a nun, Adela continued to exercise her skills as an able and literate ruler, both within and beyond her convent walls. Peter the Venerable, an abbot of Cluny who visited Marcigny, reported that the former countess was a respected spiritual guide to her sisters who once summoned a local castellan to her presence to answer accusations of having imposed unjust exactions on the nuns' lands.[188] These actions lend credence to later convent traditions that Adela became the nuns' prioress.[189] Adela also continued her correspondence with Hildebert of Le Mans, while king Henry placed Marcigny's English possessions under royal protection because his sister was a nun there.[190]

Adela likewise intervened in the domains she had ruled as countess. Since she had never implemented her proposed reform of the canons at Saint-Martin-au-Val in Chartres, Adela sent a document addressed to "all the faithful of the church" and probably wrote directly to Thibaut describing her earlier plans. Responding to Adela's missives, Thibaut implemented the reform in 1128, with the support of Hugh of Le Puiset and his wife Agnes (Thibaut's sister).[191] Sometime after 1133/34 Adela heard that the canons of Saint-Calais had re-opened an earlier dispute with the Marmoutier monks at Francheville. She thus sent sealed letters to Thibaut and the bishop of Chartres explaining how she had already negotiated a settlement between the disputants.[192] Thibaut, who had been a boy at that time, saw that Adela's original terms were upheld.

One of Adela's informants about worldly affairs was Peter the Venerable, who visited Normandy in the course of his frequent international travels. Late in 1135 he wrote to inform Adela of the circumstances of her brother's death and passed on what little he knew about the troubled state of affairs in England and Normandy caused by Henry's death without a male heir. Explaining that he had sent envoys to the archbishop of Rouen and Adela's son, then bishop of Winchester, he implied that he would keep Adela informed of events as they transpired.[193]

Henry's only legitimate son and designated heir had drowned accidently when the White Ship sank some seven months after Adela retired.[194] Failing to produce a son with his second wife, Henry eventually designated his daughter, the empress Matilda, as his successor. However, at his death, the Norman barons moved to take Adela's son Thibaut as their new lord and then readily accepted her son Stephen, after he had been been consecrated king of England with the connivance of his younger brother.[195] Thibaut supported his brother militarily in the succession dispute which ensued, but Adela died (on March 8, 1137 when she was about seventy) and was buried at Marcigny prior to the confirmation of Stephen's claims in Normandy through the homage of his son to king Louis.[196] Anniversary prayers were offered for Adela in at least nineteen churches in the centuries after her death, affirming that in both life and in death she made a lasting impression on generations of men across France and England.[197]

Henry's search for an heir after November 1120 and king Louis's continued assertiveness led to a shift in the patterns of alliance in northern France. However, Thibaut ably applied policies learned from his mother to consolidate Thibaudian power as circumstances changed. He continued to promote ecclesiastical reform, support new forms of religious life, and rely on influential churchmen as means to bolster his authority as a defender of the church — an approach to governance Orderic Vitalis claimed Thibaut learned from his mother.[198] His focus on the family's eastern domains was in part the result of the troubled state of affairs in the west caused by the wars between Stephen and Matilda, but Thibaut was also building on economic and administrative foundations strengthened by Adela, particularly during her later years as countess.[199] Yet Thibaut did not abandon his family's attempts to regain its original patrimonial honor of Tours until after 1141.[200] By that time, however, the count of Anjou was effectively duke of Normandy, and Thibaut's brother, supported by the king of France, was struggling to maintain his hold on the English crown against his cousin, the count of Anjou's wife.

In this new world, a Thibaudian–Anglo-Norman alliance on the lines conceived by Thibaut III and William the Conqueror and actively pursued by Adela and Henry I was unthinkable. Still, the significance of this alliance in the late eleventh and early twelfth centuries as a means to contain Angevin expansiveness so that the Thibaudians could set about consolidating their widespread domains in the face of powerful neighbors should not be underestimated. Only in this context can Adela's widely reported deeds fully be assessed. And only in light of Adela's accomplishments can historians fully understand how Thibaut, dubbed "the Great" by contemporaries, was able to inherit and rule, effectively and single-handedly, his family's vast domains. Nor should it be forgotten that it was Adela's relationship to William the Conqueror that gave her son Stephen a claim to the English throne. Her brother Henry's accession as king of England was largely the result of the premature death of their brother, William Rufus, and Henry's one legitimate son died in a shipwreck. Adela, as an Anglo-Norman by birth and a Thibaudian by marriage, transmitted an acknowledged claim to the English throne to her sons, one of whom took advantage of circumstances and made that claim good.

Conclusions

Aristocratic women are still too frequently thought of as passive pawns in the power plays of men. Adela's life and political career show how aristocratic women could play authoritative and decisive roles in the politics of their day. In a world where lordly households were centers of political activity, lands and titles were largely transmitted within families, and effective power depended on the ability to command the loyalty of other powerful people, the love ideally thought to bind family members to each other and followers to their lords could not be taken for granted. This love had to be actively fostered and renewed, through the exchange of gifts and favors, effective protection, and generous patronage. Women's roles in lordly households and pivotal positions in aristocratic families assured that many would find themselves well placed to enter the public political arena.

The royal-born Adela, married to a man at least eighteen years her senior to cement an alliance between two princely families, became the countess of multiple counties and acted as an acknowledged co-count with her husband as the couple strove to consolidate comital authority in their widespread domains. An active participant in the comital court, where patronage was dispensed and justice done, Adela assured that her husband treated lay followers honorably and protected influential churchmen, while at the same time confirming important comital prerogatives. Stephen-Henry, of princely rank, acted publicly with his literate wife of yet higher status to assure that the Thibaudians appeared as princes worthy of faithful service.

Yet at the same time, Adela fostered contacts with members of her natal family. Thus, when she became head of the comital family, first as regent for her crusading husband and then as a widow, Adela was in a position to reactivate the alliance confirmed in her marriage when it suited her political aims as countess of Blois, Chartres, and Meaux. Through her own astute exercise of comital authority, fostering of extended family ties, prudent management of patronage, and adroit diplomacy for over twenty years, Adela intervened decisively in the tumultuous power politics of her day. Her deeds assured the continued prosperity of the Thibaudian family, even when events after her monastic retirement rendered untenable the alliance she had manipulated to such good effect. In her last years as a nun, Adela worked to secure her monastery's possessions and intervened in the domains she had ruled as countess.

Without doubt, Adela's position as the one royal-born daughter of one of the greatest warrior-princes of her day was unique, while the opportunities presented to her during her lifetime were exceptional. But Adela was *not* exceptional in being of higher status and from a more powerful family than her husband; in being considerably younger than her husband and finding herself a widow responsible for young heirs; in having direct access to liquid and landed wealth from her dowry and dower; and in being well-educated in the language, together with the ideas transmitted by it, used by cultivated and powerful churchmen. Through their access, both direct and indirect, to diverse sources of power and lordly authority, aristocratic women at all stages of their lives could find themselves acting in situations, and affecting the distribution of power, far beyond the domestic hearth.

Only when the sources for aristocratic women are analyzed in the context of the politics of lordly families can the full historical significance of their actions be assessed. Historians must take into account the virtual conflation of "public" and "private" powers in lordly households as well as the fundamental bilaterality of medieval family structure, while avoiding unsubstantiated assumptions about women's "natural" passivity, religiosity, or domestic sentimentality. As with the case of Adela of Blois, when the sources are allowed to speak—even when the historian is not obliged to take every word at face value—historians will surely discover that women exercised more acknowledged power than has been assumed and that accounts of medieval politics are incomplete if they ignore the deeds of female lords.

2

Aristocratic Women
in the Chartrain

Amy Livingstone

EARLY ONE SPRING MORNING in the 1040s, Emeline of Châteaudun rose to prepare for a journey north to Chartres to the residence of her lord, vidame Hugh. She had heard from a traveling monk that the count of Blois-Chartres was consulting with his vassals, including Hugh, regarding the continuing conflict with the count of Anjou. Emeline also wished to make a donation to the monks of Marmoutier, one of the most prestigious religious houses of the region: she planned to give them half of the church of Saint-Lubin at Morée so the monks would pray for the souls of her relatives. Joining her on the trip was her son Herbert. As she hurried down to the hall to break her fast, she wondered whether her brother William and her niece had already arrived at the monastery of Bonneval, where Emeline and Herbert would be meeting them on their way to Chartres. Also gathering at Bonneval for the trip to Chartres were Emeline's married daughter, Rotrude, and her grandson, who were expected to witness and give their consent to Emeline's gift, as were Emeline's son, brother, and granddaughter, so that the monks could be assured that Emeline's entire family approved.

Later that day Emeline and her brother, niece, daughter, son, and grandson approached the city of Chartres, where the cathedral towers stood high in the distance. Count Thibaut — count of Blois, Chartres, Meaux, and Troyes — his family, and entourage already were present, as were representatives of the abbot of Marmoutier and several powerful people of the region who hoped to conduct business with the count or to deliberate with him over continuing Angevin aggression. Sometime during this gathering, Emeline made her gift to Marmoutier. Her family and her lords vidame Hugh and count Thibaut approved of the gift, as did Hugh's wife and sons

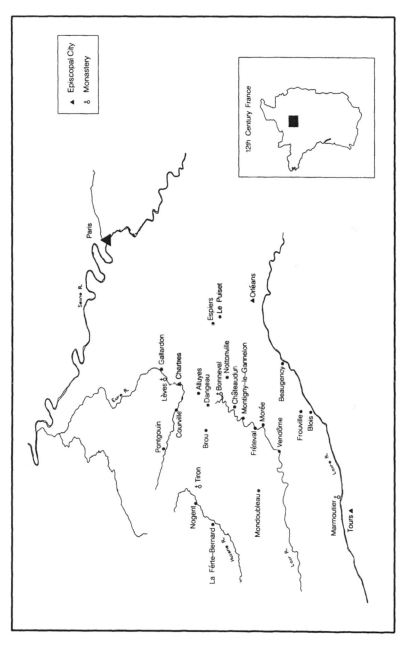

Map 2. The Chartrain.

and several of the important castellans and knights of the Chartrain. A monastic scribe recorded the event:

Let all the faithful, and especially those who succeed us, know that Emeline of Châteaudun gave to the abbey of Marmoutier half of the church of Saint-Lubin of Morée and all that pertains to that church. . . . This [gift] was authorized by her son Herbert, her daughter Rotrude with her son Hervé, and also William, Emeline's brother, and his daughter Rotrude. Hugh the vidame of Chartres from whom Emeline held this church, as well as count Thibaut [III] to whose fief it pertained, freely assented to and affirmed the gift. Witnesses to this transaction were: Adela wife of vidame Hugh, Guerric son of the same Hugh, Hugh his [Guerric's] brother, Albert [vidame Hugh's] brother; Warner Eye of the Wolf; Fulcher the son of Nivelon; Ivo of Courville, Bernard of Aisa, Ganelon the treasurer of Saint-Martin of Tours, Burchard the son of Hugo of L'Ile-Bouchard.[1]

Although my account of Emeline's day and the context of her grant is but one plausible reconstruction of otherwise undocumented events, the scribe's record of her actual donation raises some fundamental points about the experience of aristocratic women and the structure of elite families in the central Middle Ages. Here a woman donates property that she holds in fief from two lords, directly from vidame Hugh and indirectly from count Thibaut. Acting with her are her daughter, son, grandson, brother, and niece. The monastic recipient of Emeline's gift and the scribe who recorded the event viewed her family as comprising all the named persons, of both sexes, and Emeline's collateral as well as lineal relatives. In acting alone, with only the consent of her closest kin and lords, Emeline was not, in fact, unusual among Chartrain women of the medieval landholding elite. Yet historians who recognize the power women exercised through the aristocratic family in the early Middle Ages have viewed the profound changes following the collapse of the Carolingian world as resulting in restricting the power of women by the eleventh century, when they were relegated to a "domestic sphere."[2] Georges Duby argued this interpretation most effectively: he depicted the early medieval family as an open system, one in which all children and related kin enjoyed rights to family property until the eleventh century, when families attempted to prevent the successive division of their patrimonies (family holdings) and ultimate impoverishment. They consequently adopted a new family structure and new inheritance practices that restricted property to the line of the eldest male; younger sons, daughters, and extended family members thus were excluded from sharing the patrimony. Aristocratic women, according to this hypothesis, were marginalized and became powerless in a Middle Ages that Duby characterized as "resolutely male."[3] Emeline of Châteaudun and her peers would not have recognized this description of their life experience.

Like Emeline, the women discussed in this chapter were of modest status. Most were the wives, daughters, or sisters of castellans, lords, and knights; and all lived in the Chartrain, a region southwest of Paris stretching from the town of Chartres to the Loire River and Blois. To reconstruct their lives we must search out sources not concerned exclusively with the exploits of kings, bishops, and popes. Because medieval elites controlled property, they appear in documents that record the transfer of these possessions, sources that are called charters. Although most original charters have been destroyed by fires, rats, and revolution, historians are able to consult copies of the charters that the monks made in books called cartularies, which allowed abbeys to organize and administer their property. The ecclesiastical foundations of the Chartrain offer a rich collection of these documents.

A charter, at its most basic, records the transfer of property from a lay donor to the church. Because individual ownership of property did not exist in the Middle Ages, donors needed the consent of family members who had a claim to the donated property. Most charters give the name of the donor(s) as well as a list of those relatives who approved or witnessed the gift. Those who held the rights of lordship over or from the property in question also needed to approve its transfer, and therefore they are often listed in the document as consenters. To compensate relatives, lords, and vassals for the loss of the property and potential revenues deriving from it, the monks frequently awarded a countergift consisting of a small cash payment. Such a gift is an indication that the recipient exercised a right or potential right to the property.

Why did aristocrats give away their property to the monks? Most made gifts to provide prayers for their souls or the souls of their relatives, living and deceased, and to secure the intercession of the monks and local saints. Participation in these transactions also connected donors and consenters to the monastic communities, from which they derived many social and spiritual benefits. A gift could serve to remind other elites of the status of an individual or family within the community and draw attention to their particular relationship with the monks. While the act of giving meant that elites lost the use of certain property, in the end the creation of alliances with the monks and patron saints, as well as the social and spiritual rewards from such associations, more than made up for the loss of a vineyard, a mill, a meadow, or revenues.

Who were the aristocratic patrons of the monasteries? Emeline of

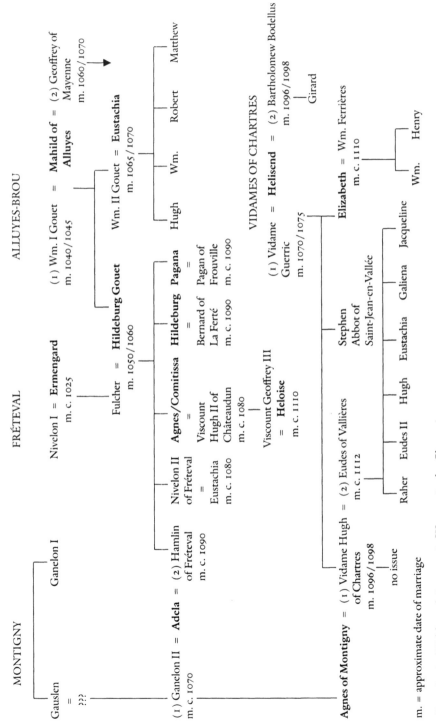

MONTIGNY   FRÉTEVAL   ALLUYES-BROU

Genealogical Table 2. Aristrocratic Women in the Chartrain.

m. = approximate date of marriage

Châteaudun and her peers would have been aware of the comings and goings of the most elite people of the region. Indeed, Emeline's gift demonstrates that she herself was personally acquainted with many of the most powerful individuals of the Chartrain. Most of the Chartrain lies in the counties of Blois and Chartres, which were under the authority of the count of Blois-Chartres. These regions, as well as lands stretching down the Loire River to Tours, had been under the control of that family since the tenth century. In the eleventh century this family lost control of the lands in the Touraine but gained the county of Champagne through inheritance. As well as being the most powerful secular lord in the Chartrain, the count was one of the most important lords in central France. Those who held their land directly from the count were an elite few. Emeline's lord vidame Hugh of Chartres was a direct vassal of Thibaut III, count of Blois, Chartres, Meaux, and Troyes. Like Hugh, the vicecomital families of Blois, Chartres, and Châteaudun held lands and lordships directly from the count. Other members of the elite, including Emeline herself, were indirect vassals of the counts. Within in this group were many influential lords of the region. Among the most prominent — and acquaintances of Emeline — were the lord of Fréteval, the lord of Montigny, the lord of Courville (all of whom took part in Emeline's grant), and the Gouet family, which controlled the lordships of Alluyes and Brou (see Genealogical Table 2).

As well as housing residences of the count and vidame, the city of Chartres was the seat of a bishop and hence the home of a cathedral. Commanding both spiritual authority and secular influence, the bishop was an extremely powerful force in the region. A testament to this power is evident in the creation of the office of *vicedominus*, or vidame, which was created to provide the bishop with a secular agent who could help him protect and administer his extensive lands. Several important monastic foundations were also situated in the Chartrain. In the eleventh century two monastic houses, Saint-Père of Chartres and the abbey of Marmoutier, were the most prominent. Although Marmoutier was located near Tours and not in the Chartrain proper, its monks established many priories and houses in the area north of the Loire River. Moreover, the counts of Chartres had been strong supporters and benefactors of Marmoutier, and many of their followers copied their example and patronized this monastic house. In the twelfth century, a wave of ecclesiastical reform swept Europe and several new monasteries were founded or reformed in and around Chartres. Saint-Jean-en-Vallée, situated just outside of the city, was reformed through the combined efforts of countess Adela and bishop Ivo of Chartres. The abbey of Notre-Dame-de-Josaphat was also founded near Chartres by bishop Geoffrey and his family, the Lèves. Far from the city of Chartres, the monastery of Tiron was established on the western fringe of the region. All these monasteries kept the documents that record the names of the landholding elite and provide the pieces needed to assemble a composite biography of the women of the Chartrain.

Charters are a very useful tool for reconstructing the lives of medieval elites. Because daughters and sons, sisters and brothers, wives and husbands exercised rights over property, they appear in these documents, and, even if they appear only once, we are given a glimpse into a medieval life.[4] In some cases, when an individual appears in several acts over the course of his or her life, a more complete picture emerges. In either instance, the charters reveal wellborn women of the landholding elite actively involved in diverse familial and lordly activities, with the same rights enjoyed by countess Adela herself at a higher level. Throughout their lives — as daughters, wives, and widows — aristocratic women exercised the powers and responsibilities of the noble-born.[5]

Daughters and Sisters

In a sample of charters from the Chartrain, 35 percent refer to daughters, primarily as consenters to their parents' gifts and sales of property and to the resolutions of disputes.[6] Daughters appeared in those transactions precisely because they shared in their family's complex web of rights.[7] When Emeline of Châteaudun alienated property in the case cited above, her married daughter attended the event and gave her consent. But unmarried daughters still living at home also consented to their parents' property transactions. When Hugh Reortarius sold his mill to the monks of Marmoutier, he secured the consent of his relative, Geoffrey of Saint-Bomert, perhaps his cousin, and of Simon, from whom Hugo held the mill.[8] The monks thought it necessary to give Hugh's wife, daughter, and son countergifts to obtain their approval of the sale.[9] Lord Ganelon of Montigny, his wife, and his nephew authorized the sale as well, since the mill pertained to Ganelon's lordship (*casamentum*). And Rainald, who may have been Simon's bastard son, also witnessed the act. Thus the rights of the closest kin, male and female, nuclear and extended, legitimate or illegitimate, were acknowledged, in addition to those pertaining to lordship. Transferral of property was a complicated and tricky business, for a gift could be challenged later by nonconsenting kin. Daughters, like sons, were included because they — and their heirs — enjoyed some future right to the property in question and might inherit a portion or even the entire patrimony. For these reasons, families secured the consent of their daughters when selling, mortgaging, or donating family property.

Did the daughters of elite families, whose rights were recognized in property transfers, actually obtain any of their family's inheritance? The evidence from both the eleventh and twelfth centuries indicates that they did. Penny Schine Gold has characterized inheritance among the landholding elite in the neighboring county of Anjou as "joint but unequal inheritance," a characterization that serves equally well for the region of Blois-Chartres.[10] In the cartulary of Marmoutier for the region of the Dunois, bishop Ivo of Chartres, for example, refers to a church held by a woman "by right of inheritance" (*jure hereditario*). There is also Mahild of Alluyes, who carries the title lord of Alluyes and holds the honor there from her father *jure hereditario*.[11] Yet, in spite of these examples, it is impossible to determine whether daughters in the Chartrain routinely shared inheritances with their brothers or inherited only in the absence of a male heir.

Daughters inherited feudal as well as allodial property (that is, property free from obligations to a lord). Although a fief was supposedly granted only for the lifetime of the recipient, in reality families often retained fiefs for several generations, and in some cases even daughters inherited fiefs. The woman named Alburg who sold to the monks of Saint-Père the fief (*feodum*) she held "through inheritance from her father" did so with the consent of her daughter Odelina, her likely heir, an indication that daughters could inherit feudal property from their mothers as well as their fathers.[12] Alburg's husband, Robert the Norman, provided the military service associated with the fief, but the fief remained her property. The monks referred to her as a "certain women of ours" (*quedam femina nostra*) in parallel usage with "certain of our men" that the monastic scribes used to refer to the abbey's fiefholders. For the monks, Alburg was a vassal who simply happened to be a woman.[13]

A daughter might even inherit the office of *vicedominus* of Chartres. Created in the tenth century, the office had become hereditary by the eleventh century. In the 1080s it was held by vidame Guerric, whose eldest son Hugh succeeded as vidame. But since Hugh had no children and his younger brother Stephen had entered the church (he later became abbot of Saint-Jean-en-Vallée), their sister Elizabeth became *vicedomina* of Chartres after her mother's death.[14] It was Elizabeth's son William who later passed the title and honors of vidame to his own son. Elizabeth's right to inherit her father's office was not usurped by her husband or her own sons, a demonstration that more distantly related male kin did not necessarily displace a more closely related woman, even in high office. Within elite families, then, even if an eldest son was preferred to succeed, that was not always possible; daughters were not thereby excluded from inheriting property, either allodial or feudal, or offices with their attendant titles.

Outright individual ownership of property did not exist in the Middle Ages, and because property was bound by a complex intertwining of familial rights the frequent disputes over gifts and their resolutions reveal the strength and legitimacy of women's claims.[15] Women participated in those disputes and were parties to the resultant quitclaims throughout the twelfth century. Let us follow one of these disputes. Rainald, an unmarried knight, lay dying. While contemplating his imminent death, he decided to become a monk of Saint-Père of Chartres. To join the monks, he needed to make a gift. So he called his sisters, his brother-in-law, and his lords (a mother and her son) to his deathbed and with their consent gave tithes to the monastery. But after Rainald's death the donation was challenged by William Pexus, who claimed that Rainald had held the tithes from his fief. William, however, eventually abandoned his claim, with the assent of his wife, sons, daughter, and sister, all those who had a possible future claim to the fief.[16] Similarly, when a certain Waldin gave up his "unjust" claim to a church, the monks paid a special visit to his sister Pagana to secure her consent to the terms of the quitclaim; later, when Waldin made a further donation in the presence of his father and uncle, Pagana not only gave her assent but jointly with her brother placed a symbol of the donation on the altar. That symbolic act, like signing the charter recording the gift, solemnized and reinforced the donation. To the monks, Pagana's consent — like her brother's — was tantamount to legitimizing the donation: "Waldin and Pagana consented to it, nay truly they gave this gift."[17] Pagana's participation in these transactions in differing capacities attests to the claim she exercised to Waldin's possessions and suggests that her interest in her family lands was not confined to her dowry. Waldin apparently considered his sister as his likely heir in the absence of his own children, and the monks were careful to obtain her consent to the quitclaim in order to ensure peace with the future lord of these properties.[18]

As daughters and sisters, aristocratic women could expect to participate with their natal families in gifts, sales, quitclaims, and disputes, and the ceremonies to implement them. Upon the death of their parents, many shared in the inheritance of family lands, fiefs, and honors. It has been suggested that once daughters or sisters married they became affiliated with their husbands' families and lost identification with their natal family. Yet women of the Chartrain maintained control of their inheritances while married, and their inheritances were not automatically absorbed into their husbands' patrimonies. While marriage represented an important transition in the lives of aristocratic women, it did not always entail a sharp break with previous attachments and social networks. Indeed, for some women marriage meant a continuation of responsibilities and an extension of social ties.

Married Women

MARRIAGE

The landholding families used marriages to create alliances, to extend or bolster family power, and to elevate their social status. Marriage into a family of a more prestigious line or with more wealth or political position could act to benefit the entire family. While neither daughters nor sons had much say about the selection of their spouses, families were bound by certain restrictions, such as making sure both children consented to the match, that they were of an appropriate age to do so, and that the marriage was not within certain prohibited degrees of kinship. Yet for most of the central Middle Ages aristocrats tended to view marriage as a political tool. Through the twelfth century marriages could be dissolved if enough pressure was brought to bear. Even though the church attempted to prevent this by insisting that marriages were indissoluble, the codes dictating marriage policy were not consistently enforced throughout Europe. Moreover there were loopholes in canon law concerning divorce and annulment, and aristocrats and kings were able to take advantage of them.[19] Consequently a child could be expected to forge several new alliances as family circumstances and agendas changed. This was particularly true for daughters, who married in their late teens and tended to be quite a bit younger than their first husbands.[20] As men also tended to die younger — in war, tournaments or hunting accidents — women, if they survived multiple childbirths, might expect to have more than one husband. A second marriage, however, usually took place later in a woman's life, when she herself may have initiated and arranged the marriage for her own interests rather than those of her parents or natal family.[21]

While a description of medieval marriage may seem cold and heartless to modern readers, and children nothing more than dynastic pawns to be wed at the whim of their family, such alliances were not necessarily devoid of affection or feeling. The Chartrain charters, although sparse, do provide glimpses into the personal relationship between husbands and wives. The knight Ansold, for example, in making a donation to the monastery of Saint-Père of Chartres at the very end of the eleventh century, said that he did so with his "beloved wife" Hildegard.[22] Agnes of Montigny, providing a perspective of an aristocratic wife, was motivated to make a donation to the abbey of Marmoutier "because of her love for her husband."[23] Noble-born women also gave gifts to insure the spiritual health of their deceased husbands, an indication of their concern for their spouses' afterlives as well as their affection and esteem. In 1103 *vicedomina* Helisend and her children made a donation to Saint-Père of the customs from Tréon to honor the anniversary of the death of her first husband, vidame Guerric.[24] Approximately ten years later, Helisend made another gift, this time to benefit the soul of her second husband who was recently deceased.[25] Such signs of affection indicate that some husbands and wives became genuinely fond of each other, if not "in love" with one another. These examples, in conjunction with evidence from the charters of wives' partnership with their husbands in these acts, suggest that some aristocratic marriages were not devoid of emotional fulfillment or attachment.

Dowry, Dower, and Inheritance

When daughters were married, their families provided them with a grant of property in the form of a dowry. The type of marriage portion accorded to brides has been used as a gauge to judge the place and importance of women in the family and society.[26] It has been argued that the adoption of dowry in place of other practices where the groom's family provided a substantial gift, particularly the morning gift or *morgengaben*, reflects a decline in the status of women.[27] The implementation of a dowry system has also been seen as characteristic of impartible inheritance and patrilineage.[28] While charters from the Chartrain contain some information on dowries, they are often vague about the regulations concerning the distribution of the property, and they contain few specifics, such as the age of the bride, that would be useful in reconstructing the experience of women. The key issue here, however, is the control of these properties. Did women retain control of dowries after marriage? Did husbands manage the lands for their wives or did women take an active role in deciding the fate of their marriage portions? Did members of the husband's family have any claims to dowries? Did the bride's natal family? In short, what can be deduced about the rights of women in their families and society from examining the provisions made at marriage for aristocratic women?

Evidence from the Chartrain suggests that married women did indeed retain rights over their dowries. The case of Hugh of Chérville is instructive. When Hugh's daughter Isenburg married Fulcaud of Dangeau, Hugh gave a dowry of two bovates of land, but land he already had donated to the monastery of Marmoutier.[29] A conflict arose, and Fulcaud responded by seizing the land and throwing the monks' plow off the property. Regretting his temper, he and Isenburg quitclaimed their right to this land in the monks' chapter house. Isenburg's approbation and participation in the resolution of this conflict demonstrates that she had to be consulted in transactions pertaining to her property, and that lay women, like lay men, did participate with monks in their chapter houses, the "sacred places" from which women were supposedly excluded.[30] Indeed, lack of a wife's or a daughter's consent to the disposition of her dowry lands was sufficient grounds for her to challenge the donation. Hildiard was another twelfth-century woman who with her husband brought suit for her dowry after her father gave it to the Church. Recognizing her right to the dowry, the monks of Saint-Père gave her and her husband 20 s. in compensation.[31]

Aristocratic wives also received property from their husbands in grants known as dowers, consisting of lands, revenues, or movable property. Women in the Chartrain could receive both dowry and dower.[32] Yet the crucial issue, as with dowries, is who exercised control of dowers after a woman's marriage. As the widow of Robert Corneus stated around 1040, when challenged by the monks of Saint-Père who tried to reclaim property they had granted to Robert, her husband had promised her lifetime use of the property.[33] She even underwent a judicial ordeal to prove her case, and continued to hold the property after remarrying. Robert Corneus's grandchildren waited until she died before taking the property, for they, like the monks, recognized her rightful entitlement to it. A woman named Roscelina, who lived about fifty years after Robert Corneus's wife, also exercised control over her dower. She gave the monks of Saint-Père a barley field which she had been given in dower (*dotis jure*) by her first husband and which she had held for more than twenty years. Her third husband Herbert and her three sons from a second marriage witnessed the gift and were compensated with "small gifts." Even though Rosecelina had twice remarried and had grown sons, her dower from her first husband remained hers. She alone initiated and made the gift of her dower to the monks.[34]

Beyond their dowries and dowers, what other rights to property did aristocratic women exercise? A series of late eleventh-century charters relating the experience of the women in the Fréteval family shows how extensive the rights of married daughters was. When lord Fulcher of Fréteval toward the end of his life made a gift to the abbey of Marmoutier, his sons and daughters, who were probably already married, consented.[35] Fulcher needed the approval of those who had a potential claim to his family property. His daughters Comitissa, Hildeburg, and Pagana continued to exercise their rights after their brother Nivelon II succeeded to the lordship. When Nivelon rectified the wrongs he had committed against the Church before leaving on the First Crusade, by abandoning certain customs to the monks of Saint-Père, both his sister Comitissa, who was married to the viscount of Châteaudun, and his brother Hamlin consented and signed the charter recording Nivelon's renunciation.[36] In recognition of their right to the property, the monks gave them countergifts for their consent, even though both were married and Hamlin had secured a lordship of his own.

At about the same time Nivelon II's brother-in-law, Bernard of La Ferté, laid claim to a *burgus* and vineyard his father-in-law had given to Marmoutier.[37] The charter does not state on what grounds Bernard made his claim or his motives for doing so, but his only claim must have been through his wife Hildeburg, who might not have consented to the original gift. Whatever his reasons, Bernard believed that he and his wife had a legitimate claim to this property. When Bernard abandoned his claim, his two sons, daughter, and grandsons consented to the quitclaim and were awarded countergifts. The children and grandchildren of Hildeburg of Fréteval continued to count in the exercise of power over Fréteval lands. The Fréteval women and their children did not lose their interests in their natal family property, but instead passed those interests to their progeny.

A number of other cases confirm that married women continued to make claims to the property of their natal kin. Odo Borrellus, who in the mid-eleventh century was said to have "unjustly" claimed land from the monks of Marmoutier, asserted that his wife Elisind held the land by right from her father. Although Odo and Elisind dismissed their claim after prolonged quarreling, the monks allowed them life use of the land.[38] Clearly Odo Borellus and Bernard La Ferté brought suits to enforce their wives' rights to natal lands: these women of the Chartrain had not lost their rights to their patrimonies after marriage.

A well-documented case from the early eleventh century illustrates why monastic recipients of property were compelled to pay attention to the rights of married women even when consent had been obtained. A certain Raher, who described himself as a "knight of the secular realm," confirming all that he or his predecessors had previously given to Marmoutier, gave additional property to insure prayers for the souls of his mother and father:

Therefore I, Raher, a knight of the secular world, realizing my many sins and in fearing absolutely the judgment day, for the redemption of the souls of my father Raher and my mother Frodelina and myself, I concede to God and Marmoutier my worldly possessions which were left to me by my own father on his death [these and the donated lands are described]. I did [all of] this with the consent of my lord count Thibaut, and also with the assent of my sisters, namely, Milisend, Rainsoind and Adelaide, with the agreement that after I leave this world, unless I have a son with a legitimate wife, dominion over these properties will go to Saint-Martin. Moreover, I wish and I order that if any of my relatives whether by him or herself or through the agency of another person wishes to bring a claim to this donation, which I made of my free mind and my own will, that person will [have to] pay one hundred pounds of proven gold and he or she will not have a claim to what he or she wants, but rather the donation will remain firm. And so that all possible claimants surrender all grounds for bringing a claim, I, Raher, brought this charter to the court of my lord count Thibaut and by his hand and those of his sworn men, the charter was confirmed. The names of those who saw and heard this have been recorded in testimony. Signed lord Raher; Signed Milisend, his sister; Signed Rainsoind, his sister; Signed Adelaide, his sister; Signed Thibaut, count; Signed Ermenard, countess; Signed Gelduin of Breteuil; Signed Harduin, viscount of Chartres; Signed Hervé, viscount of Blois.[39]

Raher obtained the consent of his adolescent lord count Thibaut III in the presence of Thibaut's mother, countess Ermengard, as well as that of his sisters Milisend, Rainsoind, and Adelaide, but he must have suspected that his act would be contested, for the charter threatened a huge fine of 100 *l.* of gold if any of his relatives challenged the donation. Raher had taken every precaution to ensure that his gift would remain uncontested: he had obtained the consent of his lord and relatives, he made the gift in front of witnesses who were some of the most powerful people of the region, and he had his sisters, lord, and witnesses sign the charter. As he anticipated, his sister Adelaide, whom the monks describe as "younger but more cunning" than Raher, later brought a claim to the donated property:

[After Raher's death] one of his sisters, younger but more cunning, named Adelaide, brought a new claim to her brother's donation, stating that she had not consented [to the gift] when she not only affirmed the gift by her own will and plain pledge, but even by swearing to the gift by her oath. Moreover, she harassed the aforementioned brother monks until the claim was brought to litigation, and through Rainald of Espiers, whom she married, they committed a violent injury to the [disputed] estates and raised an unjust claim. Finally, through the clemency of God and referring to better counsel [i.e., that of God and the monks], [Adelaide and Rainald] accepted from the monks ten pounds and were converted from dissent to agreement and they consented to what they had [earlier] denied. And both came to Marmoutier at Holy Easter Sunday for the vigil commemorating the resurrection of the Lord, and in the presence of abbot Albert and in front of the entire chapter, accepting the benefit of these places which lord Raher had given, they were witnessed to confirm in a clear voice, not only once, but again and again that they authorized without condition the donation lord Raher had made to Saint-Martin, they gave their consent not only with audible words, but also by visible intent and a certain palpable touch when, assenting with their hands, they touched the charter on which the donation of those estates was written and as their authorization placed the gift on the altar of Saint-Martin.[40]

Adelaide asserted that she had not consented to the gift, even though she had earlier signed a charter recording her assent, and she and her husband Rainald continued to harass the monks until the claim was finally litigated. In the end, the monks paid them 10 *l.* and an array of spiritual benefits for dropping their claim.[41] The monks insisted that Adelaide and Rainald repeatedly verbally authorize the gift, as well as giving physical signs of their consent in front of witnesses, to ensure that the quitclaim remained undisputed, as Adelaide's consent was necessary for the gift to stand. That married daughters and sisters were able to bring such contestations on the grounds of not consenting to the original grant demonstrates the force of their right to natal family possessions.

The property rights of married women also extended to land acquired by their husbands.[42] Hildegard, wife of Ansold of Mongerville, gave Saint-Père the land her first husband had given her "to do with as she pleased." She made the gift while dying, with the consent of her son Pagan, his wife and children, as well as her lord viscount Hugh II of Châteaudun. Later another son — Joscelin of Mongerville — disputed the donation, claiming it as part of his patrimony even though it was demonstrated that it was not; he was excommunicated until he repented and acknowledged the invalidity of his claim.[43] Even after she was widowed, remarried, and had mature sons, Hildegard maintained control of property given to her by her husband. The monastic scribe who drew up the charter states that Hildegard could dispose of the land as she saw fit, underscoring the power that women exercised over property subject, as always, to the claim of other family members.

Marriage increased the powers and rights of aristocratic women because it increased their access to property. If endowed with a dowry or dower, a woman could expect to exercise authority over the property during her marriage. Yet the granting of a dowry did not terminate a woman's right to natal family holdings. Even if a woman herself did not inherit anything beyond her dowry, she transmitted claims to natal family property to her children. Parents and siblings were therefore well advised to secure the consent of married daughters, sisters, and their heirs, to prevent a possible dispute. Women also gained access to properties of their married family through dower grants and lands acquired by their husbands. The charters from Blois-Chartres reveal that women's claims to these lands were publicly acknowledged and that monks attempted to secure gifts by gaining the consent of women with rights, sometimes even offering countergifts to obtain it. Married women used their control of these differing properties to create important alliances with neighboring elite families and local churches.

Donors and Patrons

Ermengard, wife of Nivelon I of Fréteval, was typical of aristocratic women in patronizing local monasteries, when on her deathbed she gave the church of Saint-Lubin and its lands to the abbey of Saint-Père. The gift for her soul, according to the charter, came from "her patrimony" (*ex patrimonio suo*), that is, property she had inherited from her natal family.[44] Noblewomen also arranged life estates with the monks for their benefit and that of their kin. Between 1032 and 1037 Agnes of Montigny bought land from the monks of Marmoutier and arranged that certain vineyards and buildings she alone possessed be given to the monks after her death, for the remedy of her soul and that of her husband.[45] Agnes acted completely independently in reaching this agreement that concerned her lands. Yet Agnes was bound by the same customs as men of the elite; hence she secured the consent of her husband and her lord, count Odo II, as well as his wife and sons. Women adhered to the same family and feudal custom when making gifts or taking part in other transactions with the monks, as property was subjected to a multiplicity of claims by relatives and lords.

Wives and mothers frequently made pious bequests for their husbands, children, and parents and in their own behalf. These gifts were made to secure prayers for souls or to partake in other spiritual benefits, such as burial in the monastery or being accepted into the *societas* of the monks. Women often acted for the spiritual well-being of family members. When the wife of Bernard was approaching death, she found that her husband had taken back an allod her mother had previously donated to the abbey of Marmoutier. Bernard's action jeopardized the souls of her mother, her husband, and herself, so she confirmed the gift to the abbey.[46] *Vicedomina* Helisend made gifts to benefit the souls of her two husbands.[47] Likewise a woman named Odelina, the wife of Warin, gave land to Marmoutier on behalf of her deceased husband.[48]

Aristocratic women became enthusiastic supporters of the church in the eleventh and twelfth centuries. One of the major concerns of reformers was to expunge the church of secular or worldly influences.[49] As a consequence, lay people were encouraged by ecclesiastics, including popes and archbishops, to restore churches, tithes, and other "ecclesiastical" property thought to have been unjustly usurped.[50] The influence wives and mothers exerted over their male kin was widely recognized.[51] Anselm of Bec, the archbishop of Canterbury, enlisted the aid of queen Matilda of England, the wife of Henry I and sister-in-law of countess Adela, in intervening with her royal husband on a variety of matters. In 1105 pope Paschal himself wrote to Matilda seeking her intervention in Henry's dispute with Anselm over investitures: "Therefore, beloved daughter, we beg you to watch more carefully over his [Henry I's] keeping and to turn his heart away from wrong counsel so that he will not continue provoking God's fury so greatly against himself. Remember what the Apostle says: The unbelieving husband will be saved by the believing wife. Reprove, beseech, rebuke, so that he may reinstate the aforesaid bishop in his see and permit him to act and preach as his office demands, and also return the churches to his God lest God take from him what he has given."[52] Archbishop Anselm also appealed to countess Clemence of Flanders to help persuade her husband not to invest bishops: "It is your duty, reverend lady and dearest daughter, to mention this and other similar things to your husband in season and out of season, and advise him to prove that he is not lord of the Church, but her advocate, not her step-son but her true son. . . . Thus I beg that countess Clemence should admonish and counsel her husband in this way so that divine clemency may raise both him and her to the kingdom of heaven."[53]

Wives were aware the of the influence they could have over their husbands. In 1104 queen Matilda wrote to Anselm: "For he [Henry I] is more kindly disposed towards you than most people might think. With God's help and my suggestions, as far as I am able, he may become more welcoming and compromising towards you."[54] Women like Clemence and Matilda were recruited as allies in the attempt to reform the Church and free it from secular influence or interference. The tenets of reform were thus brought to the men of the elite through the gentle, and probably persistent, admonitions of their wives.

The charters of the Chartrain provide evidence that local monks, abbots, and holy men urged aristocratic men and women of the region to restore what they considered to be property rightfully belonging to the Church.[55] The eleventh-century woman who restored the most ecclesiastical property and who had the most profound impact on her own family's donation practices was Mahild of Alluyes. Mahild enjoyed control of her own natal properties, as well as those of her first husband, William Gouet, during her widowhood and subsequent second marriage to Geoffrey of Mayenne. Starting in the 1070s, Mahild began restoring ecclesiastical property to the monasteries of the region, at the same time encouraging her vassals to undertake similar acts of piety. One of her vassals, Odo, gave the church of Villevillon to Saint-Père with the consent of his "most noble lord (*domina*) Mahild."[56] Hugh of Brethel restored the church of Chappelle Guillaume to Marmoutier with the consent of "my lord Mahild" (*domina mea Mahildis*) in her presence in the monks' chapter house.[57] Other vassals of the Gouet and Alluyes restored ecclesiastical property, including burial fees, tithes, and a parish church and its revenues.[58] Mahild's response to the call for reform had an impact on the donation patterns of those who held property from her. It also influenced the next generation of the Gouet family.

Mahild's son William II Gouet and his wife Eustachia followed her example, restoring more ecclesiastical properties and supporting restorations by their vassals. Most of those restitutions coincided with William's absence on crusade, when Eustachia exercised sole control of the family lands and titles. Like her mother-in-law, Eustachia was influenced by the preachings of reformers and persuaded her vassals to restore ecclesiastical possessions.[59] One of those was Waldin, who in her presence returned the church and tithes of Estellieux to the monks of Saint-Père.[60] Eustachia herself was a generous patron of Saint-Père. Between 1101 and 1129 she asked the abbot if she could give part of her estate at Saint-Roman of Brou to establish a community of monks. The abbot agreed, as long as her husband and children were in agreement and consented, which they did. Eustachia's family gave many properties, including land, a mill, tithes from the mill, fishing rights, judicial rights, marketing rights, and pannage (the right to pasture pigs) to support the brothers.[61]

It was not simple piety that moved women from the Chartrain to embrace the ideas of reform and to restore ecclesiastical properties. Gifts demonstrated family prosperity and indicated a real concern on the part of these women for the present and future spiritual well-being of their natal, affinal, and conjugal families.[62] Moreover, such gifts allowed the elite to establish important "communities" or ties with the monks. These women were genuinely moved by the appeals of churchmen to aid in reform and restore ecclesiastical property to the church. Their eager response earned them the respect of the clergy. The charters reveal too that as influential patrons, aristocratic women encouraged their male kin and vassals to do the same. Aristocratic women were in many cases both the patrons and defenders of the church — a powerful and important role which both the church and their families recognized and supported. Clearly, such women stood firmly in the center of kin and lord-vassal bonds that structured aristocratic society.

WIVES AS HEADS OF THE FAMILY

In addition to using ecclesiastical patronage to benefit the spiritual well-being of their families, married women often assumed responsibility for the material well-being of their families in the absence of their husbands.[63] Late in the eleventh century, Hildegard Franca became head of her family after her husband, the knight Geoffrey, had "given up all that was secular" to become a monk, leaving her and their sons, who were in the "flower of adolescence." Eventually the sons ended up in Apulia, where one of them, Fulco, fathered a bastard child "whom he sent to [his mother, Hildegard] in his cradle."[64] Hildegard raised the child and "taught him Holy Scripture when he was a small boy." When the child turned eight, she made a generous gift for his entry into the church. This benefaction also established prayers for Hildegard's soul and those of all her relatives. Entrance of this bastard grandson into the monastery where his grandfather and another his relatives were monks is significant. This family clearly felt a strong tie to Saint-Père of Chartres, one that was supported by the entrance of family members into the house and by gifts made to the monks. Fulco's bastard was not relegated to an unknown foundation or a foundation of less importance to the family, as one might expect if elite families were interested in disowning their bastard progeny. Instead Hildegard installed him where his grandfather and one of her relatives were currently serving God and where he would continue to be identified with and nurtured by his family. Hildegard acted completely independently in making arrangements for her grandson.[65] Her mature son, instead of assuming the role of head of the family and taking responsibility for his child himself, looked to his mother for aid and entrusted her with these duties.

As heads of aristocratic households, women assumed responsibility for the family's fiefs, vassals, and titles. The trust that eleventh-century men placed in their wives to fulfill such a spectrum of responsibilities is evident in a quotation from the twelfth-century Anglo-Norman historian Orderic Vitalis. When count Geoffrey II of Perche fell ill while his son Rotrou was on crusade, he entrusted his wife, with help from their vassals, "to keep the peace and maintain order honorably, [and to] protect his land and castles for his only son Rotrou."[66] The count believed his wife would act in the best interest of the family and patrimony, and indeed Rotrou returned several years later to find the county intact and thriving.

The countess of Perche was not an exception. Lady Eustachia Gouet was an active partner with her husband William II in jointly making donations, affirming gifts made by their vassals, and judging disputes.[67] When Hilduin of Alluyes quitclaimed land and tithes, both William and Eustachia confirmed the renunciation at their court.[68] Early in the twelfth century Eustachia assumed responsibility for the family and its lordship during the extended absence of William and his eldest son in the Holy Land. Throughout the period of her rule Eustachia was called *domina*, an indication that she exercised the same powers and prerogatives her husband had. For example, she witnessed Daniel of La Ferté's quitclaim, which took place, according to the scribe, "at court in front of many witnesses, in the presence of *domina* Eustachia."[69] When the tithes of Mont-Richard were falsely claimed and then restored to Saint-Père, the guilty parties quitclaimed in the presence of *domina* Eustachia.[70] Although her two younger sons had already reached their majority before their father's departure, witnessing acts and making their own donations,[71] they did not usurp their mother's authority over the family properties: she continued until around 1120 to rule over the family's vassals and lands.

Although husbands were the natural heads of landholding families, they were not always able to fulfill these responsibilities. They might be absent for long periods of time on pilgrimage or military campaigns, especially after 1095 when many were called to go on crusade to the Holy Land. As the experience of Hildegard Franca demonstrates, men could also become monks, leaving their wives and children behind in the world. Husbands might also simply become ill or incapacitated in some way. Their sons — if they had any — might well be young children, inexperienced teen-agers, or even absent at these critical points in their family's life cycle. Charters indicate that husbands in the Chartrain turned to their wives, not other male relatives, to assume responsibilities for their families and house-holds. Indeed the evidence of wives acting as partners with their husbands suggests that noble-born men were mindful of the possibility that they would not be able or available to discharge their familial obligations. By acting jointly with their wives, men ensured that their wives were experi-enced in familial affairs so that they could act competently as heads of families should the need arise. And since the administration of aristocratic households and lands entailed overseeing knightly tenants and fiefs as well as children and allodial property, married women could find themselves acting with lordly powers.

Lordship

At the heart of lordship was the control of warriors. Because women were unable to satisfy one of the fundamental components of lordship and vas-salage, namely military protection or service, modern historians have ar-gued that women were excluded from participation in lord-vassal relation-ships.[72] Yet women did actively participate in the world of lords and vassals, and that participation is perhaps the most persuasive evidence for their roles in both aristocratic society and family. Up to this point we have considered women's authority and status within the family. Women's involvement in lordship represents their part in matters beyond the family and their inclu-sion in the relationships from which the elite drew and exercised their power. Women's access to such authority, however, was derived largely from their influential position in aristocratic households. Charters from the Chartrain demonstrate that women from various sectors of the landholding elite took part in lord-vassal relationships, together with their husbands and individually, as both lords and vassals, throughout the eleventh and twelfth centuries.

To establish women's participation in feudal matters, we must start at the most basic question: did women hold fiefs? Fiefs were portions of property and/or revenues granted out by lords to vassals. In return for the land, a vassal was expected to perform certain duties, the most important of which was military service. Powerful lords not only served kings, dukes, or counts personally, but were expected to furnish contingents of knights, and therefore awarded as fiefs the amount of land and/or revenue necessary to support a knight or mounted combatant. These men, in turn, were lords of their own men. A castellan, for example, was a powerful lord of a castle who had contingents of his own vassals and knights. Yet, this lord was frequently the vassal of even more powerful men. Participation in the realm of lordship was predicated upon the control of fiefs, which often fell to women throughout the central Middle Ages.

Late in the eleventh century, the monks of Marmoutier recorded that Roscelina gave half of her dower for the benefit of her deceased husband's soul. At the same time, she and her sons gave "the fief of three knights."[73] Agnes of Marly sold her knight's fief (*fevum militum*) at Rodon to finance her second husband's journey to Rome.[74] She acted completely independently because she alone controlled the fief. Earlier a certain Ermentrude gave some of her allods to Saint-Père with the cooperation of "her knight Hunver," who along with his wife, son, daughters, and nephew signed the charter. The gift was corroborated by "the hands of her knights," who were undoubtedly the thirteen men listed at the end of the charter.[75]

Women also inherited honors, that is, the titles, fiefs, knights and vassals that pertained to a specific lordship. Mahild of Alluyes, who inherited the "honors" of Alluyes by right or custom of inheritance from her father, was called *domina* Mahild of Alluyes.[76] She acted as lord and enjoyed possession of these fiefs for her entire lifetime, through two marriages and during two periods of widowhood. That she was called "Mahild of Alluyes" represents an affirmation not only of her natal heritage but also her control of the fiefs associated with the lordship of Alluyes. Married to William I Gouet sometime before 1050, she appeared in several charters in the 1060s without reference to William, possibly because he had died or perhaps because the acts in question pertained to her honors of Alluyes rather than to his Gouet properties. What is apparent, however, is that Mahild as both wife and widow acted as lord over these properties. Recall that she consented to the gift by her dependents to Saint-Père as the "most noble lord Mahild" and as "lord" Mahild of Alluyes.[77] After her marriage to Geoffrey of Mayenne sometime around 1070, Mahild retained lordship over the vassals she brought to her marriage and those she had from the patrimony of her first husband. After Geoffrey's death ca. 1073, she again assumed sole control of the family domains. A knight from Brou made a donation to Marmoutier for his soul and those of his wife and children; Mahild, exercising her prerogative as *domina* or lord, allowed him to make the gift.[78] The charter was drafted in her presence in the chapter house at Marmoutier, within the sacred space of the monks.

The monks of Tiron likewise dealt with lordly women. The fief they received from Gautier Pagan was held from *domina* Auberia and Robert of Blainville, who himself was not identified as a *dominus*.[79] When Pagan and his brother together made a gift to Tiron, they did so with the consent and participation of their lord, Juliana.[80] In another instance, Elizens and her husband gave all of the fiefs and lordships which she held at Osmoy to Notre-Dame-de-Josaphat.[81] Even though she had married, Elizens acted as lord over the lands; and like any lord, she obtained the consent of her vassal Hilduin, who held one of these fiefs from her.

The term *domina* was used for women who controlled fiefs, vassals, and knights' fiefs. It could be translated "lady," but a more resonant translation would surely be female lord. *Domina*, *vicedomina*, and *legedocta* are all feminine forms of titles which embodied certain powers, privileges and responsibilities.[82] The rights and obligations that went along with such offices or titles were in no way lessened by the fact that a female now controlled them. An indication of the parity that existed between *dominus* or *domina* is evident in women acting in concert with their husbands as lords. Just as count Stephen and countess Adela acted together in making gifts, mediating their vassals' disputes, and confirming their gifts, so did the wives of knights and lesser aristocrats who held fiefs with their husbands. Two acts from the twelfth century illustrate this relationship. Around 1128 viscount Geoffrey III of Châteaudun and his wife Heloise were called lords when they consented to gift of property that Rainald and Ada of Espiers held together.[83] Heloise and Ada enjoyed a partnership with their husbands over their feudal holdings. Similarly when Hugh of Levreville, his mother, and *cognatus* arranged to place certain of their lands in mortgage, they did so with the consent of their lords Bardulf and Helvise of Gallardon, "from whose fief the aforementioned land belonged" (*de quorum feodo predicte terre erant*).[84]

Twelfth-century aristocratic women also participated in courts. Remember that when Hilduin of Alluyes gave the tithes from the village of Mercasius to the monks of Saint-Père, his lords, William and Eustachia, corroborated and supported his restoration at their court.[85] When Eustachia assumed control of the family and their lordship during William II's absence in the Holy Land, part of her obligation as lord was holding courts to settle disputes among her vassals and to corroborate or witness their donations. Many of the restorations of ecclesiastical property made by Gouet vassals were done in "the presence of *domina* Eustachia, at her court."[86] Early in the twelfth century the monks of Saint-Père of Chartres recorded that the tithes and revenues pertaining to the church of Moras had been given by several donors. Among those consenting to these gifts, as well as making their own donation, were Ernald Pertuis and his wife Barbata. Sometime after giving the monks their part of the tithes, this couple evidently had a change of heart, for they claimed the revenues from Moras as well as those from another church. The monks called this couple to submit to their justice, but they refused and were subsequently excommunicated. Finally, mindful of their wrongdoing, Ernald and Barbata abandoned their claims at Eustachia's court, in her presence and in front of many witnesses.[87] Eustachia mediated this dispute and reconciled this couple with the monks. Eustachia settled disputes, heard pleas, and provided Gouet vassals with justice. In short, she fulfilled the same functions that she would have in conjunction with her husband or as a male lord. Historians have asserted that a narrowing of the definition of family to only patrilineal relatives removed such opportunities for power from women. Eustachia obviously felt no such pressure, even though she and William II had two grown sons who remained in France when their father and eldest brother went to the Holy Land. Indeed, if women were relegated to the role of housekeeper, or "kept under lock and key in the most isolated part of the house," they would not have been involved in matters of justice at all and probably not have appeared in the charters.[88]

Vicedomina Elizabeth of Chartres also acted as lord in her own right even though she had male relatives who could have assumed these duties. Sometime before 1130, in her house in Chartres, she consented to the alienation of a fief (*feuodum*) by one of her vassals to Notre-Dame-de-Josaphat.[89] Sometime later she herself donated half of the tithes at Andeville and two parts of the minor tithes from fiefs she had inherited (*ad feodum suum jure hereditario pertinebat*).[90] Her sons began to appear in her acts in the 1130s, but only in purely supportive roles. Henry, who would eventually became vidame, confirmed his mother's gift of tithes at Andeville, and himself gave tithes there.[91] This act is significant because it indicates that Henry had come of age and was holding property and fiefs, which his mother had undoubtedly provided for his support. While she was alive, Elizabeth retained control of the vicedominal title, its lands, and its obligations. Shortly before her death late in 1140 she made arrangements for the continued health of her eternal soul: in return for a generous gift, the monks of Notre-Dame-de-Josaphat were to record the anniversary of her death in their martyrology and offer an annual celebration.[92] Although this *vicedomina* had a surplus of male relatives — including a half-brother, a husband, and two grown sons — she alone held the office and its attached lands. No one attempted to displace her from the office, just as no one had displaced her mother before her.[93] Women like Eustachia Gouet and Elizabeth of Chartres enjoyed official power and informal influence; neither their families nor aristocratic society felt it necessary to prevent or restrict them from performing the lordly functions associated with their lands and titles.

The wives of many lords of the Chartrain were active and recognized participants in the world of lordship and vassalage. As part of a married couple, these women acted with their husbands in meting out justice and supervising their feudal dependents in their courts. If her husband was absent or incapacitated, a wife would be expected to assume responsibility for the family's lands and obligations as lord. Even if she had sons of age, she was entrusted with the responsibilities of family head. Even though aristocratic women could became heads of families and lords in their own right, the fact remains that sons were more likely to assume these roles. But the charter evidence from the Chartrain does reveal that women were not prevented from becoming lords and vassals because of their gender and that women could and did act as lords and vassals independently of their husbands.

Widows

Widowhood has often been assumed to be the stage in an aristocratic woman's life when she could expect to wield the most power and influence.[94] Some women certainly did assume new, more public, and influential responsibilities after the loss of a spouse, but for others widowhood represented a continuation of many of the experiences and powers they had enjoyed as wives. But whether they assumed power for the first time or continued to exercise the same authority as they had as wives, women from Blois-Chartres took on active and powerful roles as widows.

A scribe of Saint-Jean-en-Vallée recorded around 1120 that Bartholomew, his mother, his sisters, and brother-in-law joined together to abandon their claim to a meadow.[95] This collective of kin also acted in solidarity by placing an oak staff on the altar as a sign of their concession and gift, an indication that its members enjoyed an interest in the fruits of the property in question and an interest in making sure the quitclaim went uncontested.

The events recorded in these charters demonstrate that widows continued to participate with their conjugal family in making gifts and settling disputes, just as many had when their husbands were still alive.

As women made the transition from wife to widow, they continued to make benefactions to local ecclesiastical houses on the behalf of their relatives. Widows were extremely generous to the foundations of their choice. *Domina* Mahild of Alluyes was motivated by concern for the eternal souls of her two husbands when she made two gifts to Saint-Germain on their behalf: she provided for the souls of her husbands and children, her parents, and her husbands' relatives, as well as for her own.[96] Those generous grants attest to Mahild's broad concept of family consciousness and solidarity, a sense of family obligation that stretched over three generations and included natal, conjugal, and distant collateral kin.[97] Even though she held the donated land as a lord, her son William II Gouet affirmed her gifts as her heir whose assent was necessary. Mahild's gifts as a widow and wife were bound by the rights of potential heirs and claimants.[98]

Other widows earned the wrath of the monks. A woman named Aremburg acted with her sons in seizing land at *Jamba* from the monks of Marmoutier.[99] The case was heard at the courts of countess Adela and Raoul of Beaugency, but not settled. Adelicia of Le Puiset and certain of her knights (*milites ejus*) were excommunicated by bishop Ivo of Chartres in 1098–1099 for the "tyranny" she and her son were inflicting on the region. Adelicia had assumed control of Le Puiset after her husband's death and during the absence of her son on crusade. Ivo complained that she also had committed certain injuries against the church of Chartres. Although the bishop and *domina* were eventually reconciled, it took actual excommunication to bring her to heel.[100] Like Adelaide, the "younger but more cunning" sister of the knight Raher, whose claim to her brother's gift earned her Marmoutier's ire (see above), some widows also provoked clerics by contesting gifts made by their kin, in some cases, seizing the property in question. Adela, the wife of Hugh, a knight of the castle of Mantes, seized and controlled property her father-in-law had given to the Church. She "unjustly" held the village of Genainvilliers and for this presumption had suffered the "chains of anathema" for twenty years after the death of her husband.[101] Even though Hugh had died, Adela continued to withhold from the monks land that had originally belonged to her husband's family.[102] Only in old age, and facing death, did she finally renounce her claim.

Widows continued to make claims to property into the twelfth century. Hugh Berbellus and his sons swore to defend their donation to Saint-

Père against all men and women (*contra omnes homines et feminas*).[103] Other charters bear out Hugh's concern with usurpation of gifts by women. Adele Filoche was one of those who disputed the gift her husband had made on becoming a monk at Tiron. "Seduced by the spirit of avarice," the monks said, she falsely claimed the meadow her husband had given. Adela gave up her claim for 50 *s.*; her children received 6 *d.*[104] Those payments testify to her right to her husband's lands and her ability to challenge the transfer of property to the Church. The charter evidence indicates that widows, like husbands and wives, caused endless trouble by successfully challenging donations made by their relatives, male and female, natal and affinal. While such actions doubtlessly infuriated the monks, they do attest to the power and authority that widows commanded.

In nearly all the cases above, widows were granted some form of compensation in return for their quitclaim, an indication of the monks' belief that these women did in fact exercise some sort of claim to the property in question. If wholesale adoption of patrilineage had occurred by the twelfth century, the status of both married and widowed aristocratic women would have been undermined, and a widow would have been expected to fall under the domination of her son or other male natal or affinal kin. The experiences of Adelicia of Le Puiset, Adela of Mantes, and Adela Filoche prove that this was not the case for all widows.

During her marriage(s) a woman shared control over her children and family holdings with her husband. If he left on crusade or another military expedition, she assumed sole responsibility for her children, family lands, and honors. The charters also demonstrate that women controlled their dowries and dowers, and acted in donations concerning natal, conjugal and affinal properties. As widows charged with the management of heirs and lands, many aristocratic women would not have found this much of a departure from their previous life experiences and responsibilities. For other women, who for reasons having to do with family circumstances, did not share such experiences, widowhood may have been the first time they commanded such public and formal powers. Lady Philippa of Courville was one such woman. Unlike Mahild of Alluyes, Eustachia Gouet, and the *vice-dominae* of Chartres, Philippa of Courville appeared in only one charter before she became a widow in the last decade of the eleventh century.[105] She and her husband, lord Gerogius of Courville, had at least one son, over whom Philippa acted as guardian during his minority. A charter of 1094 reveals that Philippa had taken on her husband's duties and responsibilities.[106] The act states that she and her son gave the ban over the village of La Pommerae, which their predecessors lord Ivo and lord Gerogius had passed down to them. She also persuaded five vassals (*fideles feodalesque nostri*) to grant their vicarial rights there to the abbey. And as a faithful vassal herself Philippa had her "lord and patron" consent to her gift. Philippa exercised the same rights and prerogatives enjoyed by all other previous male lords of Courville. As is also indicated by the monk's later reference to her as the *domina* of Courville.[107] Her husband's kin evidently did not attempt to challenge Philippa's right to act as lord and guardian, even though Gerogius had four brothers who could have assumed this responsibility. Even pope Paschal, in his 1104 confirmation of episcopal possessions in Pontgouin, decreed that "neither the male lord (*dominus*) nor female lord (*domina*) of Courville" had the right to destroy or lay waste to lands there, lands which were a bone of contention between the bishop and the Courvilles.[108] Clearly, female lords exercised the same disruptive and potentially destructive abilities as their male counterparts.

Widows exercised diverse powers within their families. They acted with family members in making donations and resolving contestations. They made pious gifts to benefit their souls and those of their natal, conjugal, and affinal families. And they exercised dominion over vassals and were themselves vassals to their lords. Women like Mahild of Alluyes, Philippa of Courville, and Adelicia of Le Puiset were active, influential, and powerful members of familial and lordly networks through which power over others in the region was exercised, disputed, and maintained. Yet the charters indicate that such power was not a new experience for most widows, who as wives had been partners with their husbands and commanded significant authority in their own right. For such women, widowhood represented a continuation of, not a dramatic increase in, the powers they were expected to command. But the experience of elite widows was grounded in family circumstance. If families needed leadership, widows stepped up and assumed control of the family. If male members assumed these responsibilities, the women of the family may not have enjoyed such public powers. Yet it appears that widowed mothers were preferred as guardians of minor children over more distant male kin. Even widows who had not before been active stepped in to fill the void and take charge of the family.

Conclusion: The Rhythms of Life

In their groundbreaking article, "The Power of Women Through the Family in Medieval Europe, 500–1200," Jo Ann McNamara and Suzanne Wemple argued that women of the of the late eleventh and the twelfth century were "confined to the role of housekeeper, a role whose boundaries were shrinking."[109] They and others have postulated that by the twelfth century the introduction of primogeniture and patrilineage had come to restrict women from assuming powerful roles either in their families or in aristocratic society in general. The charters from the Chartrain reveal no such abrupt change in either women's roles or family structure. Indeed, the evidence indicates continuity in the experiences of most women of the landholding elite from the eleventh into the twelfth century.

Throughout their lives the women of the Chartrain landholding elite were influential members of their families. According to the charters recording property transactions, daughters, sisters, wives, mothers, and widows participated with their families in various capacities. They made donations, acted to quitclaim disputes, received countergifts for their approbation of gifts and quitclaims, were involved in ceremonies to solemnize gifts, participated in grants concerning feudal property, and acted to create bonds with monasteries and lords alike through their participation in the donation and resolution / dispute processes of the eleventh and twelfth centuries.

Through marriage women became part of yet another family complex, and their participation in the web of relationships that defined, extended, and elevated both natal and conjugal family members was vital to the natal, affinal, and conjugal family's well-being. Further, upon marriage wives received property over which they would exercise control for the remainder of their lives. They could donate the property to the Church or make provision for it to pass to whomever they designated as heir. But marriage did not terminate a woman's involvement in her natal family: married daughters and their children still exercised a claim to hold family property and might inherit a portion of it. Marriage also made women heads of household and partners with their husbands in lordship and vassalage. As wives, women also created and maintained relationships with the Church. Through patronage and intercession, wives and mothers forged important spiritual and political ties with the monasteries of the region.

In the absence of their husbands, by either distance or death, aristocratic wives exercised autonomous control over children and family lands. They acted as lords in holding courts, dispensing justice, and resolving conflicts. Like wives, widows were influential and powerful members of their families and class. The charters do suggest, perhaps not surprisingly, that a woman's influence increased with maturity and marriage. Although this was the experience of many wives and widows of the elite, there were surely others who remained in the background and did not come to enjoy such prominence in society. The particular circumstances of the family played a profound role in determining the sorts of powers that women would enjoy and the positions that they could expect to assume.

Why were women of the elite so powerful in the eleventh- and twelfth-century Chartrain? The deciding factor seems to have been their families. Most elite families did not seek to restrict or impoverish their daughters, sisters, or mothers and in some circumstances women at all stages of their life cycle assumed powerful positions within their families and society. The charters from the region of Blois-Chartres allow for a fairly complete reconstruction of the life cycle of a woman of the land holding class, even if it is difficult to know the actual experience of individual women at every stage; no longer can we conceptualize women as being "under the strictest subordination" or the Middle Ages as "resolutely male." The lives that are recoverable from these documents demonstrate that women were vital participants in their families, in the world of lords and vassals, as well as important allies for the Church. The experience of the elite women of the Chartrain points to a diversity of experience, but also to the prominence that many women enjoyed in the society of eleventh- and twelfth-century France.

3

Aristocratic Women in the County of Champagne

Theodore Evergates

THE COUNTY OF CHAMPAGNE is best known today for the brilliant literary flowering of its court under the patronage of count Henry the Liberal (1152–81) and countess Marie (1164–98).[1] While the imaginative literature associated with that court continues to entertain us as it did medieval audiences, it is not entirely clear what those stories, especially the romances of Chrétien de Troyes, reveal about the lives of contemporary aristocratic men and women in Champagne.[2] Literary historians have attempted to ground Chrétien within his late twelfth-century society by identifying many of his references to contemporary events and places; they have also deduced a model of social organization from Chrétien's depiction of conflicts within the aristocracy, and even have exposed Chrétien's profoundly unsettling portrayal of discourse and violence between men and women.[3] These contributions certainly enlarge our understanding of Chrétien's romances, but they shed little light on the society and institutions specific to Champagne. To understand the social practices in Champagne, and especially the role of aristocratic women within that society, we must turn to the rich collection of nonliterary documents upon which the history of the county and its most prominent lineages rests.

Although Champagne lacks the chronicles that make the medieval societies of Flanders and the Anglo-Norman realm so vivid to modern readers, it does possess an exceptionally large and informative collection of documents describing aristocratic practices in the twelfth and thirteenth centuries. As in other regions, the voluminous property records drawn up by religious institutions throw considerable light on society at the local level where women, because of their property rights, often appear in transactions with those institutions. Even more valuable in revealing secular practices are the sealed documents drawn up by aristocratic families for their private affairs: marriage contracts, dower letters, sales and mortgages, letters of

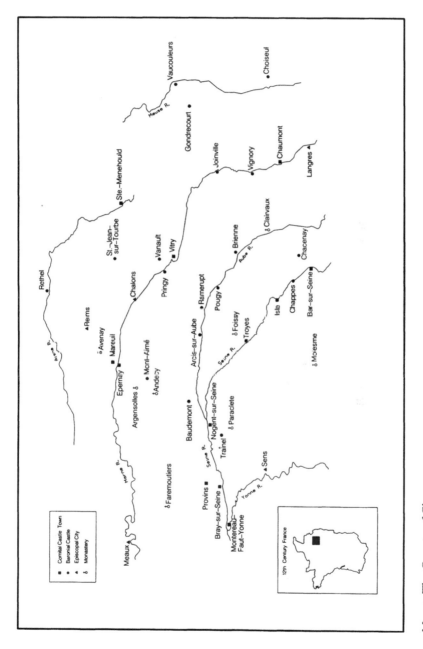

Map 3. The County of Champagne.

homage done and received, requests and permissions, and notifications regarding feudal tenure, all dealing with strictly secular transactions. The comital chancery, too, generated thousands of letters and grants in addition to its internal administrative registers, which are a font of information about the count's relations with the aristocracy. The feudal registers are especially important here: as the longest series of their kind for a French principality, extending from about 1178 to 1275, they reveal the highly visible role of women as feudal tenants in Champagne. The presence of women in those administratative registers, as well as in ecclesiastical charters and aristocratic letters, resulted from women's fundamental rights as daughters, wives, and widows. The evidence from this vast collection of diverse materials clearly shows that noble-born women were far from being marginalized in the twelfth and thirteenth centuries; they in fact shared the rights and privileges of noble-born men by virtue of birth and marriage, and participated in a wide range of activities largely ignored by modern historians.[4]

This chapter explores three distinctive roles of aristocratic women in Champagne: as countesses, as married women, and as religious. It begins with the countesses, who shaped the political history of Champagne through regencies lasting more than a third of the county's existence as an autonomous principality. Regencies loomed large in Champagne because the age of majority for counts was twenty-one, rather than fifteen as it was for other men, and maternal regencies preceded the rule of four of the six counts. Aristocratic women below the rank of countess appear in the documents primarily in their roles as proprietors and feudal lords and tenants. They appeared in those documents in observance of their considerable rights as heirs (inheritance and dowry) and spouses (joint property, dower, and wardship). Despite common familial practices, aristocratic women experienced markedly diverse lives, as illustrated here by brief biographies of seven related women. The chapter concludes with religious women, for Champagne was a region profoundly marked by the new spirituality of the twelfth century, and a large number of noble-born women, like their male counterparts, chose a religious life.

The Countesses

MARIE OF FRANCE

Countess Marie remains the best known of all the countesses because of her associations with Chrétien de Troyes, who claimed he wrote *Lancelot* at her request, and Andreas Capellanus, who described her "court of love" where high-born women dispensed amatory judgments.[5] Beyond her role as literary patron—and even if she did not hold mock courts to entertain her women friends and relatives—Marie was an important personage in her own right as the eldest child of Louis VII and Eleanor of Aquitaine. Born in 1145, Marie was promised in marriage two years later to the twenty-year-old count Henry, whom Louis had befriended on the Second Crusade. She stayed in Paris after her parents divorced (March 1152) and the next year, on reaching the canonical age of consent, was formally betrothed to Henry.[6] Soon thereafter she was sent to the old Benedictine convent of Avenay, near Epernay in Champagne, for instruction and acculturation under the tutelage of abbess Alice of Mareuil.[7] Marie remained cloistered for eleven years until 1164, when at the age of nineteen she took up residence with Henry in his newly built palace in Troyes.[8] During her sixteen-year marriage Marie appeared in only a handful of documents relating primarily to her own small benefactions, which tell us very little about her life. She had three children in her twenties and another at thirty-four, all of whom seem to have remained with her until they came of age or married. She took no part in the governance of the county, since Henry had selected his principal officers—seneschal, constable, butler, marshals, chamberers, and chancellor—when he came to office in 1152, and continued to rely on them during the twelve years he ruled before Marie's arrival in Troyes.

In May 1179, when Henry decided to revisit the sites of his youthful adventures in the Holy Land, he left Marie, then thirty-four, in charge of the county. His eighteen-month absence (June 1179–February 1181) coincided with the accession of Marie's half-brother as king, the fourteen-year-old Philip II, who soon turned against his maternal relatives and upset the close royal-comital relations forged between Louis VII and Henry I thirty years earlier. Philip unceremoniously displaced his dying father (who was Marie's father as well), confiscated the dower lands of his mother, queen Adele (count Henry's sister), and married Isabel of Hainaut (who had been betrothed since 1171 to Marie's own eldest son). Count Henry's return in early 1181 temporarily defused tensions, but, after his death in March, Marie and her disgruntled in-laws—the queen mother Adele, the royal seneschal count Thibaut V of Blois, count Stephen of Sancerre, and archbishop William of Reims—plotted against the king. That bitter conflict was resolved by mid-May with the betrothal of Marie's oldest son to queen Isabel's younger sister, and thereafter Marie and Philip had an untroubled relationship; he freely pursued his aggression against Flanders and the Plantagenets, while she had a free hand in Champagne at a time of vigorous

economic and urban expansion, when the trade fairs were becoming international centers of commerce and finance.

For six years, from March 1181 to May 1187, Marie exercised the
comital office as regent for her son Henry (II). She did so vigorously and
alone, without restriction by a regency council. In the great hall of her
palace in Troyes, which served as the political and administrative center of
the county, as well as in her other castle towns, Marie sat with a small
council of barons and administrative officers to discharge all the routine
business of medieval rulers: receiving petitioners, arbitrating and settling
disputes, making benefactions to churches, confirming private transactions,
receiving homages, confiscating fiefs and granting new ones.[9] Since her acts
continued to be drawn up by the same chancery officials who had served her
husband, they remained the same in form and content. With the notable
exception of appointing a new marshal, Geoffroy of Villehardouin, in 1185,
she made no discernible changes in her husband's officers or policies. Although feudal tenure by women apparently increased precisely during her
rule, we cannot say whether she fostered that practice. Her court, however,
was perceived as being receptive to women, several of whom sought her
confirmations at critical junctures in their lives.[10]

In 1181 Marie found herself widowed with four young children —
Henry II was fifteen, Marie seven, Scholastique five or six, and Thibaut III
only two. She considered marrying the recently widowed Philip, count of
Flanders (1168–91), the son of her husband's old friend and crusade companion count Thierry. Philip and Marie were about the same age and well
acquainted: a decade earlier he had sponsored the betrothal of her two
oldest children, Henry II and young Marie, to the children of his sister
Margaret, countess of Hainaut. Philip went so far as to seek a papal dispensation for his marriage to Marie, since they were indirectly related, but
then, for unknown reasons, broke off negotiations.[11] Marie, at thirty-nine,
seems not to have sought another marriage. Thereafter she was preoccupied with completing the marriages between her children and the children of Margaret and count Baldwin V, who had renewed, broken, revised,
then delayed carrying out the marriage contract between his only son and
Marie's daughter. Countess Marie called on her in-laws to force the elusive
count to deliver the groom; Gislebert of Mons describes the scene at Sens
where the countess, the archbishop of Reims, the counts of Blois and Sancerre, and the duke of Burgundy cornered Baldwin, perhaps threatening
him, if he did not follow through with the marriage, which finally did take
place (January 1186). Marie then trumped Baldwin at his own game by

ignoring the second part of the contract and arranging her own son's marriage to the infant heiress of Namur instead of to Baldwin's daughter.[12]

When Henry II (1187–90) assumed the countship, Marie retired to Meaux, probably with her youngest son Thibaut, then eight. The forty-two-year-old countess could not have imagined that she would ever rule again. But the fall of Jerusalem to Saladin on October 2, 1187 electrified France, and young Henry II was swept up by the wave of enthusiasm for a new crusade to recover the holy city. In May 1190 the unmarried count departed with a large contingent of barons and knights on the Third Crusade, leaving his mother as regent once again. Marie ruled in his absence (he died overseas in September 1197), then continued to rule until her death in March 1198 at fifty-three. In all, she had ruled the county over fifteen years — in her husband's absence, as guardian for her oldest son and then in his absence, and finally in the last months of her life as guardian for her second son, Thibaut.

Although she was countess of Champagne for over thirty years, half of them as ruler, we know little about Marie's life and personality beyond her official acts. She seems to have been close to her half-brothers Geoffroy Plantagenet, for whom she dedicated an altar in Paris, and Richard the Lionheart, with whom she shared Adam of Perseigne as confessor, as well as with her half-sister Margaret, who spent Christmas 1184 with Marie and queen mother Adele. Perhaps Marie saw her sister, countess Alix of Blois, and her mother, Eleanor of Aquitaine, after her parents were divorced in 1152, but there is no firm evidence of any meeting.[13] For her husband Henry she ordered a sumptuous tomb placed in the center of the church of Saint-Etienne of Troyes next to the comital palace, but she herself chose to be buried at Meaux.

Marie's role as literary patron now seems secure.[14] She could read vernacular French and probably Latin as well, given her education at Avenay, and she had a personal library, although its contents are not known. Chrétien de Troyes and Gace Brulé state that they wrote at her request, and she seems also to have patronized Conon de Béthune and Huon d'Oisy. The collegiate chapter of Notre-Dame-du-Val, which Marie founded in Provins with thirty-eight prebends, seems to have supported not only Chrétien but also his continuator Godfrey of Lagny, as well as the earliest known copyist of Chrétien's romances, Guiot of Provins.[15] Perhaps Marie's interest in lyric poetry and romances dates from her married years, for the works she is know to have commissioned as a widow in the 1180s are all translations of religious texts: Psalms (*Eructavit*), Genesis, and possibly a collection of sermons by Bernard of Clairvaux.[16]

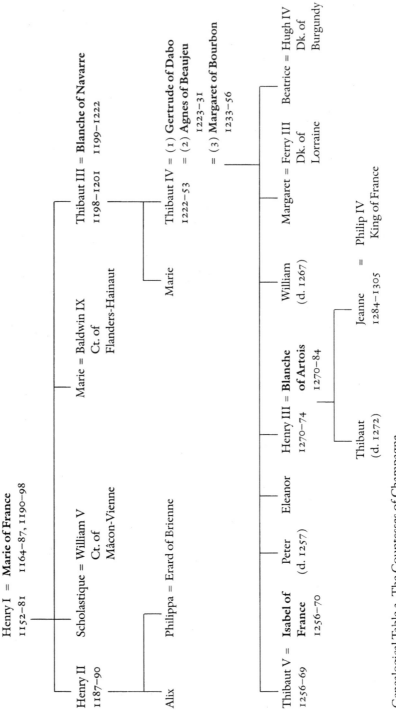

Henry I = **Marie of France**
1152–81   1164–87, 1190–98

Henry II
1187–90

Scholastique = William V
Ct. of
Mâcon-Vienne

Alix

Philippa = Erard of Brienne

Marie = Baldwin IX
Ct. of
Flanders-Hainaut

Marie

Thibaut III = **Blanche of Navarre**
1198–1201   1199–1222

Thibaut IV = (1) **Gertrude of Dabo**
1222–53   = (2) **Agnes of Beaujeu**
1223–31
= (3) **Margaret of Bourbon**
1233–56

Thibaut V = **Isabel of
France**
1256–69   1256–70

Peter
(d. 1257)

Eleanor

Henry III = **Blanche
of Artois**
1270–74   1270–84

William
(d. 1267)

Margaret = Ferry III
Dk. of
Lorraine

Beatrice = Hugh IV
Dk. of
Burgundy

Thibaut
(d. 1272)

Jeanne
1284–1305

= Philip IV
King of France

Genealogical Table 3. The Countesses of Champagne.

BLANCHE OF NAVARRE

A month after Marie's death in March 1198, a throng of barons accompanied nineteen-year-old Thibaut III to Melun, where he did homage for his lands and was knighted by the king. A year later the young count married Blanche of Navarre, the younger sister of Richard the Lionheart's widow Berengaria. Attending the magnificent ceremony in Chartres cathedral were the dowager queens Berengaria of England and Adele of France (Thibaut's aunts), as well as many prelates and barons.[17] The jubilation was short-lived, however, for Thibaut died in May 1201 while preparing to lead the Fourth Crusade. He left twenty-year-old Blanche a widow in the last week of her second pregnancy. For the next twenty-one years she would guide the county through the most perilous internal and external threats it had yet faced.

Whereas countess Marie clearly had possessed the requisite qualifications to act as regent — intimate connections with the Capetian and Plantagenet royal families, eleven formative years preparing to be countess, and sixteen years as countess consort — countess Blanche must have seemed singularly unsuited for such a role. A Navarrese speaker with a strong religious temperament, she had little experience as countess.[18] She also faced an extraordinary challenge from the start: were her children, in fact, the legitimate heirs to the county? In 1190, when the unmarried Henry II left on the Third Crusade, the barons had sworn to accept his younger brother Thibaut III as count if Henry himself did not return. No one had anticipated that Henry would remain overseas seven years, marry there, and have children. Thus it was a legitimate question, in May 1201, whether Henry II's own daughters had better rights to Champagne than his brother Thibaut's infant daughter (see Genealogical Table 3).

Blanche skillfully mastered a difficult situation. Mindful of king Philip's attempt to seize Flanders in 1191 in the absence of a male heir, she quickly made an alliance with the king the cornerstone of her regency.[19] Within days of Thibaut's death she found Philip at nearby Sens, did homage — the first homage ever rendered by a countess — for her right of wardship and her dower lands, and promised not to remarry without his permission. As security for her conduct, she surrendered two castles bordering the royal domain (Bray-sur-Seine and Montereau-faut-Yonne) and her one-year-old daughter to be raised at the royal court.[20] Several days later the birth of a son, Thibaut IV, confirmed the soundness of her strategy: he was born heir apparent under royal protection.

The mass exodus of Champenois barons and knights on the Fourth Crusade in 1202 allowed Blanche several years to establish her rule without baronial opposition. She forcefully took charge of the comital administration, exacting oaths of loyalty from her provosts under threat of her "wrath and ill-will."[21] She vigorously pursued Thibaut III's initiatives to expand comital influence both within the county and in the border lands between the kingdom of France and the empire of Germany, from Sainte-Menehould in the Argonne to Chaumont in the Bassigny, where she installed castles to extend a direct comital presence beyond the county's traditional eastern border.[22] And she imposed liege homage on younger sons who had been accustomed to hold their castles from older brothers, effectively dismantling the intrafamilial networks of the most powerful families within the county.[23] Yet her most symbolic act was to commission an elaborate tomb for her husband that she had placed in the center of Saint-Etienne of Troyes, directly in front of the tomb countess Marie had erected for Henry the Liberal. Along the sides of the tomb, surrounding the reclining effigy of Thibaut III, were silver plaques depicting his father and mother, his brother and sisters, his children, his wife and her brother (the king of Navarre), and the kings of France and England.[24] By linking her children to the royal lines in France, England, and Navarre, Blanche left no doubt about her son's legitimacy and her determination to preserve his inheritance.

As with her predecessor Marie, we know very little about Blanche's personal life, despite her long regency and wide-ranging activities. The early years were probably the most difficult, given her young age and recent arrival in Champagne. She received moral support and perhaps practical advice as well from her husband's aunt, the aging dowager queen Adele (d. 1206), whose "friendship and affection" Blanche later memorialized in an annual Mass.[25] Above all, Blanche seems to have retained a strong religious identity from her childhood. She asked countess Marie's confessor, the well-known spiritual writer Adam of Perseigne, for a copy of his sermons, which he sent in the original Latin fearing, he said, that they would lose their flavor in translation.[26] Even more telling was the fact that Blanche was admitted "as a nun" to the convent of Ligueux, whose chapter offered daily prayers for her and her son in each of its sixty affiliated convents. Cluny associated her with its orders, as did the Cistercians, who promised to remember her in death.[27] Whether for personal reasons or political expediency, Blanche seems never to have considered remarrying, and the king's restriction in that regard was never mentioned again after the treaty of 1201. The probity of her widowed life is underlined by an anecdote dating from

1212: when the highly reputed master of Langres, Walter of Mussy, tried to disport with her, "not with her mind but by touching her body," she took him to ecclesiastical court.[28]

Beyond her active involvement in the routine responsibilities of the comital office — receiving petitioners, resolving disputes, confirming private agreements, granting fiefs, and receiving homages — Blanche remained preoccupied with her son's succession. In 1209, shortly after Thibaut entered his ninth year, she obtained the king's promise to accept the boy's homage at twenty-one and to defer to that time any challenge to his succession, since that was the custom in France, as the king acknowledged. But Philip exacted a large cash payment for that pledge and obliged Thibaut to reside at the royal court during the next four years.[29] In June 1213, however, the issue of succession took an unanticipated turn when a prominent young baron, Erard of Brienne, lord of Ramerupt, announced his departure for the Holy Land in order to marry count Henry II's younger daughter Philippa and claim Champagne as her inheritance. The fact that Erard belonged to one of the premier lineages in Champagne and that his cousin, Jean of Brienne, had recently become king of Jerusalem made his challenge a serious one.

Blanche responded with characteristic vigor, no doubt with the active assistance of her new chancellor, Remi (1211–20), the illegitimate son of her brother Sancho the Strong. First she renewed her agreement with the king.[30] Then she prevailed on ecclesiastical authorities to undertake a series of inquests on Thibaud's right to succeed. Not surprisingly, they found for her on all points: the county was legitimately transferred to Thibaut III, and so to his son; Henry II's marriage overseas was invalid, and his daughters therefore illegitimate; and Erard of Brienne was related consanguineously to Philippa and thus ineligible to marry her.[31] But Blanche came to realize that on these issues, at least, papal influence within the episcopacy of both Champagne and the Latin Levant had reached its limit, and that the most effective resolution of the matter was for the king to accept the twelve-year-old Thibaut's homage for Champagne. Although Philip resisted her proposal, claiming that Thibaut could not do homage to anyone before reaching his majority, Blanche extracted a key proviso: "unless by the king's will."[32]

With the expiration of Thibaut's enforced residence in Paris in 1214, the king bowed to Blanche's persistent entreaties to accept the boy's homage, and Thibaut, in an unprecedented arrangement, promised to remain under his mother's tutelage until he reached twenty-one.[33] By this act Blanche effectively shifted the legal issue from one of familial rights and ecclesiastical norms to one of feudal tenure.[34] And so when Erard of Brienne returned to Champagne with Philippa in 1216 he found himself outmaneuvered: the royal court of peers that met at Melun refused to consider the merits of his suit because Thibaut already had rendered homage and, "according to the custom of France," an inheritance could not be challenged before the heir was twenty-one.[35]

Erard took up arms in a rebellion that was largely a regional affair confined to his relatives and disaffected barons of the eastern borderlands of Champagne. Several prelates also were implicated, notably Guy of Joinville, bishop of Langres (1209–19), who was related to Erard, and Hervé, bishop of Troyes (1207–23), who had a longstanding contentious relationship with Blanche. Unwavering papal support for Blanche neutralized the uncooperative prelates, while papal excommunications and interdicts took their inevitable toll on the rebel barons. Blanche immersed herself in military affairs and joined forces with emperor Frederick II to combat her ablest opponent, Thibaut I, duke of Lorraine. In May 1218 she personally led her army to Nancy, torched the town, and witnessed the duke's humiliating surrender. The defeated barons quickly made their separate peace, and Erard of Brienne was bought off by a large pension and a substantial fief. Blanche's ultimate triumph came in 1220, when she arranged Thibaut's marriage to the duke of Lorraine's sixteen-year-old widow, whose dower included Nancy and Gondreville, two important castle towns in Lorraine. Blanche not only had secured the succession, she had projected comital influence far beyond its traditional eastern limits.

When Thibaut succeeded in late May 1222, Blanche was about forty-one, the same age as countess Marie at the end of her first regency in 1187. Blanche spent her retirement years at Argensolles, the Cistercian convent she founded with the substantial revenues provided by the seven castellanies of her dower lands.[36] Her good relations with the Cistercians allowed her to circumvent the Chapter General's recent restrictions on the foundation of new convents: Argensolles was authorized to accept ninety women, perhaps the largest community of its kind.[37] As a memento of her regency, she took with her a copy of the documents stored in the chancery archives that pertained to her rule, a volume known as the "Cartulary of Blanche."[38]

Blanche's most enduring legacy beyond the political arena was her statute regarding female succession to castles and fortified residences. What circumstance prompted her to convene a baronial assembly on that issue in 1212, we do not know, but the proliferation of fortified sites, encouraged and funded in part by Blanche herself in the first decade of her rule, gave some urgency to the question. Should a fortification, in the absence of a direct male heir, pass to daughters or to the closest male relative? Since most military structures were held as fiefs from the countess, or were renderable to her at her need, it was imperative to establish clear principles of succession. Certainly women had inherited castles in the twelfth century, but they did so by ad hoc arrangements, not mandated procedures. With the assent of thirty-four barons representing the most important families of the county, Blanche announced a new custom for Champagne: when a baron died without a son, his castle and other fortified residences would be apportioned among his daughters according to age-rank (the eldest daughter having first choice); the rest of the property was to be divided equally among the same daughters.[39] That decision preserved the integrity of military structures while maintaining the strongly held principle of partible inheritance (equal shares among all siblings). Twelve years later, in 1224, a baronial assembly under Thibaut IV applied the same principles to male heirs.[40] The two decisions effectively precluded eldest sons and daughters from amassing fortified places to the exclusion of their siblings: only fortifications, not patrimonies, were immune from division; baronial lands would continue to be subject to partible inheritance among all heirs.

The Later Countesses

No later countess would rival Blanche's impact on the county. The three wives of Thibaut IV left no imprint whatsoever during their marriages. Countess Blanche had arranged Thibaut's first marriage, to Gertrude of Dabo, the sixteen-year-old widow of the duke of Lorraine (May 1220), but incompatibilities resulted in divorce within two years.[41] In 1223, as count in his own right, twenty-two-year-old Thibaut IV (1222–53) married his cousin of about the same age, Agnes of Beaujeu, eldest daughter of Guichard IV of Beaujeu. In his testament Guichard had asked prince Louis of France to provide his cousin Agnes a suitable dowry, and it is possible that Louis brokered the marriage between Agnes and Thibaut.[42] Their nine-year union coincided with a tumultuous period of Thibaut's life: he was accused of betraying—then poisoning—the king, of having an affair with the regent queen Blanche of Castile, and of being disloyal to the barons of northern France. Of Agnes we can say only that she had a daughter and died in 1231, shortly after Thibaut's major political problems were resolved.[43]

A year later, in September 1232, thirty-one-year-old Thibaut married fifteen-year-old Margaret of Bourbon, eldest daughter of his constable.[44] She brought a handsome dowry and seven children during their twenty-year marriage, but beyond that little is known about Margaret's married life. Only during her three-year regency (1253–56), while in her mid-thirties, does she emerge from obscurity.[45] Like Blanche of Navarre, Margaret faced a succession crisis at the start of her regency, this one involving the kingdom of Navarre, which Thibaut IV had inherited through his mother in 1234. Although Thibaut had spent much of his reign in Navarre, the barons there opposed his son's accession as king. Countess Margaret promptly took young Thibaut V to Pampelona, the capital of Navarre, where his presence averted open rebellion. She revealed similar resolve in terminating a longstanding conflict with the Templars, who had been acquiring vast tracts of land in Champagne against her husband's wishes: she prohibited them outright from buying any more feudal property in the county.[46] When count Thibaut V (1256–70) attained his majority, forty-year-old Margaret retired to her substantial dower lands, where she died two years later.[47]

In one important matter countess Margaret had deferred to her son: his desire, which he declared to Louis IX in 1254, to marry the king's second daughter, Isabel. Twelve-year-old Isabel, an ascetic from an early age who had seriously considered a conventual life, completely captivated young Thibaut, who shared her strong religious feelings. After their marriage in April 1255, Thibaut spent much time in Paris with his father-in-law, who treated him as a son.[48] When Thibaut succeeded as count in 1256, fourteen-year-old Isabel became the youngest countess of Champagne. But she took no part in the public affairs of the county, absorbed as she was by her religious life, which included, according to the royal confessor, secret self-mortifications.[49] King Louis was especially fond of Isabel, who reminded him of his own sister of the same name, and even wrote in his own hand a short treatise on personal conduct addressed "to my dear and beloved daughter, Isabel, queen of Navarre."[50] Naturally, she and Thibaut V joined Louis on his last crusade, where they both succumbed to disease: Thibaut died in November 1270, and the childless Isabel followed him a few months later while accompanying his remains home. Their embalmed bodies were placed in the Franciscan house in Provins, but Isabel's heart was sent to Clairvaux, where her two predecessors, countesses Agnes of Beaujeu and Margaret of Bourbon, were buried.

When Henry III (1271–74) succeeded his brother as count, his wife of eighteen months, Blanche of Artois, became countess.[51] The young couple in their early twenties soon suffered a cruel fate: their infant son, Thibaut, died in 1272 when his nurse accidentally dropped him from a castle wall. Henry III's own death two years later at twenty-five left countess Blanche regent for their one-year-old daughter, Jeanne. For the first time in the history of the county, a regency was established for an heiress (1274–84). Blanche did homage to the king, explored several possible marriages for her daughter, then acceded to Philip III's intense pressure to engage Jeanne to one of his own sons.[52] The marriage contract is notable in that it required both parties to convince their children to accept the marriage upon reaching the age of consent:

Philip, by the grace of God, king of the French, to all who see this letter, greeting. Be it known that I and my dearest relative Blanche, queen of Navarre and countess palatine of Champagne and Brie, have drawn up this contract of marriage between her daughter Jeanne, sole heiress of Navarre and Champagne, and one of my two oldest sons [Louis or Philip], who will obtain a papal dispensation in order to marry her. These are the terms of the agreement:

> I and the queen will conscientiously entreat my son and Jeanne to betroth themselves to each other when they reach the minimum age of consent for a betrothal. When Jeanne becomes nubile, my son will accept her in marriage and she will accept him, unless serious illness, deformity, or other reasonable impediment appears in either of them before their marriage.
>
> If my son who marries Jeanne does not succeed to the kingdom, I will grant Jeanne an annual revenue of 4000 *l.*, money of Paris, as her dower, which my son will assign. But if that son succeeds me to the kingdom, she will be assigned a larger dower, according to my wishes or my son's, if I should die before they are married.
>
> I swore to observe this agreement in good faith, obligating myself and my heir who will succeed to the kingdom to implement it faithfully. The queen swore on Holy Scriptures to carry out this agreement fully and to implement it faithfully, and that neither she nor anyone else will challenge it in the future.

We also agreed that this contract in no way prejudices the queen's guardianship of her daughter, her own dower, or the acquisitions which she ought to have in her lands, or any other of her rights. In testimony of which I have had my seal affixed to this letter. Done at Orléans in the year of our Lord 1275, in the month of May.[53]

The death of the king's oldest son in 1276 left prince Philip, then nine years old, as the designated husband of three-year-old Jeanne, who was being raised at the royal court in anticipation of her marriage.

With the future of the county secured, countess Blanche, then about twenty-five, decided to remarry. Her new husband was thirty-year-old Edmund of Lancaster, widowed brother of king Edward I of England and a personage of international repute. Blanche surrendered the regency of

Champagne to him but he, with few interests in Champagne, appointed agents to run the county in his place until Jeanne came of age. In 1284 king Philip III, anxious to bring Champagne into the royal domain as soon as possible, ordered an inquest to prove that Jeanne could inherit the county at eleven, rather than at twenty-one as was customary for men.[54] And so, when she married fifteen-year-old prince Philip in August 1284, he assumed the comital title in her name. At Philip IV's accession in October 1285, Jeanne became queen of France (1285–1305). Although Champagne retained its institutions and separate identity as the queen's inheritance, its independence and prosperity were subsumed by royal interests: effectively, it had become a royal province. Countess Blanche enjoyed her dower lands for another seventeen years and died only three years before her daughter Jeanne.

In Champagne a countess did not ordinarily share in her husband's routine governance of the county. Only during his absence or during an heir's minority did she rule, but when she did so she wielded the full plenitude of comital authority, without limitation by a regency council, male relatives, or feudal lords.[55] On only one occasion was a countess restricted in her regency, in 1201 when Blanche agreed not to remarry without royal consent, but at no time — not even in 1201 — did the king or any other feudal lord exploit a regency in Champagne to intrude into the county's internal affairs. The four regent countesses saw themselves primarily as custodians, continuators of their husbands' policies and guardians for their heirs. Beyond their active participation in all matters of governance, their most consequential decisions were in the marriages they arranged for their children, for every count between 1152 and 1285 married after his father's death. Three marriages were particularly significant in this regard. Thibaut III's marriage to Blanche of Navarre (presumably arranged by countess Marie) made the counts at once kings of Navarre and absentee counts of Champagne, a role that brought fundamental change to the very structure of comital government in the thirteenth century. The marriage arranged by Blanche of Navarre between Thibaut IV and Gertrude of Dabo, had it lasted, might well have altered the political history of eastern France. And the marriage Blanche of Artois contracted for Jeanne and prince Philip of France sealed the county's fate as an independent territorial state.

A group portrait of the seven countesses reveals few commonalities, as their characters and personal lives differed fundamentally from one another. All except Blanche of Navarre came from neighboring linguistic and cultural areas. Four carried royal blood, three as daughters of kings (Marie of

France, Blanche of Navarre, Isabel of France) and one as close relative to the Capetians (Blanche of Artois). The three wives of Thibaut IV were exceptional in this respect, all being nonroyal and one, Gertrude of Dabo, being a child widow. Although the countesses married in their mid- to late teens (Isabel of France, at twelve, was the youngest), they had relatively small families, with an average of two children surviving to adulthood. Age differences between the countesses and their husbands were notably small: the two Blanches were about their same age as their husbands, Gertrude of Dabo and Agnes of Beaujeu were three years younger than Thibaut IV, and Jeanne was four years younger than prince Philip. Only Marie of France and Margaret of Bourbon were significantly younger than their husbands, separated by eighteen and sixteen years respectively.

The latter two countesses, Marie and Margaret, had the longest marriages and largest families. Married in their teens, Marie at nineteen and Margaret at fifteen, they had four and seven children respectively during marriages lasting seventeen and twenty years. Both outlived their husbands, but neither remarried. The remaining five countesses, all closer in age to their husbands, had considerably different experiences. Blanche of Navarre's marriage lasted only three years and was followed by the longest widowhood (twenty-eight years) and regency (twenty-one years), which indelibly marked the course of the county's history. Blanche of Artois might have followed a similar pattern, a five-year marriage followed by a ten-year regency, had she not remarried and surrendered rulership to her new husband; she was the only countess to remarry. One countess, Agnes of Beaujeu, predeceased her husband, and one, Gertrude of Dabo, was divorced after a two-year marriage. With an average lifespan of about forty years, the countesses died younger than many of the aristocratic women discussed below, who lived well into their sixties.[56]

Aristocratic Women

From about 1270 the High Court of Champagne provided explicit statements of the principles governing familial and property rights within the county. Three of those "customs," as they were called, were of particular importance to noble-born women: partible inheritance, community property, and the dower.[57] As was the case in much of northern and eastern France, a family's allodial property (property held in full possession, free from lordship) was shared equally among all siblings. Feudal property, by contrast, was divided unequally in an implicit recognition of the male nature of feudal tenure: sisters received only half as much as their brothers and were barred entirely from the collateral inheritance of fiefs. Nevertheless, from the mid-twelfth century women received a substantial amount of feudal property as dowries — technically early distributions of their inheritances — and thus became proprietors in their own right of both fiefs and allods. Community (or joint) property rights and the dower were formalized at the marriage ceremony, when a husband promised his future wife an equal share of all property acquired during their marriage[58] and assigned her a dower consisting of a residence and half his property for her lifetime use.[59] A widow, consequently, retained not only her dowry (her inheritance) but also her community property and usufruct of her dower lands (acquired by marriage), as well as exclusive control of her minor children unabridged by male relatives or feudal lord. These customs affirming the rights of the wife and widow, rather than the husband's patriline or feudal lord, assured married women a central role within the aristocratic family.

The Marriage Contract

Noble-born women appear to have been married young, perhaps in their early teens, in accordance with canon law, which allowed girls of twelve and boys of fourteen to contract legitimate marriages provided they gave their "present consent." The canonists also devised a provisional category of consent by which children from the age of seven could give "future consent" to a marriage that would be consummated in the future.[60] Although the meaning of consent in a society of arranged marriages, at least of first marriages, might range from reluctant acquiescence to willing acceptance, certainly some marriages must have produced satisfying relationships, if the expressions of sentiment in legal documents ("my dearest husband/wife") were more than formulaic.[61] The actual age at marriage, however, remains difficult to verify, and it is not at all certain that aristocratic women cohabited with their husbands from the minimum age of marriage, or even after the marriage ceremony; the fact that a number of women had relatively small families suggests delayed cohabitation.[62] A recent study of Plantagenet marriages finds that, although girls were thought to be ready for marriage at about fifteen, they often were kept apart from their spouses for several years and did not immediately bear children.[63] It is not surprising that outside learned circles marriage was generally thought to require the consent of the parents and to begin with the establishment of a household rather than with the couple's declaration of consent.[64]

The unhappy experience of Anselm II of Traînel illustrates some of the risks incurred by arranged marriages. The twenty-five-year-old Anselm, newly appointed butler of Champagne in 1153, contracted to marry the very young daughter of Geoffroy of Donzy, a powerful baron from the Auxerrois, who promised a castle as her dowry.[65] After the marriage ceremony, Anselm left the girl in her father's custody, apparently in deference to her tender age. But her father, who had not yet delivered the dowry, soon found his daughter a more prestigious husband in the younger brother of count Henry the Liberal, count Stephen of Sancerre, who consummated the transaction without scruple. Jilted, dishonored, and out of pocket for the 500 *l.* he had given his father-in-law, Anselm brought suit for the unpaid dowry. He appealed to count Henry, who in turned complained to king Louis VII, and together they led an assault on Geoffroy of Donzy's castle where the wedding party was celebrating. Although Anselm recovered the promised dowry, the affair reverberated sixty years later when the lord of Donzy's grandson tried to reclaim the dowry as an illicit alienation from his inheritance.[66]

From the late twelfth century written marriage contracts attempted to preclude such blatant disregard of oral agreements by specifying the dowry, the dower, and other contingencies, such as nonfulfillment of the contract or the death of a spouse without children. Such was the case in 1239 when Margaret, lady of Dampierre, arranged an advantageous marriage for her daughter Jeanne to the count of Rethel: she stipulated that Jeanne's 6000 *l.* cash dowry be refunded if the count died without children, as he did four years later.[67] Archambaud of Bourbon inserted a similar clause in the contract for his daughter Margaret's marriage to count Thibaut IV, but allowed a prorated repayment if she died childless within nine years.[68]

The amount of a dowry (*maritagium, mariage*) generally reflected a family's wealth: the daughter of a knight could expect about 100 *l.*, the daughter of a baron 500 *l.* or more. Invested in income-producing property, as most marriage contracts stipulated, those dowries provided 10–50 *l.* annual revenue at a time when the average fief produced about 26 *l.*[69] Cash dowries seem to have been preferred, as they could be invested near the new household, although their very portability carried risks. When the brothers of Margaret of Buzancy discovered that the 500 *l.* dowry they had given for her marriage had not been invested, they forced her husband to designate part of his *own* property as her dowry so that it would revert to them if she died without children.[70] But dowries were also assigned on real property, both allodial and feudal, to which the wife held legal title. In fact, women who took landed dowries — in essence, their inheritances — retained a strong attachment to them, often seeking to preserve them for their own daughters. Elizabeth, heiress of the viscounty of Mareuil-sur-Ay, passed that inheritance to her daughter, who in turn gave it as a dowry to her own daughter, also named Elizabeth.[71] Elizabeth of Traînel, sister of the butler Anselm II of Traînel, gave her patrimonial lordship of Pâlis to her daughter Capraria.[72] Emeline of Broyes held her dowry, an entire village, for her daughter, at least until her second husband sold it to the Templars without her permission; Emeline's mother and brother intervened to force her husband to provide compensation.[73]

Aristocratic women frequently conveyed their allodial properties to monastic institutions. Alice of Briel, wife of the substantial proprietor Pierre of Briel, gave her entire allod at Essoyes "free from any claim by her heirs" to the new monastery of Molesme; her husband, three sons, and two daughters consented but did not otherwise participate in that donation. Alice even sent the abbot a letter confirming her absolute gift.[74] Helia of Villemaur, widow of the former marshal of Champagne, made a deathbed bequest of 10 *l.* annual revenue "from her own patrimony" to the Paraclete, while Alice, lady of Mallet, gave land from her inheritance to Clairvaux, with the consent of her husband (a knight), her children, and a niece.[75] When Elizabeth, the viscountess of Mareuil-sur-Ay, donated "land that I possess from my patrimony," as she said, to Avenay, she acted alone, with the consent of her brother and husband.[76] And when Alice, heiress of Venizy, drew up her own will, she assigned various bequests "from my own revenues which are from my inheritance" and sealed the document with her seal without any mention of consenters or witnesses.[77]

When a woman's inheritance or dowry consisted of feudal property, as was increasingly the case in the twelfth century, her husband ordinarily took possession of the fief and performed the requisite homage and service.[78] The young heiress of Nogent-sur-Seine, for example, exercised lordship over her castle only after her husband and son died, while the heiress of Bar-sur-Seine never exercised lordship over her castle because first her guardian and then her husband ruled in her name.[79] Lesser fiefs as well, although titled to women, were held by men; the lord of Montmirail, for one, held his wife's fief from the abbess of Faremoutiers.[80] The scribes in charge of the count's feudal registers assumed that feudal property in a woman's inheritance or dowry would be held by her husband, who was named as holding the fief "through his wife" (*ex parte uxoris sua*). The two daughters of the knight Itier of Lasson illustrate the practice: the husband of the married daughter did homage for her half of Itier's fief, while the widowed daughter did homage herself for the other half.[81]

If a woman's dowry or inheritance represented her right to share the assets of her natal family, her dower (*dos, dotalicium, douaire*) assigned by her husband at the time of their marriage represented her new right, as a legitimate wife, to share his properties.[82] Even though a woman did not exercise her dower rights until her husband died, those rights were usually assigned at the beginning of the marriage when her husband presented her a sealed document describing the dower lands. A letter drawn up in 1176 for the marriage of the knight Stephen of Pringy with his bride Comitissa survives today as the oldest original dower letter from Champagne. The bishop of Châlons-sur-Marne, who performed the marriage ceremony, reminded Stephen and his guests, including his lord and several knights, that "a man leaves his father and mother to cling to his wife, and the two will become one in flesh; what God has joined, no man may sunder." Stephen then repeated from the prepared text:

I, Stephen of Pringy, with the approval of my friends, receive you, my dearest Comitissa, as my wife. And with the advice of my friends I give you in dower (*dotem tibi assigno*) one-half of Pringy and its fortified residence. Should I ever leave that house to build another, I will give you the latter in dower. I also give you one-half of all that I possess elsewhere, and one-half of all that I will acquire.

After the ceremony the bishop's chancellor presented the document to the bride, who apparently deposited it at the episcopal chancery for safekeeping.[83]

Stephen gave his wife what was considered to be the "customary" dower in northern and eastern France: lifetime use of his main residence and half of his current and future possessions.[84] The half-dower became the "general custom" of the realm after Philip II enacted it for the entire kingdom in 1214.[85] That practice was so widespread in Champagne that some marriage contracts stipulated simply that the dower be "according to the custom of Champagne." That was the clause written into the marriage contract between Alice of Grandpré and seven-year-old Jean of Joinville, the future seneschal of Champagne and biographer of Louis IX.[86] In some cases the dower was set to equal the value of the bride's dowry.[87] But the wealthiest barons, including the counts themselves, often preferred to assign their wives "devised" dowers, that is, specified lands worth substantially less than half their assets, in order to preserve the integrity of their baronies and simplify successions. The dowers of countesses Blanche of Navarre and Margaret of Bourbon consisted of seven castellanies, perhaps one-third of the count's revenues.[88] The count of Rethel dowered his daughter-in-law with a single castle so that the chief castle of Rethel would pass unrestricted to his son, while the seneschal Simon of Joinville dowered his wife Ermengard of Montclair with his castle of Vaucouleurs, allowing his son to inherit Joinville without delay.[89] But whether devised or customary, a dower of some kind was expected for married women. And in the absence of a devised dower, the High Court declared, a widow would enjoy "by customary right" both her husband's principal residence and half of his property (that is, the customary dower).[90]

Feudal Tenure

Strictly secular dower letters became more common by the late twelfth century as dower lands were increasingly assigned on fiefs, an action that required the consent of the lord from whom the fief was held. Artaud, treasurer of Champagne, was among the first to solicit such a letter in 1171, when he assigned his wife, Hodierne of Nangis, dower lands containing the new castle he had recently constructed at Nogent-sur-Marne: Artaud presented her two identical dower letters, one sealed by count Henry the Liberal, the other by countess Marie.[91] Thereafter, husbands often requested their feudal lord to seal a brief letter describing—and confirming—the dower. Countess Blanche, for example, vouched for the dower that the knight Thibaut of Isle granted to his wife Adeline, while count Thibaut IV guaranteed the dower that the knight William of Bernon assigned to his wife Lucy.[92] Renard II, lord of Choiseul, on the other hand, presented his wife with his own sealed letter describing her dower: his castle and half of his current and future possessions.[93]

   The dower custom had enormous ramifications, for it brought women into the extrafamilial network of men whose relationships were based on loyalty, military service, and feudal tenure. Certainly most fiefs continued to pass to sons, brothers, or nephews, or, in the absence of close heirs, were regranted to unrelated men who could perform the requisite service. And when dowries were assigned on feudal property, husbands did the attendant homage and service in their wives' names. But a dower was fundamentally different from an inheritance or dowry because a widow herself retained exclusive control over her dower for the remainder of her days in the secular world. By the late twelfth century the consequences of feudal dowers had become evident to comital officials, who began inserting in the feudal registers the names of women who held their husbands' fiefs "in dower."[94]

It is not entirely clear whether women in Champagne did homage when they first acquired fiefs. The earliest examples of homage by women date from around 1200, about the time countess Blanche did homage to the king.[95] Faceria, widow of Nocher of Silvarouvres, did homage (*hominium*) to the Cistercian abbot of Mores for her husband's fief.[96] Ermengard of Montclair did liege homage (*homagium ligium*) to countess Blanche for the dower assigned by her husband Simon of Joinville, the seneschal.[97] And Alix of Dreux did homage to the bishop of Langres for the dower granted by her husband, Renard II of Choiseul; the bishop received her as his liegewoman (*femina ligia*) for the castle of Choiseul and all the property pertaining to that fief.[98] Most women, however, did homage as widows, when they took possession of their dower lands, and if they held comital fiefs they would declare their dowers at the comital chancery in Troyes and be registered in the count's Book of Homages.[99] Chancery scribes noted that Margaret, widow of the marshal Erard of Villy, did liege homage for both her dower lands and her own inheritance, while Isabel of Tours-sur-Marne did likewise for her dower and the wardship of her sons.[100] The widow of Ponce of Mont-Saint-Jean presented her dower letter to chancery officials, then "did liege homage for her dower as described in the letter of Ponce which established it."[101] Thereafter women — who represented about one-fifth of the feudal tenants throughout the thirteenth century — routinely did homage for their fiefs.[102]

In the feudal inquest of 1249–50, the most systematic and comprehensive feudal survey of its kind in Champagne, women appear as a normal part of the feudal tenurial system. Count Thibaut IV had directed his "barons, castellans, knights, and other feudal tenants" to give sworn statements about their fiefs; in fact many women — wives, daughters, widows — gave the requisite testimony.[103] The wife of Jean of Flaix reported that he was in the Holy Land and that she held their house with land, woods, rights of justice, and so on, all yielding about 30 *l.* annual revenue; she named their five rear-fiefholders but said she was unsure as to whether her husband owed annual guard duty.[104] Emeline, recently widowed by Robert of Fontette, described her own inheritance at Ville-sur-Arce (her great-grandmother's property) as consisting of a fortified residence, lands, and tenants producing about 160 *l*. annual revenue and owing one month castle guard.[105] The widowed lady of Vanault reported that she held half of the castle there as well as other properties yielding 140 *l*. annual revenue, and had fourteen rear-fiefholders; the lady Isabel of Le Buisson-sur-Saulx said that her dower consisted of a fortified residence and half of all that her husband Itier had held, which she thought was worth about 100 *l*. annually.[106] Sybil of Traînel, who had been widowed a decade earlier, sent the count's officials a sealed letter in the vernacular naming her thirteen rear-fiefholders because, she said, she had been ill during the inquest.[107] And Agnes of Dampierre-le-Château, widowed for six years, sent a letter with her bailiff, who reported in detail on her thirty-two rear-fiefholders.[108]

These and other letters from women regarding fiefs are known because they were addressed to comital officials, who sent them to the chancery archives for preservation. It is difficult to gauge the volume of correspondence between lay people, as few letters were preserved after serving their intended purpose, but it is clear that aristocratic women had individual seals from the early thirteenth century and sealed a wide variety of letters and documents, of which the extant examples offer only a glimpse.[109] The same Sybil of Traînel who responded to the feudal inquest earlier had confirmed a sale by her son, who was not yet a knight.[110] Helissand, countess of Bar-sur-Seine, added her seal to the grant her husband and son made before leaving on the Fifth Crusade, where both later perished.[111] Marie, the widowed and childless countess of Rethel who had transferred her dower to her brother-in-law, addressed a letter "to all the feudal tenants, knights, men, and the community" of her dower lands, explaining what she had done and asking them to "do what you owe him in both homages and other obligations and obey him as your lord."[112] Beatrice, lady of Marnay, made a 200 *l*. loan to the abbot of Saint-Urbain and later, unable to locate his letter of debt when he redeemed the loan, gave him another sealed letter voiding the one she had misplaced.[113] Euda, lady of Pougy, confirmed in a sealed letter the bequests of Alice of Venizy, who had died in her castle of Pougy.[114] And Philippa, wife of Erard of Brienne, explained in her own letter that the two seals she used concurrently, a large one for official business and a small one for her private affairs, were both valid despite the conventional practice of keeping only one valid seal.[115]

The instances in which women sealed their letters suggests that they could in fact represent themselves in a wide range of legal matters. Whether they pleaded their own causes to the High Court is not entirely clear, as only a few cases have survived in which women were directly involved.

Agatha, lady of Damery claimed that her second husband had deprived her of her first husband's inheritance; she won her case and the bailiff of Vitry was charged with enforcing her rights.[116] But Helissand of Arcis-sur-Aube failed to convince the court that she deserved to share an escheated castellany with her four brothers: the court upheld the custom excluding women from the collateral inheritance of fiefs except in the absence of male heirs.[117] Whether these selected cases were typical or exceptional cannot be determined, as only fragments of the High Court's registers have survived.

SEVEN LIVES

While aristocratic women all shared the rights and privileges of their social rank, their individual lives, like those of the countesses, varied considerably according to circumstance, temperament, and choice. Reconstructing those lives remains a daunting task, as it is seldom possible to assemble more than a handful of references to individuals below the comital level. Critical facts such as dates of birth, marriage, and death must be deduced, while attitudes and personalities remain virtually unrecoverable. Still, despite these limitations, it is possible to recapture the basic patterns of a few lives as counterparts to those of the countesses.

The seven noble-born women described here were related by blood, marriage, or proximity of residence. Born between the 1130s and 1180s, they appear to have been first married in their mid-teens but, unlike the countesses, to considerably older men. Although their marriages lasted twenty years or more, they produced few surviving children. Of the six who outlived their husbands, four remarried: they chose widowers about the same age or younger, with whom they had lengthy second marriages and three to six additional children. All four remarried widows outlived their second husbands, had extended second widowhoods, and died in their sixties.

Elizabeth of Nogent-sur-Seine was in her mid-teens when she became a castle heiress in 1147. Her father, Milo I, was a prominent local baron whose small castellany, with about a dozen enfeoffed knights, was strategically located on the main road between the count's twin capitals of Troyes and Provins.[118] A generous benefactor, Milo was among the founders of the Cistercian abbey of Vauluisant in 1127, and two years later contributed the land for Heloise's first oratory, the Paraclete, which he encouraged his knights to support by donating the fiefs they held from him. When in 1146

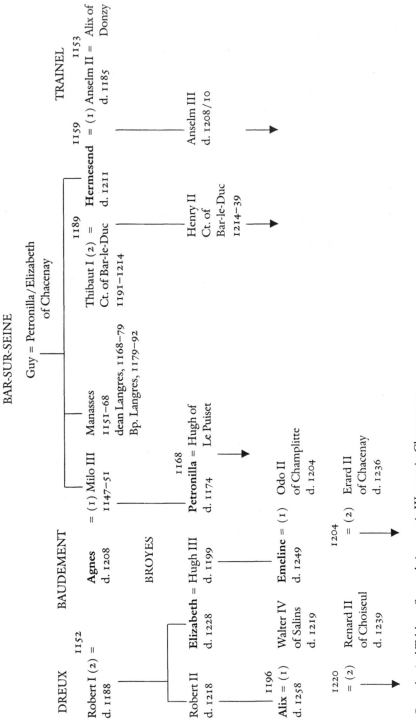

Genealogical Table 4. Some Aristocratic Women in Champagne.

the widowed Milo decided to go on the Second Crusade, Elizabeth was his only surviving child, married but still childless; so Milo took four nephews, his next closest relatives, along with Elizabeth and her husband to the Paraclete to witness his sale of property to finance his journey.[119] Milo's death during the forced crossing of the Meander River in Turkey left Elizabeth's husband as lord of Nogent (1147–71) in her name.

Elizabeth does not appear in any extant record during her twenty-four-year marriage, nor during the fifteen-year rule by her second son, Milo II (1171–86); only after the childless deaths of Milo II and his younger brother Jean, a knight, does she reappear in the documents. Then in her mid-fifties, the grief-stricken Elizabeth took her daughter-in-law Elvissa to the court of countess Marie at Provins, where, according to a chancery scribe, she made a substantial offering to the Paraclete "for the remission of her sins and for those of her father, her mother, her husband Gerard, and her sons Milo and Jean."[120] In recognition of her family's close association with the Paraclete, the tombs of her husband and sons were placed prominently in the Paraclete's chapter hall.[121] Elizabeth seems to have remained at Nogent for over a decade, then, in her mid-sixties and lacking close relatives, she sold the entire lordship to count Thibaut III and entered the Paraclete.[122] The nuns commemorated her with a tomb inscribed "Elizabeth, dedicated to God, lady of Nogent."[123] Elizabeth was exceptional, not in outliving all her sons, but in lacking a daughter or other close relative (nephew, grandson, or cousin) who could inherit her castle.

Slightly younger than Elizabeth was her neighbor of thirty years (1159–89) Hermesend of Bar-sur-Seine, who shared Elizabeth's interest in the Paraclete, where both chose to be buried. Hermesend was the fifth child and only daughter of Elizabeth of Chacenay and Guy, count of Bar-sur-Seine, one of the most powerful barons of southern Champagne (see Genealogical Table 4).[124] An infant of perhaps one year when her father died, Hermesend was raised by her widowed mother until 1159, then was married to Anselm II of Traînel, the thirty-three-year-old butler of Champagne who, as we have seen, had been jilted out of his first marriage. As with Elizabeth of Nogent-sur-Seine, little is known about Hermesend's married life beyond the fact that she had two children. As lady of Traînel, Hermesend certainly must have known Heloise, abbess of the nearby Paraclete, who earlier had sponsored her convent's first priory of twenty nuns at Traînel.[125] It is also likely that Hermesend accompanied her husband on his official visits to the comital capital of Troyes, where they had extensive familial ties. Anselm's brother Garnier II, lord of Marigny, often appeared with him at court in Troyes, and another brother, Milo, abbot of Saint-Marien of Auxerre, frequently sought benefactions there from count Henry. Anselm's sister Elizabeth was married to the lord of Plancy, who also frequented the court and whose brother Haice was an influential canon in the comital chapel of Saint-Etienne of Troyes and later bishop of Troyes. Hermesend's own brother Manasses was a well-known personage too. In 1168 he assumed the lordship of Bar-sur-Seine for seventeen years until his niece Petronilla (see below) could marry and take her inheritance; on resuming his clerical life, Manasses become dean of the cathedral chapter and then bishop of Langres (1179–92). Hermesend's familial connections made her one of the most prominent women of southern Champagne under count Henry the Liberal and countess Marie.

Hermesend was about forty when Anselm died in 1184. Her son had reached his majority, her daughter was married to a local lord, and if Hermesend enjoyed the customary dower of the castle residence at Traînel plus half of Anselm's estate she was generously provided for. But four years later, in her mid-forties, she married a man fifteen years her junior, Thibaut of Briey, a widower of twenty-nine and the younger brother of Henry, count of Bar-le-Duc (1174–90). As dower, Thibaut assigned her his castle of Briey, its castellany, and half of all his future acquisitions, and promised further the castle of Saint-Mihel should he succeed his unmarried brother as count, as he soon did.[126] Hermesend became countess of Bar-le-Duc and in her mid-forties had three more children — a son, Henry II, who would succeed to Bar, and two daughters. But her marriage ended in 1196 when Thibaut, for unknown reasons, divorced her.[127]

The fifty-year-old Hermesend left the young children of her second marriage in Bar-le-Duc to return to her original dower lands in Traînel, where she lived the last fifteen years of her life. Almost immediately she was asked to resolve a bitter dispute between the nuns of the Paraclete and the monks of Vauluisant, two monastic communities long patronized by the Traînel family. The conflict over lands and forests had passed through ecclesiastical channels all the way to the pope, who directed the archbishop and archdeacon of Sens to resolve the matter; unable to do so, they asked Hermesend to arbitrate.[128] After collecting sureties from both sides, Hermesend conducted an inquest as to the facts and, with the advice of local men, decided for the nuns; she then had a charter written to record the judgment and sealed it with her seal.[129]

Hermesend continued to be called "lady of Traînel" both in private acts and in the count's feudal registers at the same time that her son, Anselm III, and his wife, Ida, exercised lordship over Traînel.[130] When Hermesend died in 1211 at about sixty-five, her tomb was placed in the center of the Paraclete's chapter hall, as befitting her status and benefactions to the convent.[131] She had outlived her eldest son Anselm III (he died 1208/10). His widow Ida continued to represent the Traînel lineage, notably in 1213 when she appeared as the only woman among the barons of Champagne who swore their allegiance to young Thibaut IV.[132]

Hermesend may well have spent her childhood years in the castle of Bar-sur-Seine with her slightly younger niece, Petronilla of Bar-sur-Seine, who was about a year old when her father Milo III died in 1151. When her mother remarried (see below), Petronilla was left in the custody of her uncle Manasses, who postponed his ecclesiastical career to serve as her guardian and lord of Bar-sur-Seine. At about eighteen Petronilla married Hugh of Le Puiset, who assumed her inheritance and title until their son succeeded. Although Petronilla herself died in her mid-twenties (ca. 1174), the youngest of the seven women discussed here and the only one to predecease her husband, she succeeded, like most heiresses, in continuing her father's lineage.[133]

Petronilla's mother, Agnes of Baudemont, who outlived her by over thirty years, was herself an heiress twice over. From her grandfather André of Baudement, seneschal of Champagne, she inherited the castle of Baudemont, but stripped of its lands and revenues, for in a magnificent act of generosity he had given them to the new order of the Templars.[134] Agnes also inherited her grandmother's castle of Braine, a much more valuable property located on the border of Champagne and the royal domain that made an ideal base for Agnes's politically ambitious second husband, Robert I of Dreux (brother of Louis VII).[135] Robert, who had probably known Agnes's first husband on the Second Crusade, was in his mid-twenties and recently widowed with an infant daughter when he married Agnes in 1152.[136] As dower, he assigned her his castle of Dreux with its entire castellany and half the lands he might acquire in the future.[137] Agnes appeared prominently with her husband in many of his acts throughout their long marriage (1152–88); but she also celebrated her separate identity as "countess [of Braine] and lady and heir of that castle through my ancestors."[138] Together Agnes and Robert subsidized the construction of the Gothic church of Saint-Yved of Braine, where both were later buried. She had six children during a thirty-six-year marriage, and survived another sixteen years to die in her late sixties.

Agnes's castle of Baudement passed as dowry to her youngest daughter,

Elizabeth of Dreux. Elizabeth was in her mid-teens when she married Hugh III, lord of Broyes, then almost sixty and recently widowed after a thirty-four-year marriage.[139] She had two children during her twenty-one-year marriage and chose not to remarry when widowed in her mid- to late thirties. She held her dowry of Baudement (her great-grandfather's castle) for about thirty years before selling it to countess Blanche in 1211,[140] but she retained her dower castle of Châteauvillain for the rest of her life. She was in her sixties when last mentioned in 1228 — endowing a generous fund for the annual feeding and clothing of the poor who appeared at Clairvaux's gate.[141]

Elizabeth's daughter, Emeline of Broyes, followed her mother's example in marrying a much older man, Odo II of Champlitte, the grandson of count Hugh of Troyes and a prominent leader of the Fourth Crusade. When Odo perished at Constantinople Emeline was left a widow of twenty-five with an infant daughter.[142] She soon remarried, to Erard II of Chacenay, the heir of a prominent local barony then in his late teens, and had five children during their thirty-one-year marriage.[143] But Erard's emergence as a leading figure of the baronial revolt against countess Blanche, and his refusal to submit to the countess and her son despite excommunication and interdict, might have strained the marriage. Shortly after Erard made his peace with the countess in 1222 (he was the last rebel baron to do so), he sold off the dowry of his stepdaughter Euda, then about twenty, without her mother's permission, an action that may have led to talk of divorce.[144] But the marriage survived to Erard's death in 1236, and Emeline lived an additional thirteen years to her late sixties. Like Hermesend of Traînel and Elizabeth of Nogent-sur-Seine, Emeline had outlived her eldest son.

About the same age as Emeline was her cousin Alix of Dreux, one of four daughters and four sons of Robert II, count of Dreux and Braine (1188–1218), and Yolande of Coucy.[145] Alix's father was a prominent vassal of both the king (his cousin) and the count of Champagne, and her uncles Philip and Henry were bishops respectively of Beauvais (1175–1217) and Orléans (1186–98). Her brother Peter of Dreux — the leading opportunist baron of his time — played a prominent role in the political affairs of northern France after marrying the heiress of Brittany.[146] Like her cousin Emeline of Broyes and her aunt Elizabeth of Dreux, Alix was still very young when married to the recently divorced Walter IV of Vienne, lord of Salins. Their twenty-three-year marriage remained childless, however, and in 1219 Alix was left a widow in her mid-thirties. Within a year she married the forty-three-year old Renard II of Choiseul, likewise widowed without children after a twenty-five-year marriage.[147] Renard dowered her with his castle of

Choiseul and half his current and future possessions, for which she did homage to the bishop of Langres.[148] During her second marriage Alix had five children, and often appeared with Renard in his acts. She was about fifty-five when Renard died in 1239.[149] For the next seven years she acted as regent for her oldest son, Jean, and died ten years later at about seventy-four.[150]

The seven women described here represent three generations whose lives spanned the mid-twelfth through mid-thirteenth century. Three of them were exact contemporaries of countess Marie (Elizabeth of Nogent-sur-Seine, Hermesend of Bar-sur-Seine, Agnes of Baudement) and of the appropriate standing to appear at her court on official and festive occasions. Agnes of Baudemont's younger daughter (Elizabeth of Dreux) and two granddaughters (Emeline of Broyes, Alix of Dreux), grew up during countess Marie's regency and lived through countess Blanche's extended regency and into the rule of Thibaut IV. We would expect these prominent women to have interacted with the countesses, but whether and how they did so remains an open question, in the absence of narrative accounts.

While only a full prosopographical study will reveal how typical these seven women were, it is possible to draw a few conclusions about their lives. They were born into wealthy and powerful families — four were castle heiresses — and married men of comparable standing. Married in their teens to older men, they had lengthy first marriages and relatively small families.[151] Six of the seven survived their husbands, and as widows freely decided whether to remarry, enter a convent, or remain an active dowager. Two who were widowed in their late thirties (Elizabeth of Nogent-sur-Seine, Elizabeth of Dreux) remained widows for almost thirty years. Of the four who remarried, the three youngest did so within about a year (Agnes of Baudement in her late teens, Emeline of Broyes at about twenty-five, Alix of Dreux in her thirties), while Hermesend of Bar-sur-Seine, in her mid-forties, waited four years. All four widows married men of comparable social standing, three of whom had been widowed themselves (two with infant daughters). Their second marriages were as lengthy as their first ones, but produced more children. Only one of the seven was divorced (in her second marriage), but another may have considered it.

What most distinguishes these women from the countesses, besides their remarriages, is their longevity: six of the seven lived into their sixties, far longer than the countesses, whose average age was about forty (only two reached fifty). Whether any of these women were marked by early spiritual concerns, as were two of the countesses (Blanche of Navarre, Isabel of France), is difficult to ascertain. Only Elizabeth of Nogent-sur-Seine, who entered the Paraclete in her late years, is known to have adopted a conventual life. But for many other noble-born women in Champagne, the religious life remained a powerful alternative to marriage and widowhood.

Religious Women

Of the twenty-two female convents established in Champagne from the seventh century, only nine survived to 1100. The most prominent of those old convents, Avenay near Epernay, Faremoutiers and Jouarre near Meaux, and Notre-Dame-aux-Nonnains in Troyes, continued to attract women through the twelfth and thirteenth centuries.[152] But it was the new wave of spirituality, propelled largely by the Cistercians in southern Champagne, that spawned the largest number of new convents in the twelfth and thirteenth centuries: Fontevrault, which had close ties with the comital family, established six priories in the county; Molesme created ten priories for women; the Paraclete under abbess Heloise sponsored six affiliated convents; and numerous female communities imitating the Cistercians appeared spontaneously throughout the county.[153] So many women sought admission that by the end of the twelfth century several prestigious convents outstripped their resources, fell into debt, and were forced to limit their size. The Paraclete was reduced to sixty nuns and Avenay to forty.[154] Yet the pressure for placements continued unabated into the thirteenth century, resulting in the establishment of twenty new Cistercian convents despite the Chapter General's attempt to halt new female houses.[155] The largest of the new communities, with ninety nuns, was Argensolles, which countess Blanche lavishly endowed to serve as her retirement home after she left public life.[156] By the end of the thirteenth century more than one hundred convents for women existed in Champagne, primarily Benedictine, Cistercian, and Premonstratensian houses established since 1100. In all, about five thousand women, largely from aristocratic families, lived in cloistered communities.[157]

The extraordinary increase in female religious houses naturally raises the question of motivation: why did women join convents? Were they forced to take the veil by families seeking to preserve patrimonies and economic resources, or were other factors at play? Studies of female monasticism in several regions of France suggest a variety of reasons for monastic profession. Beyond familial interests in offering a child to the church for spiritual benefits or avoiding the payment of a dowry for marriage, there

were a number of more personal reasons for taking monastic vows, including flight from an unwanted marriage and individual temperament that
inclined young women to a secluded life. A widow too might retire to a
convent, and even a married woman might adopt a spiritual life with her
husband's consent.[158] In cases of mixed motives, spiritual reasons seem
to have been primary, for unlike male Benedictine monasteries that were
fueled by child oblation, female convents generally accepted only adults
(over fifteen or twenty years of age). Indeed, the close cooperation between
men and women in founding early Cistercian convents underscores the fact
that aristocratic women were affected by the same spirituality that attracted
aristocratic men to the monastic life. Herman of Tournai observed around
1150 that women

of their own free will embraced violently, nay joyfully, the Order of Cîteaux, which
many robust men and youths fear to enter. Laying aside all linen garments and furs,
they wore only woolen tunics. They did not only women's work, such as spinning
and weaving, but they went out and worked the fields, digging, cutting down and
uprooting the forest with axe and mattock, tearing up thorns and briars, laboring
assiduously with their hands and seeking their food in silence. Imitating in all things
the monks of Clairvaux, they proved the truth of the Lord's saying, that to the
believer all things are possible.[159]

The very success of Molesme and Clairvaux in recruiting adult men
created a dilemma for the families left behind.[160] Jully-les-Nonnains was
founded specifically for the female relatives of men who had joined Molesme: its first prioress was Elizabeth, wife of Bernard of Clairvaux's older
brother Guy, who had followed him to Cîteaux; she was succeeded by their
sister Humbeline. Bernard himself wrote Jully's Rule, prescribing fifteen
years as the minimum age of entrance and setting the maximum number of
nuns at seventy.[161] But many Cistercian convents lacked official sponsor-
ship, as women simply adopted the Cistercian lifestyle, including manual
labor in the fields. Nuns from Jully, for example, established a female community at Andecy before receiving a generous endowment from the local
lord, Simon of Broyes, and his wife, Felicity of Brienne: their gift of arable
land, pastures, a granary, an orchard, and assorted rents and taxes suggests
that the nuns intended to work their lands themselves.[162] Such spontaneous
communities were precluded in the next century, after the Chapter General
imposed enclosure on female houses and prohibited new foundations.[163]

The region's most notable religious woman was Heloise, who served
thirty-four years as abbess of the Paraclete (1130–64). Unlike the women

who flocked to Cistercian convents, however, Heloise found her vocation only gradually and with difficulty while she was abbess, long after she had separated from Abelard. As a natural daughter of the powerful Garlande family, Heloise entered Argenteuil as prioress in the wake of Abelard's misadventures and stayed there until 1129, when the nuns were expelled by the monks of Saint-Denis under abbot Suger, who had purged the Garlande brothers from high offices in the royal government.[164] With a few nuns from Argenteuil, Heloise set out to create a new convent at Abelard's former oratory on the Aubusson River.[165] She continued a spiritual relationship with Abelard — as evidenced by their correspondence, their vigorous debate over female monasticism, and Abelard's composition of hymns for her convent — and became a model abbess in the years after Abelard's death. She wrote a Rule for the Paraclete, rejecting a number of Abelard's proposals, and sponsored six affiliated convents, including a priory in the village of a powerful local, Anselm I of Traînel, and an abbey at La Pommeraye in association with countess Matilda of Blois.[166]

Most nuns have left few traces in the written records, often appearing only at the recording of their entrance gifts. The few who can be identified came from substantial families that are frequently mentioned as monastic donors and patrons. The prestigious old convent of Avenay, for example, where countess Marie was educated, accepted a number of daughters of knightly families after she had left it: Ferry of Vienne gave his banal oven for the admission of his two daughters, and Hugh of La Porte Marne gave land so that his daughter and *her* daughter could be nuns there.[167] Hugh of Huiron gave land to Saint-Pierre-les-Dames of Reims so that two of his three daughters "would be educated and be consecrated nuns" there.[168] The Paraclete, too, received many women from the families of knights who held fiefs from Milo I, lord of Nogent-sur-Seine, the original benefactor of the convent who encouraged them to support the community.[169] Even after 1196, when the Paraclete was forced to downsize, important families were able to reserve places for their daughters: Helia of Villemaur, widow of the marshal of Champagne, donated a 10 *l.* rent so that "one of her daughters" could enter the convent, but because limitations had been imposed on new entrants, she had to obtain the explicit consent of the abbess and the entire community.[170]

Women often chose or were placed in convents where they already had a close relative. Geoffroy of Villehardouin, marshal of Champagne and future chronicler of the Fourth Crusade, had both a daughter, Dameron, and a sister, Haye, at the convent of Foissy located just east of Troyes. They were joined by another relative, perhaps a cousin, Adeline of Briel, whose two brothers later became barons in crusader Greece under the Villehardouin princes of the Morea.[171] Geoffroy's other sister, Emeline, and second daughter, Alice, joined the wealthiest convent in Troyes, Notre-Dame-aux-Nonnains, where Alice later became abbess.[172] At that same time abbess Ermengard of the Paraclete had three of her nieces with her as nuns.[173]

Although most nuns in Champagne seem to have been unmarried, studies of other regions suggest that widowed or still-married women constituted a significant percentage of cloistered women.[174] At least one still-married woman joined the Paraclete, with her husband's consent: Benceline, the wife of Guerric of Pont-sur-Seine, brought with her a substantial entry gift that might have been her own inheritance.[175] Evidence for widows entering convents is more abundant. Helisend, the widow of Anselm I of Traînel, for example, entered Foissy as its prioress shortly after her two sons were settled on their lands. She had met Heloise at the dedication of the Paraclete's first priory in Traînel, and in 1146 had served as arbiter with her husband and his sister when Heloise and the abbot of Vauluisant came to Traînel to solve their dispute.[176] Although Helisend's achievements at Foissy are not known, she was precisely the noble-born abbess whose familial connections and personal wealth were so critical to a convent's economic viability.

Abbess Helisend of Avenay (1170–97), daughter of the viscount of Mareuil-sur-Ay, illustrates the active role played by aristocratic women as ecclesiastical administrators. After a fire destroyed the abbey church and several adjacent buildings in the 1180s, she had the entire church rebuilt: she richly furnished it with liturgical vessels and colored cloth for decorating the church on feast days; she had the refectory repaired and the granary enlarged; and she purchased vineyards and tithe revenues, all of which she accomplished in part at her own expense. Archbishop William of Reims, who dedicated the church, was so impressed that he recounted at length abbess Helisend's achievement in restoring one of the most prestigious convents of the region.[177] But abbess Helisend's vision exceeded the convent's resources: fifteen years later the same archbishop had to save the community from its creditors by limiting its size.[178]

Convent endowments consisting generally of scattered small revenues could not match the concentrated collections of land, tithes, rents, and banal taxes most male houses managed to assemble. The Paraclete's portfolio of lands, rents, transit taxes, tithes, houses, and vineyards was larger than most, yet typical in being insufficient to support all those who sought

admission there.[179] Although female convents acquired feudal properties as
well, only one — Faremoutiers — is known to have had laypeople holding
fiefs from it: thirty-two feudal tenants, including four barons, held fiefs for
which they swore fidelity (*fidelitatem*) to the abbess; among them was the
lord of Montmirail, who held his wife's dowry, one of the earliest examples
of a feudal dowry in this region.[180] The most substantial endowment, as
might be expected, was amassed by countess Blanche for the new convent
of Argensolles. She purchased its core endowment consisting of the granary, attached arable land, and 1000 *arpents* of woods, from the abbey of
Hautvillers, then added woods, tithes, rents, transit taxes, vineyards, a mill,
and another granary acquired from several knights and local proprietors.
The sum of those purchases made up a substantial, concentrated endowment appropriate to a community authorized to receive ninety nuns.[181]

Most female houses enjoyed similar rural resources, more or less, but
one notable community had its major assets located within the rapidly
expanding center of Troyes. Notre-Dame-aux-Nonnains, originally located
outside the walls of the old city, was enveloped in the course of the twelfth
century by the burgeoning new town of Troyes and its trade fairs. Little is
known about the abbey before 1188, when a fire in the city consumed its
archives, but by that date it possessed substantial urban properties, including a house where cloth merchants traded, three ovens in the city, as well as
several villages, all free of the count's taxes and jurisdiction.[182] The nuns
collected rents from houses located in the new market area adjacent to the
parish church of Saint-Jacques, over which the abbess had jurisdiction, and
continued to build a substantial portfolio of rents in the thirteenth century.
The nuns vigorously protected their economic interests, first against the
Dominicans who began to accumulate properties next to the abbey, then
against the pope himself in a remarkable case of conventual violence played
out in full view of the residents of Troyes.

Among the convent's properties was the house in which pope Urban
IV (1261–64), the son of a shoemaker, was born. Soon after his election as
pope, Urban decided to commemorate his family and natal city by constructing a new church, to be named Saint-Urbain, on the very site of his
home. Papal commissioners bought up most of the surrounding properties,
then coerced the nuns into selling their houses, revenues, and rights. The
timing was unfortunate, as the nuns were in the midst of a divisive election
of a new abbess, who was selected by a 30 to 27 vote. On appeal, however,
Urban IV reversed the election and installed the minority candidate, Isabel
of Le Châtel, the infirmarian. Tensions within the convent were exacerbated

by the pope's failure to compensate the nuns for their expropriated property, so after Urban's death the nuns decided to vent their anger. With the aid of their displaced tenants — a former provost of Troyes, a butcher, an innkeeper, among others — the nuns attacked the new church: they broke through the church doors, demolished the marble altar, and destroyed the workmen's tools and supplies in a rare act of violence by nuns. Pope Urban's successor, Clement IV, threatened excommunication, but the nuns persisted, even manhandling the archbishop of Tyre who was sent to dedicate the new church's cemetery. The nuns were excommunicated (1269) and not released from that sentence until the death of their abbess and the payment of heavy fines fourteen years later.[183]

Women and the Social Order

The practical records examined here reveal a far different picture of medieval women — at least of noble-born women — than the one refracted though misogynist literature, speculative learned treatises, and cautionary tales addressed to monastic male audiences.[184] Moreover, and contrary to what some historians have recently claimed, aristocratic women were neither marginalized by a familial obsession with the patriline nor excluded from inheritance by male primogeniture. Nor is there evidence in Champagne of a degradation of women's familial rights and legal capacity in the twelfth and thirteenth centuries. In fact, the High Court forcefully affirmed the privileges and rights of noble-born women attendant on their high birth and marriage. Those included a daughter's right to an inheritance and a wife's right to share her husband's possessions — his office and title, half of his future acquisitions, and life use of half of his own inherited property — in addition to the absolute custody of her minor children. Both secular and ecclesiastical documents record women inheriting, acquiring, disposing, and bequeathing property. Women did homage and received homage for fiefs. They responded to inquests, they sealed letters on a variety of financial and feudal matters, and they contracted marriages for their children.

In their personal lives aristocratic women displayed a variety of traits and preferences. There is no evidence that daughters were routinely married downward with small dowries or warehoused in convents as a way of preserving the patriline's resources. Although first marriages were arranged, daughters received dowries commensurate with their family's wealth, and they expected in turn comparable dowers from their husbands:

both Thibaut, count of Bar-le-Duc, and king Philip III explicitly recognized in their dower letters the relationship between the amount of the dower and the level of the husband's office and wealth.[185] Divorced or widowed women could freely remarry, and often did, choosing their husbands at will and having second families. The fact that large numbers of noble-born women opted for a conventual life, either in lieu of marriage or as widows, suggests that in a region saturated with reformed monasticism, women succumbed to the same force of spirituality as men.

The evidence from Champagne is ample and unambiguous. If historians have missed the pervasive presence of women in aristocratic society it is because they have made unwarranted assumptions about the organization of families and the descent of property. A detailed examination of the nonliterary evidence obliges us to shift the parameters of observation — from patrilineage to bilateral kinship, from primogeniture to partible inheritance, from first marriages to the longer life course. In doing so we encounter a society in which women participated in a wide range of activities too often represented as the exclusive preserve of men.

4

Countesses as Rulers in Flanders

Karen S. Nicholas

THE COUNTESSES OF FLANDERS played important political roles in the history of the county from the time of its Carolingan origins.[1] They brought their husbands not only the prestige of their natal families but often even experience in ruling, as several came to Flanders as widows of other princes. Because of deaths at war and on crusade, Flanders passed through the female line nearly as often as through the male line, and three countesses ruled by hereditary right. This chapter will examine the extensive roles of countesses in the governance of Flanders from the late eleventh through the thirteenth centuries. What assets did they bring to their marriages? How well did they work as partners with their husbands in governance? To what extent did they manage their dowers, their inheritances, and their husbands' lands? What role did they play in arranging marriages or choosing careers for their children? And how did they act as regents or as hereditary countesses?

The sources of information about ruling families in Flanders consist primarily of charters (documents attesting to grants, sales, or exchanges of property and rights, mostly to monasteries and churches) and chronicles (narrative histories, usually written by the clergy), but occasional letters and administrative documents survive as well. Charters are numerous for the twelfth and thirteenth centuries, including those isssued by the counts and countesses.[2] But it is the chronicles that supply most of the narrative information about Flanders and its political devlopment. The early twelfth-century chroniclers such as Galbert of Bruges, Walter of Thérouanne, Lambert of Waterlos, Herman of Tournai, and the authors of the deeds of the bishops of Cambrai are generally reliable, even though they present history as the acts of powerful men who exercised power primarily by the sword, and consequently had little to say about the countesses. Galbert of Bruges,

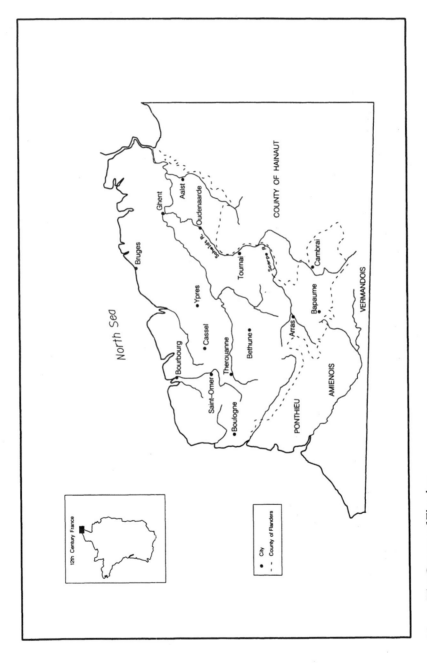

Map 4. The County of Flanders.

for example, wrote a detailed account of the murder of count Charles the Good in 1127 without even mentioning the count's wife Margaret. The bias of those chroniclers has misled modern historians, who have accepted uncritically the same attitudes, failing to appreciate the actual exercise of rule by twelfth-century women through family connections, administrative actions, and control of property. Narrative accounts written by the secular clergy, by contrast, exhibited different attitudes toward the women whom they often encountered as church patrons and lay rulers, and whom the writers frequently supported as rulers acting to further the aims of both church and state. Gislebert of Mons, the chancellor and later chronicler of Hainaut, for example, praised countess Margaret, sister of count Philip of Flanders and wife of count Baldwin V of Hainaut, for defending castles being attacked by her husband's vassals.[3] Like other secular clerics who worked closely with aristocratic women, Gislebert thought of them less in the misogynist, dualistic stereotypes of monastic authors than as individuals, each with her own particular personality and talents.

With the establishment of feudal hierarchies and the institutionalization of princely administration, private warfare virtually disappeared in Flanders by the late twelfth century. In increasingly peaceful times a countess could certainly rule, as Jeanne and Marguerite would do for most of the thirteenth century. At the same time, the hereditary position of women in feudal law also became stronger, as daughters could inherit fiefs in the absence of sons.[4] And just as few objected to Rosie the Riveter and her sisters performing additional tasks in American industry during World War II, few in medieval Flanders objected when counts and barons departing on crusade left their wives as regents, often for longer durations than originally anticipated. In this sense the crusades provided a window of opportunity for the women of northeastern France and the Low Countries.

The countesses of medieval Flanders differed in their personalities and ambitions, as well as in their methods of attaining and wielding power in the county. Their influence generally increased with time, beginning with Richilde, the widowed countess who was driven out of Flanders in 1071 (but who continued to rule in Hainaut), and Gertrude of Holland, who apparently was not active in her husband's government; growing in the twelfth century with Clemence of Burgundy, who held twelve towns as her dower and led a revolt against her son's successor, and with Sybil of Anjou, daughter of Fulk V, king of Jerusalem; and culminating in the reigns of the sister countesses Jeanne (1205–44) and Marguerite (1244–78), who inherited Flanders and Hainaut from their father and thus were independent,

Matilda = William I
King of
England

Baldwin VI
1067–70

= Richilde
1067–70
Countess of
Hainaut
1040–83

Robert I
The Frisian
1071–93

= (2) Gertrude
of Holland
1071–93

Gertrude (2) = Thierry of
Upper Lorraine

Robert of
Normandy

Robert II
1111–19

= Clemence of
Burgundy
1093–1119

Adela = Cnut IV
King of
Denmark

Thierry = (1) Swanehilde, 1128–33
of Alsace = (2) Sybil of Anjou, 1134–57
1128–68

William Clito
1127–28

Baldwin VII
1111–19

Charles the Good
1119–27

Margaret = Baldwin V of Hainaut
1191–94   (VIII of Flanders)

Philip of
Alsace
1168–91

= (1) Elizabeth of
Vermandois
1168–82

= (2) Matilda of Portugal
1183–91

Margaret of =
Clermont

Isabel = Phillip II
King of France

Louis VIII
King of France

Baldwin IX = Marie of Champagne
1194–1205

Jeanne
1205–44

= (1) Ferrand of Portugal
= (2) Thomas of Savoy

Marguerite = (1) Bouchard of Avesnes
1244–78   = (2) Guillaume of Dampierre

Guy of Dampierre
1278–1305

Genealogical Table 5. The Countesses of Flanders.

hereditary ruling princes. Hereditary countesses also ruled in Holland and Luxembourg at that same time.

Richilde

Richilde was forty-nine years old when she became countess of Flanders, much older than the other countesses discussed here. She spent eleven years as countess of Hainaut (1040–51), then sixteen years with her second husband, Baldwin of Flanders, before he succeeded his father as count Baldwin VI of Flanders (1067–70). From the beginning of her marriage to Baldwin, Richilde actively sought to retain her first husband's inheritance in her own hand. She placed the children of her first marriage in the church: Gertrude entered a convent and Roger, who is described by Gislebert of Mons as "debilitated in body," joined the secular clergy, from which he later was elected bishop of Châlons-sur-Marne. Richilde then devoted all her attention and ambition to the sons of her second marriage, Arnold and Baldwin, who were expected to inherit Hainaut as well as Flanders. Gislebert of Mons later criticized her for a lack of maternal feeling for the children of her first marriage.[5] But Roger might well have been physically disabled and Richilde, by her second marriage, would have acted decisively at a time when her rule in Hainaut was threatened; in effect, she turned the disaster of her widowhood into the victory of a prestigious second marriage to the future count of Flanders.

At the death of Baldwin VI in 1070, Richilde's position in Flanders was challenged by her husband's younger brother, Robert the Frisian (Genealogical Table 5). Robert had married the widow of the count of Holland and was ruling there as regent for his stepson. As soon as his brother died, Robert sent agents to Ghent, Bruges, and maritime Flanders to secure northern Flanders for him. According to "Flandria Generosa," Robert summoned men from the cities and towns of the north, while Richilde appealed to the southern towns and surrounding counties.[6] Robert marched on Flanders with surprising speed, so that Richilde and her sons could not gather their troops to confront him until he reached Cassel. But Richilde was not without resources. She recruited men from Hainaut, who rallied round their countess, then appealed to king Philip I of France, her feudal lord for Flanders, who in the company of three bishops brought an army composed of men from northeastern France. But the royal army, gathered in haste, was not especially large, and Richilde's son Arnold, who held the castle of Cassel, was ambushed and captured after being lured outside the castle by Robert's feigned retreat. The battle of Cassel proved decisive. Arnold soon died, at the hands of his own servants or vassals according to some Flemish sources,[7] and Richilde herself was captured.

Within weeks of the battle of Cassel, king Philip I became reconciled to Robert the Frisian and invested him with the county of Flanders. Soon thereafter the king married Robert's stepdaughter Bertha, at which point many lords and barons of southern Flanders deserted Richilde. Richilde was unable to retake Flanders for her younger son Baldwin. Although she persuaded the bishop of Liège to support her by infeudating the county of Hainaut to him in return for a large sum of money and raising an army to invade Flanders, the bishop and her other allies deserted her after the emperor Henry IV also recognized Robert as count of Flanders. Only count Henry II of Louvain, whose daughter Ida was married to Richilde's son Baldwin, remained loyal to her. Richilde's campaign to reconquer Flanders had become hopeless. The Flemings clearly preferred the energetic brother of the deceased count to a widow ruling as regent for her minor son, and they refused to support Richilde's proposed invasion.

Richilde had been countess of Flanders for only three years, and so lacked the long association with her subjects necessary to build networks of support, as she had been doing in Hainaut since 1040. She may also have been unpopular in maritime Flanders for trying to impose there the kind of hierarchical power that existed in Hainaut and in the Flemish heartland. The unruly men of maritime Flanders preferred the rule of Robert the Frisian, who knew and ruled a similar untamed land in the north, whereas the people of Hainaut, who had long known Richilde as countess, accepted her. Many Flemings who had remained loyal to her also came to live under her rule in Hainaut.

As countess of Hainaut Richilde built a castle at Beaumont, one of the three most important castles of the counts, and erected and endowed a chapel there in honor of St. Venantius. With her son Baldwin she acted against the abuses of advocates or "protectors" of churches and monasteries, who often usurped lands and income from churches instead of protecting them. Together they built the monastery of Saint-Denis-en-Broqueroie. And by installing hereditary household officials in Hainaut similar to the ones in Flanders, they began the task of dominating the unruly nobles of Hainaut. Richilde acted as regent until 1083, when she retired to the abbey of Messines, and died the following year. She and her son established an illustrious line of counts named Baldwin who ruled in Hainaut until 1205, when countess Jeanne inherited both Hainaut and Flanders.[8]

Gertrude of Holland

Robert the Frisian's wife, Gertrude of Holland, had been previously married to count Floris I of Holland, who was murdered in 1061. She was thirty when she married Robert in 1063, and although she ruled Flanders for over twenty years (1071–93) and lived into the reign of her grandson, she played a small political role in the county. She appears in one-twelfth of her husband's charters and one-eighth of her son's charters, a much smaller proportion than for other countesses, even through she was, like Richilde, an experienced widow. Gertrude was occupied with preserving the county of Holland for the son of her first marriage, the future count Dirk V, and arranging a brilliant marriage for her daughter Bertha to king Philip of France. Raising and marrying her five children by Robert may have kept her from a greater public role, but perhaps she also was daunted by the murder of her first husband and the aggressive ambition of her second. She apparently deferred to the distinguished dowager countess, Adele, daughter of the king of France, who had more personal and political ties in Flanders than Gertrude herself.[9] Or Gertrude might simply lacked political ambition in Flanders.[10]

Clemence of Burgundy

Clemence of Burgundy, wife of count Robert II (1093–1111), descended from a powerful French dynasty.[11] Mother of two or three sons early in her marriage, and lacking competition from a powerful mother-in-law, she easily established her authority in the ruling family and in Flanders. She was countess for twenty-six years, ruling with her husband and then her unmarried son. Her substantial dower testifies to her importance: one-third of Flanders, including twelve towns located in the maritime and southwestern regions of Flanders, and stretching from Lille to Douai to Bapaume.[12]

Clemence was a forceful ruler of Flanders during count Robert II's absence on the First Crusade. She minted coins in her own name and in 1096, shortly after Robert's departure, quelled violence in Bruges. In 1097, when bishop Lambert of Arras asked her, as ruler, to restrain her provost from assaulting pilgrims in Bapaume, she did so. Clemence retained her high visibility after Robert II's return and worked with him in governing the county, although he reserved certain rights of patronage and comital prerogatives for himself. She appeared in over half of Robert's charters, though not in letters he sent to Ghent and Bruges, the two largest and most turbulent Flemish cities, nor in documents that settled disputes or proclaimed the count's peace.[13] Together, she and Robert made six separate grants of property to the abbey of Bourbourg and founded and endowed the abbey of Faumont.[14] Their many grants to their subjects include a charter of liberties to the townspeople of Aire and the lifting of wheat payments owed by the inhabitants of Berquen and Steenwerck.

It was natural for Clemence to develop close relationships with prominent prelates: three of her brothers were in the church, two becoming archbishops, the third pope. She supported church reform, a rather more traditional Burgundian concern than a Flemish one, and personified the clerical ideal of wives influencing their husbands in supporting the church.[15] She sponsored the reformer John of Warneton as bishop of Thérouanne. She transferred the abbey of Saint-Bertin to the reforming Cluniacs and exempted it from episcopal jurisdiction, a provision Robert II removed in confirming her grant. She worked with bishops Lambert of Arras and Balderic of Tournai in founding a monastery at Straten near Bruges, and granted land to Anchin so the monks could dig a canal to facilitate trade. She founded the abbey of Bourbourg and identified the entire ruling family as its patrons: not only Robert II and their son Baldwin VII, but their successors Charles and Thierry also made donations to it. Later she founded an abbey at Avesnes near Bapaume. And in the only letter we have in her name Clemence wrote to the bishop of Cambrai approving the building of an oratory by the burghers of Oudenaarde.

In 1111 Robert II fell from his horse and was trampled to death in a battle at Meaux. Clemence continued as an active countess through the rule of her son Baldwin VII (1111–19). She appeared in all the charters of his first year of rule. Together they restored the abbey of Saint-Vaast's right to toll at Arras, and made several grants of property to the abbey of Bourbourg and one to the abbey of Ham.[16] Baldwin attempted to assert his independence, but Clemence remained influential behind the scenes. In 1112, after quarreling over her dower, Clemence staged a small revolt, which presaged the more serious events of 1119.[17] Bishop Lambert of Arras wrote to Baldwin, advising him to do as his father had done:

Lambert, by the compassion of God, bishop of Arras, to the honorable and distinguished count of Flanders, Baldwin, support and counsel from the Lord God always. Countess Clemence, your mother, complains that her dower and all the possessions which your father gave her and allowed her to have quietly, you also should permit her to have quietly and without scandal. For which we ask of your excellency so as not to provoke your mother to rage, but like the command of our Lord who said, "Honor your father and your mother so that one has a long life upon the land which the Lord God has given to you," that you should convey in clemency so that through the Lord, a long lived and a peaceful prince should live on the land. Because if you do not wish to do this, she asks us and we deliver our request for her, that you should establish a day and should call together the magnates of your land and the castellans whom she will have wished to come together in this cause, and because it will be judged by them for her in your court or in the court of the French king, success is to be expected. Farewell.[18]

Despite this incident, Baldwin continued to rule with his mother in a sharing of power. Simon of Saint-Bertin reported that abbot Lambert of Saint Peter's abbey in Ghent consulted both Clemence and Baldwin before reforming his monastery because, he said, they both ruled Flanders. They worked together against the increasing Anglo-Norman threat, as king Henry I of England made vassals of the count of Saint-Pol and other lords on the Flemish border. But Clemence began to feel displaced as co-ruler when Baldwin became closer to his cousin, Charles of Denmark, who was made castellan of Encre and governor of Amiens (his wife Margaret of Clermont's dowry). When Baldwin invaded Normandy he left Charles in charge of Flanders, and in 1119, after being mortally wounded in battle, designated Charles as his successor. Clemence favored instead William of Ypres, the illegitimate son of Robert II's brother, who had married her niece and with whom she had close personal ties. Resenting Charles as a newcomer over whom she had little influence, Clemence preferred an illegitimate contender in the male line to a legitimate male heir of an earlier female line. And she was still able, after her husband and last son had died, to raise an army against Charles.[19]

Clemence had widespread Flemish support in opposing Charles, but the tide turned against her when Charles captured four of her dower towns — Diksmuide, Aire, Saint-Venant, and Bray or Bergues — which effectively cut off her southern lands from those on the coast. Despite her peace with Charles in 1121, her failure to recover those towns marked the end of her rule in Flanders. She became a Flemish baron, attending to her holdings in southern Flanders, and remained one the rest of her life.[20]

The chronicler Herman of Tournai wrote critically of Clemence, not only for her revolt against Charles "the Good" but also for her use of contraception, with its consequences for the succession:

> When she had borne three of count Robert's children in less than three years, Clemence was afraid that if she bore any more, they would fight among themselves for Flanders. She employed a womanly art so that she could no longer become pregnant. This was punished by divine vengeance in that all of her children died a long time before her. Later, in her widowhood, seeing other women's sons as counts and suffering many evils from them, she bewailed too late that she and her offspring should be disinherited.[21]

Nevertheless, Clemence forced Charles and the next two counts of Flanders to respect her rights. Charles himself spoke of becoming count "through divine disposition with the prearrangement with Clemence," as if he had been forced to reach an accommodation with her.[22]

Clemence continued to issue charters concerning her dower lands and towns until her death in 1133.[23] She had served Flanders well. Politically active in the reigns of five counts, she had provided smooth transitions between them and continuity in policy. She supported religious reform, charitable services, and economic growth. She favored canal-building and land-clearance, especially in her dower lands, and was one of the first post-Carolingian countesses to issue coins in her own name. The Flemish remembered her as a dominant personality of her age, later referring to her rule as "the time of countess Clemence."[24]

Margaret of Clermont and Swanehilde

The continuing power of Clemence and the brief rule of count Charles (1119–27) proved disadvantageous for his wife Margaret. James Bruce Ross has described her as a shadowy figure who appears in only a few charters consenting to pious donations, and she is ignored entirely by the chronicler Galbert of Bruges. She appeared in about one-eighth of Charles's charters and issued none of her own. Indeed, she may not even have lived permanently with her husband, for they had no children.[25] It cannot have helped her that her husband was "a stranger and foreigner" to many Flemings, which made it almost impossible for her to overcome that status herself. Although she brought a huge dowry that Charles governed directly — the county of Amiens, her mother Adela of Vermandois's inheritance — Margaret received only a small dower in Flanders.

The murder of count Charles in 1127 created temporary disorder in Flanders, and once again the county passed through a female line, to William Clito, who claimed Flanders through his grandmother Matilda, a daughter of count Baldwin V of Flanders. William was the son of Robert Curthose of Normandy, who in 1106 lost Normandy to his younger brother, Henry I of England. William Clito ruled only a year before dying in battle against rival claimants to the county. His new wife, Jeanne of Montferrat (sister of queen Adelaide of France), does not appear in any of his charters, and it is unlikely that she ever set foot in Flanders.[26]

Flanders regained stability with the succession of Thierry of Alsace (1128–68). For the third time in a row, the county of Flanders had passed through the female line. Count Thierry descended from Gertrude, daughter of Robert I of Flanders, and Thierry III, duke of upper Lotharingia.[27] But Thierry was another "stranger and foreigner," and his first wife, Swanehilde, countess for only five years (1128–33), was overshadowed by Clemence, who remained an active dowager.[28] Moreover, Swanehilde produced only a daughter, Laurette, who was married to a local baron, Ivan of Aalst, who had supported Thierry during the interregnum. Swanehilde seems to have had a retiring and compliant personality, and may well have preferred to remain in the background in her husband's new principality.

Sybil of Anjou

In 1134 the widowed Thierry married Sybil of Anjou, daughter of the first marriage of count Fulk V of Anjou, who became king of Jerusalem through his second wife. Sybil had been married briefly in 1124 to William Clito before he became count of Flanders, but that marriage had been dissolved at the demand of Henry I of England.[29] Sybil's brother Geoffrey Plantagenet, who ruled Anjou, was married to Matilda, daughter and heir of Henry I of England and mother of the future English king Henry II. As the daughter of a reigning king and relative of the English royal house, Sybil brought great prestige to the new Flemish dynasty, and later would increase Thierry's power by associating him more closely with king Henry II: Thierry received a fief in Lincoln and several grants of land and money in England after attending Henry's coronation in 1154, and two years later, while visiting Henry in Rouen, received another fief in Suffolk.[30] Thierry's closer ties with England pleased the Flemish towns whose cloth industry was so dependent on English wool.

Sybil was about twenty-seven when she married Thierry. They had seven children, of whom the eldest, Baldwin, died in his teens. The youngest son, Peter, was placed in the church and later became provost of Saint Donatian in Bruges; the youngest daughter, Matilda, became a nun at Fontevrault, in her mother's homeland.[31] The other children were married to extend Flemish control over neigboring lands, especially Vermandois to the south of Flanders. Thierry's daughter Laurette by his first marriage also played a role in that marriage policy: the widowed Laurette married Raoul IV of Vermandois, and then count Henry of Namur. Sybil's daughter Margaret married Raoul V of Vermandois, and her eldest surviving son Philip married Raoul V's sister Elizabeth, who became heiress of Vermandois and Artois. The marriage of Sybil's second son Matthew to Marie, countess of Boulogne, increased Flemish influence over Boulogne. Her oldest daughter Gertrude married Humbert III of Maurienne, then, after divorce, Hugh III of Oisy; after her second divorce she became a nun at Messines.

Sybil was extraordinarily helpful to Thierry in his relations with the church. Her piety manifested itself in numerous monastic donations and in her foundation with Thierry of the chapel of Saint-Basil at Bruges, later known as the Chapel of the Holy Blood. Full of the fervor of Gregorian reform, she persuaded Thierry to reform several ecclesiastical institutions in Flanders between 1138 and 1151. Under her influence Thierry forced lay advocates or "protectors" who had usurped property and privileges from churches, abbeys, and inhabitants of ecclesiastical estates to return them to their rightful holders. Thierry attempted to impose his preferred candidates in episcopal elections at Thérouanne, Arras, and Cambrai, but was not always successful. When an opposing candidate was installed as bishop of Arras, pope Eugenius III asked Sybil to arrange a reconciliation between Thierry and the new bishop. Sybil also helped Thierry mediate between the church of Arras and Roger of Beaumetz. She was much more likely to be involved in mediation than in ordinary, everyday tasks of administration.[32]

Thierry's forty-year rule afforded Sybil many opportunities to develop close personal relationships with powerful and useful people in the county. He relied on Sybil's advice, displayed her lineage as often as possible, and proudly associated her with himself in about half of his charters. In one charter Thierry claims that it was the request of his friends and especially his dear wife, the noble countess Sybil, that prompted him to give his rights over the church of Saint-Jean at Houdain to the abbey of Saint-Remi at Reims, a monastery where Sybil was more likely than Thierry to have had connections. In 1150–51 Thierry and his son Philip acted on Sybil's request in settling a dispute with bishop Milo of Thérouanne. At pope Adrian IV's request, Thierry, Sybil, and Philip together induced William of Aarsele to return usurped land to the abbey of Lobbes.[33]

Sybil acted as regent in Flanders while Thierry made two trips to the Holy Land, in 1138–39 and again in 1147–49. His first absence proved uneventful — Thierry had the barons staying at home swear an oath of loyalty to Sybil — but in 1147, Lambert of Waterlos relates, count Baldwin IV of Hainaut tried to take advantage of Thierry's absence. Baldwin broke his treaty with Thierry, took up arms against countess Sybil, and pillaged Flanders. Remembering her royal rank, says Lambert, Sybil attacked Baldwin "with a virile heart," burned villages and towns, and pillaged the countryside. Baldwin fled and, according to Lambert, "acquired no honor in this campaign."[34] It was Sibyl who acquired all honor, as she was pregnant and about to give birth at the time of the invasion from Hainaut; she managed nonetheless to assemble an army and repel the invaders. She secured a truce by appealing to the pope and the archbishop of Reims.[35] Her son Philip, in confirming one of his mother's charters in 1168, referred to the time "when my mother Sybil, countess of Flanders, strongly governed the principality of Flanders."[36] Sybil emerges from the documents as extremely vigorous and capable, but as less imperious than Clemence.

Historians have speculated as to why Thierry made such lengthy and potentially hazardous journeys overseas while his children were still young. Some suggest that he sought to help the Christian cause and gain prestige for himself; others suggest that he hoped to acquire property for some of his children or that, being somewhat an adventurer, he had designs upon the kingdom of Jerusalem. Whatever his motives, his absences show considerable trust in Sybil and his son Philip, who was installed as count in 1157 while still in his mid-teens, perhaps in anticipation of Thierry's third trip to the Holy Land in the company of Sybil. She must have had a longstanding interest in the Holy Land, where her father had been king of Jerusalem, and her sister currently was abbess of Saint-Lazarus at Bethany. Earlier Sybil and Thierry had provided the Templars a generous grant of all relief payments from their vassals in Flanders. While in Jerusalem, Sybil decided to enter her sister's abbey. Thierry returned home alone, embittered by the selfishness and greed of the princes in Palestine and lonely for his wife. He made one last trip to the Holy Land in 1164, perhaps to see Sybil, who died in 1165. He returned to Flanders the next year and died two years later.[37]

Elizabeth of Vermandois

Count Philip (1168–91) had married the twelve-year-old Elizabeth, heiress of Vermandois, when he himself was only thirteen. Philip was known as pious, intelligent, determined, brave, and ambitious, but also cool and calculating. Raoul van Caenegem suggests that he was the model for Reynard the Fox, the clever and cunning character of medieval fiction.[38] As to Elizabeth, little has been recorded about her character, although she seems to have been a woman of courage.

Despite her very young age at marriage, Elizabeth soon worked out a successful political partnership with Philip, and she appeared in many of his charters. In 1159 Philip assigned her his castles of Saint-Omer, Courtrai, Harelbeke, and Orchies as dower, a relatively small one because countess Sybil was still alive with her large dower. Elizabeth and Philip seem to have been close during the early years of their marriage: in 1166, when they together established a commune at Chauny with the customs of Saint-Quentin, Philip referred to "my beloved wife." In confirming her brother Raoul's grant, Philip called Elizabeth an "associate of our dignity and legitimate marriage bed," and he confirmed another donation "with my dearest wife, our countess Isabel." They made a large number of donations of property and privileges to ecclesiastical and charitable insitutions and confirmed the donations made by others. Elizabeth shared Philip's virtues of piety and generosity.

Their marriage seems to have become less happy as it became apparent that they would be childless. Two English chroniclers accuse Elizabeth of committing adultery. The *Gesta Henrici* reports, and the chronicler Ralph of Diceto confirms the basic story, that Philip discovered Elizabeth in adultery at Saint-Omer with a young knight named Gautier of Fontaine. Enraged, Philip killed Gautier, first by mortally wounding him with clubs and swords and then by suspending him, head down, over a privy.[39] For Philip this kind of cruelty might not have been unusual; he was known as a proud man, prone to anger, and his wife's betrayal would have cut him to the quick, whether or not he was faithful to her. Elizabeth might have desired to seek love outside marriage because of her marital difficulties, especially in the absence of children, and felt empowered by her status as great-granddaughter of a king of France and by her vast inheritance, but it would have been terrible to live with Philip's anger afterward. Philip might slaughter his wife's lover in a rage, but not kill her, because he would lose Vermandois and Valois at her death.

We may never know whether the English chroniclers were reporting the truth in their accounts of Elizabeth's adultery or simply spreading scandalous rumors. It is significant that no Low Country source repeats the story, not even Gislebert of Mons, who was well-informed and reliable. Philip's relationship with Elizabeth may have deteriorated because of childlessness rather than adultery. Gislebert reports that when Elizabeth died Philip wept not for his countess but for all the western lands (especially Vermandois and Valois) that he would lose because they lacked children.[40] Perhaps Gislebert's testimony should be accepted, because elsewhere in his chronicle he is generally favorable both to Philip and to Elizabeth, despite Philip's rivalry with Gislebert's hero, Baldwin V of Hainaut. Even though this arranged marriage did not blossom into love, it did become a successful working partnership.

Elizabeth appears in Philip's charters much more frequently than we might expect, given what was probably a precarious personal relationship, although those difficulties may not have been fully apparent in the early years of their marriage when they still hoped for children. It is clear from the sources that Philip was a difficult man, and Elizabeth may have wearied of dealing with him. When she was dying, however, Philip acted "at the request of my beloved wife Elizabeth" in founding a chaplaincy at Notre-Dame of Arras and provided 100 *s.* for the celebration of masses on the anniversary of her death. We are left to speculate whether he was truly reconciled to Elizabeth or felt compassion as her death was approaching, or whether the cleric drawing up the document merely attributed to him appropriate terms of affection for a dying spouse. Gislebert of Mons, who did not like to criticize countesses other than Richilde, merely recorded Elizabeth's death in 1182 and said that she was loved by the people of Flanders and Vermandois.[41]

Matilda of Portugal

King Henry II of England arranged for Philip's remarriage in 1183, to Theresia, a daughter of king Alfonso I of Portugal. In Flanders she was called Matilda and "Queen," an adroit way of pointing out her prestige. "I, Matilda the Queen, by the grace of God lady (*domina*) of Flanders and Vermandois," is how she begins one charter. To Philip she was "Queen Matilda, illustrious countess of Flanders and my dearest consort," and she often appeared in his acts. In 1188 she consented to his grant of the urban liberties of Douai to the inhabitants of Orchies. In 1190 she declared that Philip had donated a chapel to the abbey of Clairvaux, and that she was donating her property in the vicinity, on condition that the abbot would never alienate it. Philip confirmed her donation soon after, adding that he and Matilda wished to be buried at the abbey.[42]

Matilda continued to play an important political role in Flanders after Philip's death on the Third Crusade and the transfer of the county to Philip's sister Margaret, countess of Hainaut. In fact, Matilda, who spent much more time as dowager countess (1191–1218) than as Philip's wife, issued more charters in her widowhood than during her husband's rule. As a royal daughter coming from an Iberian tradition of ruling queens, she had no hesitation in intervening repeatedly in her dower lands and occasionally elsewhere. She forcefully defended her dower lands against infringement by her brother-in-law,[43] and continued to issue charters in Flanders after her second marriage to Odo III of Burgundy. After the death in 1205 of her nephew, Baldwin IX, she served as guardian for his two daughters, Jeanne and Marguerite, and even chose a husband for Jeanne. Matilda's prominent role demonstrates not only her political power but also her extraordinary devotion to Flanders and to her relatives by marriage.[44]

Matilda's seven-year marriage to Philip ended without children, leaving him without a direct heir after twenty-three years of rule. His closest relative was his sister Margaret, whose eldest son Baldwin became heir apparent of Flanders. Philip seems not to have favored his nephew's succession, and made no attempt to become acquainted with or to train Baldwin as future count of Flanders. Gislebert of Mons reports that young Baldwin was on more intimate terms with the German emperors, Frederick Barbarossa and Henry VI, and with the king of France, Philip II, than with his own uncle.[45] In the strictest sense, of course, Flanders passed first to count Philip's sister Margaret, then to her son Baldwin.

Margaret of Flanders

Margaret of Flanders was a model of aristocratic virtue, vigor, beauty, and decorum. She had endured a brief first marriage to Raoul the Younger, the leprous count of Vermandois, then married Baldwin V, count of Hainaut, in 1169 shortly before he became count there. As countess of Hainaut, Margaret ruled in her husband's absences. She fortified and defended his castles against attacks by ambitious and unscrupulous vassals. She endowed religious foundations and participated in pious pilgrimages. And she often visited her homeland in Flanders, where she was loved and accepted as ruler more readily than her husband was later. In 1192 she and Baldwin together did liege homage for Flanders to king Philip II of France.[46]

Between 1191 and her death in 1194, Margaret appeared in thirty-two charters, including fifteen she issued by herself and fourteen she issued with the consent of her husband and son Baldwin. Her husband issued only three charters in his own name and three with her. In fact, it was Margaret's right that prevailed in Flanders. One charter directed to comital officials is imperious: "I [Margaret] order and command that you preserve the freedom from tolls . . . for the brothers and property of the abbey of Loos [given by] my very dear brother, most illustrious count of Flanders." Before her death Margaret made generous donations, confirmed by her husband and eldest son, to numerous abbeys and other charitable institutions. Her three-year rule facilitated the transition of Flanders to her son, Baldwin IX, in 1194.[47]

Margaret had two younger sons. Philip "the Noble," count of Namur, married king Philip II's daughter Marie; and Henry, who followed Baldwin IX on the Fourth Crusade and succeeded him as emperor of Constantinople, married Agnes, daughter of the marquis Boniface of Montferrat. Margaret's three daughters all made distinguished marriages as well: Isabel married king Philip II of France,[48] Yolande married Peter II of Courtenay, who became emperor of Constantinople, and Sybil married Guichard IV of Beaujeu.[49]

Marie of Champagne

In 1186 the future Baldwin IX married Marie of Champagne, daughter of count Henry the Liberal of Champagne and Marie of France, who was acting as regent of Champagne. The marriage has elicited interest because of the intimate details provided by Gislebert of Mons, including both the protracted negotiations leading to the marriage and the difficulty of the couple in adjusting to it:

Baldwin, son of the count of Hainaut, who was thirteen years old [actually, fourteen], married Marie, sister of the count of Champagne, who was twelve years old, at Château-Thierry on the Marne. The youthful Marie devoted herself to divine service in prayers, vigils, fasts, and alms. Her husband Baldwin, a young knight living chastely, spurning all other women, loved her alone with an ardor rarely found in any man, so that he devoted himself solely to her and was content with her alone. The marriage was solemnly celebrated at Valenciennes among many knights and ladies and men of every condition.[50]

Gislebert implies that in their arranged marriage Baldwin exhibited unusual patience and abstinence while waiting for Marie to become ready to perform her marital duties, and that many other young noblemen would have forced themselves on their wives or sought their pleasure elsewhere. Indeed, the initiation into marriage must have been traumatic for many pious young brides removed from the support of their families and thrust into a sexual relationship with a stranger. The noble emphasis on virginity of brides, because proud noblemen did not want a strange man's blood introduced into their lineages, and the rather rude behavior of young males emerging from a homosocial world of professional violence, must often have made the transition from protected and pampered girlhood into marriage a difficult one. The development of a comfortable and even loving relationship would take time. It is not surprising that Marie of Champagne sought refuge in religious ritual, but surely it is remarkable that young Baldwin treated her with consideration and compassion, even at the risk of ridicule from the courtiers of Hainaut. Baldwin's patient wait for Marie was rewarded by an unusually close relationship that produced two daughters.[51]

Marie was twenty when she became countess of Flanders in 1194. Like her predecessor countesses, she issued a number of charters, both independently and with her husband. She took the abbey of Eekhout under her protection and freed it from all public exactions. She confirmed Baldwin's charter of law and custom to Saint-Omer and called the burghers "my dearest friends." With Baldwin in 1198 she established tariffs at Ghent's Brabant Gate but exempted the townspeople from paying them. The next year she was a witness to the crucial Treaty of Dinant, which divided her brother-in-law Henry of Namur's inheritance between his daughter and Marie's husband Baldwin. In 1200 Marie and Baldwin freed the abbeys of Ninove and Bohéries from all tolls in their territories.[52]

In 1202 Baldwin IX became one of the leaders of the Fourth Crusade. Marie, who was pregnant when Baldwin departed, governed Flanders as regent during his absence (she issued nine charters between 1202 and 1204).[53] In 1204, however, she decided to follow Baldwin to the Holy Land. Leaving her infant daughters with their great-aunt countess Matilda at Lille, Marie set out to find Baldwin.[54] But not knowing that he had been elected emperor of Constantinople, she landed at Acre, where she died of plague before seeing him again. Baldwin was captured in battle and died in 1205 in a Bulgarian prison.[55]

Jeanne of Constantinople

The death of Baldwin IX, emperor of Constantinople, left his two small daughters, Jeanne (b. 1199/1200) and Marguerite (b. 1202), as hereditary countesses of Flanders and Hainaut under the guardianship of his brother Philip "the Noble" of Namur, who became regent of Flanders. It was a perilous time for the houses of Alsace and Hainaut. Philip of Namur was too chivalrous and honorable to usurp the rights of his nieces, or too respectful of feudal law, or perhaps too wary of the increasing power of the French king, to do so. King Philip II, who did not want a strong adult male count of Flanders on his northeastern border, persuaded Philip the Noble to hand over the two Flemish heiresses in return for a position of wealth and privilege and marriage to a French princess. Count Philip chose not to resist the king, the primary feudal lord of Flanders, although he later regretted handing over his nieces. The two hereditary countesses would eventually rule in Flanders and Hainaut for most of the thirteenth century, but under greater French influence than before.[56]

Jeanne and Marguerite were brought up in Paris as wards, almost hostages, of the French king. Acting on the advice of their great-aunt, countess Matilda, the king married Jeanne to Ferrand, third son of king Sancho I of Portugal, and in 1212 allowed the couple to rule Flanders.[57] King Philip required Ferrand to pay an enormous relief of 50,000 l., money of Paris. And he delayed the arrival of the newlyweds at Péronne while prince Louis took an army to conquer Saint-Omer and Aire, two Flemish towns that were part of his mother Isabel of Hainaut's dowry, a loss that marred the triumphal entry of Jeanne and Ferrand and so incensed the people of Ghent that they refused to recognize the new count.

Since Ferrand was twenty-four or twenty-five at that time and Jeanne only twelve, it was almost certainly Ferrand who controlled domestic and foreign policy from 1212 up to the battle of Bouvines in 1214. King Philip had intended Ferrand to be a puppet ruler, but Ferrand quickly realized that Flemish prosperity lay in the wool trade with England and in some independence from France. He opened diplomatic relations with England and exiled the leaders of the pro-French party, including John of Nesle and Siger of Ghent. The exiled nobles accompanied king Philip on a punitive expedition to Flanders. Ferrand fled to Walcheren and appealed to king John of England.[58] This led him to fight on the losing side of the battle of Bouvines in 1214 and to suffer a thirteen-year imprisonment in France.

Even before Ferrand's captivity Jeanne acted independently as countess. In 1213 she wrote to the Hospitallers, guaranteeing the ransom of Gerard of Mons, a captive in the Holy Land. The next year she wrote to king John of England, her "dear uncle," to say that she had received the 1,250 *l.* he sent her. She issued charters taking the hospital at Oudenaarde under her personal protection and forbidding the aldermen or townspeople to levy taxes on it, and she freed the abbey of Broekburg from tolls on any of its supplies.[59] After Bouvines, Jeanne ruled alone (1214–27). Her fourteen-year rule was nearly twice as long as the seven years Ferrand spent in Flanders (1212–14 and 1227–33). During that time she faced many difficulties at home and abroad. Having spent her youth as almost a hostage in France, she had no desire to become a French puppet, but she also wished to avoid the fate of her husband and the possible downfall of her dynasty. She pursued the sagacious policy of keeping on the good side of the French king while pursuing trade and friendly relations with England, a policy requiring especially adroit diplomacy in a period of hostile Anglo-French relations. She bought off and procured the resignation of king Philip's agent, John of Nesle, castellan of Bruges, and relied on loyal Flemish advisors such as Arnold of Oudenaarde and Michael of Harnes.[60] Jeanne's barons rushed to take advantage of her youth, inexperience, and weakness to usurp the count's privileges and property in Flanders and Hainaut, but she gradually recovered those rights and goods. To strengthen her position, Jeanne brought key nobles into the government of Flanders, making her rule more palatable to many of her subjects who had misgivings about a female prince. She overcame the threat of the False Baldwin, who pretended to be her father, and had him executed. That so many people accepted an inept imposter indicates, in Hainaut especially, distrust of a young female prince and of strong government. Jeanne, however, was a capable ruler who gradually won people's trust. She became an ally of the French queen, Blanche of Castile, and after Ferrand's death married Blanche's close relative, Thomas of Savoy. Valued for his companionship, he remained more a consort than a ruling prince.[61]

Early in her reign Jeanne forged a close alliance with the towns of Flanders. In 1216 she reached an agreement with the urban patriciate of Ghent about the exaction of *tailles* on behalf of the town government, and in a remarkable show of solidarity agreed in 1226 to banish from Flanders anyone who had been banished from that city. The townspeople rewarded her favors by contributing 1,700 *l.*, money of Paris, toward her purchase of the castellany of Bruges, and by providing sureties for 12,000 *l.* toward Ferrand's ransom. She was especially close to the cities of Courtrai and Ypres. In 1225–26 she shared her fishing rights at Ypres with the townspeople and exempted from taxation any lands the townspeople held outside the city in the castellany of Ypres. She often lived at Courtrai and favored the city in 1217 with the extraordinary privilege that any Flemings and inhabitants of countess Matilda's dower lands could come to live at Courtrai without paying taxes. This privilege protected the growing cloth industry at Courtrai and provided more competition within the county to the powerful cities of Ghent and Bruges. In 1225 Jeanne freed all the serfs at Halle and allowed the burghers of Biervliet to install aldermen each year.[62]

Jeanne's efforts to free Ferrand from imprisonment in the Louvre reveal her singular determination in liberating her husband. Seeing a chance in 1220 to redeem him, she set about securing loans from Italian financiers, including some Jews, for sums totaling more than 34,000 *l.* That large sum was, she said, for "the liberation of my dearest husband Ferrand." Her mother's Champenois relatives served as sureties for the loans. She also sought help from pope Honorius III, who had promised her protection in 1220. Honorius sent king Philip a letter promising to place all of Flanders under interdict if count Ferrand, after being freed, proved disloyal to the king; the pope asked Philip to free Ferrand in return for an appropriate ransom. The king died that very year, still vowing never to free his personal enemy, the count of Flanders. The new king, Louis VIII, was similarly intransigent, even after Honorius renewed his request, again promising to excommunicate a disloyal Ferrand who refused to submit to the judgment of peers in Paris. At the pope's request, the archbishop of Reims and bishop of Senlis wrote to the king in similar terms, but they too failed to move him. Because Jeanne was at that time childless, Louis may have hoped that by keeping Ferrand in prison he would prevent Jeanne from having legitimate children to inherit Flanders and Hainaut.[63]

Jeanne, meanwhile, had need of money for other purposes. In 1224 she bought the castellany of Bruges from John of Nesle. The next year brought the crisis of the false Baldwin; she went to Paris to ask for Louis VIII's support and promised to pay him 20,000 *l.* Her treasury depleted and her requests denied, Jeanne made for the time being no further ostensible efforts to free her husband. She governed in her own name without mentioning Ferrand. Duke Peter of Brittany asked the pope to approve a divorce between Jeanne and Ferrand, so that Jeanne could marry him, and the medieval chronicler of Tours suggests that Jeanne had forgotten Ferrand. It is difficult to know Jeanne's inner feelings, whether she was looking for new support after her husband had languished in prison for more than twelve years with little chance of release, or whether she used this marriage proposal as a ploy to force the king's hand. If it was an attempt to free Ferrand, it was a piece of brilliant strategy. Louis VIII, who lacked his father's personal hatred of Ferrand, could only look with horror at the prospect of Flanders united with Brittany. He quickly made arrangements for Ferrand's release, on condition that Jeanne would take him again as her husband. Ferrand was freed from prison on January 6, 1227. He ruled Flanders with Jeanne until his death in 1233.[64]

In the later part of Jeanne's reign, characterized by relative peace, Jeanne worked to strengthen her administration and her relationships with her subjects. She made donations to convents and to charitable institutions. She showered grants of liberties on the Flemish towns, granting many of them charters of law and custom. She contributed to the process of self-government in a number of cities by confirming the establishment of benches of aldermen. She was also notable for her contributions to women's religious orders and movements, especially to the Cistercians, the Dominicans, and the Beguines, as well as to hospices, leper houses, and hospitals. She generously supported and founded convents as well. When she died in 1244 she was buried, as she had requested, beside her first husband and daughter in her own foundation, the Cistercian convent of Marquette.[65]

The pattern of Jeanne's support for religious institutions, which her sister Marguerite followed after her death, is different from those of the male rulers of Flanders. The counts also were pious, but they tended to support male monasteries and the military orders, particularly the Templars. Jeanne and Marguerite supported women's convents of the Cistercian and Dominican orders, hospitals or hospices for the sick and dying, and Beguines who tried to live a religious life in the Flemish towns. The "princely beguinage" Jeanne built in Bruges still stands today. It is "princely" not only in its foundation but also in its grandeur. Large, attractive houses surround a green park with towering trees. Adjacent to the beguinage is the parish church, where the Beguines worshiped several times each day. Thus Jeanne supported women of genuine piety whose independence from the male-dominated church hierarchy and the traditional family caused ambivalence, suspicion, and even hostility from many male lay and ecclesiastical authorities.

It is easier to document Jeanne's religious donations and foundations than to investigate her interior spiritual life. Countesses and the wives of barons worshiped privately in the twelfth and thirteenth centuries, using a Psalter to which the Hours of the Virgin were added. The Hours of the Virgin, which dominate the Books of Hours used by lay people from the middle of the thirteenth century, focused meditation on events in the infancy and the passion of Christ, which were arranged to correspond to the seven or eight monastic hours, the services performed by monks and nuns each day.[66] Lay women meditated on the events in the life of Christ and on the sacred images contained in their books. The Flemish countesses had a tradition of Latin literacy because charters and administrative documents were usually issued in Latin, and so they could read these Latin prayer books. Also, the cult of the Virgin was growing in the French-speaking culture in which Jeanne participated. She undoubtedly heard the songs of the trouvères who were gradually changing focus from romantic love to religious devotion, especially prayers to the Virgin. Music undoubtedly played an important role in Jeanne's public and private prayers. She probably sang vernacular songs of praise, such as "Prions en chantant" ("We pray by singing to the mother of Christ"), which praises the Virgin and implores her aid, so that sinners might attain salvation.[67]

For ruling successfully and capably under difficult circumstances, Jeanne deserves much more credit than historians have traditionally given her.[68] Unlike other countesses of Flanders, who began ruling in their twenties, thirties, or forties by marriage, Jeanne became hereditary countess at twelve. Her guardian, king Philip, had virtually held her as a hostage and then tried to thwart her power as soon as she was installed as countess, but Jeanne worked patiently to neutralize the French threat to her power without alienating the French king, a task requiring skillful diplomacy. She overcame the challenge of the False Baldwin, whose supporters might have crushed her power. She was patron and friend to the Flemish towns and presided over their rapid and prosperous development. By her many donations to convents, beguinages, and hospitals, she helped to provide important services for the people of Flanders. After the turbulent period following the battle of Bouvines, Jeanne provided stable government and promoted economic growth in Flanders.

Marguerite of Constantinople

Because Jeanne's only child, a daughter Marie, had predeceased her, Marguerite succeeded her sister in 1244. She ruled in Flanders for thirty-four years, until 1278 when she abdicated in favor of her son Guy, but continued to rule in Hainaut until her death in 1280. Three aspects of her rule stand out: the quarrels between the Avesnes and Dampierres, the sons of her first and second marriages; the successful policy of expansion she and her son Guy pursued in the middle years of her rule; and the trade war with England, from 1270 to 1275.

Marguerite's contending sons contributed a tension that waxed and waned throughout her rule.[69] She has been criticized for inconstancy in leaving her first husband, Bouchard of Avesnes, who was about forty in 1223 when he enticed her as a ten-year-old to leave her sister's court and marry him. Marguerite probably realized after she matured that she had been taken advantage of. Her marriage also estranged her from her sister, who instigated the excommunication levied against Marguerite and her husband. Jeanne was justifiably enraged by the elopement because Bouchard, as bailiff of Hainaut, owed her primary loyalty. After Marguerite left her husband and returned to the Flemish court, Jeanne had the marriage invalidated and married her to a French noble, Guillaume of Dampierre. Marguerite could not have forseen that the early death of Jeanne's only child would leave her to inherit Flanders and Hainaut, and that her two marriages would allow Louis IX of France to divide the two counties. In 1246 Louis awarded Flanders to Guillaume of Dampierre (and after his death, to his brother, Guy of Dampierre) and Hainaut to John of Avesnes after their mother's death. The Avesnes brothers held on to Hainaut, while the Dampierres kept Flanders and acquired some other territories in the Low Countries.[70] Louis IX was happy to break up the large coalition of principalities looming on his northeastern border.[71]

Having repudiated her first husband, Marguerite remained unswervingly loyal to her second husband and the sons of her second marriage. Despite her elopement, she had been brought up as a dutiful younger sister, and in her own documents she was more inclined than Jeanne to defer to others. In 1249 she declared that the abbot of Saint Bavo at Ghent had allowed her, just this once, to provide a chaplain for the Beguines at Aardenburg, and later allowed her to found a second chaplaincy at Saint Elizabeth's beguinage at Ghent. In 1275 she notified count Henry of Luxembourg that Saint Bavo's abbey in Ghent had bought a house at Deinze in the fief that Henry held of her, "if you will allow it" (*se vous le voleis souffrir*). But she could also be more forceful: in 1266 she made Hugh of Roubaix promise not to infringe on the rights of the church at Waterlos and to guarantee his promise by giving up his fief to her as feudal lord until he compensated the church for his damages.[72]

The trade war with England from 1270 to 1275 resulted from Marguerite's demand that the English king pay her the traditional money fief held since 1100 by Flemish counts, and that the king make good the payments that had fallen into arrears. She apparently felt that king Henry III owed her a great deal for her support during the revolt led by Simon de Montfort. In 1264 she had allowed queen Eleanor of England to settle at Damme in Flanders and to recruit mercenary soldiers from her counties and elsewhere in the Low Countries, from France, and from Savoy.[73] Marguerite undoubtedly hoped that her good will would be rewarded by resumption of money fief payments from England, but she did not send soldiers at her own expense to fight for her lord, as a true vassal would do, and thus Henry III did not see sufficient reason to restore the fief. She retaliated by seizing possessions of English merchants in Flanders. Henry and his son Edward I in turn seized possessions of Flemish merchants in England, but since the countess had forewarned her merchants, their goods were worth much less than those of the English merchants. Edward I then stopped exports of English wool to Flanders, hoping that the townspeople in Flanders, who depended heavily on the textile trade, would put pressure on the countess to desist from her demands. The pressure forced Marguerite and her son Guy of Dampierre to agree to humiliating peace terms in 1274: restitution of 4755 *l.* to English merchants and payments from the Flemish towns. As a result of the war, Flemish carriers no longer dominated the transport of goods between the continent and England. The conflict also displayed the economic vulnerability of the Flemish economy and set a precedent for the English kings to use control of wool exports as a weapon in their foreign policy. This vulnerability to English reprisals would help cause the decline of the Flemish cloth towns in the late Middle Ages.[74] In 1278, when she was nearly seventy-five years old, Marguerite abdicated as countess of Flanders in favor of Guy of Dampierre. Although her actions in the trade war and in her quarrel with her Avesnes descendants were not always wise, her alliance with the Flemish towns helped to increase their security and prosperity and to make Flanders a better, more peaceful place to live.

Conclusions

The twelve countesses in Flanders faced some common difficulties. Most Low Country clerics and barons were prejudiced against rule by women, whom they saw as weak by definition, and many modern historians have uncritically echoed these prejudices.[75] The ambiguous attitudes of male nobles toward female princes weakened the military capacity of the Flemish countesses. Richilde, for example, was deserted by almost everyone and Clemence's revolt failed. A degree of military insecurity among the countesses forced them, especially Jeanne and Marguerite, into alliance with the Flemish towns, which they showered with privileges that greatly enhanced urban growth and prosperity.[76] But prejudices against female rulers among townsmen and peasants made it even more necessary for the countesses than for the counts to be associated with powerful men in order to make their rule more palatable to their subjects. Countesses also developed close relationships with the region's bishops and abbots.

While the countesses faced common difficulties, their personalities and circumstances varied widely. Charles the Good's wife Margaret and Thierry's first wife Swanehilde had relatively retiring personalities so that we know little about them, while Richilde, Clemence, Sybil, and Matilda were much more forceful. Clemence and Matilda sound particularly imperious in their documents, but Sybil was more successful in commanding an army. Jeanne was more assertive and more prudent than her sister Marguerite. A hereditary countess, Jeanne succeeded in situations where many male princes would have failed. Most of the countesses, in fact, acted as successful regents for their husbands or minor sons: Richilde, Clemence, Sybil, Matilda, and Marie of Champagne all were successful in that role. Inspired by love as well as ambition, they accomplished difficult things in the male-dominated world of politics and war.

Despite their disadvantages as female rulers, the countesses enjoyed certain advantages that enhanced their power. Princely or especially royal status, such as that of Sybil and Matilda, brought outside prestige to the comital dynasty. Longevity of married life or of independent rule gave them time to develop networks of support within their principality: Sybil was married for twenty-four years, and Richilde and Clemence were both married for nineteen, although Richilde was countess for only three of them. Serving as regent for a crusading husband or a minor son created challenges while it temporarily turned a count's wife into an independent ruler: Richilde, Clemence, Sybil, Matilda, and Marie all excelled in this role. Extensive dower lands provided assets during marriage and income and subjects during widowhood: Clemence, Sybil, and Matilda had extremely large dowers that allowed them to be politically prominent after the deaths of their husbands.

Several countesses displayed extraordinary diplomatic ability, which also contributed to their success as rulers. They fostered urban development and chose favorites among the thriving Flemish towns, to which they granted special privileges. Most countesses also developed a close relationship with the church and its leaders, sponsoring especially women's convents and beguinages as well as hospices and hospitals, in contrast to the counts, who favored male monasteries and the military orders.[77] Their patronage to charitable institutions provided important social services for townspeople and villagers. Finally, their documents show the countesses as more interested in domestic policy, endowment of religious and charitable institutions, and the welfare of their subjects than in external expansion or military aggression. Unlike their husbands, few of the countesses excelled in warfare, but when their territory and subjects were threatened they were capable of decisive and effective action in defense of their own rights, lands, and people.

5

Women, Poets, and Politics in Occitania

Fredric L. Cheyette

LET US IMAGINE OURSELVES in the great hall of a noble family somewhere in southern France around the year 1300. Rich cloths cover the trestle tables where bowls overflow with fresh fruit; from the kitchen across the courtyard come servants with roasted meats; other servants kneel by their master and mistress at the head table to fill their cups with wine from silver ewers. At another table the lord's young squires gather, along with knights and ladies who have come for the evening from their own houses in town. This is a special occasion. A minstrel troupe has come to entertain. The lord of this house has a special fondness for the troubadour songs of an earlier age, and these minstrels are known for performing them well.

Just as modem jazz musicians or pop singers may introduce a piece by telling who composed it and when, so the head of the minstrel band begins by telling a little story:

Peire Rogier was from Auvergne and was a canon of Clermont. He was a noble man, handsome and charming, well versed in letters; he had a natural wit, and he was good at composing and singing verses. He left his canonry and became a minstrel and went from court to court. Everywhere his songs were praised. One day he came to Narbonne, to the court of lady Ermengard, who was known in those days as a woman of great worth and merit. She welcomed him warmly and showed him great favor. He fell in love with her and composed songs about her; and she welcomed them. He called her "Tort-n'avez" ("You are wrong"). For a long time he remained at her court. And the people of the region believed that he received the pleasures of love from her, for which they blamed her. And so, for fear of what people were saying, she told him to leave. Sad and thoughtful, troubled and downcast, he departed and went to the court of Raymond, lord of Orange. . . . There he stayed a long time. Afterwards he was in Spain with the good king Alfonso of Castile and the good king Alfonso of Aragon, and then with the good count Raymond of Tou-

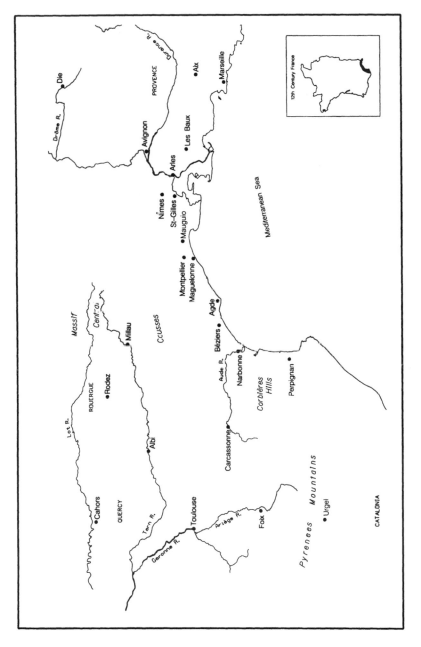

Map 5. Occitania.

louse. He had great honor in the world as long as he stayed in it. At last he entered the order of Grandmont, and there he died.[1]

The audience immediately knows that he will begin this evening with songs that Peire Rogier dedicated to his lady of Narbonne. Perhaps "Tant ai mon cor en joy assis":

Tant ai mon cor en joy assis,	My heart is so fixed on joy
per que no puesc mudar no·n chan,	that I cannot help but sing,
que joys m'a noirit pauc e gran;	for as a child and an adult, joy has
e ses luy non seria res,	nourished me.
qu'assatz vey que tot l'als qu'om fay	Without it, I'd be nothing.
abaiss' e sordey' e dechai,	I see that everything else that people do
mas so qu'amors e joys soste.	degrades, dishonors, and defames
. . .	if love and joy do not sustain it.
	. . .
Mon Tort-n'avetz en Narbones	To my Tort-n'avetz in Narbonne
man salutz, si tot luenh s'estai,	I send greetings, though she is far away,
e sapcha qu'em-breu la veyray,	and may she know that I'll soon see her
si trop grans afars no·m rete.	if great matters don't keep me away.
Lo senher, que fetz tot quant es,	May the Lord who made all that is
guart lo cors de lieys cumsi·s fay,	keep her body as he does,
qu'ilh mante pretz e joy veray,	that she maintain worth and true joy
quan tot' autra gens s'en recre.	when all others abandon it.[2]

Or perhaps "Ges non puesc en bon vers fallir":

Ges non puesc en bon vers fallir	I will never fail to make a good verse
nulh'hora qu'ieu de midons chan;	when I sing of my lady;
cosi poiri'ieu ren mal dir?	for how can I say ill of her?
Qu'om non es ta mal essenhatz,	Not even a churl is so badly taught
si parl'ab lieys un mot o dos,	that, if he speak with her a word or two,
que totz vilas non torn cortes;	he will not become courtly;
per que sapchatz be que vers es,	so understand this truth:
que·l ben qu'ieu dic tot ai de liey.	whatever I say well I owe to her.
. . .	. . .
Mon Tort-n'avetz mant, s'a lieys platz,	I send to my Tort-n'avetz, if it please her,
qu'aprenda lo vers, s'el es bos;	that she learn my song, if it be good;
e puois vol que sia trames	and then I wish that it be sent
mon dreit-n'avetz lai en Saves:	to my "dreit-n'avetz" there in the Savès:
Dieus sal e guart lo cors de liey.	may God protect and guard her body.[3]

We all recognize the plot of the minstrel's tale and how, like the dialogue of a modern musical comedy, it leads directly to the songs: boy meets girl, boy loves girl, boy loses girl; in the closing scene he walks down the road, rejected, heartbroken, and alone, toward a distant horizon. In this version of the tale, however (as in so many film "biographies" from the 1930s and '40s), the boy and girl are not entirely fictional. One is a great poet and composer of songs and the other one of the great aristocrats of her age. What, then, do the tale and the songs represent? What, if anything, do they and the many other songs and tales like them tell us about twelfth-century aristocratic women and about the world — especially the world of the courts — in which they lived? Behind all these questions looms the modern concept of medieval "courtly love" and the relation of literature to life.

Twelfth-century lyric poets and singers spread before us a brilliant spectacle of erotic relations between a lyric "I" and his lady (or ladies), most often a woman or women of high station. The tone of their poetry covers the gamut from bawdy to tearful, high serious to satiric. Some, like the first known troubadour count William IX of Aquitaine, boast of their sexual exploits in ways that smell of the warrior's campfire (or, as we would say, of the locker-room); others, like Marcabru, castigate or mock the lasciviousness of the knightly world; yet others present love as a school of virtue. Some speak of "rules" of love and debate questions such as whether lovers should treat each other as equals or whether the man should always be subservient to his lady. Others put an ironic twist on the debates and "rules" and appear to call into question the very assumptions on which they are built. In this game of love, serious and comic, issues of power — especially the power of women — are rarely far beneath the surface.

The voice in these songs always sings in the first person singular, and a long tradition going back to thirteenth-century Italy, if not before, makes that voice the voice of the poet/composer/performer himself (or herself, since there were also women poets and performers). The apparent sincerity of some poets, such as Bernart de Ventadorn, strongly reinforces our desire to follow that tradition, to make the "I" of the poem the real person of flesh and blood who composed it, and its sentiments a literal account of that person's feelings. Identifying the voice in the poem with the poet's own voice appeals to our own post-Romantic sensibilities as well; for even if we don't hear the personal voice of Irving Berlin in every performance of "White Christmas" or of Cole Porter in "Begin the Beguine," even if we are not likely to confuse the real personalities of our favorite movie stars with the characters they play on the screen, serious lyric poetry is different: the words claim to speak from the heart, and that is the way we have learned to hear them.[4]

If it is the real poet who speaks, if it is the real authorial voice we hear, it is then but a small step to say that the world evoked by that voice, a world of amorous dalliance and jealous husbands, of scandalmongers and deceivers, of knights who desire to learn virtue and ladies who are ready to teach them, was the real world in which they lived. Such was already the way in the later thirteenth century that the writers of the so-called biographies of the troubadours (such as that of Peire Rogier) and "explanations" of their songs — what are known to students of this Occitan literature as *vidas* and *razos* — heard the songs or wanted them to be heard. Such is the way they have frequently been read ever since.

It is, of course, impossible to know how much of the story of Peire and Ermengard is true and how much is fiction: there is no other evidence on which to rely, nothing more than whatever conviction the story itself will bear. The "lives" of the troubadours give each of them a kind of identity badge, a specific place of origin and social rank; they tell us that one is from the Auvergne, another from Gascony, a third from the Gevaudan; one is a noble baron, another a poor knight, a monk, a minstrel, or a son of a baker. And often some of the details in these "lives" can be confirmed by other documents, especially when the poets were landed noblemen or clerics whose activities were recorded by chroniclers and whose pious donations were preserved in church archives. It would be easy to convince ourselves that other, unconfirmed details also have some reason to be there, that they were not invented. Although the biographies were written down a century or more after the deaths of their subjects, they could very well represent an oral tradition that went back to the days of the poets themselves, information they gave out themselves or what their contemporaries knew about them. Did Peire in fact spend time at the court of Ermengard of Narbonne? It would be surprising if he did not, for she was one of the great patrons of her age.

The story of the love affair, however, is the common matter of many of the troubadour biographies. Its substance appears to have been drawn from the songs themselves (with the aid of much imagination), giving real names to the mysterious ladies and coded names (known generically as *senhals*) that they use in their songs; thus "Tort-n'avetz," "You-are-wrong," became Ermengard of Narbonne. (If the identification was accurate, was this name a private joke? a thrust of ill humor? a reference to a debate he once had with the viscountess? As usual, there is no way to know.) To accept these romances as true history requires us to make a special leap of faith, to imagine the songs to be entries in private diaries or fragments of confessional literature. The very conventionality of the tales and the public nature of the songs makes that a doubtful proposition. The lyrics, after all, are not texts found under beds or in secret drawers after the poets die; they are songs their authors sang to make a living as they traveled from court to court or in some cases, such as those of count William IX or the Countess of Die, songs that great lords and ladies sang to entertain their companions after dinner or to lighten the arduous marches of their military campaigns.[5] The "I" of the poems claims to be discreet about his love affair, but that discretion is publicly broadcast; he claims to hide his true feelings from his lady, but if this were true, she would be the only one left in the dark. The poet claims sincerity to give literary force to his lyrics, but the claim does not guarantee the lyrics' historical veracity.

For the audience who first heard the "life" of Peire Rogier, his songs and those of his fellow troubadours were already part of an old, we might even say a classical, tradition; to them, the events of his life were as far away as the events of the nineteenth century are to us, and hearing about them would have been something like our listening to an aging blues singer tell stories he has heard from his teacher about his teacher's teacher. Both the poets and the minstrels who a century later sang their songs were professional entertainers; they told stories their audiences wanted to hear and in response to a smile or a laugh were always ready to elaborate.

Nevertheless, that imaginary love affair between Peire and Ermengard, and the many others like it, cannot be ignored. The poetry that gave rise to such stories is there, and it is overwhelmingly preoccupied with matters of the heart. Occasionally it exudes a strong whiff of imagined adultery, as when the woman poet we know only as the Countess of Die sings to her "good friend,"

cora·us tenrai en mon poder,	when will I have you in my power,
e que iagues ab vos un ser,	lie with you one night,
e qu·us des un bais amoros?	and give you a loving kiss?
Sapchatz, gran talan n'auria	Be sure, I'd have a great desire
qu·us tengues en luoc del marit.	to hold you in place of my husband.[6]

Even when the lyrics are not so overt, they find a place for the *lauzengier*, the liar and scandalmonger, among their characters.

More often their theme is of love abused or deceived, leaving clothed in ambiguity the exact relation of the poetic "I" to his or her beloved: it is distant, both socially and physically, a space that translates the distance of emotional longing, as when Jaufre Rudel sings in one of his most famous songs:

Rembra·m d'un' amor de loing;   I remember a love from afar;
vauc de talan enbroncs e clis,   I go sad and bent with desire
si que chans ni flors d'albespis   so that neither song nor hawthorn
no·m platz plus que l'inverns gelatz.   flower
                                        pleases me more than icy winter.[7]

It is easy enough to see how such songs could give rise to stories like that of Peire and Ermengard.

The questions presented by Peire Rogier's *vida* are thus presented by many of the poems. And so we must ask again: What do their love stories represent? What should we read into them? Within a real world of the twelfth century they created an imagined world. Was that imagined world an exact replica of the real one? An exaggeration? A fantasy of the taboo and forbidden? A form of wish fulfillment? These are but a small number of the possibilities that critics and historians have suggested. They are all ways of asking how we should understand these troubadour songs and the amorous lives they imagined, how we should understand them as an historical phenomenon, as the creation of men and women who lived in a particular place at a particular time. These are the issues we will explore in this chapter.

*   *   *

Within a generation after their songs began to circulate, the poets of Occitania were imitated by French-speaking poets and soon afterward by poets of German-speaking lands; eventually they became the inspiration for Dante and Petrarch. Their themes became the themes of the European lyric. The forms they invented can still inspire the poetic imagination eight hundred years later. From Hollywood to country-western singers, their descendants are still with us. But those themes and forms were first created by men and women who lived in the region that English speakers now call southern France and the French call "Languedoc." It was a region where people spoke a Romance language closely related to Catalan, a language usually called Old Provençal or Old Occitan, the language of the troubadours; and throughout the twelfth century—the great age of the troubadours—this region had only the most tenuous connections to the Capetian kings of Paris. The name Languedoc is a later creation of the northern French. They took their own name for the language — the *langue d'oc*, the language that uses "oc" instead of "oïl" (> "oui"), like northern French, or "si," like Italian, to say "yes" — and applied it to the land where it was spoken. In the eleventh and twelfth centuries this land had no name of its own; following the usage of other recent historians, I will call it Occitania.

In the twelfth century, this region was a battleground over which a handful of great lordly families attempted to assert their dominance. The counts of Barcelona gained the title of count of Carcassonne by purchase in 1067–68; they became counts of Provence by marriage in 1112 and kings of Aragon, again by marriage, in 1150; from the early twelfth century until the Albigensian Crusades in the early thirteenth, they maintained a tight alliance with the most important lordly families of the Occitan coastal plain: the viscounts of Narbonne, the lords of Montpellier, and the family we know as the Trencavels, viscounts of Albi, Béziers, Agde, and Nîmes and effective rulers of Carcassonne and the mountainous region to its south.

The counts of Toulouse, who were popularly known as the counts of Saint-Gilles, after their castle in the important port and pilgrimage center at the mouth of the Rhone river, also claimed rights to Provence through their marriage into its comital house in the early eleventh century; from the days of the great crusader Raymond IV they asserted their dominance in the region by taking the title "Count of Toulouse, Duke of Narbonne, Marquis of Provence." The counts of Poitiers, who also claimed the title of duke of Aquitaine, likewise laid claim to the county of Toulouse through the marriage of count William VII of Poitiers with Philippa, whom they asserted inherited the county in 1094 on the death of her father count William IV of Toulouse. This claim passed on to Eleanor of Aquitaine when her father, William VIII, died in 1137, and through her was reasserted by her two royal husbands, Louis VII of France and Henry II of England.

Members of all these families were patrons of the troubadours. Indeed the first known troubadour was Philippa's husband, count William VII of Poitiers (also known as duke William IX of Aquitaine), who, though Occitan was probably not his native tongue, chose that language for his songs. Two sons of king Henry II of England — the young Henry and his brother Richard the Lionheart — as well as Raymond V and Raymond VI of Toulouse, Ermengard of Narbonne, Eleanor of Aquitaine, various Trencavels and various Williams of Montpellier and their brothers, as well as the kings of Aragon and Castile and lesser lords of Occitania, Provence, and northern Italy, all appear under their real names or pseudonyms in the dedications of the songs or in the *vidas* of the troubadours. Theirs is the historical world that welcomed the imagined world of the troubadour lyric. It is in their courts that we must place the poets and their poetry and the men and women they entertained. These were the people for whom the poets created their game of love.

Before we can reconstruct how their original audience may have heard and understood these love lyrics, we must ask who that audience was and what the songs may have touched in their culture and their social and political experience. Where were the responsive chords? What were their overtones? Were troubadour songs more than entertainment, more than play? Were there connections between the lyrics' themes and the place of their audience in the social order that would help explain why this poetry in particular found such success?

These questions are not new; they have been debated for several generations. The answers have tended to gather around two related positions. One has seen the central paradox of courtly love in its renunciation of sexual fulfillment. The German scholar Erich Köhler has called this the "sublimated projection of the petty nobility's lack of property." The twelfth-century nobility, this school has argued, was a class that encompassed people of great power and wealth and people of little or none, as economic and political pressures increasingly led to a concentration of wealth in ever fewer hands. The strengthening of feudal power, the argument goes, required this concentration to defend it against the encroachment of kings on the one hand and the burgeoning mercantile population of cities on the other. In the imaginary world of amorous courtly poetry, in contrast, neither rank nor possessions mattered; within its borders the noble class reached a harmonious and unified class consciousness.[8]

For another group of historians and critics, courtly love arose in what the French historian Georges Duby called the "fault line" between youths (*juvenes*) and elders (*seniores*) in the aristocratic world, as the matrimonial practices of a new patriline-focused nobility restricted the inheritance rights of younger sons and sent bands of them off to search for heiresses to wed and lands to win. In the households of their patrons, the game of love expressed a mock competition among these young bachelors for the favors of the lady; it drew its excitement from the way it flouted the strict prohibition of adultery. By letting herself be wooed, the lady helped her husband gain a stronger hold over these young warriors. She domesticated them so he could use them in his battles.[9]

There is much in these views to captivate us. They draw strength from two of the ideological giants of the nineteenth and twentieth centuries,

Marx and Freud, whose dominating position in our intellectual world is only now beginning to fade. The one assures us that the paradoxical appeal of idealized sexual frustration to an audience of tough young warrior males was that it served as an ideological salve to their marginal economic position. The other explains away the paradoxical popularity of a literature that is said to have idealized adulterous love in a society that ranked adultery as a crime equal to murder, rape, and arson. Both see the lyric world as a fantasy, a game that reconciles its players to the delayed or impossible achievement of their social, economic, and sexual desires. With a brilliant flourish they whisk away the veil of lyric illusion to reveal the real social truth beneath.

Yet questions remain. Literary questions first of all. Was the love of which the poets sang always, or even usually, adulterous love? We have seen one example that seems to leave little doubt; but is every reference to a *dompna*, a "lady," a reference to a married woman or, more specifically, to the lady of the house? The issue will probably always be debated.[10]

Was the amorous world of poetry one of noble equality? When Casteloza sings:

anz pens qan mi sove
del ric pretz qe·us mante
e sai ben qe·us cove
dompna d'aussor paratge.

rather, when I remember
the great merit that sustains you,
I know you deserve
a lady of higher lineage than mine.[11]

or Peire Vidal:

Bona domna, vostr'ome natural
podetz, si·us platz, leugieramente aucir,
mas a la gen vo·n faretz escarnir
E pois auretz en peccat criminal.
Vostr'om sui be, que ges no·m tenc per
    meu . . .

Good lady, your bound man
you can easily kill, if you wish;
but everyone will blame you
and then you will be in mortal sin.
I am truly your man; I no longer
    belong to myself . . .[12]

we know that their poetic game depends on a steeply graded hierarchy.

But does that hierarchy include women as well as men? Despite what appears to be the clear meaning of the texts, even this has been denied. For such critics, troubadour poetry is "homosocial"; it expresses an eroticized social competition among men.[13] For others the social context in which the poets composed their words and music is irrelevant; it should be read through the ahistorical lens of Freudian psychology.[14] For these critical views, like those of Köhler and Duby, the poetry is fundamentally a distorting mirror, a sublimated representation of real drives, economic and status-oriented for some, sexual for others — drives that lie elsewhere, on the plane of social relations or economic forces or deep psychology, where real history occurs. Ultimately, to follow such reasoning is to assert that the poetry itself is irrelevant, charming perhaps, but historically of little consequence. And because what is taken to be the principal theme of that poetry — a play with adulterous love — runs so much against the grain of medieval aristocratic society, the audience to which that theme appealed must have been marginal. It could not have been mainstream. The songs could not have been composed to entertain mature, married men and women, great lords in command of estates and fighting men who were concerned, among other things, with the legitimacy of their progeny.

This last assumption leads to a more troubling question. Did such marginalized groups — the landless nobles of the one interpretive schema or the unmarried household knights of the other — really exist? Were the courts to whom the troubadours sang, the courts of those great Occitan and Catalan lords and ladies, composed of young footloose males in search of women, wealth, and honor?

Such men can be found aplenty, to be sure, in medieval literary texts. How familiar to readers of *chansons de geste* and Arthurian tales is the figure of the loyal knight waiting for a gift of land and wife: William Shortnose in the *Charroi de Nîmes*, Gibouin of Mans in *Raoul de Cambrai*, Marie de France's Lanval. Georges Duby's path-breaking article on the "youth" in medieval society turns to another kind of literary text, the metrical histories of William the Marshal and the counts of Guines.[15] If the landless youthful hero is present nearly everywhere in twelfth-century literature, including "romanced" histories, was he not also present in real noble courts? If what he desires and sometimes gets is a wife as well as land, were sex and property not inseparable? Do the commonplaces of literature — especially when their subjects are the lives of real historical figures — not reflect the common experiences of social processes? Do the forms of Art not correspond to the forms of Life? For the historian the question is at least as old as the work of Johan Huizinga.[16] It will not go away.

We are here face to face with the same problem the "lives" of the troubadours presented. The world created by medieval literature, though its genres varied, is self-contained, largely self-referential. There is little outside of it by which we can test how truly it represents historical reality, or to phrase the issue more exactly, what it represents and how it goes about doing so. In the case of the landless nobility or the youth, this is particularly the case; for the very nature of the evidence we normally use to reconstruct eleventh and twelfth-century social structures necessarily excludes them.

Before the appearance of royal and comital administrative and judicial documents in the later twelfth century, our primary access to medieval society is through documents concerning land (and, in Italy, commercial transactions); we depend for our knowledge on accounts of dispute settlements, occasional testaments and marriage contracts, and, above all, land conveyances — sales, mortgages, and gifts. For the very reason we have them — because they provided titles to property and were therefore carefully stored away in treasure chests — they do not involve people without property. Unless the propertyless and the wandering bachelors happen to appear coincidentally in such documents, they necessarily remain invisible. This does not mean, of course, that we should reject their existence out of hand, however much Ockham's Razor might urge us to do so. It does mean that the arguments for their existence must be exceptionally solid: those arguments must depend on something more than general ideas about the medieval family or medieval social structure, and they should not be based on the very literary texts they are being used to explain.

What do these land conveyances, then, tell us about the membership of Occitan courts? What do they tell us about the men and women who listened to the troubadours, enjoyed their play with words and melodies and rules of love, and gave them the cloaks and horses and coin they sometimes insistently demanded? What sort of people surrounded Ermengard of Narbonne and her contemporaries, Raymond V and VI of Toulouse, Raymond Trencavel, Roger of Béziers, William of Montpellier, Alfons of Aragon?

The Court of Ermengard of Narbonne

If we are to go beyond the stylized and debatable images of the *chansons de geste*, the romances, and the Breton *lais* (all, it is important to add, from the north, and therefore from a different kind of court society), we must turn to the only other documents we have, those that survive from lay archives of Occitania in the formative period of troubadour song. These documents, in addition to telling us who gave or sold or mortgaged what to whom, who gave oaths of fidelity to whom, and who made peace with whom, also tell us who was present when these things happened. Witness lists were an important part of all such records, and they are rarely absent. They tell us, by naming names, exactly who was in the company of individual lords at important moments — when they arbitrated disputes, made treaties, contracted marriages, confirmed donations, and made gifts themselves. They are our only window into the community of people who surrounded the great lords of the region, the community we refer to as "the court." Identifying these witnesses is tedious but not impossible.

Let us take one court, an important one for troubadour poetry, that of Ermengard of Narbonne. Ermengard succeeded her father in 1134 and effectively ruled as viscountess from 1143 until she was forced into exile by her impatient nephew in 1192 or 1193, dying in Perpignan in 1196 or 1197. She appears to figure in the songs of Bernart de Ventadorn, Peire d'Alvernhe, Azalais de Porcairagues, Giraut de Bornelh, and Peire Rogier.[17] Her fame as "she who protects joy and youth," who gives "joy and merit," spread to the far reaches of the Latin world. Even a Norse skald of the Orkney Islands, north of Scotland, knew of the legendary beauty named "Ermingerda" who ruled the sea-town of "Nerbon."[18]

Sixty-three surviving documents testify to Ermengard's activities. Though small, this is a respectable number, even in comparison with the 158 extant for her exact contemporary count Raymond V of Toulouse, for Raymond exercised power in a far larger region, with many more ecclesiastical foundations to record his benefactions, while almost all of Ermengard's surely numerous benefactions are lost.[19] What percent do these sixty-two represent of all the documents that once bore her name? There is no way to tell, but it would be surprising if it were more than 0.1 percent. Only two of the oaths of fidelity that must have been given to her (and which were regularly recorded), have survived; for our purposes, that is surely the greatest loss; those that survived until the eighteenth century were carried off from the archives of the royal Court of Accounts of Montpellier or went up in flames in the great revolutionary bonfire of August 10, 1793.[20] And of what was probably never recorded, how dearly we would like to have her dinner invitations and the seating charts of her table. The number of documents we do have to work with, a little over one per year of her effective rule, gives a sense of the uncertainty that attends our investigation. Though the conclusions we draw must necessarily be cautious, let us proceed.

We begin with a list of all those people whom we know appeared with Ermengard at one time or another, especially those who witnessed her acts. Among these, the clergy form a special group. They appear as witnesses to documents involving ecclesiastical property; they are nearly absent, however, from all documents that concern exclusively lay affairs. Priests, monks, and prelates therefore did not belong to her regular entourage; their presence in her company is purely adventitious. In order to be sure we have Ermengard's court we must also remove from our full list all those people whom we can identify as belonging to the entourage of other great lords with whom Ermengard met. Once we have done this we are left with the names of 102 persons. Sixty-three of them bear family names taken from villages in the vicinity of Narbonne, such as Boutenac, Cazouls, Laredorte, Leucate, Minerve, Ouveilhan; they are from the families of the lords of these villages. The others bear patronymics or cognomens that may also be on their way to becoming family names. Of the 102, 73 appear only once in Ermengard's presence. Many of these individuals appear in other documents, however; they are local notables in the countryside or in the city or both, present as witnesses on such occasions because they are important people in the neighborhood, or because they are lords, clients, or friends of the parties involved.

It is the remainder, those who appear twice or more over several years, who are the most interesting for our purposes. They are the ones most likely to belong to Ermengard's closest entourage, to be members of her "court." Of some we know little more than that they were local landholders and military men, like William of Argens, who gave some tithes in a nearby village to the abbey of Fontfroide, a man of sufficient stature to be accompanied by his squire when he made the donation.[21] Others came from powerful families with ties to other great regional lords, like Bernard and William of Durban and William's son Raymond. William was also an intimate of the Trencavels; we can find his ancestors in the councils of the great already in the mid-eleventh century.[22] Yet others — like Hugh of Plaigne, who served as Ermengard's *vicarius*, her chief administrator, in 1176 — were notables in the city as well as the countryside. Hugh's brother William was made a canon of the cathedral in 1144, taking with him substantial property in both the countryside and the city; their grandfather had already been a major patron of the cathedral. Hugh's son became sacristan of the abbey of Saint-Paul, the other ecclesiastical power in the city. Hugh himself, we know, owned two grist-mills under the old Roman bridge and a shop on the bridge (and doubtless much other property as well).[23] Raymond of Ouveilhan was another of the same breed. His family had substantial holdings in and around the village from which he took his name; Raymond, in addition, was a major suburban real-estate developer around the ancient walls of Narbonne.[24]

Peter Raymond of Narbonne was one of Ermengard's closest companions and for a decade or more her *vicarius*; thanks to his testament we know more about him than any other member of her court. He left nearly 1000 *s.* as alms to the Cistercian abbey of Fontfroide just outside Narbonne (where he asked to be buried), to the Templars, the Hospitallers, several nunneries, and the various hospitals of the city. His three daughters received an inheritance of 11,000 *s.* in cash. His sons inherited his landed property, which spread all the way from east of Béziers to deep in the Corbières, the mountain range southwest of Narbonne; it included four mills in Narbonne, three of which he had bought from Ermengard, shops on the bridge, and houses in various parts of the city.[25] Peter Raymond's family we can likewise trace back to the mid-eleventh century, when they held Gruissan, an important coastal castle in the fidelity of the archbishop of Narbonne, as well as properties in and around the city— mills already among them.[26] Peter Raymond was every inch himself a lord of high standing.[27]

It would be difficult to argue that troubadour poetry served as a projection or sublimation of the frustrated economic or political desire of men like Peter Raymond of Narbonne, Raymond of Ouveilhan, or Hugh of Plaigne. They and their colleagues were neither propertyless petty nobles nor landless bachelor youths.

Youths there assuredly were in the armies that rode back and forth across Occitania. And the household manners of these men were certainly not the most genteel. When the canons of the cathedral of Maguelone appealed to the pope against their bishop in 1168, one of their complaints was that the bishop had his fighting men eat at table with them, doubtless disturbing due decorum; one has to wonder whether they also walked off with the cutlery, for its disappearance was another cause of complaint.[28] For those young men not yet married, a wealthy heiress was surely better than a women only modestly endowed. But the most rapacious predators on truly wealthy heiresses in twelfth-century Occitania were not wandering youths but the counts of Toulouse themselves, especially Raymond V, who could have taken as his motto (if twelfth-century aristocrats had had mottos), *tu felix Tolosa nubet*, "Others conquer by force of arms, but you, O happy Toulouse, conquer by marriage." Through his own marriages and those he arranged for his sons, he extended his power over lands that ranged from the neighborhood of Montpellier to the high Alps.[29]

Cadets, whether from wealthy families or those but modestly endowed, did not have to abscond with widows or other men's wives to establish themselves, for Occitania throughout the twelfth century was a land of partible inheritance. Wills, the joint oaths of brothers and cousins for castles, and the common references to halves or quarters, or halves of quarters, of property rights— family property divided generation after generation — are all there to prove it. That such division and subdivision led to dwindling landed resources among some families was probably true. But, as we have seen, the expropriation of peasant surpluses was not the only source of wealth, at least in coastal Languedoc. Enterprising lords who were willing to invest— and there were others besides Raymond of Ouveil-han and Peter Raymond of Narbonne — had plenty of opportunity. And they formed the core of Ermengard's entourage.

If there were remarkable absentees from Ermengard's court it was clergy, monks, and the men of new money in her city of Narbonne — the Bis-tani, for example, probably the wealthiest family in the city, who, even though they often associated with Hugh of Plaigne, did not enter the visco-mital court until Pedro de Lara succeeded his aunt in 1192–94.[30] Men such as this had no place in a narrow courtly society drawn essentially from an old well-established elite, an elite who were ready to deal with them in the market but not allow them to enter the privileged circle of their viscountess.

Women Dynasts in Twelfth-Century Occitania

ERMENGARD

I have focused on the court of Ermengard of Narbonne not just because she was a patron of the troubadours but because she was a woman patron. Troubadour songs and their amorous themes have frequently been con-sidered problematic because of the role they ascribe to women and the relation — commonly subservient and often frustrated — of the male poetic voice toward her. The troubadour's lady exercises power over her lover, and that relationship is often expressed in the same language and gestures of fidelity that bound warriors to their lords. If medieval aristocratic society was a patriarchal society, male dominated, one where women were ex-cluded from power, it is often argued, then there is a serious disjuncture between the poetry and the roles of men and women in the real world of the nobility who patronized that poetry; the gender imagery must therefore be paradoxical or ironic. For some critics, the lady is not really there; she is but "a mirror in which the poet sees his ideal self."[31] For others, compounding paradox with paradox, the poetry is really the instrument of female subjec-tion, misogyny disguised.[32] For yet others the mode of love expressed in the poems is simply "absurd." "Who in his right mind could believe such things?" Frederick Goldin once asked. "And how can any literature extolling such love be anything but ridiculous?"[33] In the male Middle Ages, the *domna* — the female lord — of the lyric must be a metaphor or a mask for something else.

In Occitania, however, there was no such disjuncture between poetic image and the realities of power. Ermengard was exceptional by the length of her reign, but she was not alone of her sex to play a powerful role in the region's dynastic politics. When the child Ermengard inherited the viscounty of Narbonne on July 17, 1134, she almost immediately became the plaything of local and regional aristocratic parties. In 1139 count Alphonse Jordan of Toulouse took control of her city, dispensing rewards to his supporters, the most important of whom was his old friend the archbishop of the city, and in 1142 he forced Ermengard to marry him.[34] The marriage did not last long, however; the threat that Ermengard's city would enter the domains of the house of Toulouse was enough to spur the regional nobility into action. Soon the allied troops of the Trencavels, the count of Rodez, William of Montpellier, and the counts of Provence and Barcelona, supported from a distance by the pope, were in the field against Alphonse Jordan, who was joined by the Genoese, the archbishop of Arles, and the lords of Les Baux. There were skirmishes all over the region, on both sides of the Rhône. The bourgeois of Montpellier, suborned by Alphonse, expelled William from his city. In the midst of these flourishing drums and trumpets of war, king Louis VII made an abortive raid on Toulouse to support the claims of his wife, Eleanor of Aquitaine, to that city. A year later, however, in 1143, William retook Montpellier and the Trencavel viscount Roger of Béziers forced Alphonse to give up both Ermengard and Narbonne.[35] Almost immediately after her "liberation" Ermengard was married again, this time to Bernard of Anduze, a companion of her father, cousin of William of Montpellier and follower of the Trencavels.[36]

Had Alphonse Jordan stayed in Narbonne he might have absorbed the city into his own territories: the marriage contract indeed provided for his right of survivorship should Ermengard die before him. That was precisely what spurred his enemies into action. But had that occurred it would have been attributable to Alphonse's power rather than to law or custom. For, although Occitan lordships sometimes disappeared into the domains of heiresses' husbands when dowries or wills so stipulated, it was not a common practice, especially among the greatest dynasties. When Gerberga, heiress to the county of Provence, married the viscount of Millau, he took the title count of Provence alongside his wife, and his portion of the familial lands of Millau and the Gévaudan fell to her, through whom they passed in 1112 to their daughter Douce and her husband Ramon-Berenguer of Barcelona.[37] The Barcelonese now bore the title "count of Provence," but Provence remained a separate territory and the countship a separable title.

Similarly, Narbonne did not disappear into the domains of Ermengard's second husband Bernard of Anduze. It is rather Bernard who seems to have disappeared from Narbonne. Though he remained active around Montpellier, we know of his activities in Ermengard's city only through the chance survival of a single oath of fidelity. Although Ermengard is about as well documented as any lay lord of twelfth-century Occitania, male or female, Bernard's name does not appear in any written act concerning her. And indeed the one surviving oath of fidelity that was sworn to him carefully reserves the rights of Ermengard's younger sister Ermessend, implying that were there to be no heirs from Ermengard's marriage to Bernard, Ermessend — rather than any of Bernard's relatives — would succeed to the viscounty.

And so it turned out. Ermengard had no children. By 1167 she had associated her sister's son Aimery in her rule. When he died, ten years later, she replaced him with his brother, Pedro. The two nephews — Aimery and Pedro — had a place at Ermengard's side that her husband never occupied.

Note that the first nephew's name was Aimery, the name of his maternal grandfather and great-grandfather, the name which a powerful legend associated with Narbonne and which, beginning with the great-grandfather, the viscomital family adopted as the name of choice for its eldest sons. Ermengard's brother, who died young, also bore that name. Had Ermessend, though married to one of the most powerful barons of Castile, designated one of her sons in this way as heir to Narbonne? It seems likely. Yet another Aimery, Pedro's son, would become viscount three years after Ermengard's death, and after him a line of Aimerys would stretch into the fourteenth century.[38]

What we have in Ermengard's story is a powerful sense of dynasty — patrilineal, to be sure, yet not transportable by marriage into another patriline. In the absence of a male heir, it was women who were expected to maintain dynastic continuity, to train their sons or nephews or daughters in the traditions and rights of their maternal line. This sense of women's dynastic role was made quite explicit in the alliance put together in 1177 to expel Alphonse Jordan's son Raymond V from Narbonne after he had momentarily captured it:

... never by my will or consent [the allies swore to each other] will count Raymond or his son acquire Narbonne or the lands of the lady Ermengard. And if they do acquire it, I will do all I can with you to bring evil war upon them until a man or woman of the lineage of Aimery of Narbonne or the king of Aragon shall recover Narbonne and its lands.[39]

Heiresses were expected to fulfill the demands of their family's position, to honor inherited alliances, in short, to do everything a man would do in their place.

Accordingly, we find Ermengard's army before the walls of Tortosa in 1148, she herself at the siege of Les Baux in 1162, at another moment (after a momentary shift in alliances) promising king Louis to lead her army in aid of the count of Toulouse. She was deeply involved in all the military and diplomatic quadrilles of the region for nearly half a century. So central was she to the Barcelonese alliance in Occitania that when Raymond Trencavel was captured by count Raymond V of Toulouse in 1153 and feared for his life, though he left his wife and children in the guardianship of the count of Barcelona, his eldest son Roger he left "in God's custody and in Ermengard's and in her service."[40]

Nineteenth-century scholars may be pardoned for seeing our Ermengard behind a legendary Ermengard, the one in the poem *Aliscans* who boasts:

... I myself will ride there
wearing my coat of mail, my shining helmet laced on,
shield at my neck, sword at my side,
lance in hand, ahead of all others.
Though my hair is grey and white,
my heart is bold and thirsts for war.[41]

STEPHANIA OF LES BAUX

When Ermengard camped with her troops before the walls of Les Baux in 1162, she was helping the forces of the king of Aragon settle a dispute that had begun with the machinations of another woman: Stephania of Les Baux.

From its perch high on the southern rim of the Alpilles hills east of Arles, the castle of Les Baux stands sentinel over what was once the vast stony flood plain of the Durance river. The place has given its name to bauxite, the ore from which aluminum is made; the hills have been immortalized in Vincent Van Gogh's *Starry Night*, painted while the artist was hospitalized at Saint-Rémy, on the plain just to the north. In the twelfth century Les Baux was principally known for the powerful family who ruled from its stone keep. Along with families such as the viscounts of Marseille and the lords of Fos, they considered themselves to be—after the Barcelonese count of Provence and the Toulousain marquis of Provence—the head of the region's aristocracy.

Their prominence was recognized when sometime before 1113 Raymond of Les Baux married Stephania, the younger daughter of Gerberga, countess of Provence, and sister of the Douce who took the county with her when she married count Ramon-Berenguer of Barcelona. Stephania was dowered and—so it was claimed much later when she was defeated—excluded from any further claims to her mother's and father's rights and titles.[42] This exclusion, however, did not deter her and her husband from suddenly advancing their own claims to the county in 1144, after decades of loyal service in the entourage of Alphonse Jordan. Provence was a land of the Empire, and Stephania and her husband had dispatched one of their children to the imperial court to cultivate the patronage of those near the throne. Their care paid off. The emperor bestowed on them a diploma appended with his golden seal which accepted them as immediate vassals of the crown not only for the traditional lands of Les Baux but also for the "honors" of Stephania's mother and father—implying in this term the couple's rights to the county of Provence itself, the very rights exercised for thirty-two years by the Barcelonese dynasty.[43] The imperial diploma was a declaration of war.

The revolt was put down by 1147, but Stephania and her four sons did not take their oaths of peace and fidelity until 1150, and her son Hugh reopened the conflict in 1156 with a new diploma from emperor Frederick I. It was not until 1162, after Frederick had abandoned Hugh in an effort to enlist count Ramon-Berenguer IV of Barcelona in his own battle against pope Alexander III, that a Catalan army—supported by the Trencavels and Ermengard of Narbonne at the head of their troops—besieged and captured Les Baux itself and finally squelched the family's pretensions.[44] Though their forces and possibly they themselves were often on opposite sides on the battlefield, Stephania of Les Baux and Ermengard of Narbonne came from the same mold.

The models for these two women, if they or their nurses and tutors had needed to look for them, were not hard to find. There was Ermessend, countess of Barcelona in the first half of the eleventh century, herself of the line of the counts of Carcassonne, who twice ruled as regent — once for her son, once for her grandson — and at last, in her seventies, had to be bought out of her stronghold in Gerona with a thousand ounces of gold.[45] There was Almodis of La Marche, who deserted the count of Toulouse to marry Ermessend's grandson, count Ramon-Berenguer I, and turned herself into the effective co-ruler of the county.[46] There was Almodis's contemporary, an earlier Ermengard, who had brought Béziers and its viscounty into her marriage with Raymond-Bernard, viscount of Albi and Nîmes, and after the death of her husband became the architect of Trencavel power in Occitania.[47] There was Cecilia, wife of this Ermengard's son, Bernard-Ato, who joined her husband in many of his political acts and on his death received the oaths of fidelity for his castles, even though her three sons had already come of age.[48] These were exceptional women all, without doubt; but social practice made similar life chances possible — albeit on a more modest scale — for every aristocratic woman.[49] We need only look at the career of Beatrice of Mauguio, especially its spectacular end.

BEATRICE OF MAUGUIO

Mauguio is now a forgotten village a few miles east of Montpellier. In the Middle Ages it was home to a line of counts who claimed to include among their ancestors the eighth-century Saint Benedict, founder of the revered monastery of Aniane and promoter of a monastic reform that eventually spread throughout the Carolingian Empire. Beatrice inherited the county when her father died in 1132; she too became an object of war, between Alphonse Jordan and William VI of Montpellier,[50] which William eventually won by marrying Beatrice into the family of his closest ally, the house of Barcelona: Beatrice's husband was the future count of Provence. Though her husband was by birth and necessity one of the major actors on the stage of regional politics, Beatrice seems to have stayed in the wings, leading a quiet life as lady of her tiny county. From this marriage to Berenguer-Ramon she had one son, Ramon-Berenguer, who on the death of his father in 1144 succeeded to the countship of Provence. Beatrice remained countess of Mauguio. Two children, Bertrand and Ermessend, came from her second marriage to Bernard Pelet, lord of Alès.

Beatrice associated both her husbands in her rule; they both enjoyed the title of count of Mauguio, though neither acted independently of her within her lands. Then in 1170 came the first signs of a family feud; her husband Bernard Pelet and their son Bertrand made an important grant to the lords of a nearby village without mentioning Beatrice, with the son styling himself "count of Mauguio." The following year, his father now dead, Bertrand "count of Mauguio" allied himself with William of Montpellier. To Beatrice this was an act of defiance, perhaps even of treachery. She was countess of Mauguio, and no one, not even her son, would take the title without her good grace. She responded by disinheriting him.[51]

Beatrice's granddaughter Douce, the daughter of Ramon-Berenguer III of Provence, had long since been betrothed to the son of Raymond V of Toulouse, the future Raymond VI. On April 1, 1172, Beatrice divided her county between Raymond V, on behalf of his future daughter-in-law, and her own daughter Ermessend and her husband.[52] Of her son Bertrand she made no mention. The following December, on the death of Ermessend's husband, Beatrice and count Raymond V quickly settled any possible disputed succession; it was now Ermessend who married Raymond's son, excluding Douce, and Beatrice gave the entire county, undivided, to Raymond V. Thus she eliminated both her son and any possible Catalan claims through Douce.[53]

Was this an act of spite? Or did Beatrice fear that Bertrand would allow Mauguio to be absorbed into the expanding lordship of her family's neighbors and rivals, the lords of Montpellier? Alas, the motives of twelfth-century politicians are just as opaque as those of our own politicians. Whatever her motivations, for Raymond V of Toulouse it was an astounding coup. Now in a position to pressure the lords of Montpellier and to undermine the Trencavel viscounty of Nîmes, he proceeded to unhinge the Catalan alliance in Occitania. Thanks to Beatrice, the vast collection of lands he had worked so mightily to assemble, from Toulouse to the high passes of the Alps, reached its apogee. For Beatrice the rewards were doubtless equally sweet. She had vindicated her dynastic self-esteem and she quietly retired on a pension of 4000 s. per year.

The Image of Women in Law and Poetry

How were these women viewed by their contemporaries? We cannot, of course, conduct an opinion poll. In any case, whatever individual opinions may have been, they did not stop Ermengard from ruling her city and commanding the admiration and support of her contemporary lords, Stephania from raising troops to vindicate her claim to Provence, Beatrice from successfully disinheriting her traitorous son. All three were accepted as superiors by their subordinates and as powerful allies or opponents by their fellow aristocrats; indeed, as the testament of Raymond Trencavel demonstrates, sometimes they could be favored allies. But in what imagined guise were they accepted? As women or as surrogate men? Were they considered unusual or perhaps even deformed by their power? Or were they admired and exalted? These questions take us down a difficult slope, one strewn with traps for the unwary.

In other climes, a medievalist's first resort in trying to answer these questions might be to monastic chronicles. Such narratives are of no avail to us here, however, for the nearest chroniclers are far to the north, in the Limousin, Anjou, Normandy, the Paris basin, England, and Germany. Even in the Limousin, Geoffrey de Vigeois pays scant attention to Occitanian events except when his neighboring clergy or warriors are involved. What news reaches farther north is a dim, distorted echo indeed. Nor would words from a monastic pen necessarily get us very far. The stream of monastic misogyny ran deep, and many professed religious found the language of sex a limber tool with which to castigate both men and women. We are hardly surprised to read on the pages of the English monk William of Malmesbury that Almodis of La Marche was driven by a "furious and godless female itch" when she left the count of Toulouse for a more powerful role as wife of the count of Barcelona.[54]

In the absence of chronicles we are left with only the flotsam of sales, donations, oaths of fidelity, and dispute settlements that have washed ashore in Occitan archives. And we have the songs of the troubadours.

Archival documents are for the most part highly conventional and formulaic, but in this case it is their very conventionality that comes to our aid. Their formulae tell us that women were expected to participate fully in political life, in waging feuds and calming disputes, in pressing and defending claims to property and rights. Whenever an Occitan castle changed hands — either a new person taking control of the place or a new overlord succeeding to that position — an oath of fidelity was given and received. From the end of the tenth century until the thirteenth (when oaths of homage and fealty on a northern model replaced the traditional oaths) the texts changed very little. The oath taker, after swearing to protect his or her lord's body, promised likewise to protect the castle of which he or she was taking possession. An essential part of this oath was the statement:

If a man or a woman (*si homo aut femina*) should take this castle by force, I [the oathtaker] will make no agreement nor associate with them nor come to their aid without the consent of [you, the overlord].[55]

Similarly, in contracts of sale and gift, texts that from the tenth century to well into the twelfth were also highly formulaic, a subtle but significant addition begins to appear early in the eleventh century. In the guarantee clause, in which the vendor or giver declares that "if anyone seeks to break [the terms of this agreement] he shall not be allowed to do so" and promises punishment ranging from heavy fines to eternal damnation, where earlier texts had been satisfied with a simple neutral pronoun, or references to heirs, or to "any man," who might try to break the contracts provisions, eleventh-century scribes started to add women to men: "if a man or a woman or any person seeks to break this agreement. . . ." (*si quis autem venerit, sive homo sive femina aut ulla persona . . .*).[56]

Both are attempts to be all-inclusive. That is exactly what makes them interesting. There were grammatically gendered but semantically neutral words ready at hand: Latin "homo" had already given the pronoun "om / hom" to Old Occitan, with the same meaning as French "on" or English "one." Latin "persona," as in the phrase just quoted, while grammatically feminine, likewise had an ungendered meaning, just like its derivatives in modern Romance languages. But to cast the net as widely as possible and reduce the holes through which prevaricators might slip, the oath formula, and sometimes the guarantee formula as well, specified "any man or woman."

The reason is simple: women as well as men might take matters into their own hands and attack a castle or try to take back a piece of property. Occitan charters are nowhere near as garrulous as those of the Loire valley, for example, but on rare occasions they do tell stories of the violence that preceded a settlement. One of those from the region of Béziers tells how a woman named Rixendis de Parez joined a posse of village lords in attacking some mills on the Orb river; she was one of a group who claimed the mills and their tenants to be their own. Another tells how the wife of Bernard of Nissan took revenge on her husband's enemy when the two men were fighting over a castle they jointly held.[57] Women would engage in such depredations for the same reason that they would collect dues and fines from their tenants, or get into legal squabbles with their brothers, or become money lenders.[58] They had rights as heiresses or widows, rights they had to manage and sustain; and this was a world where self-help, most often violent self-help, was — as it long continued to be — a first line of defense.

Women also held castles under normal obligations of fidelity and service. We can document a handful in the twelfth century: Laureta of Durban, who at the very beginning of the twelfth century held from the Trencavels the castle of Ornaisons (on the major road from Carcassonne to Narbonne) as well as an extensive spread of properties stretching from Roussillon to Agde; Ricsovendis of Termes, who in 1163 (with viscountess Ermengard's assistance) successfully pursued her right to share with her brothers her paternal inheritance to that major fortress in the Corbières; Alda, Duoda, Ermessend, and Almodis, the four sisters to whom the childless Arnold of Fenollèd bequeathed all his castles in 1173.[59] Among the castles held of the lords of Montpellier, six had a woman castellan at some time during the twelfth century. Even the powerful vicariate of the city fell to an heiress at the very end of the century.[60]

In the absence of bureaucratic record-keeping it is impossible to tell how many castles were in women's hands at any given moment in the twelfth century, but the practice of allowing women to inherit castles or take them as dowries continued into the thirteenth and fourteenth centuries, and by then the professional quill-pushers were hard at work. The administrators of the viscounts of Narbonne kept a record of oaths of fidelity and homage given from 1272 to 1298. In the fragment that survives in a seventeenth-century copy, seven out of sixty-four of those oaths were rendered by husbands in the name of their wives and six by women themselves (with *homo* in the text of the oath regularly changed to *femina*).[61] Among the people viscount Amalric summoned to join him for the war in Flanders in 1302 were "Lady Cecilia," "the widow of Peter *majoris*," Thorela Roys and her brothers, and Fina of Durban — four women out of a total of thiry-nine. On the day of the muster, lady Cecilia was represented by her husband while Thorela Roys appeared for herself and her brothers. Over the following days several other women were summoned to come themselves or to send someone in their place.[62] Even later, in 1343, the lady of Saissac, a village north of Carcassonne, could sue in the king's high court of Parlement to force the lords of the neighboring village of Oupia "to muster and march in her company and under her banner" to the king's wars; she won her suit.[63] Lordship, with all its powers of constraint and command and with its assimilation of power to property, remained familial, and thus under proper circumstances as much the right of women as of men.

At the same time as we note the presence of these women in the records of the age, we must also note their limited numbers. This was not a society of equal opportunity. By the twelfth century, daughters were no longer of equal status with their male siblings, if indeed they ever had been. Increasingly, their dowries were explicitly identified as their part of the family inheritance, and they were asked to wait in line behind their brothers for any chance to succeed to the principal portion.[64] But the dice-throw of reproduction and risks of mortality meant that some would succeed. Ermengard, Stephania, and Beatrice — our trio of lady dynasts — are exceptional by their status; but the expectations placed on them by their society, and doubtless by themselves, were the expectations of every heiress writ large.

As castellans, women would have exercised all the rights that went with such positions: rights of justice over market disputes, over petty crimes (or even over major ones), over mines or roadways in their "district"; rights to bears' paws, deer haunches, and cuts of boar hunted in the castle's territories; rights to honorific offerings of cheese, hens, and lambs; rights to annual service by ox-carts; rights to a place of honor at village weddings.[65] They would have sworn the oaths of fidelity that castle-holding required — oaths to their lord, whether male or female, and oaths to their fellow castellans.[66] As the thirteenth- and fourteenth-century documents still demonstrate, they would likewise have done the military service implied by those oaths and regularly demanded.

The first frontal assault on women's role as lords entered Occitania with the renewed study of Roman law. Knowledge of some aspects of Roman law had never entirely disappeared from Italy — or from Occitania, for that matter. When drafting contracts (a use of writing that continued unabated through the early Middle Ages) Mediterranean scribes kept alive a tradition little changed since Antiquity; in eleventh-century northern Italy, a fortunate student of rhetoric might likewise find Justinian's *Code* and the elementary legal textbook, the *Institutes*, added to his curriculum of Cicero and Virgil. Here in these late-Antique Byzantine texts the professional judges and notaries of Pavia (where Lombard kings and their Frankish and Ottonian successors had once had their residence) found intellectual guides and occasionally a supplement to their understanding of the Lombard laws it was their duty to apply.[67] When a sixth-century manuscript of the *Digest* — the most difficult part of Justinian's legal corpus — was discovered in the 1070s or 1080s, most likely in the papal library or the abbey of Montecasino, the professionals of the judicial world were ready to struggle with its complexities.[68]

The *Digest*, an anthology of selections from the greatest ancient juris-consults, quickly became the focus of teaching along with the *Code* and the *Institutes*, at just the moment when the polemical demands of the Investiture Controversy and the growing commerce of Pisa, Genoa, and Venice created a growing market for lawyers to argue the case for empire or papacy or draft new kinds of instruments to hedge the risks of long-distance Mediterranean trade. Thanks to Pepo and Irnerius, the two earliest teachers who settled there, Bologna became the primary center for instruction. By the 1120s, interest in Roman jurisprudence had spread westward along the Alpine trade route to Valence in the Rhône valley, and by mid-century masters in the subject were working and teaching in Arles, Saint-Gilles, and Montpellier.[69]

Early in the 1160s, when Occitanian politics were in a state of exceptional flux, Berenger of Puisserguier, lord of a village about fifteen miles north of Narbonne and follower of the Trencavels and possibly of the viscounts of Narbonne as well, decided he could make a bid for independence.[70] Berenger held the profitable right of "safe-conduct" — police duty or protection racket, depending on one's degree of skepticism — on the segment of the old Roman road, the Via Domitia, that connected Narbonne and Béziers. One day, on his own initiative, he decided to increase the tolls he collected on this road. When Ermengard of Narbonne, ever mindful of threats to her city's commerce, tried to bring him to justice, he took refuge with count Raymond V of Toulouse, who sent him with his blessing and a strong letter of recommendation to his brother-in-law, King Louis VII. In Paris Berenger claimed to hold his castle of Puisserguier directly as liegeman of the king. Louis was just beginning to build political bridges to Occitania, traveling through the region on his return from a pilgrimage to Santiago de Compostello in 1155, marrying his sister to the count of Toulouse, and eventually raining privileges and empty grants of fiefs on the great lords, bishops, and monasteries of the region.[71] Berenger's claim was just extravagant enough to be welcomed.

Somewhere in the Rhône valley Berenger had probably been counseled by one of those newly minted experts in Roman law and picked up a rule he thought he could argue against Ermengard: according to Roman law, women were barred from acting as magistrates. The classic text was a comment of Paulus included in Justinian's *Digest*, a version of which figured prominently in a Provençal treatise on Roman law, *Lo codi*, which may have just appeared at Saint-Gilles or Arles when Berenger was passing through.[72] King Louis first found in Berenger's favor, doubtless both to please his brother-in-law and to make a forceful claim for power in a region that still escaped his grasp. But Ermengard's messengers were close behind, and along the way they picked up the support of pope Alexander III and cardinal Hyacinth, the papal legate. Louis reversed himself and wrote to Ermengard:

The custom of our kingdom is much kinder [than Roman law]. Here, if the better sex be lacking, it is allowed to women to succeed and to administer an inheritance. Therefore remember that you are of our kingdom . . . [and] sit in judgment and examine matters with the diligent zeal of Him who created you a woman when He could have created you a man and of his great goodness gave the rule of the province of Narbonne into a woman's hands.[73]

One has to wonder what Ermengard made of Louis's reference to "the better sex" and to God "who created you a woman when He could have created you a man." Neither of these expressions was in the Roman law text, and the author of *Lo codi* explicitly ascribed women's disability to law and not to nature (still less to God). As if in ironic anticipation, Ermengard had already responded to an earlier admonition from Louis that she keep the peace with the count of Toulouse; she had assured the king that "on August 30 I will march with my army against his enemies."[74]

In practical terms, all this bustle between Narbonne, Toulouse, and Paris came to naught. Ermengard didn't need Louis's permission to administer justice; she had been doing so for years, even with Roman lawyers in her entourage. She summoned Berenger back to her court, and after some more squabbling the two came to terms. When Berenger died a few years later he left to his mother all his properties and rights, including his right to guard the highway and his two castles with all their attendant judicial powers, and ordered that if his brothers (who were to succeed after their mother's death) should themselves die without heirs of their body the castles should then be divided between his two sisters.[75] So much for insistence on legal principle. Berenger's arguments had caused a lot of fluttering in noble, royal, and papal chanceries, but against the power of longstanding custom even the prestige of ancient Rome was powerless.

In contrast, the lyrics of the troubadours (like Berenger of Puisserguier on his deathbed) accepted the power of women, indeed they enlarged upon it, and it is against the backdrop of women rulers and women castellans that we should now try to answer the set of questions with which this essay began. What should we read into the love stories these lyrics tell? What might have been the relation of the imagined world the poetry created to the real world it entertained? How should we understand these songs as the creation of men and women who may have known Ermengard and ladies like her?

*   *   *

Ermengard regularly received oaths of fidelity from the men and women who held castles of her. Every political alliance in which she was involved (and they were many over her long career) was likewise sealed with the exchange of oaths of fidelity. Here is a surviving fragment of one of those oaths:

From this hour forward, I Bernard, son of Fida, will be faithful to you Ermengard viscountess of Narbonne daughter of Ermengard, by true faith without deceit as a man should be faithful to his lady to whom he has commended himself by his hands.[76]

No English translation can do justice to both the meaning and the rhythms of oaths such as this, hundreds of which have survived, some of them in the Occitan in which they were given (rather than in Latin translation), and all cast in the same mold. The play of those rhythms is perhaps best represented in print as a poem:

nel ti tolrai
ne t'en tolrai
ni om ne femena ab mun consel;
e se om o femena
od omes o femenas
lot tollian
ne t'en tollian,
ab aquel
ne ab aquella
ne ab aquels
ne ab aquellas
fin ne societad non auria
for per lo castel a recobrar.
Et aitoris t'en serai
per fe e sanz engan.

(I will not take it [the castle] from you, nor take of it from you, nor will any man or woman with my consent; and if any man or woman or men or women should take it from you, or take of it from you, I will have no peace with him or her or them except to recover the castle. And I will come to your aid in this matter in faith and without deceit.)[77]

Here now is the poet Bernart de Ventadorn following lines of a most fleshly eroticism with the image of himself as the oath-taker:

Ara cuit qu'e·n morrai	Now I think that I shall die
del dezirer que·m ve	of the desire that comes upon me
si·lh bela lai on jai	if the fair one, there where she lies,
no m'aizis pres de se,	does not welcome me next to her
qu'eu la manei e bai	to caress and kiss her
et estrenha vas me	and press to me
so cors blanc, gras e le.	her white body, plump and smooth.
. . .	. . .
Bona domna, merce	Good Lady, show mercy
del vostre fin aman.	to your true lover.
Qu'e·us pliu per bona fe	for I pledge you in good faith
c'anc re non amei tan.	that never did I so love anyone.
Mas jonchas, ab col cle,	Hands joined, head bowed,
vos m'autrei e·m coman.	I give and commend myself to you.[78]

In another poem he lifts a line directly from the oath:

Per bona fe e ses enjan	In good faith and without deceit
am la plus bel' e la melhor.	I love the fairest and the best
Del cor sospir e dels olhs plor,	from the heart I sigh and from the eyes weep,
car tan l'am eu, perque i ai dan.	for I love her so much that I'm wronged.[79]

Such language, taken from the world of politics and military alliance, from the court society of great lords (male and female) and their fighting men (and women), infuse the lyrics of many troubadours with a troubling air. Bedroom and battlements seem incongruously joined. The world of amorous embraces slips without break into the world of political alliance and back again. Genders likewise become confused, when the lady turns into a lord:

Bona domna, re no·us deman	Good lady, I ask nothing from you
mas que·m prendatz per servidor,	but that you take me as your servant
qu'e·us servirai com bo senhor.	who will serve you as his good lord.[80]

or bears as a *senhal* — a pseudonym — a name that is grammatically male — "mon Estriu," "Azimen," "mo Cortes," "mos Bels Vezers."[81]

A hundred years ago, the image of men kneeling before their ladies, heads bowed, hands joined, provoked French literary historians to invent the idea of "courtly love" in order to explain it, so distant did it seem from normal relations between the sexes, so strange, so medieval. More recent historians have found this image impossible to accept as reality, and so have invented diverse ways to explain it away, to make it mean something very different from what it appears to say. Is either explanation necessary, or even appropriate?

*   *   *

Joglar, que aves cor gai	Joglar, you who have a joyous heart,
ves Narbona portas lai	carry there to Narbonne
ma chanson ab la fenida	my song with its conclusion
lei cui jois e jovens guida.	to her who is a model of joy and youth.[82]

So Azalais de Porcairagues dedicates one of her lyrics.

Lo vers mi porta, Corona,	Carry this song for me, Corona,
lai a midons a Narbona	there to my lady at Narbonne,
que tuih sei faih son enter	for all her actions are perfect,
c'om no·n pot dire folatge.	so that one cannot speak foolishness of of her.[83]

So Bernart de Ventadorn dedicates one of his. In both cases the lady is most likely viscountess Ermengard of Narbonne.

Let us then place these poets in Ermengard's court when Bernard of Durban or some other baron put his hands in hers and — in a decidedly unerotic setting — pledged his fidelity "per bona fe e ses enjan." Let us have them witness a young man enter her service and speak the very words that Bernart de Ventadorn employs: "Bona domna, re no·us deman mas que·m prendatz per servidor." Or let us imagine the troubadour Raimon de Miraval present when a fellow castellan swears fidelity for his castle to a woman, or Raimon even doing so himself, as so many did, if not to Ermengard of Narbonne or Beatrice of Mauguio then to one of the various Trencavel widows: Ermengard at the end of the eleventh century, her daughter-in-law Cecilia, or the widowed Saura and Guillelma later in the twelfth century.[84] For the troubadours and their audience such occasions were commonplaces of aristocratic life, ready, like the oaths of fidelity themselves, to be put to poetic use, as Raimon de Miraval does:

Mas d'una chan e d'una·m feing,	But I sing of one, and of one I have concern
e d'aquella Miraval teing.	of her I hold Miraval.[85]

What seem to us to be problematic images were drawn directly from reality.

Lines such as these are images, however, and they exist in poetic space. That space is not a replica of reality; it uses reality for its own ends, whether playful or serious or both at the same time. Troubadour lyrics are sophisticated poetry, composed for an audience of connoisseurs capable of appreciating their difficult forms and complex rhymes, capable of comparing a poet's compositions with those of his or her contemporaries and predecessors, capable likewise, we must imagine, of appreciating the poets' transformations of words and sentiments they, the listeners, could remember speaking.

For this audience of aristocrats and castellans, fidelity and service and the expectation of reward in return were at the heart of their social being. The loyalty of village lords, of castellans and knights, without which dynastic politics would have become a masquerade and armies a sham, depended on these ideals and expectations. Here was the substance of honor and worthiness; here were the actions that won praise; here was the graciousness that fostered the troubadours' "joy." To these ideals the troubadours constantly returned, sometimes in a voice tinged with irony or anger, as in the lyrics of Bertran de Born:

Vostre reptars m'es sabors,	Your accusations I find delicious,
ric, quar cuidatz tant valer	rich men, because you think so much of
qe sens donar, per temer,	yourselves
volriatz aver lauzors.	that without giving anything, simply
. . .	from fear,
	you would have people praise you.
	. . .
Mas faitz vostres faitz tan gens	Act nobly
qe·us en sega digz valens.	and you will be called worthy!
. . .	. . .
Ric ome voill qu'ab amors	I wish rich men knew how
sapchan cavaliers aver	with love to hold knights,
e qu·ls sapchan retener	knew how to retain them
ab ben far et ab honors,	with rewards and landed honors,
e qu·ls trob om ses tort faire,	I wish one found them blameless —
francs e cortes e chauzitz	open and gracious and polished,
e larcs e bos donadors :	generous and good givers.
Qu'aissi fo prez establitz:	For merit was established for this:
qu'om guerreies ab torneis	that men should fight in tournaments,
e Quaresma ez Avenz	and Lent and Advent
fesson soudadiers manenz.	should make mercenaries rich.[86]

In the voice of other poets, these ideals could take on the coloration of sentimental confession or erotic hope. What should the loyal lover do if his service is not rewarded? What does a lady (lord) risk if devotion is not recognized and recompensed? Such are the questions the lyrics sometimes asked. Then the poet played the part, shadowing the troubled retainer, the man who had promised "good faith without deceit," through all his waves of desire, despair, and hope.

Of this mode, Bernart de Ventadorn is the master. Here is one of the songs in which he mimes the *servidor* waiting for his lady (lord) to be "open, gracious, and polished, generous and a good giver," tacking between desertion in one verse and, in the next, a fidelity that resists all ills in the hope of better things to come:

Si tot fatz de joi parvensa,	Though I make a show of joy,
mout ai dins lo cor irat.	in my heart I have great anger.
Qui vid anc mais penedensa	Whoever saw someone do penance
faire denan lo pechat?	before he had committed sin?
On plus la prec, plus me's dura,	The more I beg her, the harder she is to
mas s'in breu tems no·s melhura,	me,
vengut er al partimen.	and if she's not better to me soon
	the time will have come to leave.
Pero ben es qu'ela·m vensa	But it is good that she has defeated me,
a tota sa volontat,	forced me to do her will,
que s'el' a tort o bistensa,	for if she is wrong, if she hesitates,
ades n'aura pietat;	soon she will have pity;
que so mostra l'escriptura:	for thus the scriptures show,
causa de bon'aventura	in matters of good fortune
val us sols jorns mais de cen.	one day is worth more than a
	hundred.[87]

There is little in the language here, though much in the meaning, to recall the tough world of power. In "La dousa votz ai auzida" Bernart is far more direct, and the two worlds of erotic love and the mutual love of lords and knights fuse into one. His lady is a *traïritz de mal linhatge*, a "traitoress of base lineage," evoking the worst possible breach of the oath of fidelity and thus the most grievous dishonor to both the individual and (her) family.

Mout l'avia gen servida	I most nobly served her
tro ac vas mi cor volatge,	until she showed me her fickle heart;
e pus ilh no m'es cobida,	since she is not in agreement with me,
mout sui fols si mais la ser.	I am a great fool if I serve her longer.
Servirs c'om no gazardona,	Service unrewarded
et esperansa bretona	and Breton hope[88]

fai de senhor escuder	make a squire of a lord
per costum e per uzatge.	by custom and practice.
Pois tan es vas me falhida,	Since she is so at fault toward me
aisi lais so senhoratge . . .	I leave her lordship.[89]

This is the song Bernart sends to "my lady at Narbonne . . . whose every act is so perfect that one cannot speak foolishness of her."[90] The compliment is indirect, but clear: his lady at Narbonne is the exact opposite of the traitorous lady in the lyric. Time and time again, the poets thus implicitly contrast or compare their patron — the king of Aragon, the count of Saint-Gilles, the marquis of Montferrat, the viscount of Marseille — to the invented lady of the lyric. Directly, as Bertran de Born, or indirectly, as Bernart de Ventadorn, through the devices of their lyric art they schooled their audience in social graces and political virtue, rendering in high emotional colors the polar opposites of aristocratic deportment: fidelity and service, and their contraries, deceit and discord.

Here, as one striking example, is a song on the subject of faith despised and hope denied, attributed to the Countess of Die.

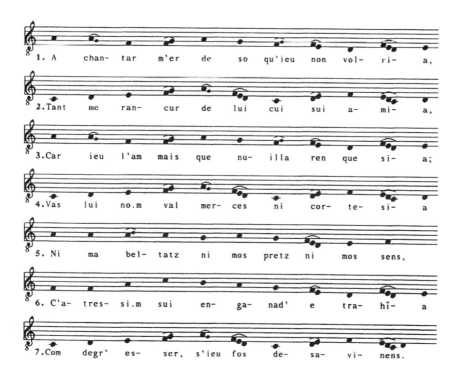

I

A chantar m'er de so qu'ieu non volria,
tant me rancur de lui cui sui amia.
car eu l'am mais que nuilla ren que sia;
vas lui no·m val merces ni cortesia
ni ma beltatz ni mos pretz ni mos sens,
c'attressi·m sui enganad'e trahïa
com degresser, s'ieu fos desavinens.

1

I must sing of what I'd rather not,
I'm so angry about him whose friend I
      am,
for I love him more than anything.
mercy and courtliness don't help me
with him, nor does my beauty or my
      rank, or my mind;
for I am every bit as betrayed and
      wronged
as I'd deserve to be if I were ungracious.

II

D'aisso·m conort car anc non fis
      faillenssa,
amics, vas vos per nuilla captenenssa,
anz vos am mais non fetz Seguis
      Valenssa,
e platz mi mout que eu d'amar vos
      venssa,
lo mieus amics, car etz lo plus valens;
mi faitz orguoil en digz et en parvenssa,
e si etz francs vas totas autras gens.

2

It comforts me that I have done no
      wrong
to you, my friend, through any action;
indeed, I love you more than Seguis
      loved Valenssa;
it pleases me to conquer you with love,
friend, for you are the most valiant.
Yet you offer prideful words and looks
      to me
but are gracious to every other person.

III

Meravill me com vostre cors s'orguoilla,
amics, vas me, per q'ai razon qe·m
      doilla;
non es ies dreitz c'autr'amors vos mi
      tuoilla
per nuilla ren qe·us diga ni·us acoilla.
e membre vos cals fo·l comenssamens
de nostr'amor, ia Dompnedieus non
      vuoilla
qu'en ma colpa sia·l departimens.

3

It amazes me how prideful your heart is
toward me, friend, for which I'm right
      to grieve;
it isn't fair that another love take you
      away
because of any word or welcome she
      might give you.
And remember how it was at the
      beginning
of our love; may the Lord God not
      allow
our parting to be any fault of mine.

IV

Proessa grans q'el vostre cors s'aizina
e lo rics pretz q'avetz m'en ataina,
c'una non sai loindana ni vezina,
si vol amar vas vos no si aclina;
mas vos, amics, ez ben tant conoissens

4

The great valor that dwells in your
      person,
and the high rank you have, these
      trouble me,
for I don't know a woman, far or near,

que ben devetz conoisser la plus fina
e membre vos de nostres covinens.

who, if she wished to love, would not
    turn to you;
but you, friend, are so knowing,
you surely ought to know the truest one,
and remember what our agreement was.

V
Valer mi deu mos pretz e mos paratges
e ma beutatz e plus mos fins coratges,
per q'ieu vos man lai on es vostr'
    estatges
esta chansson que me sia messatges,
e voill saber, lo mieus bels amics gens,
per que m'etz vos tant fers ni tant
    salvatges,
no sai, si s'es orgoills ni mals talens.

5
My rank and lineage should be of help
to me, and my beauty and, still more,
    my true heart.
This song, let it be my messenger.
Therefore, I send it to you, at your
    dwelling.
and I would like to know, my fine, fair
    friend,
why you are so fierce and cruel to me.
I can't tell if its from pride or malice.

VI
Mas aitan plus voill li digas, messatges
q'en trop orgoill ant gran dan maintas
    gens.

6
I especially want you, messenger, to tell
    him
that too much pride brings harm to
    many persons.[91]

Discord is present from the beginning of the song, in the contraried will of the poetic first person, the "I" in the first line who is forced to sing of what she would not. Discord is formally announced in the second line in the reflexive verb *me rancur*, "I am bitter/angry," a word that as a noun— *rancur*— means a dispute or conflict (it appears this way in charters as the equivalent of the Latin *discordia* or *controversia*).

Discord is amplified in the contrast between the singer's merit in lines 4 and 5 and her lover's treason in line 6. The discord is also represented aurally by the tension between the structure of rhyme and that of the melody. The first four lines of each stanza have one rhyme sound, let's label it A; their melodies have repeating cadences, let's call them 1, 2, 1, 2. The fifth line has a new melody, 3, and a new rhyme sound, B. Line 6, after an initial melodic change falls back to cadence 1 and we hear again rhyme A. We are led to expect melodic cadence 2, which we get; that leads us to expect a concluding rhyme A as well; instead we get rhyme B. The melody sets up expectations in our ears that are deceived by the rhyme. That places even more emphasis on the last two lines of each stanza at the very moment that the tune reaches its highest note and emotional pitch and its final resolution.

The subject of this discord is the lover's pride; the lady's *merces* and *cortesia*, her *beltatz*, *pretz*, and *sens* have gained her nothing. But the entire complaint is set out as if it were a dispute over land or rights, between the *rancur* in line 2 and the remembered *covinens* — the *convenientia* or *concordia* that was the standard name for the agreements that ended conflicts in eleventh- and twelfth-century Occitania. And indeed the word *dreitz* appears about half way between those two words. In *enganad* of line 6 she recalls in its exact word what the faithful man promises by oath that he will avoid (as in the oath of Bernard of Durban to Ermengard) placing that word at the most dramatic turn of the melody. She returns to that oath with *tuoilla* in line 18; for a critical part of all such oaths was the promise *non te decebrai nel ti tolrai ne t'en tolrai*, "I will not deceive you, nor take it from you, nor take of it from you." Finally, in verse 5 she turns her lover into her fighting man doing castle guard, for a common meaning of *estatges* is the dwelling of a person doing guard duty; to him she orders her song to go as a messenger, the messenger so often mentioned in oaths of fidelity, who will serve notice that the castle should be rendered to its overlord. And she ends with a commonplace from many a *chanson de geste*: excess pride brings people to a bad end.

Here is an amorous song, but also a song to remind a man of his duty of fidelity and love to his lord (who may be female). Here is a lesson in proper amorous behavior that is also proper courtly behavior, in the sense of proper behavior toward one's lord and lady and fellow knights: do not out of pride defraud or betray; do not break covenants. Do not give others to whom you are linked by *amor* any cause for *rancura*. Simple lessons, to be sure, and delightfully embellished, but how essential.

Poets such as the Countess of Die could so easily use the language of lordship to talk of romantic sentiment or the language of eroticism to talk of lordship, because the sentiment of "love" was central to both. We have seen Bertran de Born wish for barons to hold their knights with love. The expression was a commonplace. The most courteous complement that William of Tudela, author of the Song of the Albigensian Crusade, could imagine for the young viscount of Béziers was that:

. . . avia ab totz amor,
e sels de son païs, de cui era senhor,
no avian de lui ni regart ni temor,
enans jogan am lui co li fos companhor.

. . . he had love for all;
and those of his lands, over whom he was lord
did not dread or fear him
but played with him as their companion.[92]

Indeed, the unity of the love between lord and follower, the shared love of political allies, of those who fought side by side, and the love of man and lady is most succinctly expressed in the word "drut."

Look this word up in any dictionary or glossary of the Occitan language and you will see it defined as "lover," and so it is almost always translated when it appears — as it frequently does — in poetry.[93]

De totz drutz suy ieu lo plus fis	Of all lovers I am the most faithful,
qu'a midons no dic re ni man	for to my lady I say nothing nor do I
ni·l quier gen fait ni bel semblan;	command her to do anything;
cum qu'ilh m'estey,	I ask neither kind favors nor pretty
sos drutz suy et ab lieys dompney	pretence;
totz cubertz e celatz e quetz.	however she is toward me
	I am her lover and pay court to her
	secretly, discreetly, quietly.[94]

So sings Peire Rogier in a song addressed to his "Tort-n'avetz" (Ermengard of Narbonne, so we are told), and "lover" is surely meant both here and in the other two lines where it appears in this lyric.

"Drut," however, had far wider connotations than our modern word "lover" in its romantic or erotic sense. It was also the word Bertran de Born summoned to his lips in one of his most bloodthirsty lyrics as he let his song imagine "a thousand shields and hauberks and coats of mail pierced through." It is with good cause that Anthony Bonner translates these lines as he does.

E desse que serem vengut	And when we've all arrived,
mesclar s'a·l torneis pel cambo,	the tourney in the fields will start,
e·ll Catalan e·ll d'Arago	and the Catalans and Aragonese
tombaran soven e menut,	will fall thick and fast;
qu no·ls sostenran lor arso,	their saddlebows won't hold them,
tant grans colps lor ferrem, nos drut![95]	we'll hit them so hard, *me and my mates*![96]

"Drut" is derived not from Latin — which provided Old Occitan with the perfectly good "amador" and the frequently used "amics" to mean the same thing — but from an old Germanic source, Frankish "druht," Old English "dryht," Old Norse "drótt." In all these ancient languages the primary meaning of this word had nothing to do with erotic or sentimental relations of men and women. It was the word for "war band," and to Old High German, medieval Latin, French, and Occitan it gave the meaning "faithful friend," in the sense of one who had sworn fidelity.[97] The poetic meaning it gained as "lover" testifies to the emotion that was believed to infuse such military and political relationships. And so when William of Tudela used "drut" to describe the relation of the viscount of Béziers and his followers to the king of Aragon — *Ilh eran sei ome, sei amic, et sei drut* — he was playing on the complex range of meanings the word carried with it. And so, as with the phrase of Bertran de Born, this line must be translated, "they were his men, his friends, and his mates/war companions."[98]

"Drut" appears in political documents of the region as early as 1065, long before the first extant "courtly lyric," when count Raymond IV of Toulouse in an alliance with the redoubtable archbishop Guifred of Narbonne confirmed the prelate's claim to half the city and fortifications of Narbonne and then (the scribe slipping his familiar Occitan into loose Latin dress) made a further grant of rights *per drudarium*, "out of love/in return for military aid."[99] This is surely the word we should hear even when a scribe has translated it into real Latin, as when the lord of Montpellier and count Bernard of Mauguio agreed in 1125 that if the count could prove that the father of the lord of Montpellier had sworn fealty to him, the current lord would also swear fealty and "along with the honor which [the lord of Montpellier] has from the count he shall come into the power and love of the count," *venerit in potestate comitis vel amore*.[100] Love was not out of place in far more modest circumstances, as when in 1114 Peter William of Pignan gave his castle to William V of Montpellier, and for this gift, "Ermessend, wife of William of Montpellier, g[a]ve me 500 s. of Mauguio and 40 s., *pro drudo meo*, "for my love/service," or when, around 1185, an obscure noble family recorded that in the bourg of Millac in Perigord *an lor omes a amar et a chaptener e a rasonar e tener ab eus, o que il los aen, de totas lor naugas*, "in all their quarrels they have love from their men, support in deed and word and loyalty [literally "holding to them"] or they should have them."[101] The word "drut" and the emotion it signified spring into lyric poetry from this far more ancient usage.

*   *   *

When we put this common language of loyalty and love into a society where women could and did rule as territorial lords, we may not answer the major perplexing questions about the origins of troubadour poetry, but we do make its principal thematic material far less problematic. It is not paradoxical that the poetic male first person singular should consider himself the *drut* of his lady, or speak of her as his *douc'amiga*, or of the *fe qu'ieu li dey*, for somewhere in Occitania sometime during the poet's life he had probably heard these very words uttered in a decidedly un-erotic court setting. The widespread use of the language of love to contain ideas of loyalty — sometimes between equals, more often between lord and follower — should also strongly suggest that what we have in the poetry is not a borrowing of terms for metaphorical purposes across some imaginary boundary of discourse, but rather a continuum of linguistic use from the formalized legal at one extreme to the formalized poetic at the other, with everyday speech covering a broad but, alas, ill-illuminated range between them.

If we accept this position, it means that when we see the language of power relations — of loyalty and faith, of treason and deceit — used in what are clearly erotic contexts we have (as has often been seen) a projection of those relations of power and status into the world of intimacy. But by that very move we have likewise a counter-reflection of the force of sexual longing back into the world of power, an eroticization of the ideology of faith and loyalty. By eroticizing those ties, troubadour poetry gave them powerful reenforcement, served both to implant the proper ethos and to elaborate the code of behavior that made it visible. And how powerfully it did so. For that code continued to dominate noble life and speech for half a millennium.[102]

Did it also serve to strengthen the power of women such as Ermengard of Narbonne? Certainly we have the example of queen Elizabeth I in England to show how amorous courtliness could be turned into a powerful tool of royal power. We have no such direct testimonies from the courts of the twelfth century. Yet is the emotive heartbeat of Ermengard's or Beatrice's courts or those of other lordly ladies completely closed to us? Troubadour poetry did accomplish two things, both of which could only have enhanced the power of women rulers. On the one hand it sharply eroticized the values of faithfulness, trust, and open-handedness, of faithfulness even in adversity, even when unrewarded. On the other hand, instead of sharply contrasting the relations of the courtly lover to his lady from the world of manly camaraderie, it made each the extension of the other. Both could only serve to promote the legitimacy of the *domna*, the lady lord. With all its playfulness, its irony and distancing, with all the seeming formulaic quality of its sentiments, in troubadour song we are perhaps indeed hearing — directly and intimately — the beat of that courtly Occitan heart.

Notes

Abbreviations

AD	Archives Départementales (France)
BM	Bibliothèque Municipale (France)
AN	Archives Nationales (Paris)
BN	Bibliothèque Nationale de France (Paris)
GC	*Gallia Christiana in Provincias Ecclesiasticas Distibuta.* Ed. P. Piolin. 16 vols. Paris, 1715–1765.
l., s., d.	*libra, solidus, denarius,* in coins of Paris, Provins (for Champagne) and Mauguio (for Occitania).
MD	*Cartulaire de Marmoutier pour le Dunois.* Ed. E. Mabille. Châteaudun, 1874.
HGL	Claude Devic and Joseph Vaissete. *Histoire générale de Languedoc.* 16 vols. Toulouse, 1872.
MGH, SS	*Monumenta Germaniae Historica: Scriptores.* 31 vols. Hannover, 1826–1933.
OV	Orderic Vitalis, *The Ecclesiastical History* of Orderic Vitalis. Ed. and tr. Marjorie Chibnall. 6 vols. Oxford, 1969–1980. Citations are to book, chapter, and (in parentheses) Chibnall's edition. Paris, 1878.
PL	*Patrologia cursus completus . . . Series Latina.* Ed. J.-P. Migne. 221 vols. Paris, 1844–64.
RHF	*Recueil des historiens des Gaules et de la France.* Ed. Martin Bouquet. 24 vols. Paris, 1738–1904.
SPC	*Cartulaire de l'abbaye de Saint-Père de Chartres.* Ed. B.E.C. Guérard. 2 vols. Chartres, 1840.

Introduction

1. "The Power of Women Through the Family in Medieval Europe, 500–1100," *Feminist Studies* 1 (1973): 126–42, reprinted in revised form in *Women and*

Power in the Middle Ages, ed. Mary Erler and Maryanne Kowaleski (Athens, Ga., 1988), pp. 83–101, at p. 94.

2. *The Chivalrous Society* (essays), tr. Cynthia Postan (Berkeley, 1977); *Medieval Marriage: Two Models from Twelfth-Century France*, tr. Elborg Forster (Baltimore, 1978); *A History of Private Life*, vol. 2: *Revelations of the Medieval World*, tr. Arthur Goldhammer (Cambridge, Mass., 1988), pp. 56–85; and *Love and Marriage in the Middle Ages* (essays), tr. Jane Dunnett (Chicago, 1994). For some evaluations of Duby's models and further reading, see Jack Goody, *The Development of the Family and Marriage in Europe* (Cambridge, 1983), pp. 222–39; Susan M. Stuard, "Fashion's Captives: Medieval Women in French Historiography," in *Women in Medieval History and Historiography*, ed. Stuard (Philadelphia, 1987), pp. 68–76; Kimberly A. LoPrete, review of Georges Duby, *Love and Marriage in the Middle Ages*, *Speculum* 70 (1995): 607–9; and Theodore Evergates, "The Feudal Imaginary of Georges Duby," *Journal of Medieval and Early Modern Studies* 27 (1997): 645–51.

3. See Stuard, "Fashion's Captives," pp. 68–76.

4. Yannick Hillion, "La Bretagne et la rivalité Capétiens-Plantagenêts: un exemple: la duchesse Constance (1186–1202)," *Annales de Bretagne et des pays de l'ouest* 92 (1985): 111–44; Penelope D. Johnson, "Agnes of Burgundy: An Eleventh-Century Woman as Monastic Patron," *Journal of Medieval History* 15 (1989): 93–104; Marjorie Chibnall, "Women in Orderic Vitalis," *Haskins Society Journal* 2 (1990): 105–22; Theresa M. Vann, ed., *Queens, Regents, and Potentates* (Dallas, Tex., 1993); Pauline Stafford, "Women and the Norman Conquest," *Transactions of the Royal Historical Society* 6th ser. 4 (1994): 221–49; Susan Johns, "The Wives and Widows of the Earls of Chester, 1100–1252: The Charter Evidence," *Haskins Society Journal* 7 (1995): 117–32; Marjorie Chibnall, "The Empress Matilda and her Sons," in *Medieval Mothering*, ed. John Carmi Parsons and Bonnie Wheeler (New York, 1996), pp. 279–94; Stephanie Moers Christelow, "The Division of Inheritance and the Provision of Non-Inheriting Offspring Among the Anglo-Norman Elite," *Medieval Prosopography* 17 (1996): 3–44; Kathleen Hapgood Thompson, "Dowry and Inheritance Patterns: Some Examples from the Descendants of King Henry I of England," *Medieval Prosopography*, 17 (1996): 45–61; and Judith A. Green, "Aristocratic Women in Early Twelfth-Century England," in *Anglo-Norman Political Culture and the Twelfth-Century Renaissance*, ed. C. Warren Hollister (Woodbridge, 1997), pp. 59–82.

5. Stuard, "Fashion's Captives," p. 73.

Chapter 1: Adela of Blois

I would like to thank Nora Bartlett, Dáibhí Ó'Cróinín, and in particular Theodore Evergates and Fredric Cheyette for their efforts to improve the legibility of this chapter; difficult passages that remain are the result of my concern to represent the complexities and ambiguities of both the sources and the unfolding events in which Adela participated.

1. "[Understanding how men exchange women] should not be allowed to obscure the fact that women were not purely passive objects," asserted Dominique

Barthélemy ("Kinship," in *A History of Private Life*, Vol. 2, *Revelations of the Medieval World*, ed. Georges Duby [Cambridge, Mass., 1988], p. 119), but his warning has been too little heeded. For studies that emphasize the actions of women see Pauline Stafford, *Queens, Concubines and Dowagers: The King's Wife in the Early Middle Ages* (Athens, Ga., 1983); Eleanor Searle, *Predatory Kinship and the Creation of Norman Power, 840–1066* (Berkeley, Calif., 1988), esp. pp. 159–89, 237–49; Martin Aurell, *Les noces du comte: mariage et pouvoir en Catalogne (785–1213)* (Paris, 1995), esp. pp. 223–95; and Marion Facinger, "A Study of Medieval Queenship: Capetian France, 987–1237," *Studies in Medieval and Renaissance History* 5 (1968): 3–48.

2. Three documents penned by members of the comital household have also survived; I have found no significant surviving nontextual sources that can be linked directly to Adela. For analysis of these sources, especially concerning authorship, date, and the identification of people and places mentioned, see my doctoral dissertation, "A Female Ruler in Feudal Society: Adela of Blois (ca. 1067–ca. 1137)," 2 vols. (University of Chicago, 1992), 2: 467–547; minor corrections and documents discovered since that time are treated in a book I am preparing about Adela.

3. See Chapter 2 of this volume for the activities of lower-ranking lordly women in the Chartrain; and LoPrete, "A Female Ruler," passim, for another thirteen politically active women in northwestern France during Adela's lifetime.

4. I use "rank" to refer to one's place in a social group relative to other social groups; "status" to indicate personal attributes (including birth) that condition one's relations to other individuals, whether those within the same social rank or those in another.

5. For discussion and further literature, see Jane Martindale, "The French Aristocracy in the Early Middle Ages: A Reappraisal," *Past and Present* 75 (1977): 5–45; and Theodore Evergates, "Nobles and Knights in Twelfth-Century France," in *Cultures of Power: Lordship, Status, and Process in Twelfth-Century Europe*, ed. Thomas N. Bisson (Philadelphia, 1995), pp. 11–17, 29–35. Gender cut across rank and status, and the lordly powers of noble women could readily be reconciled with their gender-based social roles, though women who used their powers in ways that harmed the interests of articulate men could find themselves condemned in terms of negative gender-based stereotypes that suggested the very powers they exercised were a transgression of acceptable gender roles. Interestingly, Adela is one lordly woman for whom no gender-based negative judgments of her powers are extant, despite her occasional recourse to violence.

6. Godfrey of Reims, "Ad Ingelrannum archidiaconum de moribus eius," lines 17–38, in André Boutemy, ed., "Trois oeuvres inédites de Godefroid de Reims," *Revue du moyen âge latin* 3 (1947): 343. For Godfrey's connections, see LoPrete, "A Female Ruler," 1: 22–32.

7. Ivo of Chartres, ep. 5 (to Adela), in *Yves de Chartres: correspondance*, ed. and trans. Jean Leclercq (Paris, 1949), p. 14. Adela's royal blood from her mother is well attested; for Adela to carry royal blood from her father, he had to have been a king at the time of her conception.

8. Orderic Vitalis, *The Ecclesiastical History of Orderic Vitalis*, ed. and trans. Marjorie Chibnall, 6 vols. (Oxford, 1969–80), 5.11 (3: 116) (cited hereafter as OV); and *Gesta Ambaziensium dominorum*, in *Chroniques des comtes d'Anjou et des*

seigneurs d'Amboise, ed. Louis Halphen and René Poupardin (Paris, 1913), pp. 96–98; for dates and further discussion see Kimberly A. LoPrete, "The Anglo-Norman Card of Adela of Blois," *Albion* 22 (1990): 572–75.

9. All these possessions (with the exception of minor acquisitions in Berry) had been inherited by Odo II from his father and hence could be considered "patrimonial" lands when inherited in turn by Thibaut III; see Michel Bur, *La formation du comté de Champagne, v. 950–v. 1150* (Nancy, 1977), pp. 154–73, 180–81, 238–41; and Guy Devailly, *Le Berry du Xe siècle au milieu du XIII: étude politique, religieuse, sociale et économique* (Paris, 1973), pp. 131–34, 359.

10. These lands had been acquired by Odo II through inheritance from a childless distant cousin and blood relative of his paternal grandmother (Bur, *La formation*, pp. 157–58). Thibaut first controlled them in the name of his nephew Odo; after conflict between uncle and nephew when Odo came of age in the early 1060s, Odo left his family lands to join William the Conqueror and received rich rewards for his service: arguably a resolution to a family conflict facilitated by Thibaut's growing cooperation with William (LoPrete, "A Female Ruler," 1: 52–53).

11. Louis Halphen, *Le comté d'Anjou au XIe siècle* (Paris, 1906), pp. 47–48. The Thibaudians also lost comital rights in Reims and Châlons-sur-Marne (Bur, *La formation*, pp. 203, 209), though Thibaut acquired further rights in northern Burgundy ("Chronicon breve autissiodorense," in *RHF*, 11: 292b; and Yves Sassier, *Recherches sur le pouvoir comtal en Auxerrois du Xe au début du XIIIe siècle* [Auxerre-Paris, 1980], pp. 47–57).

12. See n. 200 below.

13. The sources for, and more detailed discussion of, the events of this and the next two paragraphs can be found in LoPrete, "The Anglo-Norman Card of Adela of Blois," pp. 572–75; and LoPrete, "A Female Ruler," 1: 40–59.

14. Thibaut III's "second marriage," perhaps never fully solemnized, to one Agnes (most likely Agnes of Burgundy, newly-divorced wife of the count of Anjou and mother-in-law of the emperor Henry III), has been overlooked by historians; see, in particular, the 1050–51 letter of John of Fécamp to pope Leo IX (*PL*, 143: 799–800); *Chartes et documents pour servir à l'histoire de l'abbaye de Saint-Maxient*, 2 vols., ed. Alfred Richard, Archives historique du Poitou, 16 (Poitiers, 1886), 1: 140–41, no. 112; and Jean Dhondt, "Henri Ier, l'Empire et l'Anjou (1043–1056)," *Revue belge de philologie et d'histoire* 25 (1946–47): 104–6 (for context). The union lasted from 1049 to ca. 1056 and produced no children; in 1058–60 Thibaut married Adelaide of Valois, likewise to strengthen his position in the east (Bur, *La formation*, pp. 209–11, 214–17).

15. Thibaut did skirmish with Geoffrey Martel the count of Anjou in the Vendômois in these years, perhaps in order to allow Bertha and her son to escape to Normandy (*Cartulaire de l'abbaye cardinale de la Trinité de Vendôme*, ed. Charles Métais, 5 vols. [Paris, 1893–1904], 1: 202–203, 210, 247, nos. 105, 109, 141).

16. William was supported by local men with ties to the Thibaudians, and again Stephen-Henry made no claim to the county in his own right. It was probably also about this time that William found a husband for Stephen-Henry's illegitimate daughter among his supporters in Maine (Kimberly A. LoPrete, "Adela of Blois as

Mother and Countess," in *Medieval Mothering*, ed. John Carmi Parsons and Bonnie Wheeler [New York, 1996], p. 329 n. 22).

17. Geoffrey is attested as a negotiator for the marriage (*Gesta Ambaziensium dominorum*, pp. 96–98); having held Chaumont from Thibaut, he joined William in 1066 and fought with him in the 1070s, at a time when he also visited the Thibaudian court (LoPrete, "Anglo-Norman Card," pp. 574–75); for Simon of Crépy, also a distant relation of queen Matilda, who helped reconcile William and his son, see "Vita beati Simonis comitis Crespeiensis," chs. 11 and 5 (*PL*, 156: 1219, 1215); *Recueil des actes de Philippe Ier, roi de France (1059–1108)*, ed. Maurice Prou (Paris, 1908), pp. 318–21, no. 126; Frank Barlow, "William I's Relations with Cluny," *Journal of Ecclesiastical History* 32 (1981): 137; and H. E. J. Cowdrey, "Count Simon of Crépy's Monastic Conversion," in *Papauté, monachisme et théories politiques: études d'histoire médiévale offertes à Marcel Pacaut*, 2 vols., ed. Pierre Guichard, et al. (Lyon, 1989), 1: 261–66.

18. William had other daughters of marriageable age: Constance, not married until 1086, Matilda (who died by 1113), and perhaps even Adeliza/Adelaide who died at a nubile age by 1087 and had apparently consecrated herself to God though she had been the object of marriage negotiations by her father on other occasions.

19. For Adela providing cash for Stephen-Henry's first crusade venture, see n. 48; of contemporaries who noted Adela's great wealth see particularly Hugh of Fleury, epilogue to the first version of his "Historia ecclesiastica" (*PL*, 163: 829b): "When [William the Conqueror] died, he left the ruling of his duchy and his kingdom to his sons, your [Adela's] brothers, by hereditary right, as is proper; and he bestowed on you that wealth which always accompanied him."

20. *Cartulaire de Marmoutier pour le Dunois*, ed. Emile Mabille (Châteaudun, 1874), pp. 78–92, no. 92, and pp. 60–62, nos. 67–68 (where land donated by Adela is referred to as *dos ejus*) (cited hereafter as *MD*).

21. See OV, 5.11 (3: 116); David C. Douglas, *William the Conqueror: The Norman Impact upon England* (Berkeley, 1964), pp. 243–44, 346–63; and LoPrete, "Anglo-Norman Card," p. 575.

22. For Chartres and the death of Matilda, who had met with one of the negotiators, see OV, 5.11, 7.9 (3: 116, 4: 44/46); Adela was certainly married by 1085 (*Cartulaire du prieuré de La Charité-sur-Loire (Nièvre), ordre de Cluny*, ed. René de Lespinasse [Paris-Nevers, 1887], pp. 201–3, no. 94), but does not appear to have been married by January 1083 (Henry d'Arbois de Jubainville, *Histoire des ducs et des comtes de Champagne*, 7 vols. [Paris, 1859–69], 1: 497–99, no. 59). See also John Carmi Parsons, "Mothers, Daughters, Marriage, Power: Some Plantagenet Evidence, 1150–1500," in *Medieval Queenship*, ed. Parsons (New York, 1993), pp. 63–68, for twelfth- and thirteenth-century evidence of delaying marriage and/or sexual consummation of aristocratic brides until fifteen and mothers' roles in arranging daughters' marriages.

23. See n. 8 above.

24. See LoPrete, "Adela of Blois as Mother," pp. 315–16; these points will be developed more fully in my book.

25. See LoPrete, "Adela of Blois as Mother," p. 315, for sources and further literature.

26. Lespinasse, *La Charité-sur-Loire*, pp. 201–3, no. 94; for a variant version of the same act, see Arbois de Jubainville, *Histoire*, 1: 499–500, no. 60.

27. See below, pp. 25–26; LoPrete, "Adela of Blois as Mother," pp. 317–19, 323–24.

28. For Adela's role in educating her children see LoPrete, "Adela of Blois as Mother," pp. 318–20.

29. See LoPrete, "Adela of Blois as Mother," pp. 316–17.

30. The traditional view (Bur, *La formation*, p. 233) that William the Conqueror was responsible for this division is unlikely, as he had been dead for two years by 1089; that Stephen-Henry inherited other patrimonial lands near Meaux indicates Thibaut was assuring that his son inherit a more territorially cohesive portion of the family's eastern domains than he himself had (see LoPrete, "A Female Ruler," 1: 76–79).

31. LoPrete, "A Female Ruler," 1: 76–79.

32. Jean Bernier, *Histoire de Blois* (Paris, 1682), *preuves*, pp. xiii–xiv (reprinted in Arbois de Jubainville, *Histoire*, 1: 504–5, no. 65), a charter Adela also validated; and BN, Fr. 12021, pp. 8–10, a charter Adela also subscribed.

33. For Adelaide, see n. 14 above and acts cited in LoPrete, "A Female Ruler," 1: 88 n. 7.

34. Ivo of Chartres, ep. 5 (Leclercq, pp. 14/16); see further discussion in Kimberly A. LoPrete, "Adela of Blois and Ivo of Chartres: Piety, Politics, and the Peace in the Diocese of Chartres," *Anglo-Norman Studies* 14 (1991): 135–36.

35. *MD*, pp. 133–34, no. 145.

36. Ivo of Chartres, ep. 17 (Leclercq, p. 74) to the canons of St. Quentin, Beauvais, the community to which he belonged before his episcopal election: "I am bound by the love of the clergy, by the devotion of the people, and by the benevolence of the prince (*benevolentia principis*) which were granted to me so freely that even the countess, without my even asking—or rather, over my protestations—devotedly swore an oath in my hand on behalf of both herself and the count, to serve me in all faith and not to abandon me in any persecution I might suffer while upholding divine law"; see also LoPrete, "Adela of Blois and Ivo," p. 135.

37. *Marmoutier cartulaire blésois*, ed. Charles Métais (Blois, 1889–91), pp. 77–78, no. 67 (1094) (cited hereafter as *MB*): "count Stephen and his wife countess Adela consented to this"; and *Recueil des chartes de l'abbaye de Saint-Germain-des-Près des origines au début du XIIIe siècle*, ed. René Poupardin (Paris, 1909), 1: 114–15, no. 70 (1096): "[the bishop] . . . persuaded also by the prayerful requests of count Stephen and his wife Adela."

38. Notcher of Hautvillers, "Miracula sanctae Helenae apud Altumvillare," in *Acta sanctorum ordinis Sancti Benedicti in saeculorum classes distributa*, ed. Jean Mabillon (Paris, 1680), 4^2: 156: "Thereupon, censing the holy ashes with the fragrant thurifer, we extracted from inside [the old reliquary] the label on which we read written, 'the body of St. Helen, queen, mother of Constantine, without head.' Then the label both was read out by countess Adela, the wife of count palatine Stephen, and interpreted by other powerful persons"; earlier in the narrative Adela was called "the daughter of William, king of the English." The only documentary evidence for the market is the passing reference in Paschal II's bull of 9 March 1102 confirming

the house's possessions in which Stephen alone was named as its founder (see Jean-Baptiste Manceaux, *Histoire de l'abbaye et du village d'Hautvillers* [Epernay, 1880], 1: 377–80), although Notcher describes his consultation with Philip and Constance, as well as the consent of the viscount of Mareuil-sur-Ay, Dudo.

39. BM, Reims, MS 15, fol. 12; the land alienated was at Fismes.

40. *Cartulaire de Notre-Dame de Chartres*, ed. Eugène de Lépinois and Lucien Merlet, 3 vols. (Chartres, 1862–65), 1: 98–99, no. 21 (cited hereafter as *NDC*); this document is in a form developed at the Anglo-Norman court and thus might reflect the influence of chaplains from her brothers' court imported by Adela; for one "imported" chaplain, see n. 105 below; *Cartulaire de l'abbaye de Saint-Père de Chartres*, ed. Benjamin E. C. Guérard, 2 vols. (Paris, 1840), 2: 295, no. 39 (cited hereafter as *SPC*); this charter was apparently validated by Adela alone.

41. Noël Mars, *Histoire du royal monastère de Sainct-Lomer de Blois de l'ordre de Sainct-Benoist* (1646), ed. Alexandre Dupré (Blois, 1869), p. 113; Bernier, *Blois*, p. 293 and plate: "Count Stephen and countess Adela and their heirs remitted in perpetuity to the men of this land the tax on wine sales (*butagium*) on condition that they close the gate in the walled fortification (*castellum*); let whosoever violates this agreement be anathema and cursed like Dathan and Abiron."

42. "Miracula sancti Aigulphi," in *Acta Sanctorum quotquot orbe coluntur*, 67 vols. (imprint varies, 1643–1940), at Sept., 1: 758; the author, perhaps referring to a now-lost charter, also noted that the couple were to retain their customs on vehicles journeying to trade at the fair.

43. *Cartulaire de l'église de Notre-Dame de Paris*, ed. Benjamin E. C. Guérard, 4 vols. (Paris, 1850), 2: 265–66, no. 3; the advocates' customs, from land at Rozay-en-Brie, southwest of Coulommiers in the county of Meaux, were granted to the cathedral of Paris; the participating sons were William and Stephen.

44. *MD*, pp. 134–35, no. 146; see also n. 35 above. There are several passing references in letters and documents of others to further actions of Stephen; the evidence discussed here suggests that Stephen at least would have consulted his wife before acting.

45. See especially *MD*, pp. 60–62, 67–68, 68–71, 78–82, nos. 67, 76, 77, 92; *MB*, pp. 114–16, no. 118; BN, Lat. 12776, pp. 247–48; *Cartulaire de l'abbaye de Conques en Rouergue*, ed. Gustave Desjardins (Paris, 1879), pp. 340–42, no. 470; Notcher of Hautvillers, "Miracula," 4²: 156; Guibert of Nogent, *Gesta Dei per Francos*, 2.15, in *Recueil des historiens des croisades, historiens occidentaux*, 5 vols. (Paris, 1841–1906), 4: 148; Hugh of Fleury, "Historia ecclesiastica" (*PL*, 163: 824b, 829a); William of Nangis, "Chronicon" (*RHF*, 20: 726d); Baudry of Bourqueil, *carmen* 129, lines 43–44, and *carmen* 134, lines 7–8, in *Baldricus Burgulianus, Carmina*, ed. Karlheinz Hilbert (Heidelberg, 1979), pp. 145, 149; Geoffrey Grossus, "Vita beati Bernardi Tironiensis," ed. Godefrey Henskens, ch. 9 (*PL*, 172: 1413b); Hildebert of Lavardin, *carmen* 15, in *Hildeberti Cenomannensis Episcopi, Carmina Minora*, ed. A. Brian Scott (Leipzig, 1969), p. 5; the anonymous poem discussed and published by André Boutemy, "Deux pièces inédites du manuscrit 749 de Douai," *Latomus* 2 (1938): 123–27. For Baudry on Adela's literacy, see his *carmen* 134, lines 37–42 (Hilbert, p. 150).

46. See Andrew W. Lewis, "Anticipatory Association of the Heir in Early

Capetian France," *American Historical Review* 83 (1978): 911–25 (though his information on the practice in the Thibaudian family must be revised in light of documents concerning William, unknown to him, and discussed below at nn. 69–70).

47. Because of his princely status, maturity, military experience, and reputation for generosity and wise counsel, Stephen was chosen as a leader of the combined Christian army (Heinrich Hagenmeyer, ed., *Die Kreuzzugsbriefe aus den Jahren 1088–1100* [Innsbruck, 1901]), pp. 149–52, ep. 10; and further discussion in LoPrete, "A Female Ruler," 2: 558–78).

48. Hagenmeyer, *Die Kreuzzugsbriefe*, pp. 149–52, ep. 10: "Know for certain, my beloved, that I now have double the gold and silver and other great wealth, which your love had bestowed on me, than I had when I left you." The wealth Stephen acquired after his initial travel expenses was in part the result of his close relationship to the emperor Alexios (Hagenmeyer, *Die Kreuzzugsbriefe*, pp. 138–40, ep. 4).

49. Hagenmeyer, *Die Kreuzzugsbriefe*, pp. 149–52, ep. 10: "mando, ut bene agas et terrae tuae egregie disponas et natos tuos et homines tuos honeste, ut decet te, tractes"; the letter was addressed "Adelae dulcissimae atque amabilissimae coniugi, carissimisque filiis suis atque cunctis fidelibus suis tam maioribus quam minoribus."

50. OV, 11.5 (6: 42); and *Gesta Ambaziensium dominorum*, p. 109.

51. Frank Barlow, *William Rufus* (Berkeley, 1983), pp. 32–35, 331–36, 355–59, 362–63; Hugh of Flavigny, "Chronicon," ed. George Pertz, bk 2 (*PL*, 154: 354C); and OV, 9.3, 10.4 (5: 26, 208).

52. Robert Latouche, *Histoire du comté du Maine pendant le Xe et le XIe siècle* (Paris, 1910), pp. 41–51; Barlow, *Rufus*, pp. 331–36, 355–59, 362–63, 381–88, 390–92, 402–4; and OV, 8.11, 10.8 (4: 192/98, 5: 228/32).

53. See Arbois de Jubainville, *Histoire*, 1: 510–14, no. 72 for the reprint of an edition from the original or a copy of the original; an edition of a twelfth-century cartulary copy of the act is published in *MD*, pp. 78–82, no. 92. The original document, showing autograph crosses, the slits, and Adela's "signature," can be consulted in AD, Loir-et-Cher, 16 H 105, no. 2; the discussion here is based on my examination of the original. The monks' use of solemn diploma form matches the magnitude of the grant. The last donation of western land in extant documentation was Thibaut III's 1059 gift of a parcel of the Blémars forest to round out earlier family grants (*MB*, pp. 38–40, no. 32), though the family continued to give Marmoutier monks lands from their eastern domains.

54. The drafters of the act incorrectly identified these ancestors as Stephen's grandfather (*avus*), Odo (II); Odo's brother Hugh, archbishop of Bourges; and their unnamed mother. The now incomplete later copy of the Marmoutier necrology (Paul Nobilleau, ed., *Necrologium beatissimi Martini Turonensis (804–1495) et obitarius (sic) Majoris Monasterii* [Tours, 1875], pp. 51, 53, 56) indicates that Odo I (Stephen's great-grandfather); his wife, Bertha of Burgundy; Odo I's brother, the archbishop Hugh; and Odo II's wife, Ermengard, were buried in the abbey church. Since the necrology is missing entries for November, the month in which Odo II died in battle at Bar-le-Duc, it is not impossible that Odo II was also buried at Marmoutier, but the mother of Odo I and archbishop Hugh was buried at St. Père, Chartres. The important point here is that, by any reckoning, those named in the

charter were not Stephen's direct male patrilineal ascendants. Thibaut III was buried in 1089 in Epernay, at a house of canons restored by his father and dedicated, like Marmoutier, to Saint-Martin (see Arbois de Jubainville, *Histoire*, 1: 468–70, no. 35, and 3: 417, no. 84).

55. Here, the land donated is called a part of *allodium nostrum*; in *MD*, p. 62, no. 68 (a notification of Adela's settlement of a dispute on the same land in 1101), the land is called Adela's *dos*. When the crusader Nivelo II of Fréteval gave the monks his customs on the land granted, he stated that it had been donated by both Stephen and Adela (*MD*, pp. 56–57, no. 64).

56. "Unde ut presentem cartam sive preceptum tuitionis gratia immunitatisque impressione sigilli mei, ex auctoritate viri mei atque mea sigillatum, et assensu liberorum nostrorum + in presentia testium circumstantium, quorum nomina subscribuntur, dominice crucis impressione + propriis manibus facta roboratum et auctorizatum ipsis, id est monachis Majoris Monasterii tradidi + +." The terms *sigillare / sigillum* did not necessarily mean "seal" at this time; they could also refer to a monogram or other symbolic sign (R. Allen Brown, "Some Observations on Norman and Anglo-Norman Charters," in *Tradition and Change: Essays in Honour of Marjorie Chibnall*, ed. G. D. Greenway, C. Holdsworth, and J. Sayers [Cambridge, 1985], p. 154). Most of the witnesses were lay followers and household officials from across the Thibaudian domains.

57. The crosses were not labeled, but were probably made by Adela's sons William, Thibaut, Stephen, and Odo. For another original document on which Adela wrote her own name, see AD, Loir-et-Cher, F 246 (1106–7, donation to Saint-Lomer, Blois). Stephen's seal has been lost, but was described and sketched by Noël Mars when he made a copy of the original in the seventeenth century for Roger Gaignières (BN, Lat. 5441², pp. 129–32, 137); this sketch was lithographically reproduced in *MB*, plate XI, no. 3. It is similar in appearance and mode of sealing to the seal of Fulk IV le Réchin, count of Anjou (Oliver Guillot, *Le comte d'Anjou et son entourage au XIe siècle*, 2 vols. [Paris, 1972], 2: 11–12 and n. 33, 235; *MB*, plate XII, no. 12; and next note).

58. For sealed letters Adela sent from Marcigny, see AD, Loiret, 2 mi 785 (olim H182, item KI) and AD, Loir-et-Cher, 16 H 109, no. 15; the seals were attested in the sixteenth and seventeenth centuries respectively, but have since been lost. Adela's practice of using her husband's seal on an official document and her own seal after her retirement appears at first sight to parallel that of her contemporary, Bertrada of Montfort, who was both countess of Anjou and queen of France prior to her monastic retirement, though there are also indications suggesting that Adela occasionally sealed documents prior to her retirement. Bertrada's seal, with her royal title, is the first seal of a French woman for which at least a sketch survives (see Brigitte Bedos-Rezak, "Women, Seals, and Power in Medieval France, 1150–1350," in *Women and Power in the Middle Ages*, ed. Mary Erler and Maryanne Kowaleski [Athens, Ga., 1988], p. 63). Bertrada's first husband was the first count of Anjou to seal documents, as Adela's husband was the first Thibaudian count to use a seal. The seal of Adela's sister-in-law, Matilda, wife of Henry I and queen of England from 1100, survives in impressions made ca. 1116, while she was still active in the royal court; it was apparently similar in appearance to the seal of Adela's sister, Cecilia, as

abbess of La Trinité, Caen, in 1113–27 (T. A. Heslop, "Seals," in *English Romanesque Art, 1066–1200* [London, 1984], pp. 299, 305, no. 336). Adela may well have been the first countess in France to use a seal, and she is as likely to have been influenced by Anglo-Norman usages as by 'French' ones; I am developing these points in my book on Adela.

59. *MD*, pp. 148–49, no. 158, and for the name, p. 62, no. 68.

60. The synod was held on 26 October 1096 (Ivo of Chartres, ep. 62 [Leclercq, p. 258] and, for date, Harmut Hoffmann, *Gottesfriede und Treuga Dei*, Schriften der Monumenta Germaniae Historica, no. 20 [Stuttgart, 1964], p. 196); the exact date of Stephen's departure in October is unknown. For more on peace statutes and their enforcement in Chartres, see LoPrete, "Adela of Blois and Ivo," pp. 136–41.

61. BN, Lat. 12776, pp. 247–48; in exchange, Adela received prayers for her husband's safety on crusade as well for the couple's eternal salvation.

62. *MB*, pp. 85–86, no. 74, concerning Geoffrey of Chaumont-sur-Loire, who, after the death of William the Conqueror, is reported to have ceded his English possessions to his nephew Savaric before returning to France to live primarily at the court of Stephen and Adela, where he would die ca. 1109, when about 100 years old (*Gesta Ambaziensium dominorum*, pp. 97–98); this act indicates that he was acting as lord of Chaumont while his great-nephew Hugh was on crusade; it also noted that Geoffrey had accompanied Adela on a trip to *Francia*. And *MD*, pp. 146–47, no. 156, concerning Hugh, the viscount of Châteaudun and second son of Rotrou II of Nogent; the document specified that the priory concerned was in Adela's *custodia*.

63. Ivo of Chartres, ep. 70 (*PL*, 162: 90b), datable to ca. 1098; the bishop of Meaux, unlike Ivo, was a royal nominee; for details, see LoPrete, "A Female Ruler," 2: 301–3.

64. For a review of the sources concerning Stephen's behavior on crusade, see LoPrete, "A Female Ruler," 2: 548–628; for sanctions, see James A. Brundage, *Medieval Canon Law and the Crusader* (Madison, Wis., 1969), pp. 37–39, 127–29.

65. OV, 10.12, 10.20 (5: 268, 5: 322/24); the words put into Adela's mouth in the second of these passages were those of Orderic, writing some thirty-five years after the purported conversation took place; see also Guibert of Nogent, *Gesta Dei*, 7.24 (*Recueil des historiens des croisades, historiens occidentaux*, 4: 243); and Desjardins, *Conques*, pp. 340–42, no. 470, for the names of some who accompanied Stephen. Guibert's crusade history is available in an English translation by Robert Levine, *The Deeds of God Through the Franks* (Woodbridge, 1997).

66. The text of the privilege is most readily accessible in the composite edition in *NDC*, 1: 104–8, no. 24; for discussion of the various issues and copies of them, see LoPrete, "Adela of Blois and Ivo," pp. 141–43; see also Ivo of Chartres, ep. 94 (*PL*, 162: 114).

67. See Augustin Fliche, *Le règne de Philippe Ier, roi de France (1060–1108)* (Paris, 1912), pp. 40–51; and Karl F. Werner, "Kingdom and Principality in Twelfth-Century France," in *The Medieval Nobility: Studies on the Ruling Classes of France and Germany from the Sixth to the Twelfth Century*, ed. Timothy Reuter (New York and Amsterdam, 1978), pp. 281, 254 n. 34 (an article originally published in German in 1968).

68. *Recueil des chartes de l'abbaye de Cluny*, ed. Auguste Bernard and Alexandre

Bruel, 6 vols. (Paris, 1876–1903): 5: 63–64, no. 3717 (after original, BN, Collection de Bourgogne, vol. 79, fol. 14); for acknowledgment of Adela's intervention in earlier phases of the dispute see Urban II, ep. 286 (PL, 151: 538–39); see also LoPrete, "A Female Ruler," 1: 114–22. Related measures were taken by Stephen and Adela in Provins and their lands in northern Berry (LoPrete, "A Female Ruler," 1: 122–27.)

69. *Cartulaire l'abbaye de Saint-Corneille de Compiègne*, ed. Emile-Epiphanius Morel (Montdidier, 1904), 1: 54–55, no. 23, a document now known only from cartulary copies; the estates concerned were at Goussancourt. An analogous presentation of Stephen, Adela, and sons speaking in unison is found in the privilege for Chartres cathedral (n. 66 above), though in that instance William and his participating brothers were named only with their subscriptions. For Alexander see also Hagenmeyer, *Die Kreuzzugsbriefe*, p. 152, ep. 10; and "Chronicon Sancti Petri Vivi Senonensis," in *Chronique de Saint-Pierre-le-Vif de Sens, dite de Clarius*, ed. Robert-Henri Bautier and Monique Gilles (Paris, 1979), pp. 184/86.

70. Orderic described William as a boy too young to fight in 1101 (OV, 11.15 [6: 156/58]), though by 1103 he appeared acting as a man (Ivo of Chartres, ep. 134, 136 [PL, 162: 144b, 145b]). For acts in which William appeared with his parents at this time, see AD, Eure-et-Loir, H 613 (Thibaut IV's 1118 confirmation of two earlier grants for Bonneval); and Morel, *Saint-Corneille de Compiègne*, 1: 54–55, no. 23; see also the act cited in n. 66 above.

71. *Cartulaires de l'abbaye de Molesme, ancien diocèse de Langres, 916–1250*, ed. Jacques Laurent, 2 vols. (Paris, 1907–11): 2: 141, no. 143; and *GC*, 8, *instrumenta*: 548–89, no. 3. Regent as a title was extremely rare at this time and no formal office of regent yet existed in aristocratic households.

72. Laurent, *Molesme*, 2: 25–26, 31–32, nos. 18, 21.

73. See LoPrete, "Adela of Blois as Mother," p. 319.

74. See below, pp. 31–32, 35; the evidence for Adela's children and their activities is discussed in greater detail in LoPrete, "Adela of Blois as Mother," pp. 317–24.

75. Robert of Torigni, *Gesta Normannorum Ducum*, in *The "Gesta Normannorum Ducum" of William of Jumièges, Orderic Vitalis, and Robert of Torigni*, ed. Elisabeth M. C. van Houts, 2 vols. (Oxford, 1992–95): 8.39 (2: 276): "Mortuo autem Stephano comite Blesensi marito Adele, filie Willelmi regis Anglorum, ipsa aliquandiu nobiliter rexit comitatum, quia filii sui adhuc minus habiles ad procurandum regimen erant. Quibus adultis ipsa sanctimonialis habitum . . . assumens."

76. *NDC*, 1: 131–34, no. 43: "In quo intervallo [between ca. 1107 and 1128] contigit ipsum papam [Paschal II, d. Jan. 1118] et ipsum episcopum [Ivo, d. Dec. 1115] de hoc mundo migrasse, et matrem meam vitam monachicam accepisse [April/May 1120] et dominium Carnotensis comitatus in manum meam devenisse."

77. For charters involving Thibaut as count at Chartres during the 1111–13 or 1117–19 wars, see *MD*, pp. 83–86, 163–66, nos. 93–94, 173, and *SPC*, 2: 299, no. 455; some of his charters were simply confirmations of acts of his parents, for example, AD, Eure-et-Loir, H613 (1118, concerning Bonneval), and BN, Lat. 12878, fol. 306r, no. 352 (ca. 1107–20, at Meaux).

78. *SPC*, 2: 454–55, no. 60 (1107, with Odo and the doctor [*medicus*] Albert); see also *SPC*, 2: 309–10, no. 57 for Adela and the *medicus* Bernard. For anniversaries,

see *NDC*, 1: 104–8, no. 24; BN, Lat. 12878, fol. 306r, no. 352; and *Un manuscrit Chartrain du XI siècle*, ed. René Merlet and the abbot Clerval (Chartres, 1893), p. 149.

79. See LoPrete, "Adela of Blois as Mother," p. 318.

80. Robert of Torigni, 8.38 (van Houts, 2: 276); see also OV, 1.26 (6: 304).

81. For the earliest dated (1103) anniversary bequest, one by Hugh and Constance, see *Chronique de Saint-Pierre-le-Vif*, pp. 264–65, no. 9; for Adela's bequests, see *SPC*, 2: 309–10, 323–24, 408–9, 411–12, nos. 57, 78, 10, 14; Merlet and Clerval, *Un manuscrit*, p. 164; *MD*, pp. 68–71, no. 77; Mars, *Sainct-Lomer*, pp. 142–45; *Recueil de chartes et documents de Saint-Martin-des-Champs, monastère Parisien*, ed. Jacques Depoin, vol. 1, Archives de la France monastique, 13 (Paris, 1912): 1: 159, no. 98; AD, Cher, 13 H 36 (at Saint-Satur-sous-Sancerre); and BN, Lat. 12878, fol. 306r, no. 352 (at a Marmoutier priory in Meaux).

82. Mars, *Sainct-Lomer*, pp. 142–45; Laurent LePelletier, *Rerum scitu dignissimarum a prima fundatione Monasterii S. Nicolai Andegavensis ad hunc usque diem, Epitome*, 2nd ed. (Angers, 1635), p. 59; AD, Seine-et-Marne, H 824; see also her later grants: *Chartes et documents de l'abbaye Cistercienne de Preuilly*, ed. Albert Catel and Maurice Lecomte (Montereau, 1927), pp. 3–5, 15–17, nos. 1, 15 (1118); Laurent, *Molesme*, 2: 440, no. 524 (1119); and *NDC*, 1: 113, no. 29 (1120). As a nun, Adela was asked to pray for the salvation of her brother Henry (Peter the Venerable, ep. 15, in *The Letters of Peter the Venerable*, ed. Giles Constable, 2 vols. [Cambridge, Mass., 1967], 1: 22).

83. For 1100–1102, see Ivo of Chartres, ep. 91 (*PL*, 162: 112 [1100–1102]); and "Miracula sancti Agili, resbacensis abbatis," ed. Jean Mabillon (*AASS, OSB*, 2: 331; also rpt. in *AASS*, at Aug. 6: 591). For 1105, see Eadmer, *Historia novorum in Anglia*, ed. Martin Rule, Rolls Series, no. 81 (London, 1884), bk 4, p. 164.

84. See LoPrete, "A Female Ruler," 1: 137–79; and LoPrete, "Adela of Blois and Ivo," pp. 143–46.

85. *MD*, pp. 56–57, 60–62, 67–71, nos. 64, 67–68, 76–77; *MB*, pp. 56–57, 111, nos. 44, 111; Mars, *Sainct-Lomer*, pp. 142–45; see also Jean Martin-Demézil, "Les forêts du comté de Blois jusqu'à la fin XVe siècle," *Mémoires de la Société des Sciences et Lettres de Loir-et-Cher* 34 (1963): 221–36; 35 (1974): 134–48.

86. Details on these points (which correct and supplement the findings of Bur, *La formation*, p. 425) will be provided in my book.

87. See above, pp. 20, 25, 27–28, 39, for Adela represented as ruling; for Adela as a prince, see the letters of Ivo and Anselm quoted in nn. 36, 110; as a ruling duke, see below, n. 185.

88. OV, 11.15 (6: 156/58).

89. Ivo of Chartres, ep. 91, 116, 121, 133, 141, 168, 173, 179, 187 (*PL*, 162: 112, 132, 134–35, 141–43, 148, 170–72, 176–77, 180–81, 190); and LoPrete, "Adela of Blois and Ivo," pp. 131–52.

90. Hildebert, ep. 1[3] (*PL*, 171: 144–45; rpt. in Peter von Moos, *Hildebert von Lavardin, 1056–1133: Humanitas an der Schwelle des höfischen Zeitalters* [Stuttgart, 1965], pp. 341–43): "Absentia mariti, laboriosior tibi cura consulatus incubuit. Eam tamen et femina sic administras et una, ut nec viro, nec precariis consiliis necesse sit adiuvari. Apud te est quidquid ad regni gubernacula postulatur. . . .

Quippe formosa pudica sibi providet; mitis autem principatus regnum servat incolume. Huius profecto virtutis locus est apud potentes, qui iure parentum, vel vi, vel electionis beneficio caeteris principantur. Apud populum vero non ita, cui nulla est potestas puniendi"; later in the letter Hildebert links the exercise of clemency to the use of reason, the divinely-bestowed faculty that distinguishes humans from animals.

91. Hildebert, ep. 3^8 (*PL*, 171: 288–89), as translated in n. 98, below; see also Ivo of Chartres, ep. 141 (*PL*, 162: 148).

92. BN, Lat. 13900, fols. 94r–v.

93. Martin-Demézil, "Les forêts," 35: (1974), 197–203, no. 2; La Ferté-Hubert is the modern La Ferté-St.-Cyr.

94. Desjardins, *Conques*, p. 354, no. 487.

95. Desjardins, *Conques*, pp. 353–54, no. 486, as corrected against AD, Seine-et-Marne, H 824; Gerard was called one of Adela's *fevales* who held the land from her.

96. Desjardins, *Conques*, pp. 34–42, no. 470 (January 28, 1101).

97. For Adela presented as a *domina* who exercised comital authority in 1111–12 and 1117–19, see Lucien Merlet, ed., "Lettres d'Ives de Chartres et d'autres personnages de son temps, 1087–1130," *Bibliothèque de l'Ecole des Chartes* 16 (1835): 470, no. 35; and *Cartulaire de l'abbaye de la Sainte-Trinité de Tiron*, ed. Lucien Merlet, 2 vols. (Chartres, 1883): 1: 28–29, no. 14, together with AD, Eure-et-Loir, H 1374, fol. 30r, in which Thibaut referred to Adela as his *domina et mater*.

98. Hildebert, ep. 3^8 (*PL*, 171: 288–89 [1104]): "In your husband's absence [Stephen was in fact dead when Hildebert wrote], care for the county lies more heavily upon you. Such care for diverse things obliges you to rely more on agility of mind than bodily endowments. I don't know where to find you, but I'm certain that wherever you are I'll find service to honorable conduct. Since I'm at home, I send letters to the lord (*domina*), which can be summarized as follows: 'I understand you provided the bishop of Chartres an armed escort to travel to a council; if this be so, I pray that you grant me the same benefice of grace (*gratia beneficium*).' As Symmachus says: 'Experience teaches persons wanting something to fly to proven decision-makers and judges.' Thus I wing my way to your protection (*patrocinium*) because, more than all other women, you are both an example and an instrument of *virtus*. The good things of past times are alive in you, through which both your sex is glorified and your ancestors retain their dignity. I could be accused of lying, except that some of the best and most powerful men (*optimates*) concur in this judgment." Hildebert also included a long chain of classical citations in his letter on clemency and again stressed the intellectual over the physical components of rulership (see n. 90, above).

99. Hugh the Chanter, *The History of the Church of York, 1066–1127*, ed. and trans. Charles Johnson, rev. Michael Brett, C. N. L. Brooke, and M. Winterbottom, 2nd ed. (Oxford, 1990), p. 152.

100. Ivo of Chartres, ep. 91, 101, 121, 136, 179 (*PL*, 162: 112, 120, 134–35, 145, 180); see also his letters to Stephen-Henry (ep. 49, 86 [*PL*, 162: 60, 107]), and note Ivo's description of Adela as "burning with the flame of divine love (*amor*) and inflamed with the desire to augment religion," in his confirmation of her privilege for the canons of Bourgmoyen, Blois (Ivo of Chartres, *diplomata* no. 1 [*PL*, 162: 289–90]).

101. *MD*, pp. 60–62, 67–68, 150–51, nos. 67, 76, 161; significantly, this language of love appears only in third-person notifications written by Marmoutier monks, not in first-person charters in Adela's name (also drafted by Marmoutier scribes).

102. BN, Lat. 12776, pp. 247–48.

103. See chap. 5 in this volume for detailed discussion of this language of lordly love, though it should be noted that here the examples are from the letters and documents of churchmen. See also Stephen D. White, "*Pactum . . . Legem Vincit et Amor Judicium*: The Settlement of Disputes by Compromise in Eleventh-Century Western France," *American Journal of Legal History* 22 (1978): 281–308; Michael Clanchy, "Love and Law in the Middle Ages," in *Disputes and Settlements: Law and Human Relations in the West*, ed. John Bossy (Cambridge, 1983), pp. 47–67; C. Stephen Jaeger, "L'amour des rois: structure sociale d'une forme de sensibilité aristocratique," *Annales: Economies, Sociétés, Civilisations* 46 (1991): 547–71; and idem, *The Envy of Angels: Cathedral Schools and Social Ideals in Medieval Europe* (Philadelphia, 1993), pp. 103–6, 193. C. Stephen Jaeger, *Ennobling Love: In Search of a Lost Sensibility* (Philadelphia, 1999), which explores these points further, appeared too recently to be included in the present discussion.

104. See Hildebert, ep. 1³, 3² (*PL*, 171: 144–45, 284c), and *carmina* 10, 15 (Scott, pp. 4–5); and Baudry, *carmen* 135, lines 63–90 (Hilbert, pp. 150–51); I have discussed these texts in greater detail in "The *Domina* Adela: Female Lord or Courtly Lady?" unpublished paper presented to the Early Medieval Seminar, Institute of Historical Research, London, in November 1996.

105. For the cleric Roger, see Desjardins, *Conques*, pp. 340–42, no. 470 (1101); and Charles Johnson and Henry A. Cronne, eds., *Regesta Henrici Primi, 1100–1135* (Oxford, 1956), pp. 12–14, nos. 544, 547; by 1107 Adela had recruited Roger as one of her chaplains, a post he held until at least 1119 (Desjardins, *Conques*, pp. 352–53, no. 485, as corrected against AD, Seine-et-Marne, H 824 [1107]; Mars, *Sainct-Lomer*, pp. 142–45 [1106–7]; and Laurent, *Molesme*, 2: 440, no. 524 [1119]). For the legates, see *NDC*, 1: 107–8, no. 24 (as corrected against the seventeenth-century copy of the original in BN, Lat. 17033, pp. 64–66). For the chronology and context, see LoPrete, "A Female Ruler," 1: 182–85.

106. OV, 1.23, 11.15 (1: 160, 6: 156/58); Louis had been christened Louis-Thibaut at his birth—at about the time of Adela's betrothal—as a sign of the solidarity between the Thibaudians and king Philip (OV, 1.23, 11.34 [1: 160, 6: 154]; and "Vita sancti Arnulfi episcopi Suessionensis" [*PL*, 174: 1406]).

107. OV, 8.24 (6: 40); see LoPrete, "A Female Ruler," 1: 185–87, for date (1102–3).

108. See LoPrete, "A Female Ruler," 1: 63–64, 102–3, 187–89, 196–97, for details.

109. Anselm, ep. 286–87, in *S. Anselmi cantuariensis Archiepiscopi, Opera Omnia*, ed. Franciscus S. Schmitt, 6 vols. (Edinburgh, 1938–61): 4: 205–7; Eadmer, *Historia novorum*, bk 3, bk 4 (Rule, pp. 151, 164); Ivo of Chartres, ep. 134, 127 (*PL*, 162: 144, 138 [supplemented by BN, Lat. 28871, fols. 66v–67r]); see also LoPrete, "Adela of Blois and Ivo," pp. 147–48.

110. Anselm, ep. 340 (Schmitt, 5: 278), to pope Paschal II: "That the countess,

more than the princes of Gaul (*super principes Galliae*), honors your legates and acknowledges your precepts I believe is so well known to your holiness that you do not need me to say so." My translation here is more literal than that by Walter Fröhlich, *The Letters of Saint Anselm of Canterbury*, vol. 3, Cistercian Studies Series, 142 (Kalamazoo, Mich., 1994), pp. 67–68.

111. See Ivo of Chartres, ep. 147, 179 (*PL*, 162: 152–53, 181a); Paschal II, "Epistolae et privilegia," no. 403 (*PL*, 163: 364); and *NDC*, 1: 112; as part of the settlement terms, Adela swore to renew the peace she had broken during the dispute.

112. For the council, see Theodor Schieffer, *Die päpstlichen Legaten in Frankreich (870–1130)* (Berlin, 1935), pp. 172–74; and Arbois de Jubainville, *Histoire*, 2: 82–85. Thibaut was with his mother near Châteaudun sometime in 1104 (*MD*, pp. 68–71, no. 77). For affairs of concern to Adela, see Laurent, *Molesme*, 2: 26–28, 31–32, nos. 18, 19, 21; and LoPrete, "A Female Ruler," 2: 359–61. Adela also provided escorts for Ivo of Chartres and Hildebert of Le Mans, two bishops who had declared their support for Henry in Normandy (Ivo of Chartres, ep. 141, 154 [*PL*, 162: 148, 157–58]; Hildebert, ep. 3[8] [*PL*, 171: 288–89]; and LoPrete, "A Female Ruler," 1: 200–201).

113. M. Gemähling, *Monographie de l'abbaye de Saint-Satur près Sancerre (Cher)* (Paris, 1867), pp. 137–38, no. 2, as corrected against original in AD, Cher, 13 H 36: Adela, at the consecration of the abbey church, restored customs she had granted to a knight, confirmed the *libertas* of the canons, and established an annual fair. For Henry at Domfront, see OV, 11.7, 10 (6: 46, 56/60); Hildebert was the son of a knightly follower of the Thibaudians from Lavardin (*Cartulaire de Marmoutier pour le Vendômois*, ed. Charles Auguste de Trémault [Paris, 1893], pp. 321–22 [appendix], no. 29).

114. *Cartulaire du prieuré bénédictin de Saint-Gondon-sur-Loire (866–1172) tiré des archives de l'abbaye de Saint-Florent près Saumur*, ed. Paul Marchegay (Les Roches Baritaud, 1879), pp. 28–30, no. 8 (1096): "Fecit itaque ipse Gilo quod comes Stephanus, in cujus dictionem honor ejus, si sine herede obierit, per successionem dicitur evenire, hoc concederet in camera sua, apud Blesim"; and Marchegay, *Saint-Gondon*, pp. 28–30, no. 10 (first transaction): "Post mortem Gilonis de Soliaco, comes Stephanus, Tebbaldi filius, habuit hereditatem predicti Gilonis."

115. For Giles with Adela see *MB*, pp. 85–86, no. 74, and *MD*, pp. 146–47, no. 156 (both 1097–98); AD, Eure-et-Loir, G 709 (first issue, 1099); for Giles as an old man in 1098 see OV, 10.8 (5: 240). Giles died after the act he issued in April 1100 (Prou, *Recueil des actes de Philippe Ier*, pp. 366–67) and before Stephen's second departure (Marchegay, *Saint-Gondon*, pp. 28–30, no. 10 [first transaction], as quoted in previous note). For Agnes as "a noble girl in the service of [Adela]" see Aubri of Trois-Fontaines, "Chronicon" (*MGH, SS*, 23: 905).

116. Robert-Henri Bautier, "La prise en charge du Berry par le roi Philippe Ier et les antecedents de cette politique de Hugues le Grand à Robert le Pieux," in *"Media in Francia": recueil de mélanges offert à Karl Ferdinand Werner à l'occasion de son 65ième anniversaire* (Paris, 1989), pp. 44–46, 49–54, 58–60 (though Bautier is unaware of Giles's relations to the Thibaudians and of the fact that William continued to act as count alongside his mother until 1107); see also Prou, *Recueil des actes de Philippe Ier*, pp. 366–67.

117. Marchegay, *Saint-Gondon*, pp. 28–30, no. 10 (second and third trans-actions, probably June 2, 1101, but perhaps May 18, 1102, at Saint-Gondon; Adela confirmed at the house of a knight (*miles*), William and Agnes at the tower there); for the arrangements confirmed, see *Le Cartulaire de Vierzon*, ed. Guy Devailly (Paris, 1963), pp. 191–94, no. 66, and *pièces annexes*, pp. 257–58 (1095).

118. Albert of Aachen, *Historia Hierosolymitana*, 9.6 (*Recueil des historiens des croisades, historiens occidentaux*, 4: 594).

119. Bautier, "La prise en charge," pp. 54–56, though Bautier misdates the viscount's return. The correct date is provided by Albert of Aachen, as cited in n. 118.

120. See AD, Cher, 13 H 36, for William and Agnes as husband and wife in November 1104; few acts of William in his Sully domains have survived, though some unpublished ones may have escaped historians' notice.

121. For Henry's campaigns see Charles W. David, *Robert Curthose: Duke of Normandy* (Cambridge, Mass., 1920), pp. 161–68; and C. Warren Hollister, "War and Diplomacy in the Anglo-Norman World: The Reign of Henry I," *Anglo-Norman Studies* 6 (1983): 72–88 (rpt. in his *Monarchy, Magnates and Institutions in the Anglo-Norman World* [London, 1986], pp. 278, 280). For relations between Henry and Anselm and the papal letter, see Sally N. Vaughn, *Anselm of Bec and Robert of Meulan: The Innocence of the Dove and the Wisdom of the Serpent* (Berkeley, 1987), pp. 283–92; and Richard W. Southern, *Saint Anselm and His Biographer: A Study of Monastic Life and Thought, 1059–c.1130* (Cambridge, 1963), pp. 176–77.

122. Eadmer, *Historia novorum*, bk 4 (Rule, pp. 163–64): "During these con-versations Anselm *in reply to her inquiries* [emphasis added] told the Countess the reason for his return to France and made no secret of the fact that he had come to excommunicate her brother Henry, King of England, for the wrong which now for two years and more he had been doing to God and to the Archbishop himself. On hearing this the Countess was greatly distressed that her brother should be so condemned and determined instead to do all she could to reconcile him to the Archbishop" (as translated by Geoffrey Bosanquet, *History of Recent Events in En-gland* [London, 1964], pp. 175–76). The pope's hesitation in excommunicating Henry would not have prevented Anselm himself from excommunicating the king.

123. Eadmer, *Historia novorum*, bk 4 (Rule, pp. 163–64); for independent confirmation of Anselm at Chartres on June 24, 1105 see Ivo, *diplomata* no. 1, *PL*, 162: 289–90.

124. Eadmer, *Historia novorum*, bk 4 (Rule, pp. 165–66): "On a date agreed upon the Archbishop and the Countess together came to the fortified city called Laigle to talk with the King, as he had asked them to do. . . . Then, when they had had their talk together, the King restored to Anselm the revenues of his arch-bishopric and their former friendship for one another was re-established" (as trans-lated by Bosanquet, *History*, p. 176); Eadmer's wording allows for the possibility that Adela also participated in the talks.

125. Anselm, ep. 388 (Schmitt, 5: 331–32) to pope Paschal II: "I approached Normandy, and it was arranged by the countess of Chartres, the king's sister, one most faithful to the church of God and obedient to your precepts, that we would meet for discussions with the king and also that I had some hope for a good

outcome." My translation here is more literal than that by Fröhlich, *Letters of Saint Anselm*, 3: 145.

126. Vaughn, *Anselm of Bec*, pp. 292–304, and Southern, *Saint Anselm*, pp. 176–77; for Henry's cleric and negotiator, William of Warelwast, with Adela and count William at Chartres, see Depoin, *Saint-Martin-des-Champs*, 1: 156–59, nos. 96–97, where he was mistakenly identified in these later and inaccurate copies of acts as the chaplain of the archbishop of Canterbury.

127. David, *Robert Curthose*, pp. 170–78; and OV, 11.20 (6: 82/92, with notes to other sources).

128. See Schieffer, *Die päpstlichen Legaten*, p. 174, and Fliche, *Le règne*, pp. 70–74.

129. Prou, *Recueil des actes de Philippe Ier*, pp. 391–96, nos. 157–58; Guillot, *Le comte d'Anjou*, 1: 117–18. Bertrada had also helped eliminate the count's rebellious eldest son (OV, 11.16 [6: 74/76]; Halphen, *Anjou*, pp. 174–75; Fliche, *Le règne*, pp. 234–35).

130. LePelletier, *Epitome*, p. 59.

131. Ivo of Chartres, ep. 158 (*PL*, 162: 163–64), a letter calling for genealogies to be reviewed at a synod at Soissons on Christmas (1104); for date, see Achille Luchaire, *Louis VI le Gros: annales de sa vie et de son règne (1081–1137)* (Paris, 1890), pp. 18–19, no. 30. It is not certain who instigated the annulment proceedings at this late date (the couple's consanguinity had been noted at the time of their marriage) or for what ulterior motives, if any.

132. OV, 5.19, 11.12 (3: 128, 6: 70); Guibert of Nogent, *Gesta Dei*, 7.37 (*Recueil des historiens des croisades, historiens occidentaux*, 4: 254, n. 7; Suger, *Vita Ludovici Grossi regis*, ch. 9 in *Vie de Louis VI le Gros*, ed. and trans. Henri Waquet (Paris, 1929), p. 48. Suger's text can be consulted in English in *The Deeds of Louis the Fat*, trans. Richard C. Cusimano and John Moorhood (Washington, D.C., 1992); see also Eadmer, *Historia novorum*, bk 4 (Rule, p. 180).

133. Ivo, *diplomata* no. 1 (*PL*, 162: 289–290) (1105); still, Adela did not renounce all comital prerogatives over the house (LoPrete, "Adela of Blois and Ivo," pp. 144–45).

134. In ca. 1107; for sources see LoPrete, "Adela of Blois and Ivo," pp. 144–45.

135. In ca. 1106–7; for sources and discussion see LoPrete, "Adela of Blois and Ivo," pp. 148–51.

136. For Paschal's itinerary see Philippe Jaffé, *Regesta pontificum romanorum ab condita ecclesia ad annum post Christum natum 1198*, 2nd ed., ed. Samuel Löwenfeld, 2 vols. (Leipzig, 1885–88), nos. 6114–30; see also the discussion in Ian S. Robinson, *The Papacy, 1073–1198: Continuity and Innovation* (Cambridge, 1990), pp. 284–85, 420–24. For Adela, see OV, 11.5 (6: 42); Ivo of Chartres, ep. 179 (*PL*, 162: 181); and Samuel Löwenfeld, ed., *Epistolae pontificum Romanorum ineditae* (Leipzig, 1885) p. 74, no. 149 (= Jaffé-Löwenfeld, no. 6430; the date, authenticity, and other versions of this letter are discussed in LoPrete, "A Female Ruler," 2: 519–22).

137. Jaffé-Löwenfeld, *Regesta pontificum romanorum*, nos. 6131–36; for Provins see AD, Seine-et-Marne, H 824 (a 1692 copy of a papal bull collated against the "original," an act not known to Jaffé-Löwenfeld).

138. Suger, ch. 10 (Waquet, pp. 50/60).

139. Meaux: *GC*, 8, *instrumenta*: 548–49, no. 3; Coulommiers: Desjardins, *Conques*, pp. 352–53, no. 485; Provins: AD, Seine-et-Marne, H 824.

140. For Hugh, see Arbois de Jubainville, *Histoire*, 2: 98–100; Adela's castellan Rotrou III of Nogent and emissaries from Henry I certainly attended the council (*Bullarium sacri ordinis Cluniacensis*, ed. P. Simon [Lyons, 1680], p. 35; Paschal II, ep. 223 [*PL*, 163: 220–21]); and Eadmer, *Historia novorum*, bk 4 [Rule, pp. 184–85]).

141. Suger, ch. 8 (Waquet, p. 40); see also Luchaire, *Louis VI*, p. 27, no. 50; and Alfons Becker, *Studium zum Investiturproblem in Frankreich* (Saarbrücken, 1955), pp. 123–26.

142. See nn. 110, 125 above.

143. See discussion and sources in LoPrete, "A Female Ruler," 1: 211–34.

144. See sources in LoPrete, "Adela of Blois as Mother," p. 332 nn. 41–42.

145. OV, 5.11 (3: 116–17); see also OV, 11.5 (6: 42). This was probably a sound assessment since William appears never to have led a military campaign, fathered five or six children, and died in his forties as lord of Sully and other castles Adela arranged for him to inherit. Later historians, not always accurate in factual detail, presented a more negative image of William, claiming he had serious mental and physical disabilities for which there is no solid evidence in contemporary sources; it is not now possible to know precisely why Adela set him aside. See further discussion in LoPrete, "Adela of Blois as Mother," pp. 320–22, and "A Female Ruler," 1: 246–55.

146. Suger, ch. 11 (Waquet, pp. 68/76), presents a highly partial account of Thibaut's first attested combat, in 1107; that he took the field to aid Thibaudian followers has been shown in LoPrete, "A Female Ruler," 1: 262–74.

147. Suger, ch. 16 (Waquet, p. 104); for variant accounts of what followed, see Suger, ch. 16 (Waquet, pp. 102/110); and Anselm, ep. 461 (Schmitt, 5: 410).

148. *SPC*, 2: 460–61, no. 66.

149. *Histoire abrégée de l'abbaye de Saint-Florentin de Bonneval des RR. PP. Dom Jean Thiroux et Dom Lambert continuée par l'abbé Beaupère et M. Lejeune*, ed. V. Bigot (1715) (Châteaudun, 1875), pp. 57–58 (1109, Adela's settlement); *Recueil des actes de Louis VI, roi de France (1108–1137)*, ed. Jean Dufour, 4 vols. (Paris, 1992–94): 1: 86–90, no. 46 (1110, Louis's confirmation).

150. *Cartulaire de Saint-Jean-en-Vallée de Chartres*, ed. René Merlet (Chartres, 1906), p. 9, no. 13 (also in Dufour, *Recueil des actes de Louis VI*, 1: 98–99, no. 49, where the editor confirms that the dating clause was a willful addition on the part of the cleric drafting the act): "vivente Ivone episcopo et Adela comitissa. Testes: Teobaudus comes . . ." (1111); Adela may well have persuaded the king to make the grant; see also Ivo of Chartres, ep. 91 (*PL*, 162: 112).

151. *Gesta Ambaziensium dominorum*, pp. 104–9: "Maurice, trying to sow discord between countess Adela and Hugh, accused him of the worst crimes before her; she, rejecting the proferred incriminations, neither believed Maurice nor harbored suspicions about Hugh. . . . Maurice, repudiated by the countess. . ." For further discussion of this episode and problems in the *Gesta* account, see LoPrete, "A Female Ruler," 2: 380–84; however, since Adela acted with comital authority in charters in 1109 (and beyond), there is no reason to date these events to an earlier period, as have the editors. Hugh, in addition to holding Chaumont-sur-Loire from

the Thibaudians, also held rights at Amboise from the counts of Anjou, though the extent of Hugh's rights there was in dispute.

152. OV, 11.44 (6: 176/78); and Latouche, *Maine*, p. 53.

153. Hugh was also the viscount of Chartres; see Suger, ch. 19 (Waquet, pp. 130/42); and Luchaire, *Louis VI*, pp. 58–59, 61, nos. 108, 110, 114.

154. Suger, chs. 19, 20 (Waquet, pp. 140/42, 150); and Luchaire, *Louis VI*, p. 68, no. 128. Geoffrey Borrel was probably excommunicated before the siege of Le Puiset, but Louis continued to block attempts to have the excommunication lifted (see *RHF*, 15: 152–54, ep. 125–31; Luchaire, *Louis VI*, pp. 66–67, no. 126; and discussion in LoPrete, "A Female Ruler," 2: 334–38).

155. Suger, chs. 20, 21 (Waquet, pp. 150, 152); and R. Merlet, *Saint-Jean-en-Vallée*, p. 9, no. 14; see also LoPrete, "Adela of Blois as Mother," p. 324.

156. L. Merlet, ed., "Lettres," p. 470, ep. 35, from Guy of Gallardon to Adela, datable according to Guy's reference to Henry's fortifying activities, which were also reported by Orderic (OV, 11.44 [6: 176, 177 n. 6]).

157. Suger, ch. 19 (Waquet, pp. 146/48); for Milo's relations with the Thibaudians and earlier quarrels with Hugh of Crécy, see LoPrete, "A Female Ruler," 1: 265–71. Milo's marriage was subsequently annulled when it was discovered that he had not canonically divorced his first wife (Suger, ch. 23 [Waquet, p. 172]; and Ivo of Chartres, ep. 238 [*PL*, 162: 246]), but the annulment was after the marriage had served its political usefulness.

158. Laurent, *Molesme*, 2: 198–200, no. 217B (an act that suggests Adela also used her timely visit to William II of Nevers to dissuade him from taking up arms for the king); and Suger, ch. 19 (Waquet, p. 148).

159. Suger, ch. 19 (Waquet, p. 146).

160. *SPC*, 2: 299, no. 455; *Actus pontificum Cenomannis in urbe degentium*, ed. G. Busson and A. Ledru (Le Mans, 1901), pp. 405–7; Hildebert, ep. 2[17-18] (*PL*, 171: 255–58); Geoffrey Grossus, "Vita beati Bernardi," chs. 79–80 (*PL*, 172: 1414–15); and OV, 11.45 (6: 182).

161. OV, 11.45 (6: 180).

162. OV, 11.45 (6: 180); and Suger, ch. 23 (Waquet, pp. 170/72).

163. For discussion and sources see LoPrete, "Adela of Blois as Mother," pp. 322–23; Stephen did not join Henry's household until after 1110 (Bigot, *Bonneval*, pp. 57–58; and Dufour, *Receuil des actes de Louis VI*, 1: 86–90, no. 46).

164. See discussion and sources in LoPrete, "Adela of Blois and Ivo," pp. 145–46; and "A Female Ruler," 2: 403–5, 412–14, 427–28.

165. *Epernay et l'abbaye Saint-Martin de cette ville: histoire et documents inédits*, ed. Auguste Nicaise, 2 vols. (Châlons-sur-Marne, 1869), 2: 118, no. 5.

166. "Continuatio ad Historiam Ingulphi," in *Rerum Anglicarum Scriptorem Veterum*, ed. William Fulman (Oxford, 1684), 1: 121; although this is a thirteenth-fourteenth-century continuation of an earlier chronicle, which was itself re-worked in the fifteenth century and is notorious for unreliable details, that Thibaut traveled to England in 1114 is neither implausible nor contradicted by other evidence. For Adela ca. 1114, see Nicolas Camuzat, *Promptuarium sacrarum antiquitatum Tricassinae dioecesis* (Troyes, 1610), fols. 373v–374r (at Sézanne); *Le premier cartulaire de l'abbaye cistercienne de Pontigny (XIIe–XIIIe siècles)*, Martines Garrigues, ed.

(Paris, 1981), p. 180, no. 112 (probably at Saint-Florentin or Pontigny); Geoffrey Grossus, "Vita beati Bernardi," ch. 9 (*PL*, 172: 1413b); L. Merlet, *Tiron*, 1: 40–41, no. 24 (perhaps at Blois).

167. See Guibert of Nogent, *De vita sua*, 3.1–12, 14, in *Guibert of Nogent: Autobiographie*, ed. and trans. Edmond-René Labande (Paris, 1981), pp. 304/86, 394/416; this text is also available in John F. Benton's English translation, *Self and Society in Medieval France: The Memoirs of Abbot Guibert of Nogent* (New York, 1970, rpt. Toronto, 1984); Suger, ch. 24 (Waquet, pp. 172/78); and Luchaire, *Louis VI*, pp. 65–66, 70, 93–96, nos. 124, 132–33, 183, 188–90. For Hugh Mancellus as Adela's seneschal, see BN, Lat. 10101, fols. 75v–76r.

168. For Hugh Mancellus, the Thibaudians, and William of Nevers, see LoPrete, "A Female Ruler," 2: 408–11; for William and the homage for Normandy, see "Chronicon monasterii de Hyda" in *Liber monasterii de Hyda*, ed. Edward Edwards, Rolls Series, no. 45 (London, 1866), pp. 309–10.

169. Ivo of Chartres, ep. 275 (*PL*, 162: 277–78); Adela and Thibaut probably viewed William's capture, in part, as one way to defend their followers against aggression.

170. For fuller discussion of the course of this war, see C. Warren Hollister and Thomas K. Keefe, "The Making of the Angevin Empire," *Journal of British Studies* 12 (1973): 1–25, rpt. in Hollister, *Monarchy Magnates and Institutions*, pp. 255–56.

171. L. Merlet, *Tiron*, 1: 104–6, no. 85; Adela was probably also in Blois in early 1116 (L. Merlet, *Tiron*, 1: 40–41, no. 24).

172. Thibaut had been wounded at least once before (in 1112); see Suger, ch. 21 (Waquet, p. 168).

173. Hugh the Chanter, *History* (Brett, pp. 114/18); Hollister and Keefe, "Making," p. 255.

174. Morel, *Saint-Corneille*, 1: 80–81, no. 39 (1117, at Roucy with Thibaut); Catel and Lecomte, *Preuilly*, pp. 3–5, 15–17, nos. 1, 15 (ca. 1118, at Provins, Preuilly, and Chalautre, sometimes with Thibaut, sometimes alone); BN, Collection de Picardie, vol. 234, fols. 166r–167v (1119, at Château-Thierry, Adela alone); Laurent, *Molesme*, 2: 440, no. 524 (1119, at La Ferté-Gaucher[?], with Thibaut); and L. Merlet, *Tiron*, 1: 28–29, no. 14 together with AD, Eure-et-Loir, H 1374, fol. 30r (1117–19, at Provins, Adela and Thibaut issuing separate charters).

175. OV 12.21 (6: 252/58) and Bur, *La formation*, pp. 216 n. 74, 271; no Thibaudian attended, though Hugh of Troyes escorted the pope (a cousin of Hugh's second wife) on his side-trip for negotiations with imperial emissaries.

176. OV, 12.21 (6: 258/64).

177. Hugh the Chanter, *History* (Brett, pp. 124/46, 152/64); Hollister, "War and Diplomacy," pp. 275–77.

178. Hugh the Chanter, *History* (Brett, p. 154).

179. Hugh the Chanter, *History* (Brett, pp. 126/32, 160); OV, 12.24 (6: 282/90).

180. For discussion and sources see Hollister and Keefe, "Making," p. 256.

181. OV, 7.9, 11.5, 13.42 (4: 46, 6: 42, 6: 536 and n. 1).

182. See n. 163 above; in the course of the 1118 fighting, Stephen was also granted further castles in Maine and Perche (on the borders of Normandy and the

Chartrain). These were first granted by Henry to Thibaut, who then granted them to his younger brother as Stephen's share in their *paternal* inheritance (OV, 12.4 [6: 196]).

183. Henry became abbot of Glastonbury in 1126 and bishop of Winchester in 1129; see LoPrete, "Adela of Blois as Mother," p. 318.

184. See n. 157 above, and LoPrete, "Adela of Blois as Mother," pp. 323–34.

185. The poet is unknown; see edition by André Boutemy, "Deux pièces inédites," pp. 123–27: "Qua duce stat regni gloria et usque uiget" (line 22).

186. See Else Maria Wischermann, *Marcigny-sur-Loire: Gründungs und Frühe-geschichte des ersten Cluniacenserinnenpriorates (1055–1150)* (Munich, 1986), pp. 3–5, 78–87, 144–60, 297–98; among contemporary descriptions, see particularly Gilo, "Vita sancti Hugonis abbatis," ch. 12, in H. E. J. Cowdrey, "Two Studies in Cluniac History, 1049–1126," *Studi Gregoriani* 11 (1978): 62; and Peter the Venerable, *De Miraculis*, 1.22, ed. Dyonisia Bouthillier, *Corpus Christianorum, Continuatio Medi-aevalis*, 83: 64–68 (Turnholt, 1988).

187. See Wischermann, *Marcigny*, pp. 280 n. 4, 369 n. 2; Bernard and Bruel, *Cluny*, 4: 685–86, no. 3557; Gilo, "Vita Hugonis," ch. 15 (Cowdrey, p. 65); Ead-mer, *Vita Anselmi*, 2.46, in *The Life of St Anselm, Archbishop of Canterbury*, ed. and trans. Richard W. Southern (Oxford, 1972), pp. 123–24. For Adela's earlier rela-tions with Cluniac monks, see LoPrete, "A Female Ruler," 1: 119–21. Adela's brother, Henry, would be buried at a Cluny priory he founded at Reading soon after Adela's retirement (Johnson and Cronne, *Regesta*, 2: 152, 192–93, nos. 1238, 1427).

188. Peter the Venerable, *De miraculis*, 1.26 (*CC, CM*, 83: 80–82).

189. These traditions cannot now be verifed because most of Marcigny's early documents were destroyed in the sixteenth or eighteenth century (Wischermann, *Marcigny*, pp. 14–27, 110–11, 319).

190. Hildebert, ep. 1[4] and perhaps ep. 1[10] (*PL*, 171: 145c–148b, 162–63); see discussion in von Moos, *Hildebert*, pp. 324–25, 360, 363. For Henry see Johnson and Cronne, *Regesta*, 2: 366, no. 222 (calendared at 2: 230, no. 1599a), a writ of 1126–29 referring to Adela as a nun at Marcigny and witnessed by Adela's son Henry alongside the seneschal of her son Thibaut.

191. BN, Lat. 12776, pp. 241 (Adela's letter), 242–44 (Hugh III and Agnes); *NDC*, 1: 131–34, no. 43 (Thibaut in 1128, referring to his mother frequently be-seeching him to implement the reform).

192. *MB*, pp. 138–39, no. 146 (the editor's alternate readings are those of the original, AD, Loir-et-Cher, 16 H 109, no. 15); for the dispute settled in 1101, see *MD*, pp. 60–62, nos. 67–68.

193. Peter the Venerable, ep. 15 (Constable, 1: 22 and notes, 2: 103–5); for Peter's itinerary see Constable, *Letters*, 2: 260.

194. OV, 12.6 (6: 305).

195. R. H. C. Davis, *King Stephen, 1135–1154*, 3rd ed. (New York, 1990), pp. 12–17; Marjorie Chibnall, *The Empress Matilda: Queen Consort, Queen Mother and Lady of the English* (Oxford, 1991), pp. 50–87.

196. For Thibaut fighting in Normandy in 1135 and 1136, see OV, 13.22, 24 (6: 458, 464); for Stephen's agreement with Louis, see OV, 13.30 (6: 482 and n. 3). Adela's death is dated to the second year after the death of Henry (d. December

1135) by Robert of Torigni, 8.39 (van Houts, 2: 276); obituaries provide the day of 8 March; for her burial at Marcigny, see Peter the Venerable, ep. 107 (Constable, 1: 270), to Adela's son Henry.

197. LoPrete, "A Female Ruler," 2: 545–47.

198. OV, 11.5 (6: 42).

199. LoPrete, "A Female Ruler," 2: 400–405, 416, 421–28.

200. OV, 13.44 (6: 548): when Stephen had been captured by Matilda, Thibaut offered to recognize Geoffrey of Anjou in Normandy in exchange for Tours and Stephen's release.

Chapter 2: Aristocratic Women in the Chartrain

I would like to thank Theodore Evergates, Kimberly LoPrete, and Fredric Cheyette for their thoughtful and helpful responses to this chapter. Fred made many stylistic suggestions. Ted read many versions of the chapter and was extremely helpful in helping make sense of a vast body of material. Kim likewise read many versions of the chapter and offered advice on substantive issues surrounding the charters; she was also generous in sharing references and materials, especially those concerning queen Matilda and Adelica of Le Puiset.

1. *Cartulaire de Marmoutier pour le Dunois*, ed. Emile Mabille (Châteaudun, 1874), p. 33, no. 35 (cited hereafter as *MD*).

2. Jo Ann McNamara and Suzanne Wemple, "The Power of Women Through the Family in Medieval Europe, 500–1200," *Feminist Studies* 1 (1973): 126–42, reprinted in *Women and Power in the Middle Ages*, ed. Mary Erler and Maryanne Kowaleski (Athens, Ga., 1988), pp. 83–101.

3. Georges Duby, *Love and Marriage in the Middle Ages* (essays), tr. Jane Dunnett (Chicago, 1994), author's note, vii. For further discussion of the powerlessness of women and the domination of patrilineal kin, see his "Women and Power," in *Cultures of Power: Lordship, Status, and Process in Twelfth-Century Europe*, ed. Thomas N. Bisson (Philadelphia, 1995), pp. 69–85.

4. Amy Livingstone, "Kith and Kin: Kinship and Family Structure of the Nobility of Eleventh- and Twelfth-Century Blois-Chartres," *French Historical Studies* 20 (1997): 76–99.

5. A recent review of scholarship on the noble family is Thomas N. Bisson, "Nobility and Family in Medieval France: A Review Essay," *French Historical Studies* 16 (1990): 597–613. See also Régine Le Jan, *Famille et pouvoir dans le monde franc (VIIe–Xe siècle): essai d'anthropologie sociale* (Paris, 1995); Constance Brittain Bouchard, *Strong of Body, Brave and Noble: Chivalry and Society in Medieval France* (Ithaca, N.Y. and London, 1998). For the Chartrain, see Amy Livingstone, "Noblewomen's Control of Property in Early Twelfth-Century Blois-Chartres," *Medieval Prosopography* 18 (1997): 55–72, and "Diversity and Continuity: Family Structure and Inheritance in the Chartrain, 1000–1200," in *Mondes de l'ouest et villes du monde: regards sur les sociétés médiévales — mélanges en l'honneur d'André Chédeville*, ed. Daniel Pinchot and Bernard Merdrignac (Rennes, 1998), pp. 415–29; Stephen D. White, "Inheritances and Legal Arguments in Western France, 1050–1150," *Traditio* 43 (1987): 53–103.

6. The database of about 125 transactions was constructed from all eleventh- and early twelfth-century charters in Marmoutier's cartulary for the Dunois (*MD*). Information coded included: the sex of the donor; the type of transaction (gift, sale, mortgage, exchange, life estate); the kind and location of the property; the motivation for the transaction; and the roles of participating or witnessing kin (co-donor, consenter, witness, signer, recipient of countergift). The development of the database was funded by a Mellon Student/Faculty research grant awarded by the Appalachian College Association. The author thanks Joshua Hogan for his enthusiasm, patience, and help in constructing the database and in creating reports from the encoded data.

7. The meaning of such participation is both complex and subtle. Stephen D. White has concluded that the consent of family members was not a legal requirement but rather a customary practice in the family's best interests; see his *Custom, Kinship, and Gifts to Saints: The "Laudatio Parentum" in Western France, 1050–1150* (Chapel Hill, N.C., 1988), pp. 44–48. Constance Brittain Bouchard interprets the inclusion of family members in property transactions as indicative of their rights to the property; although those rights might have been "ambiguous," participation at the transaction proved the claim; see her *Holy Entrepreneurs: Cistercians, Knights, and Economic Exchange in Twelfth-Century Burgundy* (Ithaca, N.Y., 1991), pp. 4–8, 45–79.

8. *MD*, p. 31, no. 31. Geoffrey and Hugo bear different *cognomina*, suggesting that they belonged to separate branches of the same family and that the younger branch retained its rights to the elder's property.

9. Countergifts of cash, palfreys, goblets, or articles of clothing were frequently given to relatives of the donor/seller for two purposes: first, to fix the transaction in the memories of donors, recipients, and witnesses; second, to obviate future challenges from those who had received tangible proof of their consent. Countergifts are discussed in Bouchard, *Holy Entrepreneurs*, pp. 87–93; 148–50; White, *Custom, Kinship, and Gifts*, pp. 47–48, 66–167; Emily Z. Tabuteau, *Transfers of Property in Eleventh-Century Norman Law* (Chapel Hill, N.C., 1988), pp. 115–19.

10. Penny Schine Gold, *The Lady and the Virgin: Image, Attitude, and Experience in Twelfth-Century France* (Chicago, 1985), p. 123, 125–30. See also Dominique Barthélemy, *La société dans le comté de Vendôme de l'an mil au XIVe siècle* (Paris, 1993), pp. 527–33.

11. *MD*, p. 144, no. 155.

12. *Cartulaire de l'abbaye de Saint-Père de Chartres*, ed. Benjamin E. C. Guérard, 2 vols. (Chartres, 1840), pp. 340–41, no. 112 (cited hereafter as *SPC*).

13. In the same grant Alburg gave the monks a revenue of 14 *l.* "from one of her manses which was not held in fief." That manse might have been part of her dowry.

14. Guerric's widow Helisend remarried and had another son, Girard, who called himself vidame after the death of his half-sister Elizabeth.

15. See Barbara Rosenwein, *To Be the Neighbor of St. Peter: The Social Meaning of Cluny's Property, 909–1049* (Ithaca, N.Y., 1989), pp. 49–77; White, *Custom, Kinship, and Gifts*, pp. 41–129; idem, "*Pactem . . . Legem vincit et amor judicum*: The Settlement of Disputes by Compromise in Eleventh-Century Western France," *American Journal of Legal Studies* 22 (1978): 281–308; idem, "Feuding and Peace-Making in

the Touraine Around the Year 1000," *Traditio* 42 (1986): 195–263; Bouchard, *Holy Entrepreneurs*, pp. 129–59; Tabuteau, *Transfers*, pp. 15, 47–48, 75, 100, 113, 116–17, 137, 175, 183, 188.

16. *SPC*, pp. 494–95, no. 37.

17. *SPC*, p. 489, no. 30: *Hoc donum concessit, immo vero dedit Gaudinus et Pagana*. This quitclaim was made in the presence of Waldin and Pagana's lord, *domina* Eustachia Gouet. See below for further discussion of Eustachia's role as lord.

18. It should be noted that Pagana gave her consent at a time when both her father and uncle were still alive.

19. James A. Brundage, *Law, Sex, and Christian Society in Medieval Europe* (Chicago and London, 1989), pp. 199–203, 243–46, 288–97, 331–409; Georges Duby, *The Knight, the Lady, and the Priest: The Making of Modern Marriage in Medieval France*, tr. Barbara Bray (New York and London, 1983), pp. 57–74, 161–88; Jack Goody, *The Development of the Family and Marriage in Europe* (London, 1983), pp. 48–83.

20. It is difficult to determine the ages at which aristocratic daughters were married. The very few extant marriage contracts do not mention waiting periods before the actual marriages. The daughters or wives who appear as co-donors, co-claimants, or in other capacities in the charters were not young girls and often had children of their own. Moreover, since several documents indicate when daughters were still minors, it would appear that most women cited in charters had attained their majorities (see *Marmoutier Cartulaire blésois*, ed. Charles Métais (Blois, 1889–91), p. 55, no. 43; pp. 86–87, no. 75.

21. Remarriage is discussed in Chapter 3 of this volume.

22. *SPC*, p. 241, no. 16.

23. *MD*, pp. 90–91, no. 97.

24. *SPC*, p. 563, no. 56.

25. *Cartulaire de Saint Jean-en-Vallée de Chartres*, ed. René Merlet (Chartres, 1906), p. 6, no. 7.

26. For a discussion of the marriage portion, see J. Hajnal, "European Marriage Patterns in Perspective," in *Population in History*, ed. D. V. Glass and D. E. C. Eversley (London, 1965); John Comaroff, ed., *The Meaning of Marriage Payments* (New York and London, 1980).

27. Diane Owen Hughes, "From Brideprice to Dowry in Mediterranean Europe," *Journal of Family History* 3 (1978): 262–96.

28. Goody, *Development of the Family*, pp. 206–7; David Herlihy, *Medieval Households* (Cambridge, Mass., 1985), pp. 73–74, 84–87; John Freed, *Noble Bondsmen: Ministerial Marriages in the Archdiocese of Salzburg, 1100–1343* (Ithaca, 1995), pp. 146–80.

29. *MD*, p. 50, no. 55.

30. Georges Duby, "Communal Living," in *A History of Private Life*, vol. 2, *Revelations of the Medieval World*, ed. Georges Duby, trans. Arthur Goldhammer (Cambridge, Mass., 1988), pp. 49–50, 56. See also note 88 below.

31. *MD*, pp. 74–75, no. 83.

32. This confirms Gold's findings for Anjou (*The Lady and the Virgin*, pp. 125–30): she detects no shift in practice from dowry to dower or vice versa.

33. *SPC*, pp. 160–61, no. 33.

34. *SPC*, p. 205, no. 79.

35. *MD*, p. 76, no. 86. See Livingstone, "Kith and Kin," pp. 424–39.

36. *SPC*, pp. 428–29, no. 36. Comitissa also consented to the gift along with other relatives (*MD*, p. 75, no. 84). Freed, *Noble Bondsmen*, pp. 113–16, has also found that sisters had a continued claim to their brothers' land.

37. *MD*, p. 67, no. 75.

38. *MD*, p. 32, no. 34. The charter implies that Odo and Elisind were granted a life estate.

39. *MD*, pp. 92–93, no. 100.

40. *MD*, p. 110, no. 116.

41. *MD*, pp. 92–93, no. 100; pp. 109–10, no. 116.

42. For a discussion of the Angevin evidence, see Dominique Barthélemy, "Note sur le *maritagium* dans le grand Anjou des XIe et XIIe siècles," in *Femmes: Mariages—Lignages, XIIe–XIVe siècles: mélanges offerts à Georges Duby* (Brussels, 1992); Jean-Louis Thireau, "Les pratiques communautaires entre époux dans l'Anjou féodal (Xe–XIIe siècles)," *Revue historique de droit français et étranger* 4th ser., 67 (1989): 201–35; Gold, *The Lady and the Virgin*, pp. 116–44. For discussion of the German evidence, see Freed, *Noble Bondsmen*, pp. 146–81.

43. *SPC*, p. 425, no. 31; p. 453, no. 58.

44. *SPC*, pp. 24–25, no. 1.

45. *MD*, pp. 90–91, no. 97.

46. *MD*, pp. 97–98, no. 105.

47. See nn. 24–25 above.

48. *MD*, pp. 147–48, no. 157. See also notes 62 and 97 below.

49. See, most recently, Uta-Renate Blumenthal, *The Investiture Controversy: Church and Monarchy from the Ninth to the Twelfth Century* (Philadelphia, 1988); H. E. J. Cowdrey, *The Cluniacs and the Gregorian Reform* (Oxford, 1970); Steven Fanning, *A Bishop and His World Before the Gregorian Reform: Hubert of Angers, 1006–1047* (Philadelphia, 1988); John Howe, "The Nobility's Reform of the Medieval Church," *American Historical Review* 92 (1988): 317–39; Karl F. Morrison, *Tradition and Authority in the Western Church, 300–1140* (Princeton, N.J., 1969).

50. André Chédeville, "Les restitutions d'églises en faveur de l'abbaye de Saint-Vincent," *Cahiers de civilisation médiévale* 3 (1960): 209–17; Bernard Chevalier, "Les restitutions d'églises dans le diocèse de Tours de Xe au XIIe siècles," in *Etudes de civilisation médiévale (IXe–XII siècles): mélanges offerts à Edmond-René Labande* (Poitiers, 1974); M. Dillay, "La régime de l'église privée du XIe du XIIIe siècle dans l'Anjou, le Maine, la Touraine: les restitutions d'églises par les laïques," *Revue historique de droit français et étranger* 4th ser., 4 (1925): 253–94; Guillaume Mollat, "La restitution des églises privées au patrimoine ecclésiastique en France du IXe du XIe siécle," *Revue historique de droit français et étranger* 4th ser., 27 (1949): 399–423; Jon Sutherland, "The Recovery of Land in the Diocese of Grenoble During the Gregorian Reform Epoch," *Catholic Historical Review* 64 (1978): 377–97; William Ziezulewicz, " 'Restored' Churches in the Fisc of St. Florent-de-Saumur," *Revue bénédictine* 6 (1988): 106–17.

51. Sharon Farmer, "Persuasive Voices: Clerical Images of Medieval Wives," *Speculum* 61 (1986): 517–43. Farmer discusses the important role countess Er-

mengard played as intercessor in the foundation myths of Marmoutier, in *The Communities of Saint Martin: Legend and Ritual in Medieval Tours* (Ithaca, N.Y., 1991), pp. 90–115. For a discussion of queens' political power, see John Carmi Parsons, "The Queen's Intercession in Thirteenth-Century England," in *Power of the Weak: Studies on Medieval Women*, ed. Jennifer Carpenter and Sally Beth MacLean (Urbana and Chicago, 1995), pp. 147–77.

The example of Queen Mathilda demonstrates that women were "persuasive voices" for the ideals of reform a generation earlier than what Farmer found in the mid and late twelfth century. See Lois L. Huneycutt, "Female Succession and the Language of Power in the Writings of Twelfth-Century Churchmen," in *Medieval Queenship*, ed. John Carmi Parsons (New York, 1993), pp. 189–201; and "Intercession and the High-Medieval Queen: The Esther Topos," in Carpenter and MacLean, *Power of the Weak*, pp. 126–46.

52. *The Letters of Saint Anselm of Canterbury*, tr. Walter Frölich, 3 vols. (Kalamazoo, Mich., 1990): 3: 87, no. 352.

53. Frölich, *Letters of Anselm*, 2: 234, no. 249.

54. Frölich, *Letters of St. Anselm*, 3: 29, no. 320.

55. Reformers like Bernard of Tiron, who roamed France preaching reform, surely must have persuaded aristocrats to restore and donate property to the church; see Lester K. Little, *Religious Poverty and the Profit Economy in Medieval Europe* (Ithaca, N.Y., 1978), pp. 70–83. For examples of restorations and gifts to Bernard's reformed abbey of Tiron, see *Cartulaire de l'abbaye de la Sainte-Trinité de Tiron*, ed. Lucien Merlet, 2 vols. (Chartres, 1883): 1: 15–16, no. 4; 1: 19–20, no. 8; 1: 24–26, no. 12; 1: 79–80, no. 58; 1: 88–90, no. 71; 1: 102–3, no. 83; 1: 130, no. 90; 1: 131–34, no. 92.

56. *SPC*, pp. 163–64, no. 36. Geoffrey appeared with Mahild in this act. For information on the Gouet family, see Kathleen Hapgood Thompson, "The Formation of the County of Perche: The Rise and Fall of the House of Gouet," in *Family Trees and the Roots of Politics: The Prosopography of Britain and France from the Tenth to the Twelfth Century*, ed. K. S. B. Keats-Rohan (Woodbridge and Rochester, N.Y., 1997), pp. 299–314.

57. *MD*, pp. 34–35, no. 37.

58. *SPC*, p. 211, no. 87; pp. 163–64, no. 36; pp. 448–49, no. 25. See also *Cartulaire de l'abbaye Saint-Florentin de Bonneval*, ed. Albert Sidoisne (Bonneval, 1939), pp. 25–31, no. 3. This act is a pancarte that lists all the gifts made to the monks of Bonneval pertaining to the church at Alluyes; donations made by the Gouet family, as well as their vassals, are recorded.

59. *SPC*, p. 494, no. 36; pp. 474–75, no. 6; pp. 486–88, no. 27.

60. *SPC*, p. 489, no. 30.

61. *SPC*, pp. 472–74, no. 5.

62. Patrick Geary argues that women, in particular, were primarily responsible for memorializing their relatives; see *Phantoms of Remembrance: Memory and Oblivion at the End of the First Millennium* (Princeton, N.J., 1994), pp. 62–64. See also n. 97 below.

63. For the discussion of feudal wardship and the experience of women in England, see John Carmi Parsons, "Mothers, Daughters, Marriage, Power: Some

Plantagenet Evidence, 1150–1500," in Parsons, *Medieval Queenship*, pp. 63–78; Linda Mitchell, "The Lady Is a Lord: Noble Widows and Land in Thirteenth-Century Britain," *Historical Reflections/Reflexions historiques* 18 (1992): 71–97; Sue Sheridan Walker, "Violence and the Exercise of Feudal Guardianship: The Action of *ejectio custodia*," *American Journal of Legal History* 16 (1972): 320–33; eadem, "Widow and Ward: The Feudal Law of Child Custody in Medieval England," *Feminist Studies* 3 (1976): 104–16; eadem, "Free Consent and the Marriage of Feudal Wards in Medieval England," *Journal of Medieval History* 8 (1972): 123–34.

64. *SPC*, pp. 221–22, no. 99.

65. Like her contemporary Hildegard Franca, Gila of Perche acted autonomously in determining the fate of her children and family lands. She had been married twice and had two sons from her first marriage. She arranged for one of them to become a monk at Saint-Père. None of the boy's paternal relatives participated in the charter in any way, nor did Gila's second husband; she acted entirely on her own and had complete dominion over her children and her family property (see *SPC*, p. 228, no. 2). The evidence from Blois-Chartres challenges Duby's assertion ("Women and Power," p. 75) that widows could not act independently as guardians.

66. *OV*, 13.1 (6: 395).

67. *MD*, p. 41, no. 44; pp. 41–42, no. 45; pp. 42–43, no. 46; pp. 108–9, no. 95; pp. 156–57, no. 166; *SPC*, p. 471, no. 6; p. 475, no. 8; Souancé and Métais, *Saint Denis*, pp. 91–92, no. 30; pp. 95–96, no. 33; pp. 152–53, no. 71.

68. *SPC*, p. 494, no. 36.

69. *SPC*, pp. 474–75, no. 6.

70. *SPC*, pp. 486–88, no. 27. For other examples of Eustachia acting as lord or holding a court, see *SPC*, p. 489, no. 30; p. 477, no. 12; p. 477, no. 13; p. 480, no. 19.

71. The fact that these sons were making their own gifts demonstrates that they were of age and controlled property on their own; if a patrilineal system had been in place, they would have replaced their mother as head of the lordship and taken on these reponsibilities themselves. For acts where the sons witnessed donations for their parents, see Souancé and Métais, *Saint-Denis*, pp. 165–66, no. 81; pp. 167–68, no. 83; for their participation at Eustachia's court: *SPC* p. 489, no. 30; p. 487, no. 27, p. 474, no. 6; p. 477, no. 12; for the sons' donations, *SPC*, no. 20, p. 486; L. Merlet, *Sainte-Trinité de Tiron*, 1: 24–28, no. 21; Sidoisne, *Bonneval*, no. 3, pp. 35–31.

72. Duby, "Communal Living," pp. 68–83, and "Women and Power"; André Poulet, "Capetian Women and the Regency: The Genesis of a Vocation," in Parsons, *Medieval Queenship*, pp. 93–116; McNamara and Wemple, "The Power of Women," pp. 137–39; Shulamith Shahar, *The Fourth Estate: A History of Women in the Middle Ages*, tr. Chaya Galai (London and New York, 1983), pp. 126–40; F. L. Ganshof, "Le statut de la femme dans la monarchie franque," *Receuil de la Société Jean Bodin* 2 (1962): 1–58.

73. *MD*, pp. 35–36, no. 38.

74. *MD*, pp. 122–23, no. 132.

75. *SPC*, pp. 98–99, no. 6.

76. *SPC*, p. 194, no. 68.

77. *SPC*, pp. 163–64, no. 36; p. 211, no. 87. Sidoisne, *Bonneval*, pp. 25–31, no. 3.

78. *MD*, pp. 34–35, no. 37.

79. L. Merlet, *Sainte-Trinité de Tiron*, 1: 113–14, no. 91. At the time of this charter Auberia was married to Joscelin of Mongerville, and acted with him in donating property to the monks of Tiron (1: 159–60, no. 134). This Joscelin was probably the same Joscelin of Mongerville who disputed his mother's gift to Saint-Pére (see above). The wife of Robert of Blainville was the daughter of Adela Filoche, who incurred the displeasure of the monks of Tiron when she disputed a gift her husband had made (no. 104 below).

80. L. Merlet, *Sainte-Trinité de Tiron*, 1: 172–73, no. 148.

81. *Cartulaire de Notre-Dame de Josaphat*, ed. Charles Métais, 2 vols. (Chartres, 1911–1912), pp. 142–43, no. 111.

82. *Legadoctus* indicates a person invested with certain legal powers.

83. L. Merlet, *Sainte-Trinité de Tiron*, 1: 118–19, no. 98.

84. L. Merlet, *Sainte-Trinité de Tiron*, 1: 106–7, no. 86.

85. See *SPC*, pp. 474–75, no. 6; p. 494, no. 36; see also n. 68 above.

86. See n. 85 above.

87. *SPC*, pp. 486–88, no. 27. The monks also had Ernald and Barbata renounce their claim in their chapter house at their court in front of witnesses, among them Ernald's brother Peter and his daughter Sarracena.

88. Duby, "Communal Living," p. 77.

89. Métais, *Notre-Dame de Josaphat*, pp. 47–48, no. 31. Elizabeth also specified that this gift of tithes should benefit the souls of her brother Hugh and deceased husband William.

90. Métais, *Notre-Dame de Josaphat*, pp. 53–54, no. 37.

91. Henry, apparently the second son of Elizabeth's marriage to William of Ferrières, was endowed with properties from the maternal line; he later succeeded his brother William as vidame.

92. Métais, *Notre-Dame de Josaphat*, pp. 141–42, no. 110.

93. Elizabeth's mother Helisend had been the *vicedominus* before her. Helisend became *vicedomina* in 1107 when her husband Vidame Hugh died, and remained in control of the family honors after her remarriage.

94. Gold, *The Lady and the Virgin*, pp. 117, 122–44.

95. R. Merlet, *Saint-Jean-en-Vallée*, p. 15, no. 25.

96. *SPC*, p. 193, no. 67; pp. 403–4, no. 5.

97. For a discussion of women's role as the memorializer of her family and in remembering family history, see Geary, *Phantoms of Remembrance*, pp. 51–69. The evidence from Blois-Chartres challenges Geary's assertion that monks came to replace women as the memory-keepers of their families during the eleventh century.

98. As well as providing for the souls of their relatives, widows also restored ecclesiastical property. Church reformers had deemed possession by the secular nobility of such holdings, particularly churches and tithes, as illegal and against God's will. Restoring churches and their tithes was viewed as a pious act; it also helped solidify the relationship between widows and the monks. In 1130 Helvisa, *legedocta*, for example, gave a church of Saint-Jean of Chamars and its tithes to the monks of Marmoutier, which she held in fief from the viscount of Châteaudun (*MD*, pp. 158–59, no. 168).

99. *MD*, pp. 150–55, no. 161.

100. Ivo of Chartres, *PL*, 162: 97–98, ep. 75–76; *Yves de Chartres: Correspondance*, ed. and tr. Jean Leclerq (Paris, 1949): 1: 252–255, ep. 60.

101. *SPC*, pp. 184–86, no. 59.

102. No mention is made of any children, so Adela was probably not claiming these possessions as part of her children's rightful patrimony or inheritance.

103. *SPC*, p. 319, no. 71.

104. L. Merlet, *Sainte-Trinité de Tiron*, 2: 27–28, no. 257.

105. *MD*, pp. 127–29, no. 138; see also R. Merlet, *Saint-Jean-en-Vallée*, pp. 1–2, no. 2.

106. *SPC*, pp. 499–500, no. 43.

107. *SPC*, pp. 417–21, no. 24.

108. *Papsturkunden in Frankenreich*, vol. 6, *Orléanais*, ed. Johannes Ramakers (Göttingen, 1958), pp. 70–71, no. 18.

109. McNamara and Wemple, "Power of Women Through the Family," pp. 137–38.

Chapter 3: Aristocratic Women in the County of Champagne

I thank Fredric L. Cheyette, Kimberly A. LoPrete, and Amy Livingstone for their incisive comments on this chapter. I am also grateful to the National Humanities Center for the opportunity to work on this chapter as part of a larger study of the aristocracy in Champagne.

1. John F. Benton, "The Court of Champagne as a Literary Center," *Speculum* 36 (1961): 551–91, reprinted in his *Culture, Power and Personality in Medieval France*, ed. Thomas N. Bisson (London, 1991), pp. 3–43; Ad Putter, "Knights and Clerics at the Court of Champagne: Chrétien de Troyes's Romances in Context," in *Medieval Knighthood V: Papers from the Sixth Strawberry Conference, 1994*, ed. Stephen Church and Ruth Harvey (Woodbridge, 1995), pp. 243–66.

2. John Benton, who for many years pursued the issue, found it impossible to reconcile the literary representations of "courtly love" with the nonliterary evidence; see his "Clio and Venus: An Historical View of Medieval Love," in *The Meaning of Courtly Love*, ed. F. X. Newman (Albany, N.Y., 1968), pp. 19–42, reprinted in his *Culture, Power and Personality in Medieval France*, pp. 99–122; and "Collaborative Approaches to Fantasy and Reality in the Literature of Champagne," in *Court and Poet: Selected Proceedings of the Third Congress of the International Courtly Literature Society* (Liverpool, 1980), ed. Glyn Burgess (Liverpool, 1981), pp. 43–57, reprinted in *Culture, Power, and Personality in Medieval France*, pp. 167–80.

3. Constance Bullock-Davies, "Chrétien de Troyes and England," in *Arthurian Literature*, ed. Richard Barber (Woodbridge, 1981), 1: 1–61; Krijnie Ciggaar, "Chrétien de Troyes et la 'matière byzantine': les demoiselles du Château de Pesme Aventure," *Cahiers de civilisation médiévale* 32 (1989): 325–31; Carleton W. Carroll, "Quelques observations sur les reflects de la cour d'Henri II dans l'oeuvre de Chrétien de Troyes," *Cahiers de civilisation médiévale* 37 (1994): 33–39; Erich Köhler, *Ideal und Wirklichkeit in der höfischen Epik: Studien zur Form der frühen Artus- und Graldichtung* (Tübingen, 1956; 2nd ed. 1970), tr. as *L'aventure chevaleresque: idéal et*

réalité dans le roman courtois: études sur la forme des plus anciens poèmes d'Arthur et du Graal (Paris, 1974); Kathryn Gravdal, *Ravishing Maidens: Writing Rape in Medieval French Literature and Law* (Philadelphia, 1992), chap. 2; E. Jane Burns, *Bodytalk: When Women Speak in Old French Literature* (Philadelphia, 1993), pp. 157–96.

4. A representative selection of those documents is translated in Theodore Evergates, *Feudal Society in Medieval France: Documents from the County of Champagne* (Philadelphia, 1993), cited hereafter as Evergates, *Documents*.

5. Marie's life, especially as it relates to her cultural activities, is recounted in June Hall Martin McCash, "Marie de Champagne and Eleanor of Aquitaine: A Relationship Reexamined," *Speculum* 54 (1979): 698–711; and Edmond-René Labande, "Les filles d'Aliénor d'Aquitaine: étude comparative," *Cahiers de civilisation médiévale* 19 (1986): 101–12. For possible meanings of Chrétien's statement regarding *Lancelot*, see William W. Kibler, ed. and tr., *Chrétien de Troyes: Lancelot, or The Knight of the Cart (Le Chevalier de la Charrete)* (New York and London, 1981), pp. 297–98; a thirteenth-century representation of Marie, explaining her commission to Chrétien, is reproduced on the cover of this volume. For Andreas Capellanus, see Pascale Bourgain, "Aliénor d'Aquitaine et Marie de Champagne mises en cause par André le Chapelain," *Cahiers de civilisation médiévale* 29 (1986): 29–36. See also n. 14 below.

6. Theodore Evergates, "Louis VII and the Counts of Champagne," in *The Second Crusade and the Cistercians*, ed. Michael Gervers (New York, 1992), pp. 109–17.

7. The Alice of Mareuil whom count Henry called his wife's "tutor" in 1159 was in fact the abbess of Avenay (ca. 1130–70); text in Louis Paris, *Histoire de l'abbaye d'Avenay*, 2 vols. (Paris, 1879): 2: 82, no. 13; tr. in Evergates, *Documents*, no. 45. Abbess Alice probably was related to the neighboring viscomital family of Mareuil-sur-Ay and to abbess Helisend of Avenay (see below).

8. Marie was promised to Henry while he and Louis VII were on the Second Crusade; a marriage was contracted in 1153 but not consummated until 1164, after which Marie was called "wife" (*uxor*); see Anthime Fourrier, "Retour au *terminus*," in *Mélanges de langue et littérature du moyen âge et de la renaissance offerts à Jean Frappier*, 2 vols. (Geneva, 1970): 1: 299–311.

9. Chancery scribes noted that she ordered the confiscation of at least one fief (*Documents relatifs au comté de Champagne et de Brie, 1172–1361*, ed. Auguste Longnon, 3 vols. [Paris, 1901–14], 1: 37, no. 973: "the countess had it seized"). Peter of Courtenay, count of Auxerre-Tonnerre, recalled ca. 1204 that he had done homage to countess Marie for the castle of Mailly (ca. 1184); text in *Recueil de pièces pour faire suite au Cartulaire général d'Yonne*, ed. Maximilien Quantin (Auxerre, 1873), p. 28, no. 29.

10. See below, Elizabeth of Nogent-sur-Seine.

11. Philip married instead Theresia of Portugal; see Chapter 4 of this volume.

12. *La chronique de Gislebert de Mons*, ed. Léon Vanderkindere (Brussels, 1904), pp. 191–92, par. 123. Details of the marriage treaties are described in Jacques Falmagne, *Baudouin V, comte de Hainaut, 1150–1195* (Montreal, 1966), pp. 114, 127, 129–31, 136, 172–73, 180–81. For young Marie's life as countess of Flanders, see Chapter 4 of this volume.

13. McCash, "Marie de Champagne," argues persuasively, in the absence of firm evidence, that Marie could well have met her mother on several occasions.

14. Rita Lejeune, "Rôle littéraire de la famille d'Aliénor d'Aquitaine," *Cahiers de civilisation médiévale* 1 (1958): 324–28, presents the strongest case for Marie's role as patron; Benton, "The Court of Champagne," offers a number of reservations.

15. Putter, "Knights and Clerics," pp. 250–51.

16. Patricia Danz Stirnemann, "Quelques bibliothèques princières et la production hors scriptorium au XIIe siècle," *Bulletin archéologique du Comité des Travaux historiques et scientifiques* n.s., 17–18A (1984): 31–36.

17. *Layettes du Trésor des chartes*, ed. A. Teulet et al., 5 vols. (Paris, 1863–1909): 1: 204, no. 497 (July 1199); tr. in Evergates, *Documents*, no. 40.

18. A history of Blanche's rule is in Henry d'Arbois de Jubainville, *Histoire des ducs et des comtes de Champagne*, 7 vols. (Paris-Troyes, 1859–1869): 4: 101–97.

19. The king tried to seize Flanders after its count, Philip of Alsace, died without children, despite the fact that the count had designated his sister Margaret, wife of the count of Hainaut, as his heir. The Flemish towns resisted the king, who agreed to arbitration. Margaret was declared the rightful heir and her son Baldwin succeeded in 1194; see Pierre Paillot, *La réprésentation successorale dans les coutumes du Nord de la France: contribution à l'étude du droit familiale* (Paris, 1935), pp. 40–47, and Chapter 4 of this volume.

20. Longnon, *Documents*, 1: 469–70, nos. 6–7 (May 1201). This is the earliest reference to the comital regency as a right exercised in ward (*de baillio*) for a minor (Blanche's one-year-old daughter Marie).

21. Longnon, *Documents*, 1: 114, no. 2985 (August 1201).

22. Thibaut III acquired Sainte-Menehould in 1200, but Blanche made it a viable military structure (see Evergates, *Documents*, no. 2). Blanche also imposed her *mouvance* over the nearby castle of Saint-Jean-sur-Tourbe, which controlled the road between Sainte-Menehould and Reims (*Thesaurus novus anecdotorum*, ed. Edmond Martène and Ursin Durand, 5 vols. [Paris, 1717], 1: 784 [September 1203]); she took possession of the mortgaged castle of Chaumont after its lord died without having redeemed the debt (AN, KK 1064, fol. 121); and she made the lord of Vignory's castle (also on the Marne) renderable at her request, except against the duke of Burgundy, from whom the castle was held (*Cartulaire du prieuré de Saint-Etienne de Vignory*, ed. Jules d'Arbaument [Langres, 1882], pp. 205–6, no. 73 [July 1204]).

23. *Layettes*, 1: 320, no. 848 (1201); tr. in Evergates, *Documents*, no. 4.

24. Michel Bur, "L'image de parenté chez les comtes de Champagne," *Annales: Economies, Sociétés, Civilisations* 38 (1983): 1016–39.

25. BN, Lat. 17098 (Cartulary of Saint-Etienne), fol. 61 (October 1209): Blanche gave a 10 *l.* rent for that commemorative Mass.

26. Adam of Perseigne, "Epistolae," *PL*, 211: 691–94, ep. 30, in which he remarked on Blanche's earlier penchant for a religious life.

27. Arbois de Jubainville, *Histoire*, 4: 613–15.

28. Anonymous, "Chronicon" of Laon, *RHF*, 18: 715; the chronicler notes that Walter evaded a summons to answer charges in Rome.

29. *Recueil des actes de Philippe Auguste*, ed. H.-F. Delaborde et al., 4 vols. (Paris, 1916–79): 3: 171–72, no. 1088 (Paris, July 1209); "the custom in France," according the king, was that "no one, before reaching the age of twenty-one, ought to be forced to defend his right to his father's lands." For that affirmation, Blanche paid Philip 15,000 *l.*

30. *Recueil des actes de Philippe Auguste*, 3: 444–45, no. 1306 (Paris, July 1213).

31. *PL*, 216: 979–81, ep. 9–12.

32. *Recueil des actes de Philippe Auguste*, 3: 453–58, nos. 1313–14 (November 1213).

33. *Recueil des actes de Philippe Auguste*, 3: 463–64, no. 1321 (Melun, March 1214). The act is erroneously dated "August" in *Layettes*, 1: 404, no. 1080, and in Longnon, *Documents*, 1: 471, no. 11.

34. She had already laid out that argument to Innocent III, who in a letter dated December 14, 1213 recalled that the barons and knights of Champagne had sworn "fidelity and homage" to Thibaut III after Henry II's death (*PL*, 216: 940–41, ep. 149).

35. *Recueil des actes de Philippe Auguste*, 4: 50–52, nos. 1439–40 (July 1216).

36. Thibaut III assigned her dower lands on the occasion of their marriage in 1199; see n. 17 above.

37. *GC*, 9: *instumenta*, 132–33, no. 53 (1224); tr. in Evergates, *Documents*, no. 104. The fact that Blanche purchased most of the property from the Cistercian monks at Hautvillers probably helped her petition.

38. BN, Lat. 5993 (known as the "Cartulary of Blanche") was Cartulary-Register 3 of the comital chancery; see Theodore Evergates, "The Chancery Archives of the Counts of Champagne: Codicology and History of the Cartulary-Registers," *Viator* 16 (1985): 168.

39. *Layettes*, 1: 385–86, no. 1031 (1212); tr. in Evergates, *Documents*, no. 35.

40. *L'ancien coutumier de Champagne (XIIIe siècle)*, ed. Paulette Portejoie (Poitiers, 1956), pp. 142–44 n.

41. Gertrude (born in 1204) was the heiress of Albert, count of Metz and Dabo, whose two sons died at a tournament in 1201. In 1216 she married Thibaut I, duke of Lorraine (1213–20). In May 1220 she married Thibaut IV (Martène and Durand, *Thesaurus novus anecdotorum*, 1: 878), but they were divorced by May 1222 (Aubri of Trois-Fontaines, "Chronicon," *MGH. SS.* 23: 910 [year 1220], who claims that Thibaut dismissed her because of consanguinity). Gertrude then married Simon of Linange but died childless in 1225 at about twenty-one. She was the last of the Dabo line, whose substantial properties were subsequently dispersed; see Michel Parisse, *Noblesse et chevalerie en Lorraine médiévale* (Nancy, 1982), pp. 94–95; Michel Bur, "Les relations des comtes de Champagne et les ducs de Lorraine au début du XIIIe siècle," *Bulletin philologique et historique du Comité des Travaux historiques et scientifiques* (1964): 75–84; and Arbois de Jubainville, *Histoire*, 4: 188–89.

42. She was the eldest daughter of Guichard IV of Beaujeu and Sybil of Hainaut, sister of queen Isabel (the two sisters had been promised in marriage to count Henry II; see also Chapter 4 in this volume). M. C. Guigue, "Testament de Guichard III [IV] de Beaujeu," *Bibliothèque de l'Ecole des Chartes* 4th ser., 3 (1857): 161–67: *ut ei* [Louis] *sicut consanguinee sue debeat providere et eam maritare*. Guichard did not yet have children in 1195 (Constance Brittain Bouchard, *Sword, Miter and Cloister: Nobility and the Church in Burgundy, 980–1198* [Ithaca, N.Y., 1987], p. 294). If Agnes, the eldest of four daughters, was born in 1196, she would have been twenty-seven in 1223; but she must have already attained her legal age, which I would take to be twelve, by the time of her father's testament in 1216, since only her

youngest sister is called a minor. If Agnes turned twelve in that year, and therefore was born ca. 1204, she would have been about nineteen in 1223. Thibaut himself was twenty-two at that time, and thus it seems likely that Agnes was closer to nineteen or twenty than to twenty-seven when she married Thibaut.

43. Arbois de Jubainville, *Histoire*, 4: 342.

44. The marriage contract is in *Layettes*, 2: 245–46, no. 2231 (1233); tr. in Evergates, *Documents*, no. 29. Margaret was the fifth child and eldest daughter of Archambaud VI of Bourbon (born 1195/1196, he assumed the lordship of Bourbon in 1216, and died in 1242). Since his eldest son was born in 1216 (Alphonse-Martial Chazaud, *Etude sur la chronologie des sires de Bourbon, X^e–XIIIe siècles*, ed. Max Fazy [Moulins, 1935], p. 208), Margaret must have been born in 1217 at the earliest, and probably was about fifteen when she married in 1232.

45. Arbois de Jubainville, *Histoire*, 4: 349–64.

46. *Layettes*, 3: 246–49, no. 4184, July 1255; tr. in Evergates, *Documents*, no. 12B.

47. Her dower consisted of revenues from seven comital castellanies, 1000 *l.* rent as her share of acquisitions made during marriage, and the movable property in her husband's castles. Her son released her from the 12,000 *l.* dowry she had contracted to pay for her daughter's marriage (BN, Cinq Cents de Colbert, vol. 56, fols. 108–9 [January 6, 1256]).

48. Arbois de Jubainville, *Histoire*, 4: 356–60.

49. Geoffroy of Beaulieu, "Vie de saint Louis par le confesseur de la reine Margueret," *RHF* 20: 83.

50. Text (written between June 1267 and February 1268) in David O'Connell, *Les propos de Saint Louis* (Paris, 1974), pp. 191–94; and Charles-Victor Langlois, *La vie en France au moyen âge*, 4 vols. (Paris, 1926–28): 4: 42–46.

51. She was the daughter of Robert I of Artois (d. 1250) and Mathilda of Brabant, who married ca. 1235. Blanche's birthdate can be placed only between 1236 and 1250; at the time of her marriage in July 1269 she would have been between nineteen and thirty-three. We might assume that she was about the same age as Henry III, who married at twenty. See Arbois de Jubainville, *Histoire*, 4: 431–32.

52. Details of the succession are in Elisabeth Lalou, "Le gouvernement de la reine Jeanne, 1285–1305," *Les cahiers haut-marnais* 167 (1986): 16–21.

53. Text in *Spicilegium sive collectio veterum aliquot scriptorum*, ed. Lucas de Achery, 13 vols. (Paris, 1655–77); 2nd ed., 3 vols. (Paris, 1723; rpt 1967): 3: 682.

54. *Les Etablissements de Saint Louis*, ed. Paul Viollet, 4 vols. (Paris, 1881–86): 3: 165–68; tr. in Evergates, *Documents*, no. 38.

55. Only countess Marie ruled during the temporary absence of her husband (1179–80) and son (1190–97). In the thirteenth century a new administrative officer, the governor of Champagne, assumed that responsibility, and countesses ruled only during an heir's minority.

56. Gertrude of Dabo, Agnes of Beaujeu, and Isabel of France died in their twenties; Blanche of Navarre and Margaret of Bourbon died in their forties; and Marie of France and Blanche of Artois died in their fifties.

57. These principles of inheritance, enunciated in decisions of the High Court from the late thirteenth century, had been followed from the early decades of the

century; see Evergates, *Documents*, no. 36. Inheritance customs varied widely in France, the north and the east (including Champagne) being more favorable to women than the west (particularly Normandy), which largely excluded women from succession; see John Gilissen, "Le privilège de masculinité dans le droit coutumier de la Belgique et du nord de la France," *Revue du Nord* 43 (1961): 201–16.

58. André Lemaire, "Les origines de la communauté de biens entre époux dans le droit coutumier français," *Revue historique de droit français et étranger*, 4th ser., 7 (1928): 584–643. For the community property of countess Margaret, see n. 47 above.

59. The dower, it should be emphasized, was assigned on the husband's *own* properties at the time of marriage, not on the couple's joint acquisitions nor on the widow's own dowry/inheritance; consequently the widow enjoyed only the usufruct of those dower lands, which ultimately devolved to her husband's children. The High Court stated the general principle (Portejoie, *L'ancien coutumier de Champagne*, 154, art. 9; tr. in Evergates, *Documents*, no. 43); see also Stephen of Pringy's dower letter below.

60. Charles Donahue, Jr., "The Canon Law of the Formation of Marriage and Social Practice in the Later Middle Ages," *Journal of Family History* 8 (1983): 144–58.

61. John Gillingham, "Love, Marriage, and Politics in the Twelfth Century," *Forum for Modern Language Studies* 25 (1989): 292–303, reprinted as chap. 11 in his *Richard Coeur de Lion: Kingship, Chivalry, and War in the Twelfth Century* (London, 1994), presents a convincing case for the role of love in aristocratic marriages and a healthy antidote to modern portrayals of medieval marriages as being loveless alliances arranged without regard for the wishes and sentiments of the spouses.

62. Anglo-Norman aristocratic families of the late twelfth century also were relatively small, two-thirds of them consisting of four or fewer persons; see John S. Moore, "The Anglo-Norman Family: Size and Structure," *Anglo-Norman Studies* 14 (1991): 153–95.

63. John Carmi Parsons, "Mothers, Daughters, Marriage, Power: Some Plantagenet Evidence, 1150–1500," in Parsons, ed., *Medieval Queenship*, pp. 66–67: of eighty-seven documented marriages, forty-nine were solemnized when the bride was fifteen or older; only five of the thirty-eight brides under fifteen years had a child immediately after the marriage. Although the age of menarche was generally thought to range from twelve to fifteen years, Hildegard of Bingen (d. 1179) observed that mothers under twenty years of age produced weakly children; see Darrel W. Amundsen and Carol Jean Diers, "The Age of Menarche in Medieval Europe," *Human Biology* 45 (1973): 363–64.

64. Juliette M. Turlan, "Recherches sur le mariage dans la pratique coutumière (XIIᵉ–XIVᵉ s.)," *Revue historique de droit français et étranger*, 4th ser., 35 (1957): 477–86.

65. The Donzy, and this incident, are discussed in Yves Sassier, *Recherches sur le pouvoir comtal en Auxerrois du Xe au début du XIIIe siècle* (Auxerre, 1980), pp. 81–90.

66. Anselm later remarried; see Hermesend of Bar-sur-Seine below. The text of the inquest in 1217 that recounts the event is in Martène and Durand, *Thesaurus novus anecdotorum*, 1: 863; tr. in Evergates, *Documents*, no. 25.

67. *Trésor des chartes du comté de Rethel* (*1081–1415*), ed. Gustave Saige, Henri Lecaille, and L. H. Labande, 5 vols. (Monaco, 1902–16): 1: 139–41, no. 86 (marriage contract of 1239).

68. *Layettes*, 2: 245–46, no. 2231, 1233; tr. in Evergates, *Documents*, no. 29B.

69. Dowries are described in Evergates, *Documents*, nos. 27–28, 31. The cash value was generally calculated as ten times the stipulated annual revenue. The average annual income of a fief in 1250 was 26 *l.*; see Theodore Evergates, "A Quantitative Analysis of Fiefs in Medieval Champagne," *Computers and the Humanities* 9 (1975): 63.

70. Martène and Durand,*Thesaurus novus anecdotorum*, 1: 904 (1223); tr. in Evergates, *Documents*, no. 27.

71. See n. 76 below.

72. *Cartulaire de l'abbaye du Paraclet*, ed. Charles Lalore (Paris, 1878), pp. 94–95, no. 77 (1189).

73. Ernest Petit, *Histoire des ducs de Bourogne de la race capétienne*, 9 vols. (Paris, 1885–1900): 2: 460–62, no. 695 (1224); tr. in Evergates, *Documents*, no. 30 (see Genealogical Table 3 there). See also Emeline of Broyes below.

74. *Cartulaires de l'abbaye de Molesme, ancien diocèse de Langres*, ed. Jacques Laurent, 2 vols. (Paris, 1907–11): 1: 78–79, nos. 71 (the property came from her own inheritance: *omnium heredum suorum*), 73, both acts of 1076–1111.

75. Lalore, *Paraclet*, pp. 117–18, no. 93 (1197): *de patrimonio suo proprio*; AD Aube 3 H 10 (Cartulary of Clairvaux), p. 221, no. 25 (1206): *quod hereditas ista movebat de capite Agnetis prefate.*

76. Paris,*Avenay*, 2: 99, no. 44, 1218: *terram quam possidebam de patrimonio.*

77. Quantin, *Recueil*, pp. 108–9, no. 245 (1220): *de propriis redditibus meis qui sunt de capite meo.*

78. The earliest references in Champagne to women inheriting fiefs come from the mid-twelfth century. The dowry of the lord of Montmirail's wife was a fief held from Faremoutiers in 1144 (see n. 80 below); Agnes, daughter of Gerard of Les Ormes, held a fief in 1157 that she donated to the Paraclete (Lalore, *Paraclet*, 18–21, no. 10).

79. See Elizabeth of Nogent-sur-Seine and Petronilla of Bar-sur-Seine below.

80. BN, nouv. acq. lat. 928 (Cartulary of Faremoutiers), pp. 49–55 (1144): Louis VII's confirmation of the abbey's possessions, after fire had destroyed its archive, names the lord of Montmirail among those "who hold fiefs from the abbess and swear fidelity to the abbey and the abbess" (*qui feodos tenent ab abbatissa et iurant ecclesie eidemque abbatisse fidelitatem*).

81. Longnon, *Documents*, 1: 150, nos. 3913–14.

82. André Lemaire, "La dotatio de l'épouse de l'époque mérovingienne au XIIIᶜ siècle," *Revue historique de droit français et étranger*, 4th ser., 8 (1929): 569–80, and Régine Le Jan-Hennebicque, "Aux origines du douaire médiéval (VIᶜ–Xᶜ siècles)," in *Veuves et veuvage dans le haut moyen âge*, ed. Michel Parisse (Paris, 1993), pp. 107–21.

83. AD, Marne, G 389, no. 7, original; printed in Michel Bur et al., *Vestiges d'habitat seigneurial fortifié en Champagne centrale*, Inventaire des sites archéologiques non monumentaux de Champagne, 3 (Reims, 1987), p. 99. When the chan-

cellor presented the document he added, in his own hand, at the end of the text: "presented by Gerard the chancellor." Copies of similar marriage-dower letters have been found in the Laonnois; see Laurent Morelle, "Mariage et diplomatique: autour de cinq chartes de douaire dans le laonnois-soissonnais, 1163–1181," *Bibliothèque de l'Ecole des Chartes* 146 (1988): 225–84, and Lemaire, "La dotatio," for other regions.

84. Hervé Chabaud, "Le douaire dans les coutumes de Reims, Châlons, Vitry," *Mémoires de la Société d'agriculture, commerce, science et arts du département de la Marne* 97 (1982): 89–102.

85. The half-dower gained favor in most of northern and eastern France in the twelfth century. Philippe of Beaumanoir credits king Philip II's *establissement* of 1214 for imposing the half-dower throughout the realm (except for "baronies," which were to remain intact; wives of barons were to be granted instead "devised" dowers). Beaumanoir regarded the half dower as the "general custom" of the realm in the 1280s, his own region of the Beauvaisis, with its one-third dower, being exceptional; see Philippe de Beaumanoir, *Les coutumes de Beauvaisis*, ed. A. Salmon, 2 vols. (Paris, 1899–1900): 1: 212, par. 445; tr. F. R. P. Akehurst as *The Coutumes de Beauvaisis of Philippe de Beaumanoir* (Philadelphia, 1992), pp. 157–58, par. 445.

86. Ambroise Firmin Didot, *Etudes sur la vie et les travaux de Jean, sire de Joinville* (Paris, 1870), pp. 191–92, no. "O" (1231): *ad usum et consuetudinem Campanie dotare tenetur*; tr. in Evergates, *Documents*, no. 31.

87. AN, KK 1064, fols. 314r (1223); 362r (1221); both tr. in Evergates, *Documents*, no. 42.

88. See nn. 17, 44 above.

89. Saige, *Trésor des chartes du comté de Rethel*, pp. 27–28, no. 12 (ca. 1191); BN, Cinq Cents de Colbert, vol. 56, fol. 155r–v (1209); tr. in Evergates, *Documents*, no. 41.

90. Portejoie, *L'ancien coutumière de Champagne*, 154, art. 9 (ca. 1270): *par droit commun*; tr. in Evergates, *Documents*, no. 43.

91. *Layettes*, 5: 23–24, nos. 67–68 (1171). See also Theodore Evergates, "Nobles and Knights in Twelfth-Century France," in *Cultures of Power: Lordship, Status, and Process in Twelfth-Century Europe*, ed. Thomas N. Bisson (Philadelphia, 1993), pp. 31–33.

92. AN, KK 1064, fol. 362r (1221); 314r (1223); both tr. in Evergates, *Documents*, no. 42.

93. AD, Haute-Marne, G 76 (1221); partial text printed in André Duchesne, *Histoire généalogique de la maison royale de Dreux* (Paris, 1631), p. 261. See Alix of Dreux below. Ponce of Mont-Saint-Jean also gave his own letter to his wife in the 1220s; see n. 101 below.

94. Longnon, *Documents* 1: 25, no. 726: "His wife holds it in dower" (*Uxor ejus tenet in dotalitio*). When in ca. 1190 the scribes updated the original register of ca. 1178, they often inserted "his wife" next to the entry for a man who had died, indicating that she held his fief in dower (ibid., no. 727: "Peter of Dormans, liege and two months castle guard [added:] His wife" (*Petrus de Dormanz, ligius et II menses custodie.* [added:] *Uxor ejus*).

95. See n. 20 above for Blanche's homage. The women who acquired their husbands' fiefs between the first (ca. 1178) and the second (ca. 1190) feudal registers, and who were noted as being "liege," probably did render homage to a comital

official: Amelina of Le Grand-Rozoy, for example, was listed as being a "liege (woman)" of the count and responsible for the three months castle guard that her husband had owed (Longnon, *Documents*, 1: 34, nos. 899, 904: *Amelina de Rosoi, ligia et III menses custodie apud Rosetum*).

96. Charles Lalore, "Chartes de l'abbaye de Mores," *Mémoires de la Société académique d'agriculture, des sciences, arts et belles-lettres du départment de l'Aube* 37 (1873): 73, no. 51 (1204): *Hominium de eodem casamento . . . recognovisse et fecisse.*

97. See n. 89 above.

98. See n. 93 above.

99. The Book of Homages was maintained from the accession of Thibaut IV in 1222; see Evergates, "The Chancery Archives," pp. 168–69.

100. Longnon, *Documents*, 1: 146, no. 3842: [Margaret of Villy] *fecit homagium ligium . . . de quocunque tenet ex hereditagio suo et de dotalicio quod tenet a dicto Erardo marito suo*; 1: 182, no. 5170: [Isabel of Tours-sur-Marne] *fecit homagium ligium de dotalicio suo et de avoeria filiorum suorum.*

101. Longnon, *Documents*, 1: 156, no. 4006: *fecit homagium ligium de dotalicio suo secundum tenorem litterarum dicti Pontii de dote sua effectarum.*

102. Women represented about 24 percent of the feudal tenants in southern Champagne (Theodore Evergates, *Feudal Society in the Bailliage of Troyes Under the Counts of Champagne, 1152–1284* [Baltimore, 1975], p. 71), and about 17 percent in the county as a whole (Theodore Evergates, "The Aristocracy of Champagne in the Mid-Thirteenth Century: A Quantitative Description," *Journal of Interdisciplinary History* 5 [1974]: 5).

103. *Layettes* 3: 122–23, no. 3931; tr. in Evergates, *Documents*, no. 10A.

104. *Rôles des fiefs du comté de Champagne sous le règne de Thibaut le Chansonnier (1249–1252)*, ed. Auguste Longnon (Paris, 1877), pp. 175–76, no. 814.

105. Longnon, *Rôles*, pp. 12, no. 55.

106. Longnon, *Rôles*, p. 275, no. 1233; p. 285, no. 1258.

107. Longnon, *Rôles*, pp. 313–14, no. 1357.

108. Both her letter (BN, Cinq Cents de Colbert, vol. 58, fol. 236) and her bailiff's oral report were copied into the feudal register (Longnon, *Rôles*, p. 282, no. 1254; p. 307, no. 1349).

109. See Brigitte Bedos-Rezak, "Medieval Women in French Sigillographic Sources," in *Medieval Women and the Sources of Medieval History*, ed. Joel T. Rosenthal (Athens, Ga., 1990), pp. 1–35.

110. BN, Cinq Cents de Colbert, vol. 57, pp. 523–25 (May 1248).

111. Lalore, "Chartes de l'abbaye de Mores," pp. 83–84, no. 79 (1218).

112. Saige, *Trésor des chartes du comté de Rethel*, 1: 204–5, no. 226 (1252): *omnibus feodatis, militibus, hominibus et communitati castri et castellanie Altimontis . . . faciatis quod debetis tam in homagiis quam aliis quibuscumque, et ei tanquam domino vestro obediatis*; tr. in Evergates, *Documents*, no. 63.

113. *Chartes en langue française antérieures à 1271 conservées dans le département de la Haute-Marne*, ed. Jean-Gabriel Gigot (Paris, 1966), pp. 13–14, no. 12 (1245); tr. in Evergates, *Documents*, no. 73.

114. Quantin, *Recueil*, pp. 115–16, no. 264 (1221). Alice of Venizy had already sealed her own testament; see n. 77 above.

115. *Layettes*, 3: 545–46, no. 1535 (1222); tr. in Evergates, *Documents*, no. 59.

116. John F. Benton, "Philip the Fair and the Jours of Troyes," *Studies in Medieval and Renaissance History* 6 (1969): 305–6, no. 2 (1284) (reprinted in his *Culture, Power and Personality in Medieval France*); tr. in Evergates, *Documents*, no. 32. Two other women won cases against predatory royal officials; ibid., pp. 308–9, nos. 12, 15 (both 1285).

117. Portejoie, *L'ancien coutumier de Champagne*, pp. 221–22, art. 57 (1287); tr. in Evergates, *Documents*, no. 36C.

118. References to the Nogent-sur-Seine are in Alphonse Roserot, *Dictionnaire historique de la Champagne méridionale (Aube) des origines à 1790*, 3 vols. (Angers, 1948), 2: 1031–44, and Evergates, *Feudal Society in the Bailliage of Troyes*, pp. 189–90.

119. Lalore, *Paraclet*, pp. 70–71, no. 52 (1146 act of count Thibaut II).

120. Lalore, *Paraclet*, pp. 92–93, no. 75 (1186). Elizabeth and her husband are first mentioned in her father's act of 1146 (see n. 119 above). If she was then recently married at the minimum age of twelve, she might have been born ca. 1134, in her late thirties when widowed in 1171, and in her early fifties when her two youngest sons died shortly before 1186. In 1183 countess Marie stated that Milo II (whose wife Elvissa was present) and Jean "do not yet have children" (BN, Lat. 9901, Vauluisant, fol. 106).

121. *Obituaires de la province de Sens*, vol. 4, *Diocèses de Meaux et de Troyes*, ed. Boutellier du Retail and Piétresson de Saint-Aubin (Paris, 1923), pp. 397, 405: her father Milo and her second son, Milo II, shared one tomb, while her husband and their youngest son, Jean, shared another.

122. Nogent appeared among the dower lands of countess Blanche in July 1199 (*Layettes* 1: 204, no. 497; tr. in Evergates, *Documents*, no. 40). No doubt it was that change of lordship over Nogent that prompted the nuns of the Paraclete to seek count Thibaut III's confirmation of Milo I's sale of 1146 (Lalore, *Paraclet*, pp. 129–30, no. 109 [1202]; see n. 119 above).

123. For Elizabeth's tomb, see *Obituaires*, 4: 400 n. 10.

124. References to the Bar-sur-Seine are in Roserot, *Dictionnaire*, pp. 109–10. Hermesend's mother is first mentioned in 1139, and her father died in 1147. If she was born in 1140/1147, she would have been between twelve and nineteen at her marriage (1159), about forty when widowed (1184), in her mid-forties when she remarried (1189), about fifty when divorced (1196), and about sixty-five when she died (1211).

125. Lalore, *Paraclet*, pp. 65–66, no. 48 (undated foundation act; dated to ca. 1142 by Roserot, *Dictionnaire*, p. 1502).

126. Georges Poull, *La maison souveraine et ducale de Bar* (Nancy, 1994), plate VIII, is a photograph of the original dower letter of 1189: both Thibaut and his brother, count Henry of Bar-le-Duc, sealed it; their mother, Agnes of Champagne (sister of count Henry the Liberal), witnessed.

127. Thibaut soon married the thirteen-year-old heiress of Luxembourg; see Michel Parisse, "Les trois mariages du comte de Bar, Thiébaut Ier," *Annales de l'Est* 19 (1967): 57–61; Poull, *La maison souveraine et ducale de Bar*, p. 150.

128. Perhaps someone recalled that fifty years earlier, when lord Anselm I of Traînel mediated a dispute between the same parties, his wife Helisend and sister

Comitissa participated in the mediation with abbess Heloise (Lalore, *Paraclet*, pp. 66–68, no. 49, ca. 1144: Milo I of Nogent-sur-Seine was also present).

129. Lalore, *Paraclet*, pp. 115–16, no. 91 (1196).

130. Lalore, *Paraclet*, pp. 128–29, no. 108 (1201): Hermesend's gift to the Paraclete; Longnon, *Documents*, 1: 130, no. 3580 (ca. 1201–4): "the lady of Traînel, liege."

131. *Obituaires*, 4: 392.

132. *Layettes*, 1: 396, no. 1060 (December 1213): a standardized letter in her name probably drawn up by comital officials.

133. Petronilla of Bar-sur-Seine was born ca. 1150, was married in 1168 to Hugh of Le Puiset, and died ca. 1174 in her mid-twenties. Hugh ruled Bar-sur-Seine in his wife's name (1168–89), and was succeeded by their son Milo IV (1189–1219); see Roserot, *Dictionnaire*, pp. 109–10.

134. Michel Bur, *La formation du comté de Champagne, v.950–v.1150* (Nancy, 1977), pp. 431–32; and Bur et al., *Vestiges d'habitat seigneurial*, p. 25.

135. For Robert I and Agnes, see Andrew W. Lewis, "Fourteen Charters of Robert I of Dreux (1152–1188)," *Traditio* 41 (1985): 148–60; and Madeline H. Caviness, "Saint-Yved de Braine: The Primary Sources for Dating the Gothic Church," *Speculum* 59 (1984): 526–28, 537, 541, and *Sumptuous Arts at the Royal Abbeys in Reims and Braine* (Princeton, N.J., 1990), pp. 67–70.

136. Robert was the fourth son of king Louis VI, born probably shortly after 1124; see Andrew W. Lewis, *Royal Succession in Capetian France: Studies on Familial Order and the State* (Cambridge, Mass., 1981), pp. 248–49 n. 61.

137. Duchesne, *Histoire généalogique de la maison royale de Dreux*, 1: 234 (1153): act of Louis stating that "my brother, count Robert, received Agnes, countess of Braine, as his wife and assigned her a dower according to the custom of the church, namely: Dreux with its principal fortress, the entire castellany with all appurtenances, and half of all the lands he is able to acquire, wherever they are" (. . . *fratrem meum, comitem Robertum, in uxorem accepisse Agnetem, Brenensem comitissam, et secundum ecclesiae morem ei dotem assignasse: Drocas videlicet cum principali firmitate et totam castellariam cum omnibus appendiciis et medietatem omnium quae ubique terrarum poterit acquirere*).

138. Lewis, "Fourteen Charters of Robert I of Dreux," 176, no. 12 (1186, an act written by their chaplain): *A. comitissa et eiusdem castri a progenitoribus heres et domina*.

139. Lewis, "Fourteen Charters of Robert I of Dreux," pp. 144–79. If Aubri of Troisfontaines is correct that Hugh of Broyes (d. 1199) had been lord of Broyes for eighty years, Hugh would have been born ca. 1110/1120; he first married in 1144. See Poull, *La maison souveraine et ducale de Bar*, pp. 106–7.

140. Louis Chantereau-Lefebvre, *Traité des fiefs et de leur origine* (Paris, 1662), *preuves*, p. 42 (1211).

141. AD, Aube, 3 H 9 (Cartulary of Clairvaux), pp. 137–38, no. 13 (1228); tr. in Evergates, *Documents*, no. 108.

142. Jean Longnon, *Les compagnons de Villehardouin: recherches sur les croisés de la quatrième croisade* (Geneva, 1978), pp. 109–110.

143. Erard II was born after 1179 (date of his parents' marriage) but before 1191 (when his father died on the Third Crusade). He was "not yet a knight" in

1203 and lacked a seal (Charles Lalore, *Les sires et les barons de Chacenay* [Troyes, 1885], p. 34, no. 73). If he had attained his majority when he married in 1204 or 1205, he would have been about fifteen, the age at which noble-born men could succeed to their fathers' properties, and therefore might have been born ca. 1188/1189. If, however, he observed the majority age of twenty-one, he might have been born as early as ca. 1183/1184.

144. See n. 73 above.

145. On Alix and her husbands, see Gilles Poissonnier, *Catalogue des actes de la maison de Choiseul, 1125–1425* (Chaumont, 1990), p. 60 n. 129, p. 62 n. 132. If Alix was married at the minimum age of twelve ca. 1196, she might have been born ca. 1184.

146. Sidney Painter, *The Scourge of the Clergy: Peter of Dreux, Duke of Brittany* (Baltimore, 1937) does not mention Alix.

147. Renaud II of Choiseul (born in 1176) married Clemence of Faucogny (1192), who appeared in most of his acts throughout their married life; she died ca. 1217 (Poissonnier, *Catalogue*, p. 48 n. 96, p. 60 n. 129).

148. See n. 93 above.

149. Alix was married 1220/21; her eldest son Jean attained his majority in 1246, apparently at twenty-one. If Alix was only twelve when she first married ca. 1196, she would have been born ca. 1184 and consequently was in her late thirties at Jean's birth.

150. Her acts are catalogued in Poissonnier, *Catalogue*, pp. 184–86.

151. The average duration of the seven first marriages was almost sixteen years; the median was twenty-one years.

152. Shulamith Shahar, *The Fourth Estate: A History of Women in the Middle Ages*, tr. Chaya Galai (London-New York, 1983), chap. 3, provides a general introduction to female monasticism. Jackie Lusse, "Les religieuses en Champagne jusqu'au XIIIe siècle," in *Les religieuses en France au XIIIe siècle*, ed. Michel Parisse (Nancy, 1985), pp. 11–26, inventories female houses in Champagne.

153. The extraordinary growth of female convents after 1100 is charted in Bruce L. Venarde, *Women's Monasticism and Medieval Society: Nunneries in France and England, 890–1215* (Ithaca, N.Y. and London, 1997), p. 8 (table).

154. Pope Celestine III ordered the Paraclete to downsize (Lalore, *Paraclet*, pp. 33–34, no. 20), while the archbishop of Reims stepped in to save Avenay from its creditors (Paris, *Avenay*, 2: 94, no. 34; tr. in Evergates, *Documents*, no. 46).

155. For the development of Cistercian convents in France, see Sally Thompson, "The Problem of the Cistercian Nuns in the Twelfth and Early Thirteenth Centuries," in *Medieval Women*, ed. Derek Baker (Oxford, 1978), pp. 227–42.

156. See n. 37 above.

157. The total number of cloistered women can be estimated from the size of convents prescribed by their foundation charter (*) or imposed as a maximum after they encountered financial difficulties:

1113 70 Jully-les-Nonnains*
1196 60 The Paraclete
1201 40 Avenay (increased to 50 in 1288)
1217 60 Notre-Dame-aux-Nonnains
1222 90 Argensolles*

1229 25 Noëfort priory
1240 20 Traînel
       52 average (× 100 convents = about 5000 nuns)
See also Penelope D. Johnson, *Equal in Monastic Profession: Religious Women in Medieval France* (Chicago and London, 1991), pp. 173–76.

158. Motivations for religious professions are explored in Mary Skinner, "Benedictine Life for Women in Central France, 850–1100: A Feminist Revival," in *Medieval Religious Women*, vol. 1, *Distant Echoes*, ed. John A. Nichols and Lillian Thomas Shank (Kalamazoo, Mich., 1984), pp. 87–113; and Johnson, *Equal in Monastic Profession*, pp. 13–34.

159. Quoted in Lewis J. Lekai, *The Cistercians: Ideals and Reality* (Kent, Oh., 1977), p. 349.

160. The implications of adult conversions are discussed in Jean Leclercq, *Monks and Love in Twelfth-Century France: Psycho-Historical Essays* (Oxford, 1979), chap. 2.

161. Jean Leclercq, *Women and St Bernard of Clairvaux*, tr. Marie-Bernard Saïd (Kalamazoo, Mich., 1989), pp. 54–56.

162. Charles Lalore, "Chartes d'Andecy," in *Cartulaire de l'abbaye de la Chapelle-aux-Planches* (Paris, 1878), pp. 259–60, no. 161 (1131, foundation charter).

163. Lekai, *The Cistercians*, pp. 347–52.

164. Robert-Henri Bautier, "Paris au temps d'Abélard," in *Abélard et son temps*, Actes du colloque international organisé à l'occasion du 9e centenaire de la naissance de Pierre Abélard (Paris, 1981), pp. 219–23.

165. Abelard describes the site and the foundation of the Paraclete in his autobiography; see *The Letters of Abelard and Heloise*, tr. Betty Radice (Baltimore, 1974), pp. 86–92.

166. Heloise's debate with Abelard over the rule appropriate for a convent is analyzed in Linda Georgianna, "Any Corner of Heaven: Heloise's Critique of Monasticism," *Mediaeval Studies* 49 (1987): 221–53. Heloise's Rule is discussed in John F. Benton, "Fraud, Fiction, and Borrowing in the Correspondence of Abelard and Heloise," in *Pierre Abélard — Pierre le Vénérable*, Colloques internationaux du Centre de la Recherche Scientifique, 546 (Paris, 1975), pp. 471–506, reprinted in his *Culture, Power, and Personality in Medieval France*, pp. 421–430; and in Pascale Bourgain, "Héloïse," in *Abélard et son temps*, pp. 219–223.

167. Paris, *Avenay*, p. 86, no. 20 (1189); p. 90, no. 26 (1193).

168. Françoise Poirier-Coutansais, *Gallia Monastica: Tableaux et cartes de dépendances monastiques*, vol. 1, *Les abbayes bénédictines du diocèse de Reims* (Paris, 1974), p. 506, no. 61A (1168).

169. Lalore, *Paraclet*, pp. 98–105, no. 83 (1194, episcopal confirmation of earlier gifts).

170. See n. 75 above.

171. Dameron (1190–ca. 1227) and Haye (1202–22) seem to have remained at Foissy the rest of their lives, while Adeline of Briel stayed sixteen years (1197–1213) then left to marry a knight. See Jean Longnon, *Recherches sur la vie de Geoffroy de Villehardouin* (Paris, 1939), pp. 42, 123–24, and Theodore Evergates, "The Origin of the Lords of Karytaina in the Frankish Morea," *Medieval Prosopography* 15 (1994): 97 n. 37.

172. Jean Longnon, *Recherches*, pp. 121–23.

173. Lalore, *Paraclet*, pp. 196–197, no. 216 (1237).

174. Jean Verdon, "Les moniales dans la France de l'Ouest aux XIᵉ et XIIᵉ siècles: étude d'histoire sociale," *Cahiers de civilisation médiévale* 19 (1976): 251, 254. Verdon calculates, that of the sixty-five nuns consecrated at Marcigny-sur-Loire during almost a century (1055–1136), thirty-one were unmarried (but over twenty years old), seventeen were widowed, and seventeen were still married; that is, over half were or had been married. It is not clear, however, how representative those sixty-five cases were of a community that could number ninety-six nuns at any time.

175. It consisted of a house at Sézanne with a storage cellar, half of the adjacent house, and two-thirds of a vineyard (Lalore, *Paraclet*, pp. 89–90, no. 72 [1185]).

176. Arbois de Jubainville, *Histoire*, 3: 445, no. 117 (1155); see also n. 129 above.

177. Paris, *Avenay*, pp. 84–85, no. 18 (1186, dedication charter).

178. See n. 154 above.

179. Venarde, *Women's Monasticism*, pp. 120–24, describes Heloise's role in forming the Paraclete's endowment.

180. See n. 80 above.

181. See n. 37 above.

182. Count Henry II summarized the documents lost in the fire; Charles Lalore, "Documents sur l'abbaye de Notre-Dame-aux-Nonnains de Troyes," *Mémoires de la Société académique d'agriculture, des sciences, arts et belles-lettres du département de l'Aube* 38 (1874): 10–12, no. 7 (1189).

183. These events are described in Johnson, *Equal in Monastic Profession*, pp. 87–89, 171–72. Clement IV's bulls recounting the events are in Lalore, "Documents sur l'abbaye de Notre-Dame-aux-Nonnains de Troyes," pp. 120–21, no. 194 (1266); pp. 123–24, no. 199 (1268); both tr. in Evergates, *Documents*, no. 101.

184. See the sensible remarks in Jacqueline Murray, "Thinking About Gender: The Diversity of Medieval Perspectives," in Carpenter and MacLean, *Power of the Weak*, pp. 1–26.

185. See nn. 53, 126 above.

Chapter 4: Countesses as Rulers in Flanders

1. For the early history of Flanders, see Jean Dunbabin, *France in the Making, 843–1180* (Oxford, 1985), pp. 68–74, 207–13.

2. Particularly valuable are the charters of the counts and countesses collected for the Belgian Commission Royale d'Histoire: *Actes des comtes de Flandre, 1071–1128*, ed. Fernand Vercauteren (Brussels, 1938); *De oorkonden der graven van Vlaanderen, juli 1128–sept. 1191*, ed. Thérèse de Hemptinne and Adriaan Verhulst, vol. 1 (Brussels, 1988) and vol. 2 (in preparation); and *De oorkonden der graven van Flaanderen, 1191–aanvang 1206*, ed. Walter Prevenier, vol. 2 (Brussels, 1964).

3. *La chronique de Gislebert de Mons*, ed. Léon Vanderkindere (Brussels, 1904), pp. 113–114.

4. Karen S. Nicholas, "The Role of Feudal Relationships in the Consolidation of Power in the Principalities of the Low Countries," in *Law, Custom, and the Social*

Fabric in Medieval Europe: Essays In Honor of Bryce Lyon, ed. Bernard S. Bachrach and David Nicholas (Kalamazoo, Mich., 1990), pp. 113–130.

5. Gislebert of Mons, *La chronique*, pp. 3–4. Gislebert, writing 150 years after these events, was not in a position to know the exact circumstances of Richilde's actions. We cannot know for certain whether Roger was physically disabled or Gislebert or someone else devised this justification for Richilde's actions dispossessing him of Hainaut. Gislebert was accustomed to serving counts of Hainaut who kept all their children in secular life, so that it is not surprising that he criticized Richilde's actions. We do know that Richilde did not forget Roger, because she later helped him become bishop of Châlons-sur-Marne.

6. "Flandria Generosa," *MGH, SS*, 9: 322. This twelfth-century account may not be accurate in all its details, but it is clear that the south supported Richilde, while the north (maritime Flanders), alienated by comital concentration on the interior of the county, supported Robert.

7. Galbert of Bruges, *The Murder of Charles the Good, Count of Flanders*, tr. James Bruce Ross (Toronto, 1982), pp. 232–37. See also Charles Verlinden, *Robert Ier, le Frison, comte de Flandre: étude d'histoire politique* (Paris, 1935), pp. 57–70.

8. For Richilde's life and rule, see Thérèse de Hemptinne, "Vlaanderen en Henegouwen onder de erfgenamen van de Boudewijns, 1070–1244," in *Algemene Geschiedenis der Nederlanden* (Bussum, 1982), 2: 379–89; and Henri Pirenne, "Richilde," *Biographie nationale*, 19: 293–300. See also Gislebert of Mons, *La chronique*, pp. 3–17 and Jacques de Guise, *Histoire de Hainaut* vol. 11 (Paris, 1831), pp. 163–73. Some interesting recent comments are found in Megan McLaughlin, "The Woman Warrior: Gender, Warfare, and Society in Medieval Europe," *Women's Studies* 17 (1990): 193–209. See also Jacques Falmagne, *Baudouin V, comte de Hainaut, 1150–1195* (Montreal, 1966), pp. 49–60. For the infeudation of Hainaut to the bishop of Liège, see A. Hansay, "L'inféodation du comté de Hainaut ag l'Eglise de Liège en 1071," *Bulletin de la Société archéologique et historique de Liège* 13 (1902): 45–58.

9. See Chapter 1 of this volume for her maternal grandmother, Countess Adela of Blois.

10. For the family of Robert the Frisian, see Verlinden, *Robert Ier*, pp. 27–39, 86–95, 136, 165. That Gertrude was overshadowed by Adele is suggested by the large number of Flemish charters involving interventions by the dowager countess: Adele appears in 67 percent of Baldwin V's charters and in 50 percent of Robert I's charters, while Gertrude appears in only 8 percent of Robert I's charters and 12 percent of Robert II's charters. For the source of these figures, see note 11 below.

11. Clemence's rule is studied in Penelope Adair, "Ego et Uxor Mea: Countess Clemence and Her Role in the Comital Family and in Flanders, 1092–1133," Ph.D. dissertation, University of California at Santa Barbara, 1995. See also Thérèse de Hemptinne, "Clementia van Bourgondie, gravin van Vlaanderen," *Nationaal Biografisch Woordenboek* vol. 10 (Brussels, 1981), cols. 148–50.

12. Adair, "Ego et Uxor Mea," pp. 166–248 ("Areas of Influence: The Dower and Special Interests"), an extended and perceptive analysis of how Flemish counts assigned their wives' dowers, and specifically how Clemence used her dower lands to advance her personal, family, and political interests in Flanders. Adair (pp. 66–67) gives the proportion of each count's charters in which each countess appeared.

13. Adair, "Ego et Uxor Mea," pp. 79–105.

14. Adair, "Ego et Uxor Mea," pp. 125–65. For the religious roles of aristocratic laywomen, see Sharon Farmer, "Persuasive Voices: Clerical Images of Medieval Wives," *Speculum* 61 (1986): 517–43.

15. Vercauteren, *Actes des comtes*, p. xxvii (1096), pp. xxxv–vi (1093–1111), p. xxxvi (1093–1111), pp. 101–5 (1106–7), pp. 116–18 (1110), pp. 122–24 (1110).

16. Vercauteren, *Actes des comtes*, pp. 130–31 (1111), pp. 134–40 (1111/1112), pp. 142–43 (1112), pp. 149–50 (1114), pp. 169–71 (1115), p. 175 (1115).

17. De Hemptinne, "Vlaanderen en Henegouwen," 2: 376.

18. Translated by Adair, "Ego et Uxor Mea," p. 251.

19. Adair, "Ego et Uxor Mea," pp. 123–24, 255–59.

20. Adair, "Ego et Uxor Mea," pp. 272–98.

21. Herman of Tournai, *The Restoration of the Monastery of St. Martin of Tournai*, tr. Lynn H. Nelson (Washington, D.C., 1996), pp. 35–36.

22. Vercauteren, *Actes des comtes*, pp. 267–29 (1124).

23. Vercauteren, *Actes des comtes*, pp. 228–35 (1121); de Hemptinne and Verhulst, *De oorkonden der graven*, 1: 35–36, 170–72.

24. Adair, "Ego et Uxor Mea," pp. 295–98.

25. She appears with Charles in two charters in 1121 (Vercauteren, *Actes des comtes*, pp. 228–31, 234–35), but there is evidence that she stayed with him thereafter.

26. For the reigns of Charles the Good and William Clito, see James Bruce Ross, introduction, *Galbert of Bruges*.

27. Thérèse de Hemptinne, "Diederik van de Elzas, graaf van Vlaanderen," *Nationaal Biografisch Woordenboek* vol. 13 (Brussels, 1990), col. 224. His first wife, Swanehilde, was related to him; de Hemptinne suggests she was a daughter of Folmar, count of Metz, whose mother bore the same name. They married before 1127, when Thierry was lord of Bitche in Alsace.

28. Clemence appears in 11 percent of Thierry's charters during her lifetime, while Swanehilde appears in 17 percent of them during her lifetime, mainly to confirm Thierry's donations.

29. De Hemptinne, "Diederik," col. 224.

30. De Hemptinne, "Diederik," cols. 233–34.

31. Sybil's role in this is discussed in de Hemptinne and Verhulst, *De oorkonden der graven*, 1: 68–274. See also de Hemptinne, "Diederik," cols. 224–42.

32. De Hemptinne and Verhulst, *de oorkonden der graven* 1: nos. 47–49, 215–16, 248, 260–62; de Hemptinne, "Diederik," cols. 230–32.

33. De Hemptinne and Verhulst, *De oorkonden der graven*, 1: 133–37, 268–71, 336–38, 399–402.

34. Lambert of Waterlos, "Annales Cameracenses," *MGH, SS*, 16: 516.

35. De Hemptinne, "Diederik," col. 236; De Hemptinne, "Vlaanderen en Henegouwen," col. 381.

36. De Hemptinne and Verhulst, *De oorkonden der graven*, 2: no. 299. I am grateful to Thérèse de Hemptinne of the University of Ghent for allowing me to examine in manuscript, her edition of Philip's charters which is still several years away from publication.

37. For Sybil, see Thérèse de Hemptinne and Michel Parisse, "Thierry d'Alsace, comte de Flandre: biographie et actes," *Annales de l'Est* 5th ser., 43 (1991): 83–

113; de Hemptinne, "Diederik," pp. 224–42; and Hans van Werveke, *Een Vlaamse graaf van Europees formaat: Filips van de Elzas* (Haarlem, 1976). See also de Hemptinne, "Vlaanderen en Henegauwen," cols. 383–85.

38. Personal conversation, Harvard University, May 3, 1991.

39. Gislebert of Mons, *La chronique*, pp. 86–88, 120 (n. 3).

40. Gislebert of Mons, *La chronique*, pp. 147–48.

41. De Hemptinne and Verhulst, *De oorkonden der graven*, 1: 306–7 (1161); 2: no. 619 (1181–82). Gislebert of Mons, *La chronique*, pp. 147–48.

42. De Hemptinne and Verhulst, *De oorkonden der graven*, 2: nos. 703, 733, 778, 844, 845, 846, 850.

43. Matilda's dowry included, in addition to Aire and St-Omer, the towns of Douai, l'Ecluse, Orchies, Lille, Nieppe, Cassel, Diksmuide, Veurne, Saint-Winnoksbergen, and Bourbourg. See also Giselbert of Mons, *La chronique*, p. 164.

44. For Matilda's charters, see Prevenier, *De oorkonden*, 2: 11–31, 109–12, 124–26, 164–66, 185–86, 526–28, 559–60, 605–8, 630–31, 636–37, 639–42. Jacques de Guise, *Histoire de Hainaut*, 13: 59–60.

45. Gislebert of Mons, *La chronique*, pp. 234–41, 254, 262.

46. Gislebert of Mons, *La chronique*, pp. 99, 114, 150, 174, 276.

47. Prevenier, *De oorkonden*, 2: 50–70, nos. 11–25 (1193–94). As Margaret's heir, Baldwin IX inherited Flanders in 1194, a year before his father's death.

48. Gislebert of Mons, who was a close but not impartial observer of the negotiations that arranged the marriage between Isabel and King Philip II, claims that Baldwin V of Hainaut was reluctant to allow the marriage to take place because Isabel had long been promised to Henry of Champagne, and because Isabel would take a large portion of western Flanders as dowry, away from his son. Gislebert declares, as does the "Flandria Generosa," that it was Philip of Flanders who was determined for the king to marry his niece, since he himself had no daughter. Baldwin V may have feared that the king would use the marriage to constrain his behavior and to divert his loyalty away from the empire and toward France, and that Isabel would be unhappily caught in the middle, all of which did happen. In 1184 a coalition of French nobles, led by the Champenois party, persuaded King Philip to divorce Isabel, but with her father's help she managed to change Philip's mind. In 1187 Isabel gave birth to the future Louis VIII, and she died three years later. See Gislebert of Mons, *La chronique*, pp. 129–30, 152–53, 199, 245.

49. Their daughter Agnes of Beaujeu became countess of Champagne; see Chapter 3 in this volume.

50. Gislebert of Mons, *La chronique*, p. 192; Jacques de Guise, *Histoire de Hainaut*, 13: 243–47.

51. See André Joris, "Un seul amour . . . ou plusieurs femmes?" in *Femmes: Mariages-Lignages, XIIe–XIVe siècles: mélanges offerts à Georges Duby* (Brussels, 1992), pp. 197–214.

52. Prevenier, *De oorkonden*, 2: 98–99, 112–13, 180–81, 203–4, 226–32, 253–58, 265–66, 270–71, 319–20, 367–72, 468–70, 476–78.

53. Prevenier, *De oorkonden*, 2: 518–20, 549–52.

54. Theo Luykx, *Johanna van Constantinopel* (Antwerp, 1946), p. 69.

55. De Hemptinne, "Vlaanderen en Henegouwen," pp. 394–95. Philippe

Mousket says of Marie's devotion to Baldwin, *ki moult trés durement l'ama* ("Historia Regum Francorum," *MGH, SS*, 21: 746).

56. De Hemptinne, "Vlaanderen en Henegouwen," pp. 394–96.

57. "Flandria Generosa," *MGH, SS*, 9: 330.

58. De Hemptinne, "Vlaanderen en Henegouwen," p. 396.

59. Luykx, *Johanna van Constantinopel*, pp. 122–24.

60. Arnold of Oudenaarde's support was especially important in Jeanne's early years. Arnold, a good friend of Baldwin IX, was probably also a father figure in Jeanne's life. She had been extraordinarily badly parented: orphaned at five or six, she had been betrayed by her uncle Philip the Noble and by the French king who posed as her protector, then involuntarily abandoned by her husband for thirteen years. A phrase by Philippe Mousket (*Quar il estoit moult ses amis* ["Historia Regum Francorum,"*MGH, SS*, 26: 358]) led some later chroniclers to misinterpret Jeanne's attachment to Arnold by calling him her lover. But despite her reliance on Arnold Jeanne had the spunk in 1217 to contest his control of the *winagium* (an exaction paid for safe transport) at Yseel; see Luykx, *Johanna van Constantinopel*, pp. 155, 163. Michael of Harnes was particularly helpful in Jeanne's attempts to control the Flemish nobility, some of whom had usurped comital rights; see Luykx, pp. 161–64.

61. Luykx, *Johanna van Constantinopel*, pp. 363–83. See also Karen S. Nicholas, "Women as Rulers: Countesses Jeanne and Marguerite of Flanders, 1212–78," in *Women of Power: Queens, Regents, and Potentates*, ed. Theresa Vann (Dallas, Tex., 1993), pp. 73–89. For the affair of the False Baldwin, see de Guise, *Histoire de Hainaut*, 14: 409–21.

62. Luykx, *Johanna van Constantinopel*, pp. 170–76.

63. Luykx, *Johanna van Constantinopel*, pp. 240–47.

64. Luykx, *Johanna van Constantinopel*, pp. 247–62.

65. Luykx, *Johanna van Constantinopel*, pp. 286–320, 345–59, 390–420; Jacques de Guise, *Histoire de Hainaut*, 15: 25–27.

66. Roger S. Wieck, *Painted Prayers: The Book of Hours in Medieval and Renaissance Art* (New York, 1997), p. 23 lists the contents of Books of Hours, including the Hours of the Virgin.

67. Marcia J. Epstein, ed. and tr., *"Prions en chantant": Devotional Songs of the Trouvères* (Toronto, 1997), pp. 132–35.

68. Most Belgian historians of the past century have followed Charles Duvivier in blaming Jeanne for the loss of Flemish lands to King Philip (which occurred while she was an infant), for the affair of the False Baldwin (which was not her fault, and which she successfully handled), and for vindictiveness against Bouchard of Avesnes (which is understandable, since he personally betrayed her by abducting her ten-year-old sister).

69. Charles Duvivier, *La querelle des d'Avesnes et des Dampierre jusqu'à la mort de Jean d'Avesnes (1257)*, 2 vols. (Brussels, 1894). See also the commentary by Luykx, *Johanna van Constantinopel*, pp. 199–211. See also Jacques de Guise, *Histoire de Hainaut*, 14: 3–17, 33–35; 15: 19–27, 357–439.

70. M. Vandermaesen, "Vlaanderen en Henegouwen onder het Huis van Dampierre 1244–1384," in *Algemene Geschiedenis der Nederlanden*, 2: 400–401. Guy of Dampierre married an heiress, Matilda of Béthune, who brought Dendermonde

and Béthune to her husband. Marguerite and Guy purchased the lordship of Bornem, and in 1263/4 they bought out the rights of Baldwin of Courtenay and Henry count of Luxembourg to the county of Namur.

71. *Oorkondenboek van Holland en Zeeland tot het einde van het Hollandsche Huis*, ed. L. Ph. C. van den Bergh, 2 vols. (Amsterdam, 1866–73): 2: 234–35.

72. Cyriel Vleeschouwers, "De oorkonden van de Sint-Baafsabdij te Gent," doctoral dissertation, University of Ghent, 1986, pp. 684–86, 757–59, 949–51, 1037–39.

73. J. R. Maddicot, *Simon de Montfort* (Cambridge, 1994), p. 290.

74. David M. Nicholas, *Medieval Flanders* (London, 1992), pp. 176–79.

75. For example, the chapter on Jeanne's and Marguerite's reigns in Nicholas, *Medieval Flanders* is entitled "The Catastrophe of Medieval Flanders."

76. Luykx, *Johanna van Constantinopel*, pp. 130–34, 168–79, 274–81, 303–9, 311–14, 365–71, 390–411.

77. Luykx, *Johanna van Constantinopel*, pp. 180–98, 310–18, 345–59, 412–20. Although most countesses exhibited exemplary piety, they generally preferred the role of patron to that of nun; only Sybil ended her days in a convent.

Chapter 5: Women, Poets, and Politics in Occitania

I dedicate this essay to my late wife, Susan Ross Huston, whose many dinner-table poetry seminars first taught me how to read troubadour verse. It could not have been written without the help of Margaret Switten as well, who taught me most of what I know about the language of the troubadours, and whose comments on an earlier draft have saved me from many errors. I thank her too for transcribing the music for "A chantar m'er." My thanks also to Ekkehard Simon, whose invitation to speak to the Harvard Medieval Studies Seminar prompted me to elaborate many of the arguments presented here.

1. Translation adapted from *The Vidas of the Troubadours*, ed. and tr. Margarita Egan (New York, 1984), p. 78.

2. *The Poems of the Troubadour Peire Rogier*, ed. Derek E. T. Nicholson (New York, 1976), p. 81.

3. Nicholson, *Peire Rogier*, pp. 88–89. The reference to "dreit-n'avetz" and the district of Savès remain a mystery. An alternative manuscript reading (ibid., p. 97) replaces *en Saves* with *on ill es* ("where she is").

4. "In dealing with writers," remarks Leon Edel, "we discover quickly enough how their inner modes of thought were projected into their art. . . . [I]f the biographer reads a writer's work carefully, . . . he is aware of the singular personality who is his subject. He has seen and knows the work; and he must discover the life materials out of which it came into being. By this kind of continuing psychological approach, he can arrive at the essence of a life" (*The Age of the Archive* [Middletown, Conn., 1966], pp. 14–15). One of the central problems faced by students of troubadour song in the last generation has been to find an alternative to assumptions such as these about the connection of poetry to the poet's life. On the way troubadour poetry was understood by its audiences in the thirteenth century and after,

see Maria Luisa Meneghetti, *Il pubblico dei travatori: ricezione e riuso dei testi lirici cortesi fino al XIV secolo* (Modena, 1984).

5. Such, at least, is implied by Orderic Vitalis's account of William on crusade; see Orderic Vitalis, *The Ecclesiastical History of Orderic Vitalis*, ed. and tr. Marjorie Chibnall, 6 vols. (Oxford, 1969–80): 10.20 (5: 324–25): 10.21 (5: 342–43).

6. "Estat ai en greu cossirier," in *Songs of the Women Troubadours*, ed. and tr. Matilda Bruckner, Laurie Shephard, and Sarah White (New York, 1995), pp. 10–11.

7. *The Songs of Jaufré Rudel*, ed. Rupert Pickens (Toronto, 1978), p. 164.

8. This view was first propounded by Erich Köhler, *Trobadorlyrik und höfischer Roman: Aufsätze zur französischen und provenzalischen Literatur des Mittelalters* (Berlin, 1962); see esp. pp. 8–9.

9. The classic statement of this position is in Georges Duby, *Medieval Marriage: Two Models from Twelfth-Century France* (Baltimore, 1978); see esp. pp. 12–14, as well as his essay "Women and Power" in *Cultures of Power: Lordship, Status, and Process in Twelfth-Century Europe*, ed. Thomas Bisson (Philadelphia, 1995), pp. 69–85. A recent work of literary criticism that takes Köhler and Duby as its starting point is R. Howard Bloch, *Medieval Misogyny and the Invention of Western Romantic Love* (Chicago, 1991), chap. 7.

10. See most recently Don A. Monson, "The Troubadour's Lady Reconsidered Again," *Speculum* 70 (1995): 255–74, and the literature cited there.

11. Castelloza, "Ja de chantar non degr'aver talan," in Bruckner et al., *Songs of the Women Troubadours*, pp. 14–15.

12. Peire Vidal, "Anc no mori per amor ni per al," in *Les poésies de Peire Vidal*, ed. Joseph Anglade (Paris, 1923), p. 76.

13. Most notably, Simon Gaunt, *Gender and Genre in Medieval French Literature* (Cambridge, 1995), pp. 122–79.

14. The most recent Freudian treatment of this poetry is Rouben C. Cholakian, *The Troubadour Lyric: A Psychocritical Reading* (New York and Manchester, 1990), who asserts (p. 188) that "the psychoanalytic reading of the courtly discourse provides explanations which supersede its sociohistorical framework." C. Stephen Jaeger has challenged the Freudian approach forcefully in more recent versions of the paper originally published as "L'amour des rois: structures sociales d'une forme de sensibilité aristocratique," *Annales: Economies, Sociétés, Civilisations* 46 (1991): 547–71. Jaeger, *Ennobling Love: In Search of a Lost Sensibility* (Philadelphia, 1999), which explores these points further, appeared too recently to be included in the present discussion.

15. Georges Duby, "Dans la France du Nord-Ouest au XIIe siècle: les *jeunes* dans la société aristocratique," *Annales: Economies, Sociétés, Civilisations* 19 (1964): 835–46; tr. as "Youth in Aristocratic Society" in *Lordship and Community in Medieval Europe*, ed. F. L. Cheyette (New York, 1967) and in Duby, *The Chivalrous Society* (Berkeley and Los Angeles, 1977).

16. Johan Huizinga, *The Autumn of the Middle Ages* (Chicago, 1996).

17. The various references to Ermengard in troubadour poetry are discussed in Nicholson, *Peire Rogier*, pp. 160–64.

18. *Orkneyinga saga: The History of the Earls of Orkney*, ed. Hermann Pálsson and Paul Edwards (London, 1978). For a discussion of this text see Jacqueline

Caille, "Une idylle entre la vicomtesse Ermengarde de Narbonne et le prince Rogn-vald Kali des Orcades au milieu du XIIe siècle?" in *Hommage à Robert Saint-Jean*, ed. Guy Romestan (Montpellier, 1993), pp. 229–33, and the older bibliography listed in Nicholson, *Peire Rogier*, p. 164, note.

19. The documentation for Ermengard is widely dispersed, from the Biblio-thèque Nationale de France to the Archives of the Crown of Aragon in Barcelona; a large portion, though not all, is published in *Histoire Général de Languedoc*, ed. Claude Devic and Joseph Vaissete, 16 vols. (Toulouse, 1872–95), vol. 5 (cited hereafter as *HGL*). The surviving documents of Raymond V are inventoried in Emile-G. Léonard, *Catalogue des actes de comtes de Toulouse: Raymond V (1149–1194)* (Paris, 1932).

20. Eugène Martin-Chabot, ed., *Les archives de la Cour des Comptes, Aides et Finances de Montpellier, avec un essai de restitution des premiers registres de sénéchaussée* (Paris, 1907), p. vii.

21. AD, Aude, H 206 (1171); BN, Doat 59, fol. 58 (1171, witness with Er-mengard); Archives communales de Narbonne, AA 104, fol. 179v.

22. William appears in the Trencavel entourage repeatedly from 1139 (Société archéologique de Montpellier, ms. 10, cited hereafter as "Cartulaire des Trencavel," fol. 59) to 1163 (*HGL*, 5: 1270, 1277) and as a witness to Ermengard's acts in 1157 (*Cartulaire de l'abbaye de Silvanès*, ed. P. A. Verlaguet, Archives historiques de Rouergue, 1 [Rodez, 1910], no. 314) and several times in 1163 (*HGL*, 5: 1267, 1273; see also cols. 1275, 1277). Raymond of Durban is with Ermengard in 1163 and 1171 (*HGL*, 5: 1267; BN, Doat 47, fol. 23). A Bernard of Durban (one of the names that appears regularly in the family thereafter) made a settlement with the abbey of Mas-d'Azil in 1067 (*HGL*, 5: 547); an Ademar of Durban, who was possibly an ancestor (the name does not reappear in later generations), served as judge in the court of Aimery of Narbonne in 1097 (*HGL*, 5: 752) and appears as witness a number of times between 1080 and 1108.

23. BN, Doat 55, fols. 206, 241; Doat 59, fol. 89; G. Mouynès, ed., "Cartulaire de la seigneurie de Fontjoncouse," *Bulletin de la Commission archéologique et littéraire de Narbonne* 1 (1877), no. 24. Between 1170 and 1197, Hugh and his son Hugh appear frequently as witnesses and participants in documents from within and around the city.

24. Raymond of Ouveilhan appears as the developer of the suburb of Belveder (BN, Doat 48, fol. 28, probably around 1158). Members of this family appear from 1124 onward.

25. AD, Haute-Garonne, H Malte Narbonne, layette 1, no. 9 (1184).

26. BM Narbonne, Inventaire Rocques, Gruissan, no. 1 (1084). The docu-ment mentions an earlier generation that held the tower at Gruissan.

27. Ermengard's entourage will be discussed in considerable detail in my forth-coming book, *Lady of the Troubadours: Ermengard of Narbonne and the Politics of her Age*.

28. *Cartulaire de Maguelone*, ed. Jean Rouquette and A. Villemagne (Mont-pellier, 1912), 1: no. 135.

29. This story will be told in *Lady of the Troubadours*.

30. Already in 1162, William Bistani appears with members of Ermengard's

entourage, though not in the presence of Ermengard herself (BN, Mélanges Colbert 414, no. 42). His son John Bistani who would become, if he was not already, one of the richest men in the city (during the Albigensian Crusades the archbishop pawned half of the city's fortifications to him in return for a loan to finance Simon de Montfort's crusade [BN, Baluze 374, p. 123 and Baluze 380, no. 35]), first appears as a witness to acts of Pedro de Lara in 1193 and 1194 (*HGL*, 8: 418, no. 11; BN, Doat 59, fol. 137); he is present at a great gathering of Narbonnais and Catalan nobility and city notables in 1204 (BN, Doat 40, fol. 20).

31. Joan Ferrante, *Woman as Image in Medieval Literature* (New York, 1975), p. 67 and the references cited there.

32. Bloch, *Medieval Misogyny*, chaps. 6–7.

33. Frederick Goldin, "The Array of Perspectives in the Early Courtly Love Lyric," in *Pursuit of Perfection: Courtly Love in Medieval Literature*, ed. Joan Ferrante and George Economou (Port Washington, N.Y., 1975), p. 57.

34. The most complete account we have of these events is in an Occitan Hebrew manuscript, written about 1160: Arieh Graböis, "Une étape dans l'évolution vers la désagrégation de l'état toulousain au XIIe siècle: l'intervention d'Alphonse-Jourdain à Narbonne (1134–1143)," *Annales du Midi* 78 (1960): 25. Graböis's commentary on the events should be treated with caution. The marriage contract (in French translation) is in Guillaume Catel, *Mémoires de l'histoire de Languedoc* (Toulouse, 1633), p. 589. For more details see Jacqueline Caille, "Les seigneurs de Narbonne dans le conflit Toulouse-Barcelone au XIIe siècle," *Annales du Midi* 97 (1985): 227–44.

35. The peace treaty is printed in *HGL*, 5: 1069.

36. The only evidence for this marriage is an oath of fidelity given to him by Bernard of Porta Regia (Catel, *Mémoires*, p. 589).

37. For the complex succession to the county of Provence, see Jean-Pierre Poly, *La Provence et la société féodale (879–1166): contribution à l'étude des structures dites féodales dans le Midi* (Paris, 1976), pp. 318–20.

38. See Jacqueline Caille, "Seigneurs et 'peuple' de Narbonne (XIe–XVe siècles)," in *Histoire de Narbonne*, ed. Jacques Michaud and André Cabanis (Toulouse, 1981), pp. 119–40.

39. *HGL*, 8: 325.

40. *HGL*, 5: 1171.

41. *Aliscans*, ed. Claude Regnier (Paris, 1990), 1: ll. 3105–9. Regnier, like previous editors, dates the poem to the very end of the twelfth century (around the time of Ermengard's death). An abridged translation of the entire *chanson de geste* appears in Joan Ferrante, ed., *Guillaume d'Orange: Four Twelfth-Century Epics* (New York, 1974).

42. For Stephania's dowry we have only her statement in 1150 after her defeat by the count of Provence (Edwin Smyrl, "La famille des Baux," *Cahiers du Centre d'études des sociétés méditerranéennes* 2 [1968], 81). In her oaths of that year she pointedly includes her mother's title when she names herself "daughter of the countess Gerberga." The donations to the count of Barcelona are printed in *Liber feudorum maior*, ed. Francisco Miquel Rosell, 2 vols. (Barcelona, 1945), nos. 875, 876, 877.

43. Smyrl, "La famille des Baux," p. 36. The emperor also granted them the regalian right to coin money at Arles, Aix, and Trinquetaille (their castle across the river from Arles).

44. Smyrl, "La famille des Baux," pp. 40–44.

45. Pierre Bonnassie, *La Catalogne du milieu du Xe à la fin du XIe siècle*, 2 vols. (Toulouse, 1975–76), pp. 632–641; S. Sobrequés i Vidal, *Els grans comtes de Barcelona* (Barcelona, 1961), pp. 35–66; and Martin Aurell, *Les noces du comte: mariage et pouvoir en Catalogne (785–1213)* (Paris, 1994), pp. 222–55.

46. On all this, see Bonnassie, *La Catalogne*, pp. 639–680, 698–711 and passim; Aurell, *Les noces du comte*, pp. 257–95.

47. Fredric L. Cheyette, "The 'Sale' of Carcassonne to the Counts of Barcelona and the Rise of the Trencavels," *Speculum* 63 (1988): 854–59.

48. See the acts of Bernard Ato, especially the oaths of fidelity, in *HGL*, 5: 965–66.

49. "Les pratiques sociales et le droit ouvraient à toute dame de l'aristocratie, surtout si elle était du tempérament d'Almodis ou d'Ermessende, l'accès aux plus hautes résponsabilités. . . . Elles ont joui . . . d'un pouvoir indéniable. Le XIe siècle méridional fut-il vraiment misogyne?" (Aurell, *Les noces du comte*, p. 280).

50. *HGL*, 5: 984.

51. *HGL*, 6: 44–45.

52. Rouquette and Villemagne, *Cartulaire de Maguelone*, 1: no. 155.

53. *HGL*, 8: 293.

54. "insano muliercula pruritu et irreverenti" (William of Malmesbury, *De gestis regum anglorum*, ed. William Stubbs [London, 1889], 2: 455).

55. These texts are printed by the hundreds (usually in abbreviated form) in *HGL*, 5 and 8, as well as in the cartulary of the lords of Montpellier, the *Liber instrumentorum memorialium: cartulaire des Guillems de Montpellier*, ed. A. Germain (Montpellier, 1884).

56. Compare, for example, two donations in the Béziers "Black Book," one from 897 in which the clause reads, following a late-Antique pattern, "Si quis vero . . . si nos ipsi aut quislibet nostre posteritatis vel persona cujuscunque conditionis . . . voluerit contraire, tantum . . . componat et sua repetitio nullum vigorem obtineat," repeated in expanded or contracted form through the tenth century, and the first surviving one in the collection to use the new form in 1019: "Si quis autem venerit, sive homo sive femina aut ulla persona, sive amissa, subrogata, ad disrumpendum, non liceat eis facere sed conponat vobis tantum" (*Cartulaire de Béziers (Livre Noir)*, ed. J. Rouquette [Paris, 1918], nos. 9 and 60).

57. Rouquette, *Cartulaire de Béziers*, no. 147 (1135); *HGL*, 5: 790 (unless the *uxor* in the text is a misreading for *uxorem*, in which case the wife was victim rather than attacker, but still involved directly in battle).

58. *Cartulaires des Templiers de Douzens*, ed. Pierre Gérard and Elisabeth Magnou (Paris, 1965), no. 20 (squabbles with brothers); Rouquette, *Cartulaire de Béziers*, no. 100 (moneylending).

59. Laureta, sister of William of Durban (*HGL*, 5: 852 no. III; 5: 908); Ricsovendis of Termes (*HGL*, 5: 1277, 8: 412); the sisters of Arnold of Fenollèd (AD, Haute-Garonne, H Malte Homps 5, no. 14). Arnold seems to have recovered from

the illness or wound that prompted this first testament; the second, which he dictated on his deathbed three months later (BN, Doat 59, fol. 72), left his principal castle of Fenollèd to a nephew and two other male relations, while the sisters only inherited his other three castles. It is striking that three women castellans can be identified even in the paltry archival remains from the abbey of Quarante, north of Narbonne: Poncia of Coumiac and her husband who gave half of the castle of Coumiac with its *dominatu* to the abbey of Quarante (the order of listing of wife and husband here implying that the castle is hers [*HGL*, 5: 1273 (1163)]). Lady Calva, daughter of Aladais, *mandato eiusdem dominae matris meae*, who exchanged oaths of fidelity with the abbot and cellarer of the same abbey for the castle of Argeliers and its *forciis* (BN, Doat 58, fol. 148 [1192]). The database from which Claudie Duhamel Amado argues that women after 1130 were "exclues du fief" seems to me to rest on a misunderstanding of the nature of castle-holding; see her "Femmes entre elles: filles et épouses languedociennes (XIe–XIIe siècles)," in *Femmes, Mariages-Lignages, XIIe–XIVe siècles: mélanges offerts à Georges Duby* (Brussels, 1992), pp. 125–56.

60. Germain, *Liber instrumentorum memorialium*, nos. 348, 360, 365, 367 (Castries), no. 377 (Villeneuve), no. 421 (Pignan), no. 468 (Balaruc), nos. 482, 485, 495, 525 (Poujet), nos. 534, 535 (Clermont); no. 119 (vicariate). See also Adalais, vicar of Paulhan (no. 541).

61. BN, Doat 47, fols. 27ff. Too much should not be made of the verbal change, since the oaths survive only in seventeenth-century copies, and the change could be the work of the copyist. Note that the percentage, about 9 percent for the oaths and about the same for the actual muster of military forces (see the following note), is the same as that which Amado ("Femmes entre elles") found for women holders of noble fiefs in the Béziers cartulary. Since the documentation is fragmentary, however, and the database small, too much should not be made of these numbers.

62. BN, Doat 49, fols. 260–281v.

63. Pierre Clément Timbal et al., *La Guerre de Cent Ans vue à travers les registres du Parlement* (Paris, 1961), pp. 16–17.

64. On this, Amado, "Femmes entre elles," accurately summarizes the evidence.

65. These are among the many varieties of castellans' rights mentioned in Occitan documents. Every castle and every village was different, the dues depending on negotiation and arbitration among various claimants and, of course, on simple arbitrary imposition by those with power, which—if carried on long enough— became "customary."

66. One oath from a woman to a woman survives (*Les plus anciennes chartes en langue provençal*, ed. Clovis Brunel [Geneva, 1973], no. 8 [1103]). Every mention of a woman holding a castle implies that such an oath had been given, and several of them (see n. 59 above) would have been given to women as well; the testament of Arnold of Fenollèd, for example, specifies that his sisters are to swear such oaths to lady Ermengard of Narbonne. Oaths by women to fellow castellans: BN, Doat 58, fols. 130, 148, 154; and one in which a man holds the castle for four months of the year and the woman for the other eight: "Cartulaire des Trencavel," fol. 162v (also Doat 167, fols. 18, 20, incompletely published *HGL*, 5: 1065).

67. For a survey of this literature, see Charles M. Radding, *The Origins of*

Medieval Jurisprudence: Pavia and Bologna, 850–1150 (New Haven, Conn., 1988), whose opinions on the debated dating and origins of some of the early works (such as the *Exceptiones Petri*) must, nevertheless, be treated with great caution.

68. See Stephan Kuttner, "The Revival of Jurisprudence," in *Renaissance and Renewal in the Twelfth Century*, ed. Robert L. Benson and Giles Constable (Cambridge Mass., 1982), pp. 299–323. A more comprehensive treatment will be found in the collective enterprise *Ius romanum medii aevi* (Milan, 1961–).

69. The most complete account of this subject is in André Gouron, "La science juridique française aux XIe et XIIe siècles," *Ius romanum medii aevi*, pars 14 d–e (Milan, 1978), reprinted in his *Etudes sur la diffusion des doctrines juridiques médiévales* (London, 1987). See also the other articles in this and his other two volumes of collected studies: *La science de droit dans le Midi de la France au Moyen Age* (London, 1984), and *Droit et coutume en France aux XIIe e XIIIe siècles* (Aldershot, 1993).

70. The documents from which we can reconstruct these events were copied later in the century without their dates; their sequence—and thus the sequence of events they record—are therefore speculative (*RHF*, 16: 89–91, nos. 273, 275–280). Ermengard's uneasy alliance with Raymond of Toulouse, of which she speaks in one letter, and the presence of the king's sister Constance at Raymond's side place the events between 1162 and 1167. Achille Luchaire, *Etudes sur les actes de Louis VII* (Paris, 1885), no. 495, dates them to 1164. Berenger of Puisserguier died in 1168 (Rouquette, *Cartulaire de Béziers*, no. 225). The name persisted in the next generation and doubtless beyond, as Berenger took it from a grandfather or grand-uncle already prominent in Narbonne in 1119 (BN, Doat 55, fol. 154; *HGL*, 8: 337, 338).

71. *HGL*, 8: 279, 296. Luchaire, *Etudes sur les actes de Louis VII*, nos. 340, 366, 387–89, 446, 456, 649, 771, etc. See Marcel Pacaut, *Louis VII et son royaume* (Paris, 1964), p. 185.

72. *Digest*, bk. 5, tit. 1, cap. 12. *Lo codi, in der lateinischen Ubersetzung des Ricardus Pisanus*, ed. Hermann Fitting (Halle, 1906; reprint Aalen, 1968), pp. 32, 34. On the date and place of composition of this work, see André Gouron, "La science juridique française," pp. 89–104. Whether and by what stages this rule came to be accepted in Occitan and Provençal practice is unknown. Martí Aurell's rich article, "La détérioration du statut de la femme aristocratique en Provence (Xe–XIIIe siècles)," *Le Moyen Age* 40 (1985): 5–32, treats many other aspects of thirteenth-century developments, but not this.

73. *RHF*, 16: 91, no. 280.

74. *RHF*, 16: 90, no. 275.

75. Rouquette, *Cartulaire de Béziers*, no. 225.

76. *HGL*, 5: 1204, no. II.

77. Brunel, *Les plus anciennes chartes*, no. 25: oath of Raines, son of Rocia to his brother William Rainon, c. 1128.

78. "Pois preyatz me, senhor," in *The Songs of Bernart de Ventadorn*, ed. Stephen Nichols, Jr., Stephen G., John A. Galm, and A. Bartlett Giarmetti (Chapel Hill, N.C., 1965), pp. 145–46.

79. "Non es meravelha s'eu chan" (Nichols et al., *Bernart de Ventadorn*, pp. 132–33). Bernart's choice of "dan" as rhyme word here, whose meaning ranges from emotional "hurt" to "damage to rights" adds force to the political language of

the first line. See Glynnis M. Cropp, *Le vocabulaire courtois des troubadours de l'époque classique* (Geneva, 1975), pp. 277–80.

80. "Non es meravelha s'eu chan."

81. The first used by Raimon de Miraval, the other three by Bernart de Ventadorn.

82. "Ar em al freg temps vengut" (Bruckner, et al., *Women Troubadours*, pp. 34–37).

83. "La dousa votz ai auzida" (Nichols, et al., *Bernart de Ventadorn*, pp. 104–5).

84. Ermengard, wife of Raymond Bernard, and one of the founders of the Trencavel family fortunes (see my "'Sale' of Carcassonne," pp. 853–56); Cecilia, wife of Ermengard's son Bernard Ato and mother of viscounts Raymond Trencavel, Roger of Béziers, and Bernard Ato of Nîmes; Saura, wife of Raymond Trencavel; Guillelma, wife of Bernard Ato of Nîmes. All ruled as widows, and oaths of fidelity survive to all of them.

85. "Cel que no vol auzir chanssos," in *The Cansos of Raimon de Miraval*, ed. Margaret L. Switten (Cambridge, Mass., 1985), p. 183.

86. "S'abrils e fuolhas e flors," in *The Poems of the Troubadour Bertran de Born*, ed. William Paden, Jr., Tilde Sankovitch, and Patricia Stäblein (Berkeley and Los Angeles, 1986), pp. 254–65.

87. "Lo tems vai e ven e vire" (Nichols et al., *Bernart de Ventadorn*, pp. 129–30).

88. A proverb referring to the Bretons' wait for king Arthur to return.

89. Nichols et al., *Bernart de Ventadorn*, pp. 104–6.

90. See above, p. 168.

91. Text and translation (amended) from Bruckner et al., *Women Troubadours*, pp. 6–9; Music transcribed by Margaret Switten. In line 19, I prefer to read the verbs as third person (as Bruckner et al. allow, though they choose in their translation to make them first person). For a more detailed analysis of the words and music of this song, see Fredric L. Cheyette and Margaret Switten, "Women in Troubadour Song: Of the Contessa and the Vilana," *Women and Music* 2 (1998): 26–46.

92. *La chanson de la croisade albigeoise*, ed. Eugène Martin-Chabot, 3 vols. (Paris, 1957–63): 1: 44.

93. See Cropp, *Le vocabulaire courtois*, pp. 52–66.

94. Peire Rogier, "Per far exbaudir mos vezis" (Nicholson, *Peire Rogier*, p. 61).

95. Bertran de Born, "Lo coms m'a mandat e mogut" (Paden et al., *Poems of Bertran de Born*, pp. 106–11).

96. *Songs of the Troubadours*, ed. Anthony Bonner (London, 1973), pp. 144–45. Paden et al., *Poems of Bertran de Born*, p. 108, translate *nos drutz* exactly the same.

97. See Du Cange, *Glossarium mediae et infimae latinitatis* (sub verbo). Cropp, *Vocabulaire courtois*, p. 59 n. 37 refers only to W. von Wartburg, *Französisches etymologisches Wörterbuch* and W. Meyer-Lübke, *Romanisches etymologisches Wörterbuch*, but there is an immense literature on the semantic field of this word in old Germanic languages, where its primary meaning is associated with the war band, from which, by the time of Otfrid, it had gained the meaning "friend." Other recent work has proposed an early meaning of "festive band" or a link to Germanic "growth magic."

Michael J. Enright, *Lady with a Mead Cup: Ritual, Prophecy, and Lordship in the European Warband, from the La Tène to the Viking Age* (Dublin, 1996), pp. 71–74, attempts to reconcile these versions of the word's etymology, with full references, p. 71, n. 8. The fullest account is D. H. Green, *The Carolingian Lord: Semantic Studies on Four Old High German Words* (Cambridge, 1965), pp. 270–357 and passim.

98. Martin-Chabot, *La chanson de la croisade*, 1: 70.

99. *HGL*, 5: 535. The sense of this word given in J. F. Niermeyer, *Mediae Latinitatis Lexicon Minus* (Leiden, 1976), p. 360 (taken from Du Cange) is clearly inapplicable here.

100. Germain, *Liber instrumentorum memorialium*, p. 106.

101. William of Pignan (Germain, *Liber instrumentorum memorialium*, no. 404); Milac (Brunel, *Les plus anciennes chartes*, no. 225). For a wider view of the sentiment of love as political and social phenomenon, see Jaeger, "L'amour des rois"; Michael Clanchy, "Law and Love in the Middle Ages," in *Disputes and Settlements: Law and Human Relations in the West*, ed. John Bossy (Cambridge, 1983), pp. 47–68; Stephen D. White, "*Pactum . . . Legem Vincit et Amor Judicium*: The Settlement of Disputes by Compromise in Eleventh-Century France," *American Journal of Legal History* 22 (1978): 281–308.

102. See the comments of Lauro Martines, "Ritual Language in Renaissance Italy," in *Riti e rituali nelle società medievali*, ed. Jacques Chiffoleau, Lauro Martines, and Agostino Bagliani (Spoleto, 1994), pp. 69–75.

Bibliography

MANUSCRIPT SOURCES

Archives Communales de Narbonne, AA 104.
AD, Aube, 3 H 9, 3 H 10.
AD, Aude, H 206.
AD, Cher, 13 H 36.
AD, Eure-et-Loir, G 709, H 613, H 1374.
AD, Haute-Garonne, H Malte Narbonne, H Malte Homps.
AD, Haute-Marne, G 76.
AD, Loir-et-Cher, F 246, 16 H 105, 16 H 109.
AD, Loiret, 2 mi 785 (olim H 182, item KI).
AD, Marne, G 389, no. 7.
AD, Seine-et-Marne, H 824.
AN, KK 1064.
BM, Narbonne, Inventaire Rocques.
BM, Reims, MS 15.
BN, Cinq Cents de Colbert, vols. 56–58.
BN, Collection Baluze, 374.
BN, Collection de Bourgogne, vol. 79.
BN, Collection Doat, 40, 47, 48, 55, 58, 59, 167
BN, Collection de Picardie, vol. 234.
BN, Fr. 12021.
BN, Lat. 5993, 9901, 17098.
BN, Lat. 5441^2, 10101, 12776, 12878, 13900, 17033, 28871.
BN, Lat. nouv. acq. 928.
BN, Mélanges Colbert, 414.
Société archéologique de Montpellier. Ms. 10. "Cartulaire dit de Foix" alias "Cartulaire des Trencavel."

PRINTED SOURCES

Abelard. *The Letters of Abelard and Heloise*. Trans. Betty Radice. Harmondsworth: Penguin, 1974.
Achery, Lucas de. *Spicilegium sive collectio veterum aliquot scriptorum*. 13 vols. Paris, 1655–77; 2nd ed. 3 vols. Paris, 1723. Reprinted Farnborough, Hants.: Gregg Press, 1967.

Adam of Perseigne. "Epistolae." *PL*, 211:583–694.

Albert of Aachen. *Historia Hierosolymitana*. In *Receuil des historiens des croisades, historiens occidentaux*. 5 vols. Paris: Imprimerie Royale, 1841–1906. 4: 270–713.

Aliscans. Ed. Claude Regnier, 2 vols. Paris: H. Champion, 1990.

Anonymous. "Chronicon" of Laon. *RHF*, 18: 702–20.

Anselm of Canterbury. "Epistolae." In *S. Anselmi cantuariensis Archiepiscopi, Opera Omnia*, ed. Franciscus S. Schmitt. 6 vols. Edinburgh: Nelson 1938–61. Trans. Walter Fröhlich as *The Letters of Saint Anselm of Canterbury*. 3 vols. Cistercian Studies Series, nos. 96, 97, 142. Kalamazoo, Mich.: Cistercian Publications, 1990–94.

Arbaument, Jules d', ed. *Cartulaire du prieuré de Saint-Etienne de Vignory*. Langres: F. Dangien, 1882.

Aubri of Trois-Fontaines. "Chronicon." *MGH, SS*, 23: 674–950.

Baudry of Bourgueil. *Baldricus Burgulianus, Carmina*. Ed. Karlheinz Hilbert. Heidelberg: Winter, 1979.

Beaumanoir, Philippe de. *Les coutumes de Beauvaisis*. Ed. Am[édée] Salmon. 2 vols. Paris, 1899–1900. Trans. F. R. P. Akehurst as *The Coutumes de Beauvaisis of Philippe de Beaumanoir*. Philadelphia: University of Pennsylvania Press,1992.

Bergh, L. Ph. C. van den, ed. *Oorkondenboek van Holland en Zeeland tot het einde van het Hollandsche Huis*. 2 vols. Amsterdam and the Hague, 1866–73. Reprint 's-Gravenhage: M. Nijhoff, 1937–.

Bernard, Auguste and Alexandre Bruel, eds. *Recueil des chartes de l'abbaye de Cluny*. 6 vols. Paris: Imprimerie Nationale, 1876–1903.

Bernart of Ventadorn. *The Songs of Bernart of Ventadorn*. Ed. and trans. Stephen G. Nichols, Jr., John A. Galm, and A. Bartlett Giametti. Chapel Hill: University of North Carolina Press, 1965.

Bernier, Jean. *Histoire de Blois*. Paris: François Muguet, 1682.

Bertran de Born. *The Poems of the Troubadour Bertran de Born*. Ed. William D. Paden, Jr., Tilde Sankovitch, and Patricia Stäblin. Berkeley and Los Angeles: University of California Press, 1986.

Bigot, V., ed. *Histoire abrégée de l'abbaye de Saint-Florentin de Bonneval des RR. PP. Dom Jean Thiroux et Dom Lambert continuée par l'abbé Beaupère et M. Lejeune*. 1715. Châteaudun: Lecesne, 1875.

Bonner, Anthony, ed. *Songs of the Troubadours*. London: George Allen and Unwin, 1973; New York: Schocken Books, 1972.

Boutemy, André. "Deux pièces inédites du manuscrit 749 de Douai." *Latomus* 2 (1938): 123–30.

Bruckner, Matilda Tomaryn, Laurie Shepard, and Sarah White, eds. and trans. *Songs of the Women Troubadours*. New York: Garland,1995.

Brunel, Clovis Felix, ed. *Les plus anciennes chartes en langue provençale*. 2 vols. Paris: Picard, 1926; reprint Geneva: Slatkine, 1973.

Busson, G. and Ambroise Ledru, eds. *Actus pontificum Cenomannis in urbe degentium*. Le Mans: Société des Archives Historiques de Maine, 1901.

Camuzat, Nicolas. *Promptuarium sacrarum antiquitatum Tricassinae dioecesis*. Troyes, 1610.

Catel, Albert and Maurice Lecomte, eds. *Chartes et documents de l'abbaye Cistercienne de Preuilly*. Montereau: Claverie, 1927.

Catel, Guillaume. *Mémoires de l'histoire de Languedoc*. Toulouse: Pierre Bosc, 1633.

Chantereau-Lefebvre, Louis. *Traité des fiefs et de leur origine*. Paris: L. Billaine, 1662.

Chrétien de Troyes. *Chrétien de Troyes: Lancelot, or The Knight of the Cart (Le Chevalier de la Charrete)*. Ed. and trans. William W. Kibler. New York and London: Garland, 1981.

"Chronicon breve autissiodorense." *RHF*, 11: 292.

"Chronicon monasterii de Hyda." In *Liber monasterii de Hyda*, ed. Edward Edwards. Rolls Series, no. 45. London: HMSO, 1866.

Chronique de Saint-Pierre-le-Vif de Sens, dite de Clarius. Ed. and trans. Robert-Henri Bautier and Monique Gilles. Paris: Editions du CNRS, 1979.

"Continuatio ad Historiam Ingulphi." In *Rerum Anglicarum Scriptorem Veterum*, vol. 1, ed. William Fulman. Oxford: Sheldonian Theatre, 1684. Vol 1: 108–32.

Depoin, Joseph, ed. *Recueil de chartes et documents de Saint-Martin-des-Champs, monastère Parisien*. Vol. 1. Archives de la France Monastique 13. Paris: Jouvé, 1912.

Desjardins, Gustave, ed. *Cartulaire de l'abbaye de Conques en Rouergue*. Paris: A. Picard, 1879.

Devailly, Guy, ed. *Le Cartulaire de Vierzon*. Paris: Presses Universitaires de France, 1963.

Devic, Claude and Joseph Vaissete, eds. *Histoire générale de Languedoc*. 16 vols. Toulouse: Privat, 1872–95.

Duchesne, André. *Histoire généalogique de la maison royale de Dreux*. Paris: Sebastien Cramoisy, 1631.

Eadmer. *Historia novorum in Anglia*. Ed. Martin Rule. Rolls Series, no. 81. London: Longman, 1884. Trans. Geoffrey Bosanquet as *History of Recent Events in England*. London: Cresset Press, 1964.

———. *Vita Anselmi*. Ed. and trans. Richard W. Southern, *The Life of St Anselm, Archbishop of Canterbury*. Oxford: Clarendon Press, 1972.

Egan, Margarita, ed. and trans. *The Vidas of the Troubadours*. New York: Garland, 1984.

Epstein, Marcia J., ed. and trans. *"Prions en chantant": Devotional Songs of the Trouvères*. Toronto: University of Toronto Press, 1997.

Les Etablissements de Saint Louis. Ed. Paul Viollet. 4 vols. Paris, 1881–86. Trans. F. R. P. Akehurst as *The Etablissements de Saint Louis: Thirteenth-Century Law Texts from Tours, Orléans, and Paris*. Philadelphia: University of Pennsylvania Press, 1996.

Evergates, Theodore, ed. and trans. *Feudal Society in Medieval France: Documents from the County of Champagne*. Philadelphia: University of Pennsylvania Press, 1993.

Fitting, Hermann, ed. *Lo Codi, in der lateinischen Ubersetzung des Ricardus Pisanus*. Halle: Niemeyer, 1906. Reprinted Aalen, 1968.

"Flandria Generosa." *MGH, SS*, 9: 313–34.

Galbert of Bruges. *The Murder of Charles of Good, Count of Flanders*. Trans. James Bruce Ross. Toronto: University of Toronto Press, 1982.

Garrigues, Martines, ed. *Le premier cartulaire de l'abbaye cistercienne de Pontigny (XIIe–XIIIe siècles)*. Paris: Bibliothèque Nationale, 1981.

Gemähling, M. *Monographie de l'abbaye de Saint-Satur près Sancerre (Cher)*. Paris: Chaix, 1867.

Geoffrey Grossus. "Vita beati Bernardi Tironiensis." Ed. Godefrey Henskens. *PL*, 172: 1367–1446.

Geoffroy of Beaulieu. "Vie de saint Louis par le confesseur de la reine Marguerite." *RHF*, 20: 58–121.

Germain, A., ed. *Liber instrumentorum memorialium: cartulaire des Guillems de Montpellier*. Montpellier: J. Martel, 1884.

Gérard, Pierre and Elisabeth Magnou, eds. *Cartulaires des Templiers de Douzens*. Paris: Bibliothèque Nationale, 1965.

Gesta Ambaziensium dominorum. In *Chroniques des comtes d'Anjou et des seigneurs d'Amboise*, ed. Louis Halphen and René Poupardin. Paris: Picard, 1913. Pp. 74–132.

Gigot, Jean-Gabriel, ed. *Chartes en langue française antérieures à 1271 conservées dans le département de la Haute-Marne*. Paris: Editions du CNRS, 1966.

Gilo. "Vita sancti Hugonis abbatis." Ed. H. E. J. Cowdrey, "Two Studies in Cluniac History, 1049–1126." *Studi Gregoriani* 11 (1978): 42–148.

Gislebert of Mons. *La chronique de Gislebert de Mons*. Ed. Léon Vanderkindere. Brussels: Kiessling, 1904.

Godfrey of Reims. "Ad Ingelrannum archidiaconum de moribus eius." Ed. André Boutemy, "Trois oeuvres inédites de Godefroid de Reims." *Revue du moyen âge latin* 3 (1947): 335–66.

Guérard, Benjamin E. C., ed. *Cartulaire de l'abbaye de Saint-Père de Chartres*. 2 vols. Paris: Crapelet, 1840.

——, ed. *Cartulaire de l'église Notre-Dame de Paris*. 4 vols. Paris: Crapelet, 1850.

Guibert of Nogent. *De vita sua*. Ed. and trans. Edmond-René Labande, *Guibert de Nogent: Autobiographie*. Classiques de l'Histoire de France au Moyen Age, 34. Paris: Les Belles Lettres, 1981. English trans. John F. Benton as *Self and Society in Medieval France: The Memoirs of Abbot Guibert of Nogent*. New York: Harper and Row, 1970. Reprint: Toronto: University of Toronto Press, 1984.

——. *Gesta Dei per Francos*. In *Recueil des historiens des croisades, historiens occidentaux*. 5 vols. Paris: Imprimerie Royale, 1841–1906. Vol. 4: 117–263. Trans. Robert Levine as *The Deeds of God Through the Franks*. Woodbridge, Suffolk: Boydell, 1997.

Guigue, M. C. "Testament de Guichard III [IV] de Beaujeu." *Bibliothèque de l'Ecole des Chartes* 4th ser. 3 (1857): 161–67.

Guillaume d'Orange: Four Twelfth-Century Epics. Trans. Joan M. Ferrante. New York: Columbia University Press, 1974.

Hagenmeyer, Heinrich, ed. *Die Kreuzzugsbriefe aus den Jahren 1088–1100*. Innsbruck: Wagner, 1901.

Hemptinne, Thérèse de and Adriaan Verhulst, eds. *De oorkonden der graven van Vlaanderen, juli 1128–sept. 1191*. Vol. 1. Brussels: Palais des Academies, 1988. Vol. 2 (in preparation).

Herman of Tournai. *The Restoration of the Monastery of St. Martin of Tournai*. Trans. Lynn H. Nelson. Washington, D.C.: Catholic University of America Press, 1996.

Hildebert of Lavardin. *Hildeberti Cenomannensis Episcopi, Carmina Minora*. Ed. A. Brian Scott. Leipzig: Teubner, 1969.

———. "Epistolae." Ed. Jean-Jacques Bourassé. *PL*, 171: 135–310.

Hugh of Flavigny. "Chronicon." Ed. George Pertz. *MGH, SS*, 8: 280–503. Rpt. *PL*, 154: 21–400.

Hugh of Fleury. "Historia ecclesiastica." Ed. George Waitz. *MGH, SS*, 9: 349–64. Rpt. *PL*, 163: 821–54.

Hugh the Chanter. *The History of the Church of York, 1066–1127*. Ed. and trans. Charles Johnson, rev. Michael Brett, C. N. L. Brooke, and Michael Winterbottom. 2nd ed. Oxford: Clarendon Press, 1990.

Ivo of Chartres. "Epistolae." Ed. François Juret. *PL*, 162: 11–504. Letters 1–70 ed. and trans. Jean Leclercq as *Yves de Chartres: Correspondance*. Paris: Belles Lettres, 1949. A collection of 280 of Ivo's letters was edited and translated (though not in the same order as the Juret edition in *PL*) by Lucien Merlet as *Lettres de Saint Ives, évêque de Chartres*. Chartres: Garnier, 1885.

Jacques de Guise. *Histoire de Hainaut*. Vols. 11–14. Paris: Sautelet, 1831.

Jaffé, Philippe and Samuel Löwenfeld, eds. *Regesta pontificum romanorum ab condita ecclesia ad annum post Christum natum 1198*. 2nd ed. 2 vols. Leipzig: Veit, 1885–88. Reprint Graz: Akademische Druck- u. Verlagsanstalt, 1956.

Jaufré Rudel. *The Songs of Jaufré Rudel*. Ed. and trans. Rupert T. Pickens. Toronto: Pontifical Institute of Mediaeval Studies, 1978.

John of Fécamp. "Letter to Pope Leo IX." *PL*, 143: 799–800.

Johnson, Charles and Henry A. Cronne, eds. *Regesta Henrici Primi, 1100–1135*. Regesta Regum Anglo-Normannorum. Oxford: Oxford University Press, 1956.

Lalore, Charles, ed. *Cartulaire de l'abbaye du Paraclet*. Paris: Thorin, 1878.

———, ed. "Chartes d'Andecy." In *Cartulaire de l'abbaye de la Chapelle-aux-Planches*. Paris: Thorin, 1878.

———, ed. "Chartes de l'abbaye de Mores." *Mémoires de la Société académique d'agriculture, des sciences, arts et belles-lettres du département de l'Aube* 37 (1873): 5–107.

———, ed. "Documents sur l'abbaye de Notre-Dame-aux-Nonnains de Troyes." *Mémoires de la Société académique d'agriculture, des sciences, arts et belles-lettres du département de l'Aube* 38 (1874): 5–236.

Lambert of Waterlos. "Annales Cameracenses." *MGH, SS*, 16: 509–54.

Langlois, Charles-Victor. *La vie en France au moyen âge*. 4 vols. Paris, 1926–28. Reprint Geneva: Slatkine, 1984.

Laurent, Jacques, ed. *Cartulaires de l'abbaye de Molesme, ancien diocèse de Langres, 916–1250*. 2 vols. Paris: A. Picard, 1907–11.

Layettes du Trésor des chartes. Ed. Alexandre Teulet, Joseph de Laborde, Elie Berger, and H.-François Delaborde. 5 vols. Paris: Plon, 1863–1909.

Léonard, Emile-G. *Catalogue des actes des comtes de Toulouse: Raymond V (1149–1194)*. Paris: Picard, 1932.

LePelletier, Laurent. *Rerum scitu dignissimarum a prima fundatione Monasterii S. Nicolai Andegavensis ad hunc usque diem, Epitome*. 2nd ed. Angers: Adam Mauger, 1635.

Lépinois, Eugène de and Lucien Merlet, eds. *Cartulaire de Notre-Dame de Chartres*. 3 vols. Chartres: Garnier, 1862–65.

Lespinasse, René de, ed. *Cartulaire du prieuré de La Charité-sur-Loire (Nièvre), ordre de Cluny*. Nevers: Morin-Boutillier, 1887.

Longnon, Auguste, ed. *Documents relatifs au comté de Champagne et de Brie, 1172–1361.* 3 vols. Paris: Imprimerie Nationale, 1901–14.

——, ed. *Rôles des fiefs du comté de Champagne sous le règne de Thibaut le Chansonnier (1249–1252).* Paris: H. Menu, 1877.

Löwenfeld, Samuel, ed. *Epistolae pontificum Romanorum ineditae.* Leipzig: Veit, 1885.

Luchaire, Achille. *Etudes sur les actes de Louis VII.* Paris: Picard, 1885.

——. *Louis VI le Gros: annales de sa vie et de son règne (1081–1137).* Paris: Picard, 1890.

Mabille, Emile, ed. *Cartulaire de Marmoutier pour le Dunois.* Châteaudun: H. Lecesne, 1874.

Manceaux, Jean-Baptiste. *Histoire de l'abbaye et du village d'Hautvillers.* 2 vols. Epernay: L. Doublat, 1880.

Marchegay, Paul, ed. *Cartulaire du prieuré bénédictin de Saint-Gondon-sur-Loire (866–1172) tiré des archives de l'abbaye de Saint-Florent près Saumur.* Les Roches Baritaud: Forrest et Grimaud, 1879.

Mars, Noël. *Histoire du royal monastère de Sainct-Lomer de Blois de l'ordre de Sainct-Benoist.* 1646. Ed. Alexandre Dupré. Blois: Marchand, 1869.

Martène, Edmond and Ursin Durand, eds. *Thesaurus novus anecdotorum.* 5 vols. Paris: Sumptibus F. Delaulne, 1717.

Martin-Chabot, Eugène, ed. *La chanson de la croisade albigeoise.* 3 vols. Paris: Les Belles Lettres, 1957–61.

——, ed. *Les archives de la Cour des Comptes, Aides et Finances de Montpellier, avec un essai de restitution des premiers registres de sénéchaussée.* Paris: Alcan, 1907.

Merlet, Lucien, ed. *Cartulaire de l'abbaye de la Sainte-Trinité de Tiron.* 2 vols. Chartres: Garnier, 1883.

——, ed. "Lettres d'Ives de Chartres et d'autres personnages de son temps, 1087–1130." *Bibliothèque de l'Ecole des Chartes* 16 (1855): 443–71.

Merlet, René, ed. *Cartulaire de Saint-Jean-en-Vallée de Chartres.* Chartres: Garnier, 1906.

Merlet, René and the abbot Clerval, eds. *Un manuscrit Chartrain du XI siècle.* Chartres: Garnier, 1893.

Métais, Charles, ed. *Cartulaire de l'abbaye cardinale de la Trinité de Vendôme.* 5 vols. Paris: A. Picard, 1893–1904.

——, ed. *Cartulaire de Notre-Dame de Josaphat.* 2 vols. Chartres: Garnier, 1911–12.

——, ed. *Marmoutier cartulaire blésois.* Blois: Moreau, 1889–91.

Miquel Rosell, Francisco, ed. *Liber feudorum major.* 2 vols. Barcelona: Consejo superior de investigaciones cientificas, 1945.

"Miracula sancti Agili, resbacensis abbatis." Ed. Jean Mabillon in *Acta Sanctorum ordinis Sancti Benedicti in saeculorum classes distributa.* 1st ed. 9 vols. Paris: Louis Billaine, 1668–1701. 2: 316–34. Reprinted in *Acta Sanctorum quotquot orbe coluntur.* 67 vols. Antwerp, Tongerloo, Paris, Brussels, 1643–1940. At Aug., 6: 574–97.

"Miracula sancti Aigulphi." In *Acta Sanctorum quotquot orbe coluntur.* 67 vols. Antwerp, Tongerloo, Paris, Brussels, 1643–1940. At Sept., 1: 755–63.

Morel, Emile-Epiphanius, ed. *Cartulaire de l'abbaye de Saint-Corneille de Compiègne.* 2 vols. Montdidier: J. Bellin, 1894–1909.

Mouynès, Germain, ed. "Cartulaire de la seigneurie de Fontjoncouse." *Bulletin de la Commission archéologique et littéraire de Narbonne* 1 (1877): 107–341.

Nicaise, Auguste, ed. *Epernay et l'abbaye Saint-Martin de cette ville: histoire et documents inédits.* 2 vols. Châlons-sur-Marne: Le Roy, 1869.

Nobilleau, Paul, ed. *Necrologium beatissimi Martini Turonensis (804–1495) et obitarius (sic) Majoris Monasterii.* Tours: Ladevèze, 1875.

Notcher of Hautvillers. "Miracula sanctae Helenae apud Altumvillare." Ed. Jean Mabillon in *Acta Sanctorum ordinis Sancti Benedicti in saeculorum classes distributa.* 1st ed. 9 vols. Paris: Louis Billaine, 1668–1701. Vol. 4²: 154–56.

Obituaires de la province de Sens. Vol. 4, *Diocèses de Meaux et de Troyes.* Ed. Boutellier du Retail and Piétresson de Saint-Aubin. Paris: Imprimerie Nationale, 1923.

O'Connell, David. *Les propos de Saint Louis.* Paris: Gallimard, 1974.

Orderic Vitalis. *The Ecclesiastical History of Orderic Vitalis.* Ed. and trans. Marjorie Chibnall. 6 vols. Oxford: Clarendon Press, 1969–80.

Pálsson, Hermann and Paul Edwards, eds. and trans. *Orkneyinga saga; The History of the Earls of Orkney.* London: Hogarth Press, 1978.

Paris, Louis. *Histoire de l'abbaye d'Avenay.* 2 vols. Reims: Imprimerie Coopérative, 1879.

Paschal II. "Epistolae et privilegia." *PL*, 163: 31–444.

Peire Rogier. *The Poems of the Troubadour Peire Rogier.* Ed. and trans. Derek E. T. Nicholson. New York: Barnes and Noble and Manchester: Manchester University Press, 1976.

Peire Vidal. *Les poésies de Peire Vidal.* Ed. Joseph Anglade. Paris: Champion, 1923.

Peter the Venerable. *De Miraculis.* Ed. Dyonisia Bouthillier. Corpus Christianorum Continuatio Mediaevalis, no. 83. Turnholt: Brepols, 1988.

——. *The Letters of Peter the Venerable.* Ed. Giles Constable. 2 vols. Cambridge, Mass.: Harvard University Press, 1967.

Philippe Mousket. "Historia Regum Francorum." *MGH, SS*, 26: 718–821.

Portejoie, Paulette, ed. *L'ancien coutumier de Champagne (XIIIᵉ siècle).* Poitiers: P. Oudin, 1956.

Poupardin, René, ed. *Recueil des chartes de l'abbaye de Saint-Germain-des-Près des origines au début du XIIIe siècle.* Paris: Champion, 1909.

Prevenier, Walter, ed. *De oorkonden der graven van Vlaanderen,1191–aanvang 1206.* Vol. 2. Brussels: Paleis der Academiën, 1964.

Quantin, Maximilien, ed. *Recueil de pièces pour faire suite au Cartulaire général d'Yonne.* Auxerre: Société des Sciences Historiques et Naturelles de l'Yonne, 1873.

Raimon de Miraval. *The Cansos of Raimon de Miraval: A Study of Poems and Melodies.* Ed. and trans. Margaret L. Switten. Cambridge, Mass.: Medieval Society of America, 1985.

Ramackers, Johannes, ed. *Papsturkunden in Frankenreich.* Vol. 6, *Orléanais.* Göttingen: Vandenhoekt and Ruprecht, 1958.

Recueil des actes de Louis VI, roi de France (1108–1137). Ed. Jean Dufour. 4 vols. Paris: Boccard, 1992–94.

Recueil des actes de Philippe Auguste. Ed. H.-F. Delaborde et al. 4 vols. Paris: Imprimerie Nationale, 1916–79.

Recueil des actes de Philippe Ier, roi de France (1059–1108). Ed. Maurice Prou. Paris: Imprimerie Nationale, 1908.

Richard, Alfred, ed. *Chartes et documents pour servir à l'histoire de l'abbaye de Saint-Maxient*. 2 vols. Archives historiques du Poitou, 16, 18. Poitiers: Archives de la Vienne, 1886, 1888.

Robert of Torigni. *Gesta Normannorum Ducum*. Ed. and trans. Elisabeth M. C. van Houts, *The "Gesta Normannorum Ducum" of William of Jumièges, Orderic Vitalis, and Robert of Torigni*. 2 vols. Oxford: Clarendon Press, 1992–95.

Rouquette, J., ed. *Cartulaire de Béziers (Livre Noir)*. Paris: Picard, 1918.

Rouquette, J. and A. Villemagne, eds. *Cartulaire de Maguelone*. Vol. 1. Montpellier: Valat, 1912.

Saige, Gustave, Henri Lacaille, and L. H. Lebande, eds. *Trésor des chartes du comté de Rethel (1081–1415)*. 5 vols. Monaco: Imprimerie de Monaco, 1902–16.

Sidoisne, Albert, ed. *Cartulaire de l'abbaye de Saint-Florentin de Bonneval*. Bonneval, 1939.

[Simon, P.], ed. *Bullarium sacri ordinis Cluniacensis*. Lyon: Antonius Jullieron, 1680.

Souancé, Vicomte de and Charles Métais, eds. *Saint-Denis de Nogent-le-Rotrou (1031–1789): histoire et cartulaire*. Vannes: Lafolye, 1899.

Suger. *Vita Ludovici Grossi regis*. Ed. and trans. Henri Waquet, *Vie de Louis VI le Gros*. Classiques de l'Histoire de France au Moyen Age, 11. Paris: Belles Lethes, 1929. English trans. Richard C. Cusimano and John Moorhood as *The Deeds of Louis the Fat*. Washington, D.C.: Catholic University of America Press, 1992.

Trémault, Charles Auguste de, ed. *Cartulaire de Marmoutier pour le Vendômois*. Paris: Picard, 1893.

Urban II. "Epistolae." *PL*, 151: 283–561.

Vercauteren, Fernand, ed. *Actes des comtes de Flandre, 1071–1128*. Brussels: Palais des Academies, 1938.

Verlaguet, P. A., ed. *Cartulaire de l'abbaye de Silvanés*. Archives historiques de Rouergue, 1. Rodez: Carrere, 1910.

"Vita beati Simonis comitis Crespeiensis." *PL*, 156: 1211–24.

"Vita sancti Arnulfi episcopi Suessionensis." (Attributable to Lisiard of Soissons and Hariulf of St. Riquier.) In *Acta Sanctorum quotquot orbe coluntur*. 67 vols. Antwerp, Tongerloo, Paris, Brussels, 1643–1940. At Aug., 3: 230–59. Reprinted in *PL*, 174: 1375–1438.

William of Malmesbury. *De gestis regum anglorum*. Ed. William Stubbs. 2 vols. Rolls Series no. 901–2. London HMSO, 1887–89.

William of Nangis. "Chronicon." Partial edition *RHF*, 20: 726.

Vleeschouwers, Cyriel, ed. "De oorkonden van de Sint-Baafsabdij te Gent." Doctoral dissertation, University of Ghent, 1986.

Secondary Works

Adair, Penelope. "Ego et Uxor Mea: Countess Clemence and Her Role in the Comital Family and in Flanders, 1092–1133." Ph.D. Dissertation, University of California at Santa Barbara, 1995.

Amado, Claudie Duhamel. "Femmes entre elles: filles et épouses languedociennes

(XIe–XIIe siècles)." In *Femmes: Mariages-Lignages, XIIe–XIVe siècles: mélanges offerts à Georges Duby*. Brussels: De Boeck Université, 1992. Pp. 125–56.

Amundsen, Darrel W. and Carol Jean Diers. "The Age of Menarche in Medieval Europe." *Human Biology* 45 (1973): 363–69.

Arbois de Jubainville, Henry d'. *Histoire des ducs et des comtes de Champagne*. 7 vols. Paris-Troyes: A. Durand, 1859–69.

Aurell, Martí. "La déterioration du statut de la femme aristocratique en Provence (Xe–XIIIe siècles)." *Le Moyen Age* 40 (1985): 5–32.

Aurell, Martin. *Les noces du comte: mariage et pouvoir en Catalogne (785–1213)*. Paris: Publications de la Sorbonne, 1995.

Barlow, Frank. "William I's Relations with Cluny." *Journal of Ecclesiastical History* 32 (1981): 131–41.

———. *William Rufus*. Berkeley: University of California Press, 1983.

Barthélemy, Dominique. "Kinship." In Duby, *A History of Private Life*. Pp. 85–155.

———. "Note sur le *maritagium* dans le grand Anjou des XIe et XIIe siècles." In *Femmes: Mariages-Lignages, XIIe–XIVe siècles: mélanges offerts à Georges Duby*. Brussels: De Boeck Université, 1992. Pp. 9–24.

———. *La société dans le comté de Vendôme de l'an mil au XIVe siècle*. Paris: Fayard, 1993.

Bautier, Robert-Henri. "Paris au temps d'Abélard." In *Abélard et son temps*. Actes du colloque international organisé à l'occasion du 9e centenaire de la naissance de Pierre Abélard. Paris: Belles Lettres, 1981.

———. "La prise en charge du Berry par le roi Philippe Ier et les antecedents de cette politique de Hugues le Grand à Robert le Pieux." In *"Media in Francia": recueil de mélanges offerts à Karl Ferdinand Werner à l'occasion de son 65ième anniversaire*. Paris: Hérault, 1989. Pp. 31–60.

Becker, Alfons. *Studium zum Investiturproblem in Frankreich*. Saarbrücken: West-Ost Verlag, 1955.

Bedos-Rezak, Brigitte. "Medieval Women in French Sigillographic Sources." In *Medieval Women and the Sources of Medieval History*, ed. Joel T. Rosenthal. Athens: University of Georgia Press, 1990. Pp. 1–35.

———. "Women, Seals, and Power in Medieval France, 1150–1350." In *Women and Power in the Middle Ages*, ed. Mary Erler and Maryanne Kowaleski. Athens: University of Georgia Press, 1988. Pp. 61–82.

Benton, John F. "Clio and Venus: An Historical View of Medieval Love." In *The Meaning of Courtly Love*, ed. F. X. Newman. Albany, N.Y.: SUNY Press, 1968. Pp. 19–42. Reprinted in Benton, *Culture, Power and Personality in Medieval France*. Pp. 99–122.

———. "Collaborative Approaches to Fantasy and Reality in the Literature of Champagne." In *Court and Poet: Selected Proceedings of the Third Congress of the International Courtly Literature Society*, ed. Glyn Burgess. Liverpool: F. Cairns, 1981. Pp. 43–57. Reprinted in Benton, *Culture, Power and Personality in Medieval France*. Pp. 167–80.

———. "The Court of Champagne as a Literary Center." *Speculum* 36 (1961): 551–91. Reprinted in Benton, *Culture, Power and Personality in Medieval France*. Pp. 3–43.

———. *Culture, Power and Personality in Medieval France*. (Collected articles.) Ed. Thomas N. Bisson. London: Hambledon Press, 1991.

———. "Fraud, Fiction and Borrowing in the Correspondance of Abelard and Heloise." In *Pierre Abélard—Pierre le Vénérable*. Colloques Internationaux de Centre de la Recherche Scientifique, 546. Paris: Editions du CNRS, 1975. Pp. 471–506. Reprinted in Benton, *Culture, Power and Personality in Medieval France*. Pp. 417–53.

———. "Philip the Fair and the Jours of Troyes." *Studies in Medieval and Renaissance History* 6 (1969): 281–344. Reprinted in Benton, *Culture, Power and Personality in Medieval France*. Pp. 191–254.

Bisson, Thomas, ed. *Cultures of Power: Lordship, Status, and Process in Twelfth-Century Europe*. Philadelphia: University of Pennsylvania Press, 1995.

———. "Nobility and Family in Medieval France: A Review Essay." *French Historical Studies* 16 (1990): 597–613.

Bloch, R. Howard. *Medieval Misogyny and the Invention of Western Romantic Love*. Chicago: University of Chicago Press, 1991.

Blumenthal, Uta-Renate. *The Investiture Controversy: Church and Monarchy from the Ninth to the Twelfth Century*. Philadelphia: University of Pennsylvania Press, 1988.

Bonnassie, Pierre. *La Catalogne du milieu du Xe à la fin du XIe siècle: croissances et mutations d'une société*. 2 vols. Toulouse: Association des Publications de l'Université de Toulouse-Le Mirail, 1975.

Bouchard, Constance Brittain. *Holy Entrepreneurs: Cistercians, Knights, and Economic Exchange in Twelfth-Century Burgundy*. Ithaca, N. Y.: Cornell University Press, 1991.

———. *Strong of Body, Brave and Noble: Chivalry and Society in Medieval France*. Ithaca, N. Y.: Cornell University Press, 1998.

———. *Sword, Miter, and Cloister: Nobility and the Church in Burgundy, 980–1198*. Ithaca, N. Y.: Cornell University Press, 1987.

Bourgain, Pascale. "Aliénor d'Aquitaine et Marie de Champagne mises en cause par André le Chapelain," *Cahiers de civilisation médiévale* 29 (1986): 29–36.

Brown, R. Allen. "Some Observations on Norman and Anglo-Norman Charters." In *Tradition and Change: Essays in Honour of Marjorie Chibnall*, ed. Diana E. Greenway, Christopher J. Holdsworth, and Jane E. Sayers. Cambridge: Cambridge University Press, 1985. Pp. 145–63.

Brundage, James A. *Medieval Canon Law and the Crusader*. Madison: University of Wisconsin Press, 1969.

———. *Law, Sex, and Christian Society in Medieval Europe*. Chicago and London: University of Chicago Press, 1987.

Bullock-Davies, Constance. "Chrétien de Troyes and England." In *Arthurian Literature*. Vol. 1, ed. Richard Barber. Woodbridge, Suffolk: D. S. Brewer, 1981. Pp. 1–61.

Bur, Michel. *La formation du comté de Champagne, v. 950–v.1150*. Nancy: Université de Nancy II, 1977.

———. "L'image de parenté chez les comtes de Champagne," *Annales: Economies, Sociétés, Civilisations* 38 (1983): 1016–39.

———. "Les relations des comtes de Champagne et les ducs de Lorraine au début du XIIIe siècle," *Bulletin philologique et historique du Comité des Travaux historiques et scientifiques* (1964): 75–84.

Bur, Michel, et al. *Vestiges d'habitat seigneurial fortifié en Champagne centrale*. Inventaire des sites archéologiques non monumentaux de Champagne, 3. Reims: ARERS, 1987.

Burns, E. Jane. *Bodytalk: When Women Speak in Old French Literature*. Philadelphia: University of Pennsylvania Press, 1993.

Caille, Jacqueline. "Ermengarde, Vicomtesse de Narbonne (1127/29–1196/97): une grande figure féminine du Midi aristocratique." In *La femme dans l'histoire et la société méridionales (IXe–XIXe s)*. Actes du 66e congrès de la Fédération historique du Languedoc méditerranéen et du Roussillon. Montpellier: Fédération historique du Languedoc méditerranéen et du Roussillon, 1995. Pp. 9–50.

———. "Les seigneurs de Narbonne dans le conflit Toulouse-Barcelone au XIIe siècle." *Annales du Midi* 97 (1985): 227–44.

———. "Seigneurs et 'peuple' de Narbonne (XI–XVe siècles)." In *Histoire de Narbonne*, ed. Jacques Michaud and André Cabanis. Toulouse: Privat, 1981. Pp. 119–40.

———. "Une idylle entre la vicomtesse Ermengarde de Narbonne et le prince Rognvald Kali des Orcades au milieu du XIIe siècle?" In *Hommage à Robert Saint-Jean: art et histoire dans le Midi languedocien et rhodanian*, ed. Guy Romestan. Montpellier: Société Archéologique de Montpellier, 1993. Pp. 229–33.

Carpenter, Jennifer and Sally-Beth MacLean, eds. *Power of the Weak: Studies on Medieval Women*. Urbana and Chicago: University of Illinois Press, 1995.

Carroll, Carleton W. "Quelques observations sur les reflects de la cour d'Henri II dans l'oeuvre de Chrétien de Troyes." *Cahiers de civilisation médiévale* 37 (1994): 33–39.

Caviness, Madeline H. "Saint-Yved de Braine: The Primary Sources for Dating the Gothic Church." *Speculum* 59 (1984): 524–48.

———. *Sumptuous Arts at the Royal Abbeys in Reims and Braine*. Princeton, N. J.: Princeton University Press, 1990.

Chabaud, Hervé. "Le douaire dans les coutumes de Reims, Châlons, Vitry." *Mémoires de la Société d'agriculture, commerce, science et arts du département de la Marne* 97 (1982): 89–102.

Chazaud, Alphonse-Martial. *Etude sur la chronologie des sires de Bourbon, Xᵉ–XIIIᵉ siècles*. Ed. Max Fazy. Moulins: Desrosiers, 1935.

Chédeville, André. *Chartres et ses campagnes (XIe–XIIe siécles)*. Paris: Klincksieck, 1973.

———. "Les restitutions d'églises en faveur de l'abbaye de Saint-Vincent." *Cahiers de civilisation médiévale* 3 (1960): 209–17.

Chevalier, Bernard. "Les restitutions d'églises dans le diocèse de Tours du Xe au XIIe siècles." In *Etudes de civilisation médiévale (IXe–XII siècles): mélanges offerts à Edmond-René Labande*. Poitiers: CESCM, 1974.

Cheyette, Fredric L. "The 'Sale' of Carcassonne to the Counts of Barcelona (1067–1070) and the Rise of the Trencavels." *Speculum* 63 (1988): 826–64.

Cheyette, Fredric L. and Margaret L. Switten. "Women in Troubadour Song: Of the Contessa and the Vilana." *Women and Music* 2 (1998): 26–46.

Chibnall, Marjorie. "The Empress Matilda and her Sons." In *Medieval Mothering*, ed. John Carmi Parsons and Bonnie Wheeler. New York: Garland, 1996. Pp. 279–94.

———. *The Empress Matilda: Queen Consort, Queen Mother, and Lady of the English.* Oxford: Blackwell, 1991.

———. "Women in Orderic Vitalis." *Haskins Society Journal* 2 (1990): 105–22.

Cholakian, Rouben C. *The Troubadour Lyric: A Psychocritical Reading.* Manchester and New York: Manchester University Press, 1990.

Christelow, Stephanie Moers. "The Division of Inheritance and the Provision of Non-Inheriting Offspring Among the Anglo-Norman Elite." *Medieval Prosopography* 17 (1996): 3–44.

Ciggaar, Krijnie. "Chrétien de Troyes et la 'matière byzantine': les demoiselles du Château de Pesme Aventure." *Cahiers de civilisation médiévale* 32 (1989): 325–31.

Clanchy, Michael. "Law and Love in the Middle Ages." In *Disputes and Settlements: Law and Human Relations in the West*, ed. John Bossy. Cambridge: Cambridge University Press, 1983. Pp. 47–68.

Comaroff, John L. *The Meaning of Medieval Marriage Payments.* New York and London: Academic Press, 1980.

Cowdrey, H. E. J. *The Cluniacs and the Gregorian Reform.* Oxford: Clarendon Press, 1970.

———. "Count Simon of Crépy's Monastic Conversion." In *Papauté, monachisme, et théories politiques: études d'histoire médiévale offertes à Marcel Pacaut*, ed. Pierre Guichard et al. 2 vols. Collection d'histoire et d'archéologie médiévales, no. 1. Lyon: Presses Universitaires de Lyon, 1989. 1: 253–66.

Cropp, Glynnis M. *Le vocabulaire courtois des troubadours de l'époque classique.* Geneva: Droz, 1975.

David, Charles Wendell. *Robert Curthose: Duke of Normandy.* Harvard Historical Studies 25. Cambridge, Mass.: Harvard University Press, 1920.

Davis, R. H. C. *King Stephen, 1135–1154.* 3rd ed. New York: Longman, 1990.

Devailly, Guy. *Le Berry du Xe siècle au milieu du XIIIe: étude politique, religieuse, sociale, et économique.* Paris: Mouton, 1973.

Dhondt, Jean. "Henri Ier, l'Empire et l'Anjou (1043–1056)." *Revue belge de philologie et d'histoire* 25 (1946–47): 87–109.

Didot, Ambroise Firmin. *Etudes sur la vie et les travaux de Jean, sire de Joinville.* Paris: Didot, 1870.

Dillay, Madeleine. "La régime de l'église privée du XIe du XIIe siècle dans l'Anjou, le Maine, la Touraine: les restitutions d'églises par les laiques." *Revue historique de droit français et étranger* 4th ser., 4 (1925): 253–94.

Donahue, Charles Jr. "The Canon Law of the Formation of Marriage and Social Practice in the Later Middle Ages." *Journal of Family History* 8 (1983): 144–58.

Douglas, David C. *William the Conqueror: The Norman Impact upon England.* Berkeley: University of California Press, 1964.

Duby, Georges. *The Chivalrous Society.* (Essays.) Trans. Cynthia Postan. Berkeley: University of California Press, 1977.

———. "Communal Living." In Duby, *A History of Private Life.* 2: 35–85.

———. "Dans la France du Nord-Ouest au XIIe siècle: les *jeunes* dans la société aristocratique." *Annales: Economies, Sociétés, Civilisations* 19 (1964): 835–46. Trans. as "Youth in Aristocratic Society," Fredric L. Cheyette in *Lordship and Community in Medieval Europe: Selected Readings* (New York: Holt, Rinehart, and Winston, 1968); trans. Cynthia Postan in Duby, *The Chivalrous Society*.

———, ed. *A History of Private Life*. Vol. 2, *Revelations of the Medieval World*. Trans. Arthur Goldhammer. Cambridge, Mass.: Belknap Press of Harvard University Press, 1988.

———. *The Knight, the Lady, and the Priest: The Making of Modern Marriage in Medieval France*. Trans. Barbara Bray. New York and London: Pantheon, 1983.

———. *Love and Marriage in the Middle Ages*. (Essays.) Trans. Jane Dunnett. Chicago: University of Chicago Press, 1994.

———. *Medieval Marriage: Two Models from Twelfth-Century France*. Trans. Elborg Forster. Baltimore: Johns Hopkins University Press, 1978.

———. "Solitude: Eleventh to Thirteenth Century." In Duby, *A History of Private Life*. 2: 509–33.

———. "Women and Power." In Bisson, *Cultures of Power*. Pp. 69–85.

Dunbabin, Jean. *France in the Making, 843–1180*. Oxford: Oxford University Press, 1985.

Duvivier, Charles. *La querelle des Avesnes et des Dampierre jusqu'à la mort de Jean d'Avesnes (1257)*. Brussels, 1894.

Edel, Leon. *The Age of the Archive*. Middletown, Conn.: Center for Advanced Studies, Wesleyan University, 1966.

Enright, Michael J. *Lady with a Mead Cup: Ritual, Prophecy, and Lordship in the European Warband, from the La Tène to the Viking Age*. Dublin: Four Courts Press, 1996.

Evergates, Theodore. "The Aristocracy of Champagne in the Mid-Thirteenth Century: A Quantitative Description." *Journal of Interdisciplinary History* 5 (1974): 1–18.

———. "The Chancery Archives of the Counts of Champagne: Codicology and History of the Cartulary-Registers." *Viator* 16 (1985): 159–79.

———. "The Feudal Imaginary of Georges Duby." *Journal of Medieval and Early Modern Studies* 27 (1997): 645–51.

———. *Feudal Society in the Bailliage of Troyes Under the Counts of Champagne, 1152–1284*. Baltimore: Johns Hopkins University Press, 1975.

———. "Nobles and Knights in Twelfth-Century France." In Bisson, *Cultures of Power*. Pp. 11–35.

———. "Louis VII and the Counts of Champagne." In *The Second Crusade and the Cistercians*, ed. Michael Gervers. New York: St. Martin's Press, 1992. Pp. 109–17.

———. "The Origin of the Lords of Karytaina in the Frankish Morea." *Medieval Prosopography* 15 (1994): 81–113.

———. "A Quantitative Analysis of Fiefs in Medieval Champagne." *Computers and the Humanities* 9 (1975): 61–67.

Facinger, Marion. "A Study of Medieval Queenship: Capetian France 987–1237." *Studies in Medieval and Renaissance History* 5 (1968): 3–48.

Falmagne, Jacques. *Baudouin V, comte de Hainaut, 1150–1195*. Montréal: Presses de l'Université de Montréal, 1966.

Fanning, Steven. *A Bishop and His World Before the Gregorian Reform: Hubert of Angers, 1006–1047.* Philadelphia: American Philosophical Society, 1988.

Farmer, Sharon. *Communities of Saint Martin: Legend and Ritual in Medieval Tours.* Ithaca, N.Y.: Cornell University Press, 1991.

——. "Persuasive Voices: Clerical Images of Medieval Wives." *Speculum* 61 (1986): 517–43.

Ferrante, Joan M. *Women as Image in Medieval Literature from the Twelfth Century to Dante.* New York: Columbia University Press, 1975.

Fliche, Augustin. *Le règne de Philippe Ier, roi de France (1060–1108).* Paris: Société Française d'Imprimerie at de Libraire, 1912. Reprint Geneva: Slatkine, 1975.

Fourrier, Anthime. "Retour au *terminus.*" In *Mélanges de langue et de littérature du moyen âge et de la renaissance offerts à Jean Frappier.* 2 vols. Geneva: Droz, 1970. 1: 299–311.

Freed, John. *Noble Bondsmen: Ministerial Marriages in the Archdiocese of Salzburg, 1100–1343.* Ithaca, N. Y.: Cornell University Press, 1995.

Ganshof, F. L. "Le statut de la femme dans la monarchie franque." *Receuil de la Société Jean Bodin* 2 (1962): 1–58.

Gaunt, Simon. *Gender and Genre in Medieval French Literature.* Cambridge: Cambridge University Press, 1995.

Geary, Patrick J. *Phantoms of Remembrance: Memory and Oblivion at the End of the First Millennium.* Princeton, N.J.: Princeton University Press, 1994.

Georgianna, Linda. "Any Corner of Heaven: Heloise's Critique of Monasticism." *Mediaeval Studies* 49 (1987): 221–53.

Gilissen, John. "Le privilège de masculinité dans le droit coutumier de la Belgique et du nord de la France." *Revue du Nord* 43 (1961): 201–16.

Gillingham, John. "Love, Marriage and Politics in the Twelfth Century." *Forum for Modern Language Studies* 25 (1989): 292–303. Reprinted as chap. 11 in Gillingham, *Richard Coeur de Lion: Kingship, Chivalry, and War in the Twelfth Century.* London and Rio Grande, Oh.: Hambledon Press, 1994.

Gold, Penny Schine. *The Lady and the Virgin: Image, Attitude, and Experience in Twelfth-Century France.* Chicago: University of Chicago Press, 1985.

Goldin, Frederick. "The Array of Perspectives in the Early Courtly Love Lyric." In *In Pursuit of Perfection: Courtly Love in Medieval Literature*, ed. George D. Economou and Joan M. Ferrante. Port Washington, N.Y.: Kennikat Press, 1975.

Goody, Jack. *The Development of the Family and Marriage in Europe.* Cambridge: Cambridge University Press, 1983.

Gouron, André. *Droit et coutume en France aux XIIe et XIIIe siècles.* (Collected studies.) Aldershot: Variorum, 1993.

——. *La science de droit dans le Midi de la France au Moyen Age.* (Collected studies.) London: Variorum, 1984.

——. "La science juridique française aux XIe et XIIe siècles." In *Ius romanum medii aevi*, pars 14 d–e. Milan, 1978. Reprinted in Gouron, *Etudes sur la diffusion des doctrines juridiques médiévales.* (Collected studies.) London: Variorum, 1987.

Graböis, Aryeh. "Une étape dans l'évolution vers la désagrégation de l'état toulousain au XIIe siècle: l'intervention d'Alphonse-Jourdain à Narbonne (1134–1143)." *Annales du Midi* 78 (1966): 23–36.

Gravdal, Kathryn. *Ravishing Maidens: Writing Rape in Medieval French Literature and Law*. Philadelphia: University of Pennsylvania Press, 1992.

Green, Dennis Howard. *The Carolingian Lord: Semantic Studies on Four Old High German Words*. Cambridge: Cambridge University Press, 1965.

Green, Judith A. "Aristocratic Women in Early Twelfth-Century England." In *Anglo-Norman Political Culture and the Twelfth-Century Renaissance*, ed. C. Warren Hollister. Woodbridge: Boydell Press, 1997. Pp. 59–82.

Guerreau-Jalabert, Anita. "Sur les structures de parenté dans l'Europe médiévale." *Annales: Economies, Sociétés, Civilisations* 36 (1981): 1028–49.

Guillot, Oliver. *Le comté d'Anjou et son entourage au XIe siècle*. 2 vols. Paris: A. and J. Picard, 1972.

Hajnal, J. "European Marriage Patterns in Perspective." In *Population in History: Essays in Historical Demography*, ed. D. V. Glass and D. E. C. Eversley. London: Arnold, 1965.

Halphen, Louis. *Le comté d'Anjou au XIe siècle*. Paris: A. Picard, 1906. Reprint Geneva: Slatkine, 1974.

Hansay, A. "L'inféodation du comté de Hainaut à l'église de Liège en 1071." *Bulletin de la Société d'Art et d'Histoire du diocèse de Liège* 13 (1902): 45–58.

Heinzelmann, Martin. "La noblesse du haute moyen âge (VIIIe–XIe siècles)." *Le Moyen Age* 83 (1977): 131–44.

Hemptinne, Thérèse de. "Clementia van Bourgondie, gravin van Vlaanderen." In *Nationaal Biografisch Woordenboek*. Vol. 10. Brussels: Paleis der Academiën, 1981. Cols. 148–50.

———. "Diederik van de Elzas, graaf van Vlaanderen." In *Nationaal Biografisch Woordenboek*. Vol. 13. Brussels: Paleis der Academiën, 1990. Cols. 224–42.

———. "Vlaanderen en Henegouwen onder de erfgenamen van de Boudewijns, 1070–1244." In Algemene Geschiedenis der Nederlanden. Bussum, 1982. 2: 379–98.

Hemptinne, Thérèse de and Michel Parisse. "Thierry d'Alsace, comte de Flandre: biographie et actes." *Annales de l'Est* 5th ser. 43 (1991): 83–113.

Herlihy, David. *Medieval Households*. Cambridge, Mass.: Harvard University Press, 1985.

Heslop, Timothy A. "Seals." In *English Romanesque Art, 1066–1200*, ed. George Zarnecki, Janet Holt, and Tristram Holland. London: Weidenfeld and Nicolson, 1984. Pp. 299–305.

Hillion, Yannick. "La Bretagne et la rivalité Capétiens-Plantagenêts: un example: la duchesse Constance (1186–1202)." *Annales de Bretagne et des pays de l'ouest* 92 (1985): 111–44.

Hoffmann, Hartmut. *Gottesfriede und Treuga Dei*. Schriften der Monumenta Germaniae Historica, 20. Stuttgart: A. Hiersemann, 1964.

Hollister, C. Warren. "War and Diplomacy in the Anglo-Norman World: The Reign of Henry I." *Anglo-Norman Studies* 6 (1983): 72–88. Reprinted in Hollister, *Monarchy, Magnates, and Institutions in the Anglo-Norman World*. London: Hambledon Press, 1986. Pp. 273–89.

Hollister, C. Warren and Thomas K. Keefe. "The Making of the Angevin Empire." *Journal of British Studies* 12 (1973): 1–25. Reprinted in Hollister, *Monarchy,*

Magnates, and Institutions in the Anglo-Norman World. London: Hambledon Press, 1986. Pp. 241–71.

Howe, John. "The Nobility's Reform of the Medieval Church." *American Historical Review* 92 (1988): 317–39.

Hughs, Diane Owen. "From Brideprice to Dowry in Mediterranean Europe." *Journal of Family History* 3 (1978): 262–96.

Huizinga, Johan. *The Autumn of the Middle Ages.* Trans. Rodney J. Payton and Ulrich Mammitzsch. Chicago: University of Chicago Press, 1996.

Huneycutt, Lois. "Female Succession and the Language of Power in the Writings of Twelfth-Century Churchmen." In Parsons, *Medieval Queenship.* Pp. 189–201.

———. "Intercession and the High-Medieval Queen: The Esther Topos." In Carpenter and MacLean, *Power of the Weak.* Pp. 126–46.

Jaeger, C. Stephen. "L'amour des rois: structure sociale d'une forme de sensibilité aristocratique." *Annales: Economies, Sociétés, Civilisations* 46 (1991): 547–71.

———. *Ennobling Love: In Search of a Lost Sensibility.* Philadelphia: University of Pennsylvania Press, 1999.

———. *The Envy of Angels: Cathedral Schools and Social Ideals in Medieval Europe.* Philadelphia: University of Pennsylvania Press, 1993.

Johns, Susan. "The Wives and Widows of the Earls of Chester, 1100–1252: The Charter Evidence." *Haskins Society Journal* 7 (1995): 117–32.

Johnson, Penelope D. "Agnes of Burgundy: An Eleventh-Century Woman as Monastic Patron." *Journal of Medieval History* 15 (1989): 93–104.

———. *Equal in Monastic Profession: Religious Women in Medieval France.* Chicago and London: University of Chicago Press, 1991.

Joris, André. "Un seul amour . . . ou plusieurs femmes?" In *Femmes: Mariages-Lignages, XIIe–XIVe siècles: mélanges offerts à George Duby.* Brussels: De Boek Université, 1992. Pp. 197–214.

Köhler, Erich. *Ideal und Wirklichkeit in der höfischen Epik: Studien zur Form der frühen Artus- und Graldichtung.* Tübingen, 1956; 2nd ed. 1970. Trans. Eliane Kaufholz as *L'aventure chevaleresque: idéal et réalité dans le roman courtois: études sur la forme des plus anciens poèmes d'Arthur et du Graal.* Paris, 1974.

———. *Trobadorlyrik und höfischer Roman: Aufsätze zur französischen und provenzalischen Literatur des Mittelalters.* Berlin: Rutten and Loening, 1962.

Kuttner, Stephan. "The Revival of Jurisprudence." In *Renaissance and Renewal in the Twelfth Century.* ed. Robert L. Benson and Giles Constable. Cambridge, Mass.: Harvard University Press, 1982.

Labande, Edmond-René. "Les filles d'Aliénor d'Aquitaine: étude comparative." *Cahiers de civilisation médiévale* 19 (1986): 101–12.

Lalore, Charles. *Les sires et les barons de Chacenay.* Troyes: L. Lacroix, 1885.

Lalou, Elisabeth. "Le gouvernement de la reine Jeanne, 1285–1305." *Les Cahiers haut-marnais* 167 (1986): 16–21.

Latouche, Robert. *Histoire du comté du Maine pendant le Xe et le XIe siècle.* Paris: Champion, 1910. Reprint Geneva: Slatkine, 1977.

Leclercq, Jean. *Monks and Love in Twelfth-Century France: Psycho-Historical Essays.* Oxford: Oxford University Press, 1979.

————. *Women and St. Bernard of Clairvaux.* Trans. Marie-Bernard Saïd. Kalamazoo, Mich.: Cistercian Publications, 1989.

Le Jan, Régine. *Famille et pouvoir dans le monde franc (VIIe–Xe siècle): essai d'anthropologie sociale.* Paris: Publications de la Sorbonne, 1995.

Le Jan-Hennebicque, Régine. "Aux origines du douaire médiévale (VIᶜ–Xᶜ siècles)." In *Veuves et veuvage dans le haut Moyen Age,* ed. Michel Parisse. Paris: Picard, 1993. Pp. 107–21.

Lejeune, Rita. "Rôle littéraire de la famille d'Aliénor d'Aquitaine." *Cahiers de civilisation médiévale* 1 (1958): 319–34.

Lekai, Louis J. *The Cistercians: Ideals and Reality.* Kent, Oh.: Kent State University Press, 1977.

Lemaire, André. "La dotatio de l'épouse de l'époque mérovingienne au XIIIᶜ siecle." *Revue historique de droit français et étranger* 4th ser. 8 (1929): 569–80.

————. "Les origines de la communauté de biens entre époux dans le droit coutumier français." *Revue historique de droit français et étranger* 4th ser. 7 (1928): 584–643.

Lewis, Andrew W. "Anticipatory Association of the Heir in Early Capetian France." *American Historical Review* 83 (1978): 907–27.

————. "Fourteen Charters of Robert I of Dreux (1152–1188)." *Traditio* 41 (1985): 148–60.

————. *Royal Succession in Capetian France: Studies on Familial Order and the State.* Cambridge, Mass.: Harvard University Press, 1981.

Little, Lester K. *Benedictine Maledictions: Liturgical Cursing in Romanesque France.* Ithaca, N.Y.: Cornell University Press, 1993.

————. *Religious Poverty and the Profit Economy in Medieval Europe.* Ithaca, N.Y.: Cornell University Press, 1978.

Livingstone, Amy. "Diversity and Continuity: Family Structure and Inheritance in the Chartrain, 1000–1200." In *Mondes de l'ouest et villes du monde: regards sur les sociétés médiévales — mélanges André Chédeville,* ed. Daniel Pinchot and Bernard Merdrignac. Rennes: Presses Universitaires de Rennes, 1998.

————. "Kith and Kin: Kinship and Family Structure of the Nobility of Eleventh- and Twelfth-Century Blois-Chartres." *French Historical Studies* 20 (1995): 76–99.

————. "Noblewomen's Control of Property in Eleventh and Early Twelfth-Century Blois Chartres." *Medieval Prosopography* 18 (1995): 55–72.

Longnon, Jean. *Les Compagnons de Villehardouin: recherches sur les croisés de la quatrième croisade.* Geneva: Droz, 1978.

————. *Recherches sur la vie de Geoffroy de Villehardouin.* Paris: Champion, 1939.

LoPrete, Kimberly A. "Adela of Blois and Ivo of Chartres: Piety, Politics, and the Peace in the Diocese of Chartres." *Anglo-Norman Studies* 14 (1991): 131–52.

————. "Adela of Blois as Mother and Countess." In Parsons and Wheeler, *Medieval Mothering.* Pp. 313–33.

————. "The Anglo-Norman Card of Adela of Blois." *Albion* 22 (1990): 569–89.

————. "The *Domina* Adela: Female Lord or Courtly Lady." Paper presented to the Early Medieval Seminar, Institute of Historical Research, London, November 1996.

——. "A Female Ruler in Feudal Society: Adela of Blois (ca. 1067–ca. 1137)." 2 vols. Ph.D. dissertation, University of Chicago, 1992.

——. Review of Georges Duby, *Love and Marriage in the Middle Ages*. *Speculum* 70 (1995): 607–9.

Lusse, Jackie. "Les religieuses en Champagne jusqu'au XIIIe siècle." In *Les religieuses en France au XIIIe siècle*, ed. Michel Parisse. Nancy: Presses Universitaires de Nancy, 1985. Pp. 11–26.

Luykx, Theo. *Johanna van Constantinopel*. Antwerp: Standaard-Boekhandel, 1946.

Maddicot, J. R. *Simon de Montfort*. Cambridge: Cambridge University Press, 1994.

Martin-Demézil, Jean. "Les forêts du comté de Blois jusqu'à la fin XVe siècle." *Mémoires de la Société des Sciences et Lettres de Loir-et-Cher* 34 (1963): 127–236; 35 (1974): 117–246.

Martindale, Jane. "The French Aristocracy in the Early Middle Ages: A Reappraisal." *Past and Present* 75 (1977): 5–45.

Martines, Lauro. "Ritual Language in Renaissance Italy." In *Riti e rituali nelle società medievali*, ed. Jacques Chiffoleau, Lauro Martines, and Agostino Baggliani. Spoleto: Centro Italiano di Studi sull'alto Medioevo, 1994. Pp. 69–75.

McCash, June Hall Martin. "Marie de Champagne and Eleanor of Aquitaine: A Relationship Reexamined." *Speculum* 54 (1979): 698–711.

McLaughlin, Megan. "The Woman Warrior: Gender, Warfare, and Society in Medieval Europe." *Women's Studies* 17 (1990): 193–209.

McNamara, Jo Ann and Suzanne Wemple. "The Power of Women Through the Family in Medieval Europe, 500–1100." *Feminist Studies* 1 (1973): 126–42. Reprinted in revised form in *Women and Power in the Middle Ages*, ed. Mary Erler and Maryanne Kowaleski. Athens: University of Georgia Press, 1988. Pp. 83–101.

Meneghetti, Maria Luisa. *Il pubblico dei trovatori: ricezione e riuso dei testi lirici cortesi fino al XIV secolo*. Modena: Mucchi, 1984.

Meyer-Lübke, Wilhelm. *Romanisches etymologischer Wörterbuch*. Heidelberg: C. Winter, 1911–20.

Mitchell, Linda. "The Lady Is a Lord: Noble Widows and Land in Thirteenth-Century Britain." *Historical Reflections/Reflexions historiques* 18 (1992): 71–97.

Mollat, Guillaume. "La restitution des églises privées au patrimoine ecclésiastique en France du IXe du XIe siècle." *Revue historique de droit français et étranger* 4th ser. 27 (1949): 399–423.

Monson, Don A. "The Troubadour's Lady Reconsidered Again." *Speculum* 70 (1995): 255–74.

Moore, John S. "The Anglo-Norman Family: Size and Structure." *Anglo-Norman Studies* 14 (1991): 153–95.

Moos, Peter von. *Hildebert von Lavardin, 1056–1133: Humanitas an der Schwelle des höfischen Zeitalters*. Pariser historische Studien, 3. Stuttgart: Hiersemann, 1965.

Morelle, Laurent. "Mariage et diplomatique: autour de cinq chartes de douaire dans le laonnois-soissonnais, 1163–1181." *Bibliothèque de l'Ecole des Chartes* 146 (1988): 225–84.

Morrison, Karl F. *Tradition and Authority in the Western Church, 300–1140*. Princeton, N.J.: Princeton University Press, 1969.

Murray, Jacqueline. "Thinking About Gender: The Diversity of Medieval Perspectives." In Carpenter and MacLean, *Power of the Weak*. Pp. 1–26.

Nicholas, David M. *Medieval Flanders*. London and New York: Longman, 1992.

Nicholas, Karen S. "The Role of Feudal Relationships in the Consolidation of Power in the Principalities of the Low Countries." In *Law, Custom, and the Social Fabric in Medieval Europe: Essays in Honor of Bryce Lyon*, ed. Bernard S. Bachrach and David Nicholas. Kalamazoo: Medieval Institute Publications, Western Michigan University, 1990. Pp. 113–30.

———. "Women as Rulers: Countesses Jeanne and Marguerite of Flanders (1212–1278)." In Vann, *Queens, Regents, and Potentates*. Pp. 73–89.

Niermeyer, J. F. *Mediae Latinitatis Lexicon Minus*. Leiden: Brill, 1976.

Pacaut, Marcel. *Louis VII et son royaume*. Paris: SEVPEN, 1964.

Paillot, Pierre. *La répresentation successorale dans les coutumes du Nord de la France: contribution à l'étude du droit familiale*. Paris: Domat-Montchrestien, 1935.

Painter, Sidney. *The Scourge of the Clergy: Peter of Dreux, Duke of Brittany*. Baltimore: Johns Hopkins Press, 1937.

Parisse, Michel. *Noblesse et chevalerie en Lorraine médiévale*. Nancy: Service des publications de l'Université Nancy, 1982.

———. "Les trois mariages du comte de Bar, Thiébaut Iᵉʳ." *Annales de l'Est* 19 (1967): 57–61.

Parsons, John Carmi, ed. *Medieval Queenship*. New York: St. Martin's Press, 1993.

———. "Mothers, Daughters, Marriage, Power: Some Plantagenet Evidence, 1150–1500." In Parsons, *Medieval Queenship*. Pp. 63–78.

———. "The Queen's Intercession in Thirteenth-Century England." In Carpenter and MacLean, *Power of the Weak*. Pp. 147–77.

Parsons, John Carmi and Bonnie Wheeler, eds. *Medieval Mothering*. New York: Garland, 1996.

Petit, Ernest. *Histoire des ducs de Bourogne de la race capétienne*. 9 vols. Dijon: Lamarche, 1885–1900.

Pirenne, Henri. "Richilde." *Biographie national* 19: 293–300.

Poirier-Coutansais, Françoise. *Gallia monastica: tableaux et cartes de dépendences monastiques*. Vol. 1, *Les abbayes bénédictines du diocèse de Reims*. Paris: Picard, 1974.

Poissonnier, Gilles. *Catalogue des actes de la maison de Choiseul, 1125–1425*. Chaumont: Cahiers Haut-Marnais, 1990.

Poly, Jean Pierre. *La Provence et la société féodale (879–1176): contribution à l'étude des structures dites féodales dans le Midi*. Paris: Bordas, 1976.

Poulet, André. "Capetian Women and the Regency: The Genesis of a Vocation." In Parsons, *Medieval Queenship*. Pp. 93–116.

Poull, Georges. *La maison souveraine et ducale de Bar*. Nancy: Presses Universitaires de Nancy, 1994.

Putter, Ad. "Knights and Clerics at the Court of Champagne: Chrétien de Troyes's Romances in Context." In *Medieval Knighthood V: Papers from the Sixth Strawberry Conference, 1994*, ed. Stephen Church and Ruth Harvey. Woodbridge and Rochester, N. Y.: Boydell Press, 1995. Pp. 243–66.

Radding, Charles. *The Origins of Medieval Jurisprudence: Pavia and Bologna, 850–1150*. New Haven, Conn.: Yale University Press, 1988.

Reuter, Timothy, ed. *The Medieval Nobility: Studies on the Ruling Classes of France and Germany from the Sixth to the Twelfth Century*. New York and Amsterdam: North-Holland, 1978.

Robinson, Ian S. *The Papacy, 1073–1198: Continuity and Innovation*. Cambridge: Cambridge University Press, 1990.

Rosenwein, Barbara. *To Be the Neighbor of St. Peter: The Social Meaning of Cluny's Property, 909–1049*. Ithaca, N. Y.: Cornell University Press, 1989.

Roserot, Alphonse. *Dictionnaire historique de la Champagne méridionale (Aube) des origines à 1790*. 3 vols. Angers: Editions de l'Oust, 1948. Reprint Marseille: Laffitte, 1984.

Sassier, Yves. *Recherches sur le pouvoir comtal en Auxerrois du Xe au début du XIIIe siècle*. Auxerre: Société des fouilles archéologiques et des monuments historiques de l'Yonne, 1980.

Schieffer, Theodor. *Die päpstlichen Legaten in Frankreich (870–1130)*. Berlin: Verlag Ebering, 1935.

Searle, Eleanor. *Predatory Kinship and the Creation of Norman Power, 840–1066*. Berkeley: University of California Press, 1988.

Shahar, Shulamith. *The Fourth Estate: A History of Women in the Middle Ages*. Trans. Chaya Galai. London and New York: Methuen, 1983.

Skinner, Mary. "Benedictine Life for Women in Central France, 850–1100: A Feminist Revival." In *Medieval Religious Women*. Vol. 1, *Distant Echoes*, ed. John A. Nichols and Lilliane Thomas Shank. Kalamazoo, Mich.: Cistercian Publications, 1984. Pp. 87–113.

Smyrl, Edwin. "La famille des Baux." *Cahiers du Centre d'études des sociétés méditerranéennes* 2 (1968): 7–107.

Sobrequés i Vidal, Santiago. *Els grans comtes de Barcelona*. Barcelona: Editorial Vicens-Vives, 1970.

Southern, Richard W. *Saint Anselm and His Biographer: A Study of Monastic Life and Thought, 1059–c.1130*. Cambridge: Cambridge University Press, 1963.

Stafford, Pauline. *Queens, Concubines, and Dowagers: The King's Wife in the Early Middle Ages*. Athens: University of Georgia Press, 1983.

———. "Women and the Norman Conquest." *Transactions of the Royal Historical Society* 6th ser. 4 (1994): 221–49.

Stirnemann, Patricia Danz. "Quelques bibliothèques princières et la production hors scriptorium au XIIe siècle." *Bulletin archéologique du Comité des Travaux historiques et scientifiques* n.s. 17–18A (1984): 7–38.

Stuard, Susan Mosher. "Fashion's Captives: Medieval Women in French Historiography." In *Women in Medieval History and Historiography*, ed. Susan Mosher Stuard. Philadelphia: University of Pennsylvania Press, 1987. Pp. 68–76.

Sutherland, Jon. "The Recovery of Land in the Diocese of Grenoble During the Gregorian Reform Epoch." *Catholic Historical Review* 64 (1978): 377–97.

Tabuteau, Emily Z. *Transfers of Property in Eleventh-Century Norman Law*. Chapel Hill: University of North Carolina Press, 1988.

Thireau, Jean-Louis. "Les pratiques communautaires entre époux dans l'Anjou féodal (Xe–XIIe siècles)." *Revue historique de droit français et étranger* 4th ser. 67 (1989): 201–35.

Thompson, Kathleen Hapgood. "Dowry and Inheritance Patterns: Some Examples from the Descendants of King Henry I of England." *Medieval Prosopography* 17 (1996): 45–61.

———. "The Formation of the County of Perche: The Rise and Fall of the House of Gouet." In *Family Trees and the Roots of Politics: The Prosopography of Britain and France from the Tenth to the Twelfth Century*, ed. K. S. B. Keats-Rohan. Woodbridge, Suffolk and Rochester, N.Y.: Boydell Press, 1997. Pp. 299–314.

Thompson, Sally. "The Problem of the Cistercian Nuns in the Twelfth and Early Thirteenth Centuries." In *Medieval Women*, ed. Derek Baker. Oxford: Blackwell, 1978. Pp. 227–42.

Timbal, Pierre Clément, ed. *La Guerre de Cent Ans vue à travers les registres du Parlement (1337–1369)*. Paris: CNRS, 1961.

Turlan, Juliette M. "Recherches sur le mariage dans la pratique coutumière (XIIe–XIVe s.)." *Revue historique de droit français et étranger* 4th ser. 35 (1957): 477–528.

Vandermaesen, M. "Vlaanderen en Henegouwen onder het Huis van Dampierre 1244–1384." In *Algemene Geschiedenis der Nederlanden*. Vol. 2. Bussum: Fibula-Van-Dishoeck, 1982. Pp. 400–401.

Vann, Theresa M, ed. *Queens, Regents, and Potentates*. Dallas, Tex.: Academia, 1993.

Van Werveke, Hans. *Een Vlaamse graaf van Europees formaat: Filips van de Elzas*. Haarlem: Fibula-Van Dishoeck, 1976.

Vaughn, Sally N. *Anselm of Bec and Robert of Meulan: The Innocence of the Dove and the Wisdom of the Serpent*. Berkeley: University of California Press, 1987.

Venarde, Bruce L. *Women's Monasticism and Medieval Society: Nunneries in France and England, 890–1215*. Ithaca, N.Y. and London: Cornell University Press, 1997.

Verdon, Jean. "Les moniales dans la France de l'Ouest aux XIe et XIIe siècles: étude d'histoire sociale." *Cahiers de civilisation médiévale* 19 (1976): 247–64.

Verlinden, Charles. *Robert Ier, le Frison, comte de Flandre: étude d'histoire politique*. Paris: Champion, 1935.

Walker, Sue Sheridan. "Free Consent and the Marriage of Feudal Wards in Medieval England." *Journal of Medieval History* 8 (1972): 123–34.

———. "Violence and the Exercise of Feudal Guardianship: the Action of *ejectio custodia*." *American Journal of Legal History* 16 (1972): 320–33.

———. "Widow and Ward: The Feudal Law of Child Custody in Medieval England." *Feminist Studies* 3 (1976): 104–16.

Wartburg, Walther von. *Französisches etymologisches Wörterbuch*. 25 vols. Bonn: F. Klopp, 1928–62.

Werner, Karl F. "Kingdom and Principality in Twelfth-Century France." In Reuter, *The Medieval Nobility*. Pp. 243–90. Originally published as "Königtum und Fürstentum des französischen 12. Jahrhunderts." *Vorträge und Forschungen* 12 (1968): 177–225.

White, Stephen D. *Custom, Kinship, and Gifts to Saints: The "Laudatio Parentum" in Western France, 1050–1150*. Chapel Hill: University of North Carolina Press, 1988.

———. "Feuding and Peace-Making in the Touraine Around the Year 1000." *Traditio* 42 (1986): 195–263.

———. "Inheritances and Legal Arguments in Western France, 1050–1150." *Traditio*
43 (1987): 55–103.

———. "*Pactum . . . Legem Vincit et Amor Judicium*: The Settlement of Disputes by
Compromise in Eleventh-Century Western France." *America Journal of Legal
History* 22 (1978): 281–308.

Wieck, Roger S. *Painted Prayers: The Book of Hours in Medieval and Renaissance Art*.
New York: George Braziller, 1997.

Wischermann, Else Maria. *Marcigny-sur-Loire: Gründungs- und Frühegeschichte des
ersten Cluniacenserinnenpriorates (1055–1150)*. Munich: W. Fink, 1986.

Ziezulewicz, William. "'Restored' Churches in the Fisc of St. Florent-de-Saumur."
Revue bénédictine 6 (1988): 106–17.

Contributors

Fredric L. Cheyette is Professor of History at Amherst College. He edited *Lordship and Community in Medieval Europe* (1968) and has written a number of articles, notably "Suum Cuique Tribuere," *French Historical Studies* (1970) and "The Invention of the State," in *Essays in Medieval Civilization: The Walter Prescott Webb Memorial Lectures*, ed. B.K. Lackner and K.R. Phillip (1979). He is writing a book entitled *Lady of the Troubadours: Ermengard of Narbonne and the Politics of Her Age*.

Theodore Evergates is Professor of History at Western Maryland College. He has published several studies on medieval society in the county of Champagne, including *Feudal Society in the Bailliage of Troyes Under the Counts of Champagne, 1152–1284* (1975) and *Feudal Society in Medieval France. Documents from the County of Champagne* (University of Pennsylvania Press, 1993), as well as "Nobles and Knights in Medieval France," in *Cultures of Power: Lordship, Status, and Process in Twelfth-Century Europe*, ed. Thomas N. Bisson (University of Pennsylvania Press, 1995).

Amy Livingstone is Assistant Professor of History at Wittenberg University. She is author of "Kith and Kin: Kinship and Family Structure of the Nobility of Eleventh- and Twelfth-Century Blois-Chartres," *French Historical Studies* (1997), "Noblewomen's Control of Property in Early Twelfth-Century Blois-Chartres," *Medieval Prosopography* (1997), and "Powerful Adversaries: Aristocratic Women and Power in Medieval France," in *Women and Medieval Culture* (1998), ed. Linda Mitchell. She is preparing a book-length study on aristocratic families in the county of Blois-Chartres.

Kimberly A. LoPrete, is Lecturer in History at the National University of Ireland, Galway. Her publications include "The Anglo-Norman Card of Adela of Blois," *Albion* (1990), "Adela of Blois and Ivo of Chartres: Piety, Politics, and the Peace in the Diocese of Chartres," *Anglo-Norman Studies* (1991), and "Adela of Blois as Mother and Countess," in *Medieval Mothering*, ed. John Carmi Parsons and Bonnie Wheeler (1996). She is writing a book-length study of Countess Adela.

Karen S. Nicholas is Associate Professor of History at the State University of New York at Oswego. Her articles include "The Role of Feudal Relationships in the Consolidation of Power in the Principalities of the Low Countries," in *Law, Custom, and the Social Fabric in Medieval Europe: Essays in Honor of Bryce Lyon* (1990), "When Feudal Ideas Failed: Conflicts between Lords and Vassals in the Low Countries, 1127–1296," in *The Rusted Hauberk: Feudal Ideals of Order and Their Decline*, ed. Liam O. Purdon and Cindy L. Vitto (1994), and "Women as Rulers: Countesses Jeanne and Marguerite of Flanders, 1212–1278," in *Queens, Regents, and Potentates*, ed. Theresa M. Vann (1994). She is preparing a book entitled *Princes, Lords, and Vassals in the Low Counties, 1000–1300*.

Index

Philip II, king of France, 77, 81, 83, 93, 126, 127, 129, 133
Philip III, king of France, 87–88, 93, 110
Philip IV, king of France, 87–88
Philippa of Courville, 70, 71
Philippa (of Ramerupt) of Brienne, 83–84, 96
Philippa, heiress of Toulouse, 145
Physician, 26, 27, 189 n. 78
Pierre. See also Peter
Pierre of Briel, 92
Plaigne. See Hugh; William
Plancy. See Elizabeth of Traînel; Haice
Poetry, 3–4, 9, 10–11, 29, 39, 79. See also Sources; Troubadour songs
Ponce of Mont-Saint-Jean, 95
Pontigny, monastery, 197 n. 166
Portugal. See Ferrand; Matilda (Theresia)
Popes. See Adrian IV, Alexander III; Calixtus II; Celestrine III; Clement IV; Eugenius III; Innocent III; Honorius III; Paschal II; Urban II; Urban IV
Pougy. See Euda
Preuilly, monastery, 38, 198 n. 174
Primogeniture, 1, 109. See also Inheritance; Family structure
Pringy. See Comitissa; Stephen
Provence, 145. See also counts: 154; Barenguer-Ramon; Ramon-Barenguer III. See also Douce; Eleanor; Gerberga
Provins, 11, 34, 79, 188 n. 68, 198 n. 174; Franciscans, 86. See also Artaud; Guiot; Saint-Ayoul; Notre-Dame-du-Val
Puisserguier. See Berenger

Raher, knight in the Chartrain, 57–58, 69
Raimon de Miraval, 168
Ralph. See also Raoul
Ralph of Diceto, chronicler, 124
Ramerupt. See Erard; Philippa
Ramon-Berenguer III, count of Barcelona, 155
Ramon-Berenguer IV, count of Barcelona, 157
Ramon-Berenguer III, count of Provence, 158
Raoul. See also Ralph
Raoul of Beaugency, 33–34, 36, 69
Raoul the Younger of Vermandois, 126
Raoul IV of Vermandois, 122

Raoul V of Vermandois, 122
Raymond of Les Baux, 157
Raymond of Orange, 138
Raymond of Ouveilhan, 151
Raymond IV, count of Toulouse, 145, 176
Raymond V, count of Toulouse, 138–39, 145, 150, 152, 155, 156, 159, 164
Raymond VI, count of Toulouse, 145, 159
Raymond Trecavel, 149, 156
Raymond-Bernard, viscount of Albi and Nîmes, 158
Razos. See Vidas
Rebais, monastery, 27
Regency, 4, 23, 25–26, 27, 28, 43, 61, 63–64, 77, 78, 81–85, 86, 87–88, 10, 103, 115–16,123, 128, 136, 158, 189 n. 71. See also Widows
Reims, 11, 18, 182 n. 11; Council of, 38. See also archbishops: 34, 131; William of Champagne. See also Godfrey of Reims; Notre-Dame of Reims; Saint-Pierre-les-Dames; Saint-Remi
Relics, 17–18, 27
Remi of Navarre, chancellor of Champagne, 83
Renard II of Choiseul, 94, 95, 102
Rethel: count, 94; countesses: Jeanne of Dampierre; Marie of Garlande
Reynard the Fox, 124
Richard of Chester, 37
Richard the Lionheart, king of England, 79, 81, 145
Richilde, countess of Hainaut and Flanders, 113, 115–16, 117, 125, 136
Ricsovendis of Termes, 162
Rixendis de Parez, 161
Robert of Bellême, 30
Robert I of Dreux, 101
Robert II, count of Dreux, 102
Robert I (the Frisian), count of Flanders, 115–16, 117, 121
Robert II, count of Flanders, 117–18
Robert of Fontette, 95
Robert II, king of France, 11
Robert Curthose, duke of Normandy, 14, 20, 30, 31, 32, 33, 121
Robert of Torigni, chronicler, 26, 199 n. 191
Rodez, 154
Roger I of Béziers, 149, 154, 156
Roger II of Béziers, 176

William I Gouet of Alluyes, 61, 65
William II Gouet of Alluyes, 61, 63, 66, 69
William of Argens, 151
William of Bernon, 94
William (of Blois-Chartres), lord of Sully,
  16, 17, 25, 24, 29, 31–32, 35, 39, 185 n. 43,
  187 n. 57, 195 n. 126
William of Champagne, archbishop of
  Reims, 77, 78, 107
William of Durban, 151
William I (the Conqueror), king of En-
  gland, 7, 10, 13–14, 24, 41, 42, 182 n. 10,
  182 n. 16, 184 n. 30
William II (Rufus), king of England, 20–21,
  30, 42
William of Malmsbury, chronicler, 160

William V, lord of Montpellier, 176
William VI, lord of Montpellier, 154, 158,
  159, 176
William VII, lord of Montpellier, 159
William II, count of Nevers, 37, 38, 197
  n. 158
William of Plaigne, 151
William IV, count of Toulouse, 145
William of Tudela, 174, 176
William of Ypres, 119
Winchester. *See* Henry of Blois
Witness list, 44–47, 149–50

Yolande of Coucy, 102
Yolande of Hainaut, 127
Ypres, 131. *See also* William